INTERNATIONAL PERSPECTIVES ON THE GOVERNANCE OF HIGHER EDUCATION

An authoritative overview that questions why some systems of governance have persisted while others have changed, *International Perspectives on the Governance of Higher Education* is essential reading for policy-makers, institutional leaders, managers, advisors, and scholars in the field of higher education. The recent evolution of higher education governance is analyzed by international contributors from the United Kingdom, the Netherlands, Italy, Austria, Australia, Germany, Denmark, Canada, the US, and Ireland. The text builds towards a better understanding of developments in governance and their impact upon policy-making, and explores how governments shape higher education policy-making and how actors and institutions are affected by policies.

International Perspectives on the Governance of Higher Education builds on the conceptual and theoretical insights from different disciplines, particularly political science, public administration, and public policy. Exploring traditional governance, variations on those traditional themes, and the recent growth of a new institutional playing field wherein governance and coordination take part in a complex interaction, the book brings us to a better understanding of steering policy processes and their outcome in higher education.

Jeroen Huisman is Professor in Higher Education Management and Director of the International Centre for Higher Education Management (ICHEM), University of Bath. He is a graduate from the University of Groningen, the Netherlands (Educational Sciences, 1991), and received his Ph.D. at the University of Twente (1995).

International Studies in Higher Education
Series Editors:
David Palfreyman, OxCHEPS
Ted Tapper, OxCHEPS
Scott L. Thomas, Claremont Graduate University

The central purpose of this series of a projected dozen volumes is to see how different national and regional systems of higher education are responding to widely shared pressures for change. The most significant of these are: rapid expansion; reducing public funding; the increasing influence of market and global forces; and the widespread political desire to integrate higher education more closely into the wider needs of society and, more especially, the demands of the economic structure. The series will commence with an international overview of structural change in systems of higher education. It will then proceed to examine on a global front the change process in terms of topics that are both traditional (for example, institutional management and system governance) and emerging (for example, the growing influence of international organizations and the blending of academic and professional roles). At its conclusion the series will have presented, through an international perspective, both a composite overview of contemporary systems of higher education, along with the competing interpretations of the process of change.

Published titles:

Structuring Mass Higher Education
The Role of Elite Institutions
Edited by David Palfreyman and Ted Tapper

International Perspectives on the Governance of Higher Education
Alternative Frameworks for Coordination
Edited by Jeroen Huisman

Forthcoming titles:

Spring 2009
International Organizations and Higher Education Policy
Thinking Globally, Acting Locally?
Edited by Roberta Malee Bassett and Alma Maldonado

Fall 2009
Academic and Professional Identities in Higher Education
The Challenges of a Diversifying Workforce
Edited by George Gordon and Celia Whitchurch

International Perspectives on the Governance of Higher Education

Alternative Frameworks for Coordination

Edited by
Jeroen Huisman

NEW YORK AND LONDON

First published 2009
by Routledge
270 Madison Ave, New York, NY 10016

Simultaneously published in the UK
by Routledge
2 Park Square, Milton Park, Abingdon, Oxon OX14 4RN

Routledge is an imprint of the Taylor & Francis Group, an informa business

Transferred to Digital Printing 2009

© 2009 Routledge, Taylor & Francis

Typeset in Minion by
Keystroke, 28 High Street, Tettenhall, Wolverhampton

Library of Congress Cataloging in Publication Data
International perspectives on the governance of higher education:
alternative frameworks for coordination/Jeroen Huisman, ed.
     p. cm. — (International studies in higher education)
    Includes bibliographical references and index.
   1. Universities and colleges—Administration—Cross-cultural studies.
  I. Huisman, Jeroen.
  LB2341.I584 2009
  378.1′01—dc22   2008032786

ISBN 10: 0–415–98933–7 (hbk)
ISBN 10: 0–203–88335–7 (ebk)

ISBN 13: 978–0–415–98933–6 (hbk)
ISBN 13: 978–0–203–88335–8 (ebk)

**I dedicate this book to
Louisa, Erin and Keyan**

Contents

Illustrations

Series Editors' Introduction

International Studies in Higher Education

This Series is constructed around the premise that higher education systems are experiencing common pressures for fundamental change, reinforced by differing national and regional circumstances that also impact upon established institutional structures and procedures. There are four major dynamics for change that are of international significance:

1 Mass higher education is a universal phenomenon.
2 National systems find themselves located in an increasingly global marketplace that has particular significance for their more prestigious institutions.
3 Higher education institutions have acquired (or been obliged to acquire) a wider range of obligations, often under pressure from governments prepared to use state power to secure their policy goals.
4 The balance between the public and private financing of higher education has shifted – markedly in some cases – in favor of the latter.

Although higher education systems in all regions and nation-states face their own particular pressures for change, these are especially severe in some cases: the collapse of the established economic and political structures of the former Soviet Union along with Central and Eastern Europe, the political revolution in South Africa, the pressures for economic development in India and China, and demographic pressure in Latin America.

Each volume in the Series will examine how systems of higher education are responding to this new and demanding political and socio-economic environment. Although it is easy to overstate the uniqueness of the present situation, it is not an exaggeration to say that higher education is undergoing a fundamental shift in its character, and one that is truly international in scope. We are witnessing a major transition in the relationship of higher education to state and society. What makes the present circumstances particularly interesting is to see how different systems – a product of social, cultural, economic and political contexts that have interacted and evolved over time – respond in their own peculiar ways to the changing environment. There is no assumption that the pressures for change have set in motion the trend towards a converging model of higher education, but we do believe that in the present circumstances no understanding of "the idea of the university" remains sacrosanct.

Although this is a Series with an international focus, it is not expected that each individual volume should cover every national system of higher education. This would be an impossible task. Whilst aiming for a broad range of case studies, with each volume addressing a particular theme, the focus will be upon the most important and interesting examples of responses to the pressures for change. Most of the individual volumes will bring together a range of comparative quantitative and qualitative information, but the primary aim of each volume will be to present differing interpretations of critical developments in key aspects of the experience of higher education. The dominant, overarching objective is to explore the conflict of ideas and the political struggles that inevitably surround any significant policy development in higher education.

It can be expected that volume editors and their authors will adopt their own interpretations to explain the emerging patterns of development. There will be conflicting theoretical positions drawn from the multidisciplinary, and increasingly interdisciplinary, field of higher education research. Thus we can expect in most volumes to find an intermarriage of approaches drawn from sociology, economics, history, political science, cultural studies and the administrative sciences. However, whilst there will be different approaches to understanding the process of change in higher education, each volume's editor(s) will impose a framework upon the volume inasmuch as chapter authors will be required to address common issues and concerns.

This, the second volume in the Series, is edited by the distinguished Dutch social scientist, Jereon Huisman of the University of Bath. The general context is sufficiently varied in terms of international differences to allow both sharp contrasts and subtle differences in the modes of governance between national systems of higher education. Whilst it is possible to make an historical distinction between systems in which individual institutions were considered to be autonomous, yet in other systems they were perceived as state controlled, the reality was always more complex. Invariably autonomy was circumscribed while the tentacles of state control would encounter entrenched historical legacies and embedded institutional practices.

Within this volume we see the emergence of the state-steering model of governance, which gives rise to all sorts of interesting possibilities. How do institutions, the regulatory bodies and government interact to shape policy and practice? What are the particular policy concerns of the state and what are the mechanisms that governments use to further their policy ends? Is there a role for the market and how much encouragement is there for institutional entrepreneurialism? Is there convergence with respect to models of governance? Are national systems not only more diverse in terms of the internal interpretations of higher education but also in terms of how the varying segments of the system are governed? Are national governments increasingly of less importance in shaping the pattern of development as both international organizations and supra-national political bodies take increasing responsibility for the development of higher education?

The above issues are located in different theoretical contexts. Its editor and authors have attempted to establish a dialogue between theory and praxis in order to further our understanding of the changing governance of higher education in the contemporary world. At its best, this is what the study of higher education attempts to achieve.

David Palfreyman
Director of OxCHEPS, New College, University of Oxford

Ted Tapper
Visiting Fellow, OxCHEPS, New College, University of Oxford and CHEMPAS, University of Southampton

Scott L. Thomas
Professor of Educational Studies, Claremont Graduate University, California

Contributors

Series Editors

David Palfreyman is Bursar and Fellow, New College, Oxford, and also Director of OxCHEPS (the Oxford Centre for Higher Education Policy Studies), details of which can be seen at its website: http://oxcheps.new.ox.ac.uk. David is a General Editor for the seventeen-volume Open University Press-McGraw Hill series Managing Universities and Colleges (within which he and David Warner contribute a volume on Managing Crisis).

Ted Tapper is Visiting Fellow at the Oxford Centre for Higher Education Policy Studies and at CHEMPAS, University of Southampton. Most of his research on higher education has been concerned with issues of governance, with a particular focus on the changing relationship between the state and the universities in the British context. In recent years he has added a stronger comparative dimension to his research and this book reflects that development.

Scott L. Thomas is Professor in the School of Educational Studies at Claremont Graduate University, California. His work focuses on stratification in higher education with an especial interest in issues relating to college access and the secondary school achievement gap. Thomas also has a line of methodological work that focuses on multilevel models and social network analysis. His work in this area includes a book, *An Introduction to Multilevel Modeling* (with Ron Heck, published by Psychology Press) and related articles in a variety of refereed journals.

Contributors to this Volume

Jonathan Adams is the lead founder and a director of Evidence Ltd, which publishes the *UK Higher Education Research Yearbook*, now in its seventh edition. He worked at King's College London (1979–1980), University of Newcastle upon Tyne (1980–1983), University of Leeds (1983–1989) and Imperial College London (1989–1992) and was a science policy adviser to the Advisory Board for the Research Councils. He has published over 100 articles in research journals and books on research policy. Presentations in 2006/7 included the Royal Society, London; Academie des Sciences, Paris; and Rand Corporation meetings in Washington, USA. He chaired the New Zealand government's review of research evaluation (2008), the Monitoring Group of the European Research

Fund for Coal and Steel (2006) and the EC Monitoring Committee for the Evaluation of Framework Program VI (2004).

Alberto Amaral is Professor at the University of Porto, Portugal, and Director of the Centre for Research in Higher Education Policies (CIPES). He has been chair of the board of CHER, is a life member of IAUP, and a member of EAIR, SRHE, SCUP and IMHE. He is editor and co-editor of several books, including *Governing Higher Education: National Perspectives on Institutional Governance, The Higher Education Managerial Revolution?, Markets in Higher Education: Rhetoric or Reality?* and *Reform and Change in Higher Education.*

Ivar Bleiklie is Professor and Head of Department at the Department of Administration and Organization Theory, University of Bergen, Norway. Among his publications are: *University Governance: Western European Comparative Perspectives* (Dordrecht: Springer, 2008) (ed. with C. Paradeise, E. Reale and E. Ferlie), *Transforming Higher Education: A Comparative Study* (2nd edn, Dordrecht: Springer, 2006) (ed. with M. Kogan, M. Bauer and M. Henkel), *Governing Knowledge: A Study of Continuity and Change in Higher Education* (Dordrecht: Springer, 2005) (ed. with M. Henkel) and *Comparative Biomedical Policy: Governing Assisted Reproductive Technologies* (London: Routledge, 2004) (ed. with M. Goggin and C. Rothmayr).

Harry F. de Boer is Senior Researcher at the Center for Higher Education Policy Studies at the University of Twente, the Netherlands. He holds a Ph.D. in Public Administration (topic: university governance). His expertise lies in the area of higher education system dynamics, coordinating and steering relationships at national and institutional levels, higher education governance, leadership and management, and (theories of) policy analyses, all issues on which he has published frequently. He has carried out several national and international research and consultancy projects (e.g. for the Dutch Ministry of Education, Culture and Science, national advisory councils, the German Research Foundation, and the EU). He is also lecturing a number of courses (nationally and internationally) on the issues mentioned above.

Kees Boersma is Associate Professor and Research Manager at the Vrije Universiteit Amsterdam in the group of Culture, Organization and Management. His research interest is in science and technology studies, business history, and the organization of higher education. He has published widely on R&D history, organizational learning and organizational culture, innovation and higher education. His articles have appeared in such journals as *Enterprise and Society, Business History, Human Relations,* and *Tertiary Management and Education.* He teaches courses on Organizational Behavior, Organizational Politics, Organizational and Management Theory and Technology and Culture.

Roger Brown is Professor of Higher Education Policy and Co-Director of the Centre for Research and Development in Higher Education at Liverpool Hope University. He was previously Vice-Chancellor of Southampton Solent

University, Chief Executive of the Higher Education Quality Council and Chief Executive of the Polytechnics and Colleges Funding Council. Before that he was a senior civil servant at the Department of Trade and Industry. He has lectured and written on many aspects of higher education policy. His second book, *Quality Assurance in Higher Education: The UK Experience since 1992*, was published in 2004.

Kelly Coate is Lecturer in Teaching and Learning in Higher Education at the Centre for Excellence in Learning and Teaching at the National University of Ireland, Galway. Her research interests are focused on changes within higher education systems, particularly around such issues as teaching and learning, policy, internationalization and gender. She previously worked at the Institute of Education, University of London, as a researcher and lecturer, where she taught on the MBA in Higher Education Management program and on the research training program in the doctoral school. Her Ph.D., from the Institute of Education, was on the history of women's studies as an academic subject area in the UK, and she has an MA in Gender Studies from Middlesex University and a BA from Northwestern University in the USA.

Jürgen Enders is Professor and Director of the Center for Higher Education Policy Studies at the University of Twente, the Netherlands. Some of his recent publications are: *Public–Private Dynamics in Higher Education, Expectations, Developments, and Outcomes* (Bielefeld: Transit, 2007) (ed. with B. Jongbloed), "Public Sector Reform in Dutch Higher Education: The Organizational Transformation of the University" (2007, with H. de Boer and L. Leišytė), in *Public Administration*, and "State Models, Policy Networks, and Higher Education Policy: Policy Change and Stability in Dutch and English Higher Education" (2007, with H. Theisens), in G. Krücken, A. Kosmützky and M. Torka, eds., *The Multiversity: Universities between Global Trends and National Traditions* (Bielefeld: Transit).

Gaële Goastellec is a sociologist, and head of the research unit Higher Education Policies and Organizations at the Observatoire Science, Politique et Société, University of Lausanne, Switzerland. Some of her recent publications are: "Changes in Access to Higher Education: From Worldwide Constraints to Shared Patterns of Reform?," in D. Baker and A. Wiseman, eds., *The Worldwide Transformations of Higher Education* (Elsevier, 2008), "Globalization and Implementation of an Equity Norm in Higher Education," *Peabody Journal of Education* (2008), and "Comparative Perspectives on Access and Equity" (with P. Clancy, H. Eggins, S. Guri-Rosenblit, P.N. Nguyen and T. Yizengaw), in P.G. Altbach and P. McGill Peterson, eds., *Higher Education in the New Century: Global Challenges and Innovative Ideas* (Sense, 2007).

Leo Goedegebuure is Associate Professor at the Center for Higher Education Management and Policy, University of New England, and Academic Programs Director at the L. H. Martin Institute for Higher Education Leadership and Management at the University of Melbourne, Australia. His previous positions include Executive Director of the Center for Higher Education Policy Studies, and Deputy to the *Rector Magnificus*, both at the University of Twente, the Netherlands. With a Ph.D. in Public Administration, he has been active in higher education policy research for over two decades. His areas of expertise include governance and management, institutional restructuring, organizational change, and higher education systems dynamics. Most of his work has a strong comparative dimension. He has worked with various international organizations, including the European Commission, OECD, World Bank and UNESCO in Europe, Africa, Latin America and the Asia-Pacific region.

Peter Groenewegen is Professor of Organization Science at the Faculty of Social Sciences of VU University, Amsterdam. Key research themes are the development of research fields and cooperation between research organizations and policy; information transfer between universities and business; and the role of communication technologies in internal and external organizational networks. His research has been published in science studies journals such as *Research Policy, Science, Technology* and *Human Values,* and organization and policy journals. He supervises Ph.D. students exploring open innovation, social networks and research performance. He teaches social networks and organization, and organization theory.

Martin Hayden is Professor of Higher Education at Southern Cross University, Australia. He has had a breadth of management experience at several Australian universities. He was awarded a Ph.D. from the University of Melbourne for a thesis in the area of higher education policy. His interests in the area of higher education are diverse. His specific area of expertise relates to equity in access to higher education. He is also interested in university governance, graduate attributes, research on higher degree supervision and issues affecting the future of universities. He is widely experienced across quantitative and qualitative research methods. He has a strong working knowledge of curriculum development, quality enhancement and program evaluation processes in universities and, most recently, higher education systems in South-East Asia.

James C. Hearn is Professor in the Institute of Higher Education at the University of Georgia, USA. He holds a Ph.D. in the sociology of education from Stanford University, an MBA from the Wharton School, University of Pennsylvania, and an AB from Duke University. His research and teaching focus on organization, governance and policy in tertiary education. In recent work, he has investigated trends towards marketization and performance accountability in tertiary education policy, finance, and management; federal and state policies shaping governance and decision-making in colleges and universities, and factors affecting educational policy innovation in US states. His research has been published in sociology, economics, and education journals as well as in several books. He currently serves as associate editor of *Research in Higher Education* and serves on the editorial board of the *Teachers College Record.* In the past, he has served on the editorial boards of the *Journal of Higher Education, Sociology* *of Education* and the *Review of Higher Education*, and as a section editor for the annual volume *Higher Education: Handbook of Theory and Research*.

Jeroen Huisman graduated in Educational Sciences at the University of Groningen (1991), and received his Ph.D. at the Center for Higher Education Policy Studies (CHEPS), University of Twente. He worked as Senior Research Associate and Research Coordinator at CHEPS until 2005. In June 2005 he became Professor in Higher Education Management and Director of the International Centre for Higher Education Management (ICHEM), University of Bath, where he is involved in research, consultancy and teaching (e.g. on ICHEM's Doctorate in Business Administration – Higher Education Management). He is editor of *Higher Education Policy* and *Tertiary Education and Management* and a member of the editorial board of *Perspectives*. His research interests are: organizational change, internationalization, higher education policy and management, leadership and organizational diversity.

Michael Jaeger is deputy head of the project center for steering, financing and evaluation in higher education at the German higher education policy and research institute, Higher Education Information System (HIS), in Hanover. Following professional positions in the fields of human resources management and research management, he received a doctoral degree in Social Psychology at the University of Osnabrück. His field of interest is coordination and steering in higher education with a special focus on the questions of funding and quality assurance.

Glen A. Jones is the Ontario Research Chair in Postsecondary Education Policy and Measurement and Associate Dean, Academic at the Ontario Institute for Studies in Education of the University of Toronto, Canada. His research focuses on higher education systems, policy and governance, and he is a frequent contributor to higher education research literature. His edited books include *Creating Knowledge, Strengthening Nations: The Changing Role of Higher Education* (with McCarney and Skolnik, University of Toronto Press, 2005) and *Governing Higher Education: National Perspectives on Institutional Governance* (with Amaral and Karseth, Kluwer, 2002). An expanded version of his 1997 book *Higher Education in Canada: Different Systems, Different Perspectives* was translated into Chinese and published by Fujian Education Press in 2007. In 2001 he received the Distinguished Research Award from the Canadian Society for the Study of Higher Education.

Iain Mac Labhrainn (MacLaren) is the Director of the Centre for Excellence in Learning and Teaching at the National University of Ireland, Galway, where he has responsibility for educational technologies, civic engagement, academic staff development, pedagogic strategy and research into higher education practice and policy. He has edited a number of books in each of these areas, has participated in (and led) a number of international collaborations and has obtained funding for higher education research from a variety of national and international sources. Previously, he held a readership in Physics and has worked at various levels in universities in a number of countries.

António M. Magalhães is Associate Professor at the Faculty of Psychology and Education Sciences of the University of Porto, Portugal, and a senior researcher at CIPES (Center for Research in Higher Education Policies), Portugal. His expertise lies in the area of the regulation mechanisms of education and the relationships between state and higher education, higher education governance, and theories and methods of policy analyses, issues on which he has published in national and international journals and publishing houses.

Michael K. McLendon is Associate Professor of Public Policy and Higher Education at Peabody College, Vanderbilt University, USA. At Vanderbilt, he chairs the program in Higher Education Leadership and Policy. He studies state governance, finance and politics of higher education. His current work examines the origins and spread of new higher education finance and governance policies among the American states. His work has appeared in the *Journal of Higher Education, Educational Evaluation and Policy Analysis, Review of Higher Education, Educational Policy, Research in Higher Education, Higher Education: Handbook of Theory and Research*, and as chapters in numerous books. He serves as an associate editor of *Higher Education: Handbook of Theory and Research* and on the editorial boards of *Research in Higher Education* and *Review of Higher Education*. He holds a Ph.D. in higher education policy from the University of Michigan.

V. Lynn Meek is Professor and Foundation Director of the L. H. Martin Institute of Higher Education Leadership and Management at the University of Melbourne. He was previously Professor and Director of the Center for Higher Education Management and Policy at the University of New England. Having completed a Ph.D. in the sociology of higher education at the University of Cambridge, he has nearly three decades' experience researching higher education management and policy issues. Specific research interests include governance and management, research management, diversification of higher education institutions and systems, institutional amalgamations, organizational change, and comparative study of higher education systems. He has published thirty books and monographs and numerous scholarly articles and book chapters. He is on the editorial board of several international journals and book series, and has worked with such international agencies as UNESCO and the OECD.

Claudia Meister-Scheytt is Lecturer in the Department of Organization and Learning, School of Management, Innsbruck University (currently on maternity leave). Her main research interest lies in organizational dynamics in universities, especially changing governance and management practices, the role of middle management in organizational change and the impact of new forms of financing higher education institutions. She has carried out a number of research projects on these issues (for example, for the National Science Fund Austria and the

Austrian Ministry of Science and Research). She also lectures on a number of courses in higher and further education programs on the above-mentioned issues, and acts as a consultant to higher education institutions and policy-making bodies.

Svein Michelsen is Associate Professor at the Department of Administration and Organization Theory, University of Bergen. Among his publications are: "Apprentice Socialisation, Biography and Organisation: Societal Conditions for Vocational Training in Norwegian Industry," in A. Heikkinen et al., eds., *Work of Hands and Work of Minds in Time of Change* (University of Jyväskylä, 1999), "The New Careworker: Expanding the Apprentice System into New Fields of Work" (with H. Høst), in P. Gonon et al., eds., *Gender Perspectives on Vocational Education* (Brussels: Peter Lang Verlag, 2000), and "Some Remarks on Norwegian Vocational Education and Training Policies and Lifelong Learning" (with H. Høst), in K. Harney et al., eds., *Lifelong Learning: One Focus, Different Systems: Studien zur Erwachsenbildung* (Brussels: Peter Lang Verlag, 2002).

Dominic Orr is currently a senior researcher at the German higher education policy and research institute Higher Education Information System (HIS), Hanover. He is also International Coordinator of the European project EUROSTUDENT on the social dimension of higher education in the European Higher Education Area. Following completion of his first degree at Southbank University in London, he obtained a Ph.D. in Comparative Education at the Technical University of Dresden. He has also worked at the International Centre for Higher Education Management (ICHEM) at the University of Bath. He has worked and published in the areas of comparative studies on higher education, funding and quality assurance, social dimension in European higher education reform.

Lucia Padure is a Ph.D. candidate in Higher Education in the Department of Theory and Policy Studies in Education, Ontario Institute for Studies in Education, University of Toronto, Canada. She earned degrees in Economics from State University of Moldova, St Petersburg State University, and Northeastern University, and a Master's degree in Public Policy from Harvard University. She is the author of a number of articles and reports dealing with higher education and economic reforms in Central and Eastern Europe. She taught at Kansas State University (USA) and the International Institute of Management (Moldova), and worked as consultant for the Moldovan Parliament. In 2007 she served as a senior policy adviser in the Transformation and Integration Branch of the Ontario Ministry of Training, Colleges and Universities. Her doctoral research focuses on policy reforms in Central and Eastern European higher education, with a particular emphasis on issues of access, governance and the changing role of government in steering higher education.

Catherine Paradeise is Professor of Sociology at the University Paris Est-Marne-la-Vallée and member of the research center Laboratoire Techniques, Territoires et Sociétés-CNRS/UMLV/Ecole Nationale des Ponts et Chaussées (LATTS).

Among her publications are: *University Governance: Western European Comparative Perspectives* (Dordrecht: Springer, 2008) (ed. With I. Bleiklie, E. Reale and E. Ferlie), *Global Science and National Sovereignty* (ed. with G. Mallard and A. Peerbaye) (Abingdon: Routledge, 2008) and "Les plateformes technologiques, un instrument de politique scientifique dans les sciences de la vie" (with F. Aggeri, A. Branciard, P. le Masson and A. Peerbaye), *Revue d'économie industrielle* (December 2007).

Emanuela Reale is a senior researcher at CNR CERIS in Rome. Among her recent publications are: *The Evaluation of Public Research: An Analysis of the Three-year Research Evaluation Exercise* (Milano: Franco Angeli, 2008), *University Governance: Western European Comparative Perspectives* (Dordrecht: Springer, 2008) (ed. with C. Paradeise, I. Bleiklie and E. Ferlie), and "Evaluation of Research and Teaching Activities: Methods, Instruments and Critical Connections in the Italian Experience" (with M. Seeber), in *Rassegna Italiana di valutazione* (2007).

Gianfranco Rebora is Full Professor of Organization at the University Cattaneo LIUC, Italy, where he is currently Head of the Department of Management. From 2001 to 2007 he was Rector of the university and was previously Dean of the Faculty of Business Administration. He also lectured at the Università Bocconi and the University of Brescia. His expertise lies in the area of organization and management of human resources, public management, evaluation and change management. He has directed numerous research projects and is president of various scientific committees and evaluation units in Italian public institutions. He is on the editorial board of several scientific journals.

Alan Scott is Professor of Sociology at the University of Innsbruck. In Easter term 2008 he was a visiting fellow at the Centre for Research in the Arts, Social Sciences and Humanities (CRASSH), University of Cambridge, during which he was able to work on issues of (academic) disciplinarity. In 2009 he holds the Vincent Wright Visiting Chair in Sciences Politiques, Paris. His research and publications are in the areas of political and organizational sociology, and in social theory. With respect to higher education research, he is co-editor of and a contributor to *Bright Satanic Mills: Universities and Regional Development in the Knowledge Economy* (Ashgate, 2007).

David N. Smith is Professor of Lifelong Learning and Co-Director of the Centre for Research in Lifelong Learning (CRLL) at Glasgow Caledonian University. From 1993 to 2008 he was Principal Research Fellow at the School of Education, University of Leeds where he was also lead founder and Director of the Higher Education Policy Unit (HEPU). His research and writing reflect a broad spectrum of higher education policy in both historical and contemporary settings, including governance and leadership in universities, widening participation and research policy. His most recent research includes an ESRC-funded study (with Parry, Bathmaker and Brooks), *Universal Access and Dual Regimes of Further and Higher Education* and an AHRC Impact Fellowship (with Taylor), *Knowledge Transfer and the Creative Industries.*

Christine Teelken is Associate Professor at the Faculty of Social Sciences of the VU University Amsterdam. Her research interests focus on higher education institutions, particularly from an international perspective. She has supervised Ph.D. and Master's theses in a variety of areas. Her publications have appeared, for example, in *Public Administration, International Journal for HRM, Comparative Education, International Review of Administrative Sciences, Higher Education Policy* and *Research in Higher Education.* She is Chair of the EGOS-Standing Working Group: Organizing the Public Sector: Governance and Public Management Reform (2008–2011). She has carried out various external research projects (e.g. for the Dutch Educational Council and for McKinsey and Company). She lectures on Organizational Change and Development, Organizational Learning and many other courses.

Matteo Turri is a researcher at the Department of Economics, Business and Statistics at the University of Milan, Italy. He holds a Ph.D. in Business Economics (topic: university evaluation) from the University Cattaneo LIUC. He is Lecturer in Public Management in the Faculty of Political Science at the University of Milan. He deals with managerial and organizational topics particularly with respect to public administrations: the functioning of control and evaluation systems, the changing face of the university, governance systems in non-profit-making organizations and organizational change. He is a member of the evaluation unit at the University of Bologna.

Don F. Westerheijden is Senior Research Associate at the Center for Higher Education Policy Studies (CHEPS), where he coordinates research related to quality management and is involved in the coordination of Ph.D. students. Among his publications are: *Quality Assurance in Higher Education: Trends in Regulation, Translation and Transformation* (ed. with B. Stensaker and M. Rosa) (Dordrecht: Springer, 2007), "Disseminating the Right Information to the Right Audience: Cultural Determinants in the Use (and Misuse) of Rankings" (with L. Cremonini and J. Enders), in *Higher Education* (2007) and *Accreditation and Evaluation in the European Higher Education Area* (ed. with S. Schwarz) (Dordrecht: Kluwer Academic Publishers, 2004).

Jakob Williams Ørberg is Research Assistant on the project New Management, New Identities? Danish University Reform in an International Perspective, Danish School of Education, University of Århus. He studied the debates surrounding the reform through documentary analysis and interviews with politicians, civil servants and university leaders, with a focus on how Danish universities are imagined and enacted in the context of globalization. He has a candidate degree (M.Phil.) in Anthropology from Copenhagen University and his thesis is a fieldwork-based study of public space in relation to a World Heritage Site in Nepal. This thesis and his secondary qualification in town planning exemplify his main interest in relations between planning and practice and how institutions work in both conceptual and physical forms.

Susan Wright is Professor of Educational Anthropology, Danish School of Education, University of Århus. Her main interest is in the anthropology of large-scale processes of political transformation. Her current project is on Danish university reform and before that she focused on the role of universities in changing forms of governance in Britain. Through a multi-site ethnography in the 1980s and 1990s in central government, a local authority and an examining community, she traced the introduction of neo-liberal forms of governance in Britain, and in the *Anthropology of Policy* (co-edited with Cris Shore) (London: Routledge, 1997) proposed a new approach to political anthropology. Informing all her work are insights gained from studies of political transformation in Iran before and after the Islamic Revolution.

Foreword

Higher education institutions are part of the social furniture in almost every society, and increasingly so in today's world of "information work." But their social role varies sharply across time and space. Indeed they could almost be said to be a mirror of political life, as Napoleon Bonaparte said of budgeting.

In some societies higher education institutions are seen as organs of the state or the "establishment." They are state or nation-building institutions, guardians of political or religious orthodoxy. They can often function as instruments of ethnocratic rule as well, for instance, in the way they privilege some languages over others. In 1870 Emil du Bois-Reymond described the University of Berlin (of which he was *Rektor*, as well as President of the Prussian Academy of Sciences) as "the intellectual bodyguard of the House of Hohenzollern" (Von Mises, 1944: 101). With appropriate changes to the name of the ruling regime, that description could equally be applied to numerous universities today.

In other social contexts, higher education institutions aspire to, and may even achieve, a significant degree of autonomy as self-governing societies. We can think of them as approximating the position of the Church in medieval Europe or that of the military in those societies where the armed forces see themselves as a self-governing *Staat im Staat*. It is arguably no accident that Don Price drew an analogy with the autonomous estates of European feudal states for the title of his 1965 classic *The Scientific Estate*. And university students have often played a key part in politics as a distinct and organized social grouping in developing and transitional countries. On occasion that has even happened in developed countries too, for instance, in the famous *événements* in Paris in May 1968.

In still other social settings, higher education institutions can be seen essentially as firms in a market for the production of "knowledge services." They are concerned with economic viability and competition for business, maybe engaging in cartel and rent-seeking behavior as well, whenever they get the chance. The privately owned universities of East and South-East Asia, some of which are family businesses that form part of a conglomerate group of companies, are perhaps the purest examples of that style. But market analogies, private corporate-style governance and a business ethos for the provision of research, consultancy and even teaching have been much in vogue in a number of countries over the recent past. And the increasing population of universities in Western countries over the last forty years has perhaps helped to put the spotlight on competition to a greater extent than before.

In other circumstances, higher education institutions can be understood as "organized anarchies." That was the telling phrase used by Cohen, March, and Olsen (1972) to characterize organizations – of which they held universities to be the pre-eminent example – where goals are problematic rather than generally agreed, where links between cause and effect (particularly over governance arrangements) are unclear, and where decision-making involves an ever-changing cast of characters rather than a fixed group of participants operating within clear institutional boundaries. Business-minded reformers of course shudder at this model of university life, and you hardly have to be a fully paid-up managerialist to recognize its frustrations. But this model too offers a form of governance that is not only commonly observable, but apparently viable as a way of organizing training and research in many circumstances.

Those four types do not exhaust the possibilities. But they represent some of the most obvious contradictory models for higher educational institutions and their governance today. We can see such competing models as part of an arrow-like process of historical development of the kind favored in nineteenth-century social theory, in which the stress goes from one approach to another over time. Or we can see them as part of a more circle-like process of recurrence and return. We can see the tensions between different models as contradictions to be worked out in the interest of arriving at a clearer mission for the modern university against which its performance can be assessed, and that is a common drumbeat of advocates of reform. Or we can see them as countervailing pressures which are the only way to make such institutions controllable and avoid an unchecked embrace of any one social value – an argument made long ago by Andrew Dunsire (1978) for control over bureaucracy.

There is a need for these issues to be properly debated. And in the face of such pervasive tensions, a book that grapples seriously with the underlying theoretical issues of governance and reform in higher education across a dozen or so developed countries is timely and necessary. Equally welcome is the attempt by the contributors to this volume to link such issues in higher education with broader frameworks for understanding governance.

Christopher Hood
Gladstone Professor of Government,
University of Oxford

References

Cohen, Michael D., James G. March, and Johan P. Olsen. "A Garbage Can Model of Organizational Choice." *Administrative Science Quarterly* 17(1) (1972): 1–23.

Dunsire, Andrew. *Control in a Bureaucracy. The Execution Process: Volume 2.* Oxford: Martin Robertson, 1978.

Price, Don K. *The Scientific Estate.* Cambridge, MA: Belknap Press, 1965.

Von Mises, Ludwig. *Bureaucracy.* New Haven: Yale University Press, 1944.

1

Coming to Terms with Governance in Higher Education

JEROEN HUISMAN

Introduction

Although "system policy" is among the most popular areas for research in higher education (Tight, 2003), the use of frameworks to study higher education policy and governance rooted in public administration and public policy, sociology or political science is rare, although there are notable exceptions. This is partly due to the nature of higher education as a field of study. Tight (2004) aptly qualifies this field as an a-theoretical community of practice: the broader engagement with theory is absent and theoretical perspectives are merely implicit.

Whereas such a field may flourish – and, given the growth of the field, it undoubtedly has – it can be argued that much is lost in not linking up with the achievements and insights gained in the aforementioned disciplines. Without trying to sound overly critical of the state of the art in higher education research, a corollary of Tight's qualification is that much of the work is descriptive and/or normative. This considerably limits the learning opportunities in the field. In this context, learning particularly relates to building a better understanding of higher education, based on conceptually and theoretically sound building blocks. In slightly different words, Schwarz and Teichler (2000: 2) ask: "How can research on higher education make sure that the range of heterogeneous disciplines it refers to does not remain segmented, thus leading to simplified observations?"

The advantages of an approach that seeks to build bridges between the field of higher education and the disciplines are obvious. First of all, the disciplines have a rich and long(er) tradition of studying policy, politics, governance and organizations. It would be unthoughtful to discard this abundance of insights. One may argue that higher education is different from the subjects (sectors, actors, organizations) studied in policy studies, political sciences, etc., but it would be far-fetched to argue that higher education is so special or specific that none of the conceptual or theoretical disciplinary approaches would apply to the field of higher education. Second, and this is also another counter-argument against those arguing for a special treatment of higher education, results from applications of disciplinary devices in higher education would lead either to a further strengthening or enrichment of the disciplinary approaches. Studies would either confirm the expectations or lead to adjustments thereof. One needs to bear in mind, however, that seeking refuge in the disciplines is not a panacea for all "problems" (perceived or real) that the field of higher education is confronted with (see, e.g., Scott (1999) on the research–policy gap). Furthermore, disciplines such as public administration, sociology and political science themselves struggle with building coherent and consensual theoretical frameworks. As in the field of higher education, there are numerous competing schools, approaches and traditions, leaving the disciplines to some extent fragmented.

Nevertheless, it is argued that building bridges between the field of higher education and the policy and governance disciplines is a worthwhile exercise, and this is one of the basic objectives of this volume in the series International Studies in Higher Education. In the remainder of this chapter, concepts are elaborated upon and an overview is given of the contributions to the volume.

The Concepts of Government and Governance

One of the central notions in public administration and public policy and political science is the relationship between state and society and – more specifically – whether, and if so how, the state (government) should steer, plan, regulate and control societal sectors (and individuals). The basic questions around this relationship relate to the division of responsibilities between the nation-state – in all its different guises: governments, parliaments, ministries and other governmental agencies – and public and private institutions as well as individual citizens. In this context, public policy is roughly to be understood as "a choice made by a government to undertake some course of action" (Howlett and Ramesh, 1995: 5), whether these actions are regulative, financial or communicative in nature (Hood, 1983). There is a plentiful literature addressing the normative foundations of this relationship, discussing the formation and development of these relationships and debating its impact, e.g. in terms of efficiency and effectiveness. In the traditional literature, governance is almost synonymous with government, being the main actor and coordinator in "the act or process of governing, specifically authoritative direction and control" (Merriam-Webster dictionary online: www.merriam-webster.com). In this setting, governmental policies were the main steering instruments to give direction to the state's role in societal affairs, acknowledging that there were quite different manifestations of the state's role (see, e.g., Streeck and Schmitter (1985) on corporatism and pluralism).

In recent decades, the general role of government as the "lone coordinator," particularly in Western Europe, has changed. Partly, its steering role has been eroded by challenges to the efficiency and effectiveness – and thus the legitimacy – of the traditional state model. Also increasing social pluriformity and ongoing individualization have undermined the state governments' roles (van Heffen, Kickert and Thomassen, 2000). As such, policy arenas were opened up for other "coordinators" and new steering principles and governance modes – e.g., quasi-markets (LeGrand and Bartlett, 1993), network steering (Rhodes, 1997; Thompson et al., 1991), new public management (Ferlie et al., 1996; Pollitt, 2003), multi-level and multi-actor governance (Peters and Pierre, 2001) and interactive governance (Denters et al., 2003) – were introduced to make sense of the changes. Also conceptual and empirical attempts have been proposed to understand better how actors control public sectors (see, e.g., Hood et al., 2004).

Like many other societal sectors, higher education has not been left untouched by changing views on and manifestations of governance. Indeed, in many Western countries, higher education has been among the front-runners – although not always wholeheartedly – in experiments with changing steering approaches (but see Chapter 11, this volume). The initial change in steering in higher education in the 1980s and early 1990s are aptly perceived as the rise of the evaluative state (Neave, 1988, 1998) or steering from a distance (Neave and van Vught, 1991). In general, this change implies less governmental interference in higher education affairs or a change from *ex ante* control to *ex post* evaluation and more apparent autonomy for higher education institutions.

However, there is more to the picture than meets the eye. Whereas the general observation on the change in steering approaches applies to many systems across the globe and the observation is particularly relevant for the changes in the 1980s and early 1990s, it is worthwhile to address three sets of qualifications. First, changes across systems occur at different paces (some systems move faster towards the "steering from a distance" model). In a number of higher education systems governments are ambiguous and show different faces at the same time when it comes to their steering approaches (Gornitzka and Maassen, 2000; Maassen and van Vught, 1988) and – furthermore – some of the intentions to move towards the evaluative state have had serious side-effects (e.g. in the UK through rather rigorous quality control in research, teaching and learning) leading paradoxically to increasing state intrusion. A second qualification is that the move towards the evaluative state and steering from a distance has to some extent played down the rise of the market or quasi-markets in higher education. Particularly among the early continental European adopters of the new steering approach, the changes were mostly formulated as a recalibration of the powers of governments versus the higher education institutions. Only in the 1990s – and in the UK at an earlier stage – the concept of market mechanisms became more dominant in the policy and steering debates (see, e.g., Dill, 2000; Meek and Wood, 1997; Teixeira et al., 2004 and various contributions to this volume). A third issue, often neglected in the higher education literature, is the interplay between national and supranational steering approaches (but see De Wit, 2003; De Wit and Verhoeven, 2001; Witte, 2006), although it has to be admitted that the interference of supranational agencies in higher education is fairly recent. But there is growing evidence that there will be increasing interaction between domestic and supranational policies and steering approaches in higher education – particularly in the context of the Bologna and Lisbon processes (Corbett, 2005) and possibly in relation to GATS (Knight, 2002).

Challenges for Higher Education Governance Research

Whereas the concepts developed in the field of higher education (evaluative state, steering from a distance) and the disciplines (e.g. multi-level and multi-actor governance; quasi-markets) have certainly contributed to our understanding of the general patterns of change in the steering and governance of higher education systems, at the same time new puzzles emerged. First, various analyses have pointed out that current modes of governance in higher education are mixtures of old and new steering approaches. Maassen and van Vught (1988) were among the first to illustrate that changes of steering paradigms in practice were less clear cut than the models envisaged (see also Hood et al., 2004; Olsen, 2007).

Governments, still dominant in changing governance arrangements, have seemingly struggled to let go of public sectors; and traditional governance mechanisms were not easily, or in a straightforward manner, replaced by new mechanisms (see also Chapter 10, this volume). Second, a corollary of the former, given the current mix of governance approaches, the consequences – in terms of impact on organizations and actors in the field – are difficult to predict. Higher education institutions, institutional leaders and academics are situated in institutional contexts in which various factors stemming from different coordination mechanisms push and pull them in directions that are quite often unanticipated. In all, the field of higher education (and other public or quasi-public sectors) lends itself perfectly for further investigations – either through contemporary or longitudinal studies within one country or comparatively across systems – of governance issues in higher education. The object of analysis could be the higher education system, the organizations within the system or (groups of) actors within the system.

In this volume, the challenge to understand better governance in higher education and its (potential) impact is taken up. The general guiding question for the contributions to this volume is: *how can we, on the basis of insights from the disciplines and the field of higher education, better understand governance in higher education?* In the volume, basically three different directions are chosen. Chapters 2 to 7 – looking at the application of governance frameworks – take "traditional" governance approaches as a point of departure. The second set of chapters (8 to 12) – under the part title "Variations on a Governance Theme" – do build on existing governance insights but choose to deviate, for various reasons, from the "traditional" approaches. Reasons may range from discontent with what is on offer from the field of higher education or the disciplines, to a combination of curiosity and creativity to stimulate the search for new ways. The third set of chapters (13 to 15) – "The Invisible Hand of Governance" – addresses phenomena in higher education, where new and often complex interactions of governance and co-ordination arrangements create a changing institutional playing field where coordination imperatives may be ambiguous, vague and of different strengths. Actors within this new governance context may, on the one hand, be limited in their scope of behavior or be caught in a web of different coordination mechanisms that work as a straitjacket. But, on the other hand, such contexts (guided by a mixture of hierarchical, market and network coordination) may create space as well to experiment, to find new answers to old and emerging questions. Certainly when governments withdraw from interference in certain domains and create room for maneuver for market and network coordination – without clearly setting institutional boundary rules for such coordination – actors may find considerable leeway to devise and assemble new patterns of behavior.

The Contributions to this Volume

Part I: The Application of Governance Frameworks

As said, this set of chapters deals with the application of existing frameworks, concepts and theories in the field of higher education. Gianfranco Rebora and Matteo Turri (Chapter 2) use Olsen's institutional perspective (Olsen, 1988, 2007) to analyze the evolution of system governance in Italian higher education. They argue that the development can be captured as a change from the sovereign rationality-bounded state model to the supermarket model, but there are important nuances. Particularly the notion of pluralistic or fragmented networks, beyond the move towards the market, adds to the understanding of the current dynamics in the Italian higher education system.

Dominic Orr and Michael Jaeger (Chapter 3) return to Peters' insights in governance. Peters' (2001) approach – particularly the market model – is used to assess the state of public reform in higher education governance in German *Länder*. Particular attention is paid to changes in the funding regulations of German higher education. The analysis shows that (along the lines of Peters' expectations) the implementation of new models is not without contradictions, leading to dynamic adjustments of reform programs and potential limits to the implementation of reform (as intended).

Claudia Meister-Scheytt and Alan Scott (Chapter 4) apply Hood's (1998) conceptual view on governance, rooted in Mary Douglas' cultural theory in combination with Dumont's (1970) anthropological insights. They analyze tensions in recent reforms in Austrian higher education, with an emphasis on the functioning of boards of governance. The reform turns out to be a complex struggle between tradition (Humboldtian model) and modernization (neo-liberal model), and outcomes are uneven and context-dependent.

An anthropological perspective is (also) used by Susan Wright and Jakob Williams Ørberg (Chapter 5) to analyze recent reforms in Danish higher education. Using the concept of assemblage (Collier and Ong, 2005) – which assumes that elements of reform may be derived from multiple origins and may carry different logics, and thus become prone to negotiation and controversy – the focus is on key elements of the reform process: self-ownership (autonomy), degrees of freedom, and accountability. The chapter puts the findings of the study in the context of the broader literature on governance: does steering from a distance give universities more autonomy or is the level of autonomy merely rhetoric? And does steering from a distance lead to the hollowing out of the state?

In Chapter 6 (Catherine Paradeise and colleagues), three different theoretical perspectives from the public administration and management literature (New Public Management, Network Governance and neo Weberianism) are used to shed light on governance reform projects in a number of European countries (England, France, Germany, Italy, the Netherlands, Norway and Switzerland). The three perspectives, although not mutually exclusive, put different emphasis on the "causes" of reform policies. The chapter highlights which of the perspectives is/are able to explain higher education reform processes.

Lucia Padure and Glen A. Jones (Chapter 7) review different approaches to policy network analysis and discuss how this concept could contribute to the study of higher education reforms. The chapter argues that policy networks can help us to understand and explain the effects of globalization and multi-level governance on higher education policy-making. Incorporating critical and discursive policy network approaches, which rely on the context of policy-making (values, ideas and ideologies), unequal power dynamics and discourse analysis will increase, it is argued, our understanding of issues of power and influence in the development of higher education theory and policy.

Part II: Variations on a Governance Theme

This set of chapters deviates (sometimes profoundly) from existing governance approaches. Roger Brown (Chapter 8) addresses governance change in UK higher education. His contribution argues that, basically, efficiency and effectiveness have been the underlying drivers for higher education policy-making between the early 1980s and the mid-2000s. In terms of a conceptual and theoretical perspective this chapter links to, but also deviates from, longitudinal policy change perspectives, such as the lifecycle perspective (Peters and Hogwood, 1985) and policy generations (Namenwirth and Weber, 1987).

Leo Goedegebuure, Martin Hayden and V. Lynn Meek (Chapter 9) analyze current understandings of "good governance" in Australian higher education at the higher education system level. They address whether concepts of "good governance" rooted in the private sector organizational governance literature are transferable to the level of the higher education system. The chapter analyzes to what extent the policies of the past decade live up to the expectations of "good governance."

Michael K. McLendon and James C. Hearn (Chapter 10) contribute to our understanding of governance issues (particularly decentralization) in US higher education. The chapter focuses on (a) the deregulation of state procedural controls; (b) the loosening of state governance and state-wide coordination; and (c) the advent of charter or enterprise colleges and universities. These trends are analyzed in the context of countervailing pressures and perspectives. That is, although decentralization is seen almost as an inherent good, there are various reasons to doubt whether this assumption applies. The chapter concludes with reflections on what is lost and gained when governments forgo or diminish one form of authority for others.

The chapter by António M. Magalhães and Alberto Amaral (Chapter 11) aims to map out the general discourses on higher education governance over the past decades. After having discussed various analytical frameworks that have tried to come to terms with governance change in the past decades (e.g. Neave and van Vught, 1991; Peters, 2001; Salamon, 2002), the chapter analyzes recent and current governance trends around three central themes: (a) the role attributed to the state; (b) the role assigned to education; and (c) the role assigned to knowledge. Ultimately, the discussions around these themes lead the authors back to basic political questions: what is higher education about and what are its social and economic roles?

Kelly Coate and Iain Mac Labhrainn (Chapter 12) look at the Irish case. The developments in Irish higher education seem to be a result of various interrelated drivers, most of which relate to socio-economic factors: a belief in the economic contribution of higher education to the knowledge society and the shaping of higher education policy by external influences, such as a recent OECD review, the Lisbon agenda and a commitment to the wider European project. The chapter considers how current theoretical models are unable to explain some of the peculiarities of the Irish system as it has developed over the past four decades.

Part II: The Invisible Hand of Governance

The change in governance arrangements has created space for various actors in the higher education system to adapt to new forms of coordination or to allow for "creative" solutions in new institutional contexts. Harry F. de Boer (Chapter 13) argues that the theory of reasoned action (Fishbein and Ajzen, rooted in social psychology) can be a fruitful approach to analyze institutional reform. This theory posits that the best way to explain behavior is to discover an actor's intentions to perform an act. Thus, the attitude towards a behavior, and the social norm that the actor perceives with respect to that behavior, explains intentions. In other words, behavior is dependent on attitudes (beliefs and their strengths) towards behavior and formal rules. A third factor – informal rules that sustain safeguards to maintain professional autonomy – is added to the basic model. The case of institutional governance reform in the Dutch university sector is used to illustrate the relevance of the framework.

Christine Teelken, Kees Boersma and Peter Groenewegen (Chapter 14) look at the Dutch graduate system, focusing on the phenomenon of part-time, external Ph.D. students and the policies and strategies developed by schools and departments to cater for these students. There are no concrete national policies regarding these scholars, apart from the fact that universities (or their departments) are financially rewarded for graduating a Ph.D. student. The lack of a national policy gives actors at the local level ample room to set rules and standards. The chapter discusses how local actors deal with this leeway in a setting that is mainly dominated by the New Public Management doctrine. Surprisingly, external Ph.D. students are not (yet) part of increasingly pervasive managerial control systems.

David N. Smith and Jonathan Adams (Chapter 15) deal with university leadership and its relationship with recent changes in national steering approaches (focusing on the UK and Australia). They argue that theories and concepts of meta-level relationships between state and society have limited value in understanding the specific directions of institutional change (including leadership issues). A plea is made for an institutional view – using management theory and organizational sociology – that focuses much more on organizational structures and strategies. The development of how executive leadership is evolving in the various countries is exemplified. Evidence was found for convergence around the problem of aligning the leadership of academic structures with the leadership of the wider corporate institution.

For sure, the volume has not pretended to give the definitive answer to existing governance questions. Indeed, it may have raised more new questions. But the chapters have tried to answer pieces of particular puzzles. The richness of existing and adjusted frameworks has been accentuated and it is hoped that the insights from the analyses will prove to be a valuable input to the continuing debates on higher education governance.

Acknowledgments

I would like to thank the series editors David Palfreyman, Ted Tapper and Scott Thomas for their support to include this volume in their International Issues in Higher Education series. Special thanks to Ted Tapper for acting as the liaison between general editors and volume editor, and his willingness to edit two chapters written by contributors who do not have English as their first language. Also thanks to Jill Siddall (DBA-HEM administrator at the International Centre for Higher Education Management, University of Bath) and Mari Brookes (Ph.D. student at the Centre) for helping to prepare the full document.

References

Collier, Stephen, and Aiwha Ong. "Global Assemblages, Anthropological Problems." In *Global Assemblages: Technology, Politics, and Ethics as Anthropological Problems*, edited by Aiwha Ong, and Stephen Collier. Oxford: Blackwell Publishing, 2005, 3–21.

Corbett, Anne. *Universities and the Europe of Knowledge: Ideas, Institutions and Policy Entrepreneurship in European Union Higher Education Policy, 1955–2005.* Basingstoke: Palgrave Macmillan, 2005.

De Wit, Kurt. "The Consequences of European Integration for Higher Education." *Higher Education Policy* 16(2) (2003): 161–178.

De Wit, Kurt, and Jef Verhoeven. "The Higher Education Policy of the European Union: With or Against the Member States?" In *Higher Education and the Nation State: The International Dimension of Higher Education*, edited by Jeroen Huisman, Peter Maassen, and Guy Neave. Amsterdam: Pergamon, 2001, 175–231.

Denters, Bas, Oscar van Heffen, Jeroen Huisman, and Pieter-Jan Klok, eds. *The Rise of Interactive Governance and Quasi-markets.* Dordrecht: Kluwer, 2003.

Dill, David D. *The "Marketization" of Higher Education: Applications of the Theory of Industrial Organization.* Paper presented at NIFU, Oslo, Norway, June 19, 2000.

Dumont, Louis. *Homo Hierarchicus: The Caste System and Its Implications.* Translated by Mark Sainsbury, Louis Dumont, and Basic Gulati. Chicago: University of Chicago Press, 1970.

Ferlie, Ewan, Lynn Ashburner, Louise Fitzgerald, and Andrew Pettigrew. *The New Public Management in Action.* Oxford: Oxford University Press, 1996.

Gornitzka, Ase, and Peter Maassen. "Hybrid Steering Approaches with Respect to European Higher Education." *Higher Education Policy* 13(3) (2000): 267–268.

Heffen, Oscar van, Walter J.M. Kickert, and Jacques Thomassen. "Introduction: Multi-level and Multi-actor Governance." In *Governance in Modern Society*, edited by Oscar van Heffen, Walter J.M. Kickert, and Jacques Thomassen. Dordrecht: Kluwer, 2000, 3–11.

Hood, Christopher. *The Tools of Government.* London: Macmillan, 1983.

Hood, Christopher. *The Art of the State: Culture, Rhetoric, and Public Management.* Oxford: Clarendon Press, 1998.

Hood, Christopher, Oliver James, B. Guy Peters, and Colin Scott, eds. *Controlling Modern Government: Variety, Commonality and Change*. Cheltenham: Edward Elgar, 2004.

Howlett, Michael, and M. Ramesh. *Studying Public Policy: Policy Cycles and Policy Subsystems*. Toronto: Oxford University Press, 1995.

Knight, Jane. *Trade in Higher Education Services: The Implications of GATS*. London: OBHE, 2002.

LeGrand, Julian, and Will Bartlett. *Quasi-markets and Social Policy*. London: Macmillan Press, 1993.

Maassen, Peter, and Frans A. van Vught. "An Intriguing Janus-head: The Two Faces of the New Governmental Strategy for Higher Education in the Netherlands." *European Journal of Education* 23 (1988): 65–77.

Meek, V. Lynn, and Fiona Q. Wood. "The Market as a New Steering Strategy for Australian Higher Education." *Higher Education Policy* 10(3/4) (1997): 253–274.

Namenwirth, J. Zvi, and Robert P. Weber. *Dynamics of Culture*. Winchester: Allen and Unwin, 1987.

Neave, Guy. "On the Cultivation of Quality, Efficiency and Enterprise: An Overview of Recent Trends in Higher Education in Western Europe, 1986–1988." *European Journal of Education* 23(1/2) (1988): 7–23.

Neave, Guy. "The Evaluative State Reconsidered." *European Journal of Education* 33(3) (1998): 265–284.

Neave, Guy, and Frans A. van Vught, eds. *Prometheus Bound: The Changing Relationship between Government and Higher Education in Western Europe*. Oxford: Pergamon, 1991.

Olsen, Johan P. "Administrative Reform and Theories of Organization." In *Organizing Governance: Governing Organizations*, edited by Colin Campbell, and B. Guy Peters. Pittsburgh: University of Pittsburgh Press, 1988, 233–245.

Olsen, Johan P. "The Institutional Dynamics of the European University." In *University Dynamics and European Integration*, edited by Peter Maassen, and Johan P. Olsen. Dordrecht: Kluwer, 2007, 25–53.

Peters, B. Guy. *The Future of Governing: Four Emerging Models* (2nd edn). Kansas: University of Kansas Press, 2001.

Peters, B. Guy, and Brian Hogwood. "In Search of the Issue–Attention Cycle." *Journal of Politics* 47 (1985): 238–253.

Peters, B. Guy, and Jon Pierre. "Developments in Intergovernmental Relations: Towards Multi-level Governance." *Policy and Politics* 29(2) (2001): 131–135.

Pollitt, Christopher. "The 'New Public Management' – Revolution or Fad?" In *The Essential Public Manager*, edited by Christopher Pollitt. Maidenhead: Open University Press, 2003, 26–51.

Rhodes, Rod A.W. *Understanding Governance: Policy Networks, Governance, Reflexivity and Accountability*. London: Open University Press, 1997.

Salamon, Lester M. "The New Governance and the Tools of Public Action: An Introduction." In *The Tools of Government: A Guide to the New Governance*, edited by Lester M. Salamon. New York: Oxford University Press, 2002, 1–47.

Schwarz, Stephanie, and Ulrich Teichler. "Introduction." In *The Institutional Basis of Higher Education Research: Experiences and Perspectives*, edited by Stephanie Schwarz, and Ulrich Teichler. Dordrecht: Kluwer Academic, 2000, 1–9.

Scott, Peter. "The Research–Policy Gap." *Journal of Education Policy* 14(3) (1999): 317–337.

Streeck, Wolfgang, and Philippe C. Schmitter. *Private Interest Government: Beyond Market and State*. London: Sage, 1985.

Teixeira, Pedro, Ben Jongbloed, David Dill, and Alberto Amaral, eds. *Markets in Higher Education: Rhetoric or Reality?* Dordrecht: Kluwer, 2004.

Thompson, Grahame, Jennifer Frances, Rosalind Levacic, and Jeremy Mitchell, eds. *Markets, Hierarchies and Networks: The Coordination of Social Life*. London: Sage, 1991.

Tight, Malcolm. *Researching Higher Education*. Maidenhead: Society for Research into Higher Education and Open University Press, 2003.

Tight, Malcolm. "Research into Higher Education: An A-theoretical Community of Practice?" *Higher Education Research and Development* 23(4) (2004): 395–411.

Witte, Johanna. *Change of Degrees and Degrees of Change: Comparing Adaptations of European Higher Education Systems in the Context of the Bologna Process*. Enschede: CHEPS, 2006.

Part I
The Application of
Governance Frameworks

2

Governance in Higher Education
An Analysis of the Italian Experience

GIANFRANCO REBORA AND MATTEO TURRI

Objectives and Theoretical Background

The concept of governance has many meanings and there is no scholarly consensus on a definition. This is partly due to changes in governance, making it, to some extent, a "moving target." In the context of higher education until the 1980s, governance was more or less synonymous with government, but in subsequent decades governance became associated with the idea of networks (Bevir, Rhodes and Weller, 2003), and the introduction of markets and ideas from the corporate world has led to the focus on New Public Management (NPM) as a mode of governance (Dent, 2007). The change in governance has broadened the focus beyond solely governmental policies: current analyses include policies and different ways of influencing other stakeholders and agencies in higher education, as well as incorporating – with the diffusion of the power of the state – strategy and management at the level of higher education institutions.

This chapter deals particularly with change in the governance of Italian universities and builds on the analytical observations of Olsen (2005 and 2007), who analyzed change in university governance in Europe. His most recent model results from previous work (Olsen, 1988) that referred to the evolution of state models. An initial analysis of the experience in several European countries, including Italy, was developed by Gornitzka and Maassen (2000), who took Olsen's model as a starting point. We aim to go beyond this analysis by proposing a more in-depth study and an update on recent developments as well as presenting a different interpretation. According to Olsen's theory, two fundamental variables face each other in determining the structure of university governance:

- The first considers the university either as an instrument of the policies and intentions of different external stakeholders or as an institution mainly driven by internal requests and aims (instrumental versus institutional perspective).
- The second takes into consideration the role of the actors who influence decision-making and the fact that their aims and standards of behavior are either shared or conflicting (shared versus conflicting aims).

Crossing the two variables leads to four ideal-type university and steering models (see Figure 2.1). In the institutional version, if aims are not in conflict, the university is a community of scholars governed by shared rules. The steering model

Figure 2.1
The Two Frameworks
Proposed by Olsen
(1988, 2007)

	Institutional perspective	Instrumental perspective
Shared aims	(1988) Sovereign, rationality-bounded steering model (2007) A rule-governed community of scholars	(1988) Institutional steering model (2007) Instrument for national political agendas
Conflicting aims	(1988) Corporate-pluralistic steering model (2007) Representative democracy	(1988) Supermarket steering model (2007) Service enterprise embedded in a competitive market

is based on sovereignty and bounded rationality. If aims and behavioral norms are conflicting, the model of the university is a representative democracy. The steering model that "fits" this situation is the corporate-pluralistic model (see also Streeck and Schmitter (1985) for a similar perspective). When the university is considered as instrumental, it becomes a vector of national policies and related stakeholders' agendas when objectives are non-conflicting, but if multiple or conflicting aims and ideas predominate, it turns into a service enterprise embedded in a competitive market. The concomitant steering models are the institutional steering model and the supermarket steering model, in which market mechanisms play an important role. The perspective of the most recent work by Olsen (2007) seems to shift in the direction of the individual university, but the framework also refers to the broader (steering) context of the higher education system.

Our attempt to apply this framework to an analysis of Italian university system governance implied some modifications of the Olsen model, partly because of the rather abstract nature of the model and the particular Italian context. Regarding the latter, the framework suggests giving a preference to factual elements, such as events, political decisions, norms, behavior, etc. rather than to the ideas and concepts expressed by people and bodies involved in the university system. In Italy there is in fact a systematic gap between publicly expressed ideas and actual actions and behavior.

The Framework Adopted for the Analysis of System Governance

Our analytical framework departs from two concepts: locus and focus. In the literature the concept of locus of control, elaborated by Rotter (1966), has been widely used in behavioral research to explain human behavior in organizational settings. According to Rotter, individuals develop generalized expectations as to whether success in a particular situation will be a consequence of their own personal behavior or controlled by external forces. Individuals who have a tendency to associate outcomes with their own efforts or believe that events are under their own control are defined as internals, whereas externals believe that they cannot control events or outcomes (Spector, 1982). We adapted this concept to fit governance, permitting a more gradual scale of internal versus external control, compared to the dichotomous presentation in Olsen's model. The second dimension (focus) resembles closely the idea of shared and conflicting interests between actors that Olsen (1988) took from the literature on organizations (Simon, 1957). Decision-making may be strategically rational and driven by the shared aims and values of the people taking part or involves the multiple and conflicting aims and values of those involved. In these extremes, rational policies and strategy can develop more completely or decision-making is inclined towards negotiation, managing conflicts and heeding the emotional waves of public opinion in the search for consensus. The conceptual combination of the focus and locus of governance produces four different models (see also Figure 2.2):

• Internal locus and rational focus: internal strategic governance. Forms of "self-government driven by intellectual values" develop and are expressed by the most influential actors inside the university system, who assume leadership and define strategies.

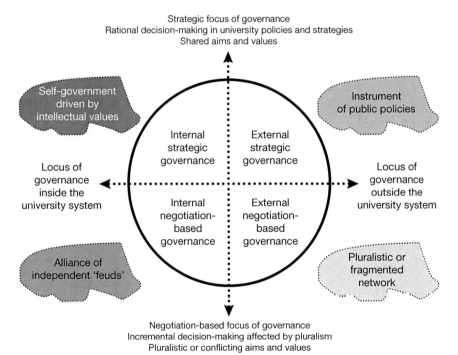

Figure 2.2 Framework for the Analysis of University System Governance

- Internal locus and conflicting focus: internal negotiation-based governance. The university system is still self-regulating in accordance with internal criteria but there is no coherent leadership and vital decisions come from multiple or conflicting processes. Governance may be interpreted as an "alliance of independent feuds."
- External locus and rational focus: external strategic governance. The university system is unable to govern in accordance with its own criteria and has to respond seriously to external requests and the influence of external actors. University action can thus be interpreted as an "instrument of public policies" when the system is coherent and the political actors governing it are able to orient it on the basis of a shared strategy.
- External locus and conflicting focus: external, negotiation-based conflicting governance. The system has to answer external requests and drives but is unable to define and carry out a unitary strategy because the different actors that make up the system follow their own objectives, which are numerous, heterogeneous and sometimes even conflicting. Complex changeable relationships thus come to light among a variety of institutional actors that lack any hierarchical order. This situation can be interpreted in terms of pluralistic or even fragmented networks.

The Four Periods in the Development of Italian University System Governance

The proposed framework will now be applied to the situation in Italian higher education. An in-depth historical analysis is not intended but rather the examination focuses on developments that have taken place since 1989, when a new era began. The following periods are taken into consideration: prior to 1989; 1989–1998; 1999–2006; and developments since 2007. The analysis draws upon previous works on the subject (e.g. Boffo, 1997; Boffo and Moscati, 1998; Moscati, 2001; and Capano, 2008). The division into periods hinges on 1989 and 1998 when important innovations took place. The period since 2007 concerns the most recent developments. It is important to note that in the period 1980–2006, the system as such underwent considerable change (data from CNVSU: www.cnvsu.it). The number of universities almost doubled (from 51 in 1980 to 94 in 2006, with a strong growth of private universities). Also the number of students grew impressively: from slightly more than 1 million (1980) to 1.8 million in 2006. The percentage of nineteen-year-olds enrolling at the university almost doubled: from 28.4 percent (in 1980) to 56.1 percent (academic year 2005/6).

Prior to 1989: Internal Negotiation-based Governance

The year 1989 was a turning point in the Italian university system as it witnessed the beginning of a wave of reforms that continued throughout the 1990s, recognizing and strengthening the autonomy of universities *vis-à-vis* the government. In 1989 the law 168/1989 was passed under the guidance of Minister Ruberti (1987–1989 and 1989–1992), who was responsible for drafting a complex plan to

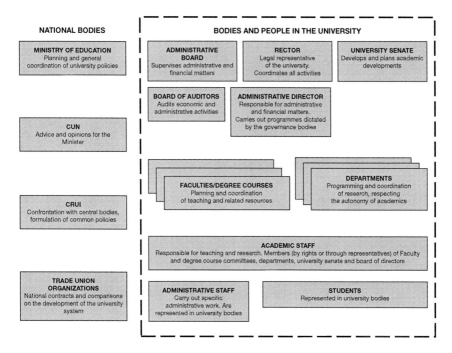

Figure 2.3 University Administration Structure, 1989

update the system. Up to that time the system had been highly centralized, with strong formal powers in the hands of the Minister of Education, who controlled and allocated public funds while the individual universities had to respect strict rules and regulations.

In 1988 university system governance was relatively simple (see Figure 2.3) and there were very few centralized institutional bodies. One of these was the CUN (National University Council), an elective assembly composed of representatives of the different professional categories and students. Its role was mainly advisory: the Ministry of Education had formal powers and allocated university funds through a long-term planning system. At this time there were only a few established universities (about forty) and approximately ten newer ones. Within the CRUI (National Association of Italian Rectors), rectors compared and discussed issues of common interest which were passed on to the Minister. In the CRUI set-up there were very few rules, which consequently left a great deal of room for adjustment and negotiation between the main actors, who knew one another directly and were on familiar terms. Internal university governance, updated by a law passed in 1980, mirrored traditional governance. It hinged on collegial bodies (the Administrative Board, the University Senate and the Faculty councils). Research Departments were added in 1980. The Rector (who was elected) and the Administrative Director (chosen by the Rector) were the key management figures. However, the greatest power was in the hands of academics. The key actors were professors who were chair-holders (*maestro* in a positive interpretation or *baron* in a negative one). Thus, a narrow circle of professors who headed academic schools or were in charge of the various disciplines played a crucial role in the recruitment or careers of teaching staff and influenced all internal university decisions. This is a distinctive trait of the Italian university "characterised by a particularly high degree of faculty authority" (Moscati, 2001: 117), which, according to Clark (1977), has been likened to that of the medieval professional guilds. The Rector was a *primus inter pares* whose main task was to facilitate the balance between the interests of the disciplinary groups. As Capano pointed out: "Individuals with formal power (such as Rectors and Deans) were expected to mediate between the different, often divergent, interests of internal groupings" (2008: 483).

This system was centralized only in theory, as in practice planning systems and control were just a formal bureaucratic structure and real decisions resulted from the interrelationship between the most important academic figures and ministerial bodies. Relations were direct and involved continuous exchanges of views, interaction and negotiation. As stated in the literature (Boffo, 1997; Boffo and Moscati, 1998; Capano, 2008), the informal relationship between chair-holders and the ministerial bureaucracy constituted the true mechanisms for coordination at local level and the whole system "was based on informal, but persistent, interrelations between the most powerful local chair-holders (or groups thereof) and the ministerial bureaucracy" (Capano, 2008: 483). Relations with the Ministry were seen in terms of interests and bargaining with "wide scope for individual universities and, in some cases individual professors, to bargain (often informally) their share of funding" (Boffo, 1997: 175), and where everything was "a useful way of avoiding responsibility" (Boffo and Moscati, 1998: 350). The CUN shows this balance more than any other body and "mainly represents individual disciplines and university staff categories before the Ministry and the universities" (Boffo, 1997: 175). University professors composed and dominated the faculties, governing council and Administrative Board, which were the few important bodies responsible for the running of the universities. Every professor had complete autonomy both as of right and in reality, with ample space for the expression of his or her force of personality.

In this situation, *locus of governance* was certainly inside the university system which was governed by an alliance between the ministerial bureaucracy and the centers of university power, thus perpetuating the Italian university tradition. The influence of external interests was extremely limited. Trade unions kept a low profile and only came forward with requests to improve the working conditions of non-academic staff. Associations of employers did not have any great expectations. University professors, on the other hand, were particularly influential and conspicuous both in the political world, where many of them were present in Parliament and frequently became ministers or premiers, and in the economic world, where they were administrators of private or state-controlled banks and firms (Regonini, 1993). Externally influential academics "protected" university interests from outside influences.

Focus of governance was characterized by decision-making aimed at the search for consensus through negotiation, settlement of conflicts and agreements between central powers. It thus developed along lines that lacked transparency and did not fully comply with formal guidelines. More often than not, decision-making was a mere formal ratification of decisions taken elsewhere. So, rationality gave way to incremental negotiation that was not particularly conflicting but oriented to the search for general agreement through continuous mediation between influential groups. The democratic structure of the system, with its elective and collegial bodies, was more of a ritual with an external appearance and a legitimizing role rather than a truly operational role. In the words of Boffo: "The Italian HE system was a typical example of the continental mode of authority distribution, a combination of faculty guilds and state bureaucracy" (1997: 181), and Capano states, "Universities as autonomous institutions simply did not exist; . . . In fact, they were not in a position to decide anything of any importance themselves" (2008: 483).

1989–1998: The Drives Towards External Governance

Law 168 set up the Ministry of the University and Scientific Research but more significantly paved the way for important reforms that were to take place in the following ten years. In the 1990s the governance map (see Figure 2.4) was redrawn by rearranging the CUN, strengthening the institutional role of the CRUI, setting up the CNSU (National Students' Committee) and creating the permanent Observatory for the evaluation of the Italian university system and evaluation units in state universities. This was the beginning of the Italian university's experience with quality assurance systems.

The system became more complex partly due to the increase in the number of universities following a series of government decrees. The policy of "relieving the congestion" of the large metropolitan universities led to the creation of new ones in cities such as Rome, Milan and Naples. The go-ahead was also given to some new private universities. The plan to strengthen university autonomy was affected by less conspicuous changes, which in reality had strong effects. Funding systems changed by lifting restrictions involving planning (Law 537/1993; 1994 Budget). This liberalized the way that university funds were to be used and made it possible to discard the old system whereby the total number of university staff was subject to ministerial approval (Potì and Reale, 2005). Funds were given as a lump sum without any particular ties or conditions. According to Moscati, this was "the first real step toward university autonomy, and it is worth noting that it was never debated but was simply imposed on the university milieu" (2001: 113). In addition, the setting up of new university courses was liberalized on condition that they were self-financed. As a result of these changes the *locus of governance* started to move towards the outside of the university system because forces that were unconnected to the university world came into play not just in the shape of stimuli but as actors directly involved in the reform process. The idea of setting up a university that would abandon its traditional detached attitude to seek a *partnership* actively in society and the economy was certainly one of the fundamental criteria that inspired the new policies put forward by Ruberti. The implementation of these early measures was reinforced by a series of external driving forces. Europe, in

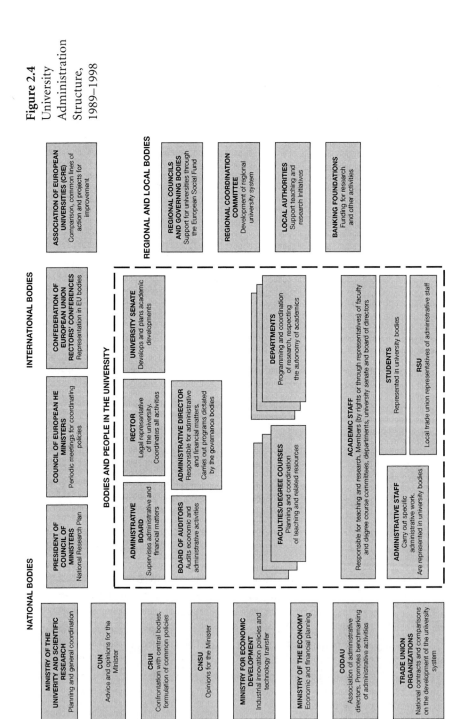

Figure 2.4 University Administration Structure, 1989–1998

NATIONAL BODIES

INTERNATIONAL BODIES

REGIONAL AND LOCAL BODIES

BODIES AND PEOPLE IN THE UNIVERSITY

MINISTRY OF THE UNIVERSITY AND SCIENTIFIC RESEARCH
Planning and general coordination

CUN
Advice and opinions for the Minister

CRUI
Confrontation with central bodies, formulation of common policies

CNSU
Opinions for the Minister

MINISTRY FOR ECONOMIC DEVELOPMENT
Industrial innovation policies and technology transfer

MINISTRY OF THE ECONOMY
Economic and financial planning

CODAU
Association of administrative directors. Promotes benchmarking of administrative activities

TRADE UNION ORGANIZATIONS
National contracts and comparisons on the development of the university system

PRESIDENT OF COUNCIL OF MINISTERS
National Research Plan

COUNCIL OF EUROPEAN HE MINISTERS
Periodic meetings for coordinating policies

ASSOCIATION OF EUROPEAN UNIVERSITIES (CRE)
Comparison, common lines of action and projects for improvement

CONFEDERATION OF EUROPEAN UNION RECTORS' CONFERENCES
Representation in EU bodies

REGIONAL COUNCILS AND GOVERNING BODIES
Support for universities through the European Social Fund

REGIONAL COORDINATION COMMITTEE
Development of regional university system

LOCAL AUTHORITIES
Support teaching and research initiatives

BANKING FOUNDATIONS
Funding for research and other activities

RECTOR
Legal representative of the university. Coordinates all activities

UNIVERSITY SENATE
Develops and plans academic developments

ADMINISTRATIVE BOARD
Supervises administrative and financial matters

ADMINISTRATIVE DIRECTOR
Responsible for administrative and financial matters. Carries out programs dictated by the governance bodies

BOARD OF AUDITORS
Audits economic and administrative activities

DEPARTMENTS
Programming and coordination of research, respecting the autonomy of academics

FACULTIES/DEGREE COURSES
Planning and coordination of teaching and related resources

ACADEMIC STAFF
Responsible for teaching and research. Members (by rights or through representatives) of faculty and degree course committees, departments, university senate and board of directors

STUDENTS
Represented in university bodies

ADMINISTRATIVE STAFF
Carry out specific administrative work. Are represented in university bodies

RSU
Local trade union representatives of administrative staff

particular, became a driver through many different channels, such as framework programs for research and international exchanges on the part of university staff and students, which started off on a small scale but then developed rapidly. And last, but not least, there was the setting in motion of the Bologna Process. As Finocchietti and Capucci affirmed: "Italy immediately transposed the principles and criteria of the Bologna Declaration into national legislation" (2004: 272).

During this period relations with Confindustria (the Italian Manufacturers' Association) and other organizations in industry developed. The newly conceived three-year vocational university diplomas offered an excellent opportunity for collaboration between the university and the world of work (Luzzatto and Moscati, 2005). The Campus Project, which later became Campus One, promoted by the CRUI with a series of non-academic partners, became a fundamental catalyst of energies, giving universities the funds for experimenting with the planning, innovation and management of degree courses (Turri, 2005; Stefani, 2006). Relationships with the trade unions became stronger after the reform of the civil service, which made the employer–employee relationship of non-academic university staff conform to civil law and gave the parties more contractual autonomy. At the same time the CRUI became more active, creating an environment that encouraged the diffusion of practices and experiences open to the outside world, and also assisted the universities in setting up new contacts and partnerships.

The focus of governance was not significantly different from the previous period and was still characterized by the prevailing incremental decision-making based on negotiation. However, the reforms passed at the beginning of the ten-year period opened the way for new vitality within the system which in turn welded to the external forces present in Europe, Italy and the different university environments. The development of the system therefore seems subsequently to have been steered from the bottom rather than guided by central planning. This period saw the emergence of a number of local leaders embodied mainly by rectors who became entrepreneurs in their own universities, playing on their relationships with the local environment and society. They strengthened their universities through a complex combination of resources brought in by numerous bodies and set up wide-ranging alliances with industrial and productive associations, the professional world, trade unions, the regions, local authorities and chambers of commerce. They carried on their work with versatility and also established relations with the political world while managing to keep initiatives in their own hands, dealing with the opening up to the outside world without compromising the autonomy of their university. As a consequence, a number of administrative executives came to the forefront thanks to the new contracts that distinguished executives from the rest of the personnel. In particular the role of administrative directors was strengthened and they felt the need to promote their own national body (CODAU), taking an active part in discussions and measuring themselves against ministerial bureaucracy more strongly than in the past.

It is significant that in 1996 the principal private secretary to Minister Berlinguer (1996–1998) was an administrative director. However, the idea of a "new university" as a conveyor of new competitiveness for the country did not materialize as expected (Conraths et al., 2003; Potì and Reale, 2005). The move from internal to external locus of governance worked, but the same cannot be said for the second variable which maintained a conflicting focus. The well-consolidated tradition of the Italian academia dominated by narrow groups that associated themselves more with disciplinary areas and with individual chair-holders than with official structures ended up by orienting the implementation of reforms according to tradition. In the absence of coherence and true shared objectives the legislation that had given more autonomy to universities opened the way for the energies present in the system but did not manage to activate the intended *steering from a distance* model that reflected the experience in other European countries. This was a prelude to the fragmentation of the system that took place in the subsequent period.

The action of the entrepreneurial rectors that characterized the 1990s not only was not steered by the state but was conditioned and maybe distracted by internal resistance in the university environment much more than by relationships with external stakeholders. According to Moscati (2001: 117): "This attitude can be explained in part as a way of protecting a number of vested interests, in part as deriving from the fear of having to change ingrained professional habits, and in part as an expression of a deeply rooted perception of the role of the university and of the academic profession." The ideas that guided university policies in Europe and subsequently resulted in the Bologna Declaration and Lisbon Agenda produced only weak partial effects in the Italian university (Egidi, 2006). Very few of the entrepreneurial rectors managed to keep their positions beyond the year 2000: some went into politics, others were not re-elected, but all of them increasingly suffered the conflicts and internal divisions among academics who tended to see the openings for their personal initiatives as short-term advantages or a mere extension of traditional academic power. At the end of this period the Italian university appeared to have abandoned the state of "alliance of independent feuds" even if its role seemed to be more one of a "pluralistic" or even "fragmented" network rather than an "instrument of public policies."

1999–2006: Pandora's Box

The year 1999 marked another turning point with two important measures that supported the drive for autonomy but also facilitated the subsequent drift towards a more marked fragmentation of the system. The first occurred when Berlinguer was Minister, and Parliament passed new laws regulating the appointment of professors, decentralizing the task to the individual universities (Law 210/1998). The second took place immediately afterwards, in the wake of the Bologna Declaration, when teaching systems were reformed with the adoption of new undergraduate and postgraduate curricula. Specific responsibility for degree courses was handed over to the individual universities with only slight coordination and control by central bodies (Finocchietti and Capucci, 2004; Agasisti, Arnaboldi and Azzone, 2008). With regard to university autonomy, this was tantamount to opening Pandora's box. The actual implementation of these two measures by the universities marked a complete surrender to fragmentation. During this stage the structure of the university system became even more complicated (see Figure 2.5).

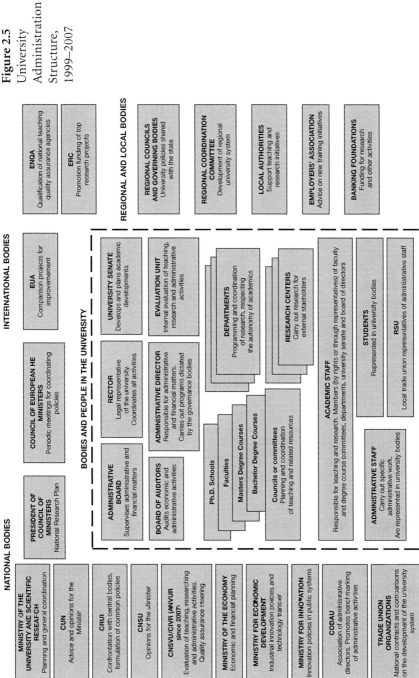

Figure 2.5
University Administration Structure, 1999–2007

NATIONAL BODIES

MINISTRY OF THE UNIVERSITY AND SCIENTIFIC RESEARCH
Planning and general coordination

CUN
Advice and opinions for the Minister

CRUI
Confrontation with central bodies, formulation of common policies

CNSU
Opinions for the Minister

CNSVU/CIVR (ANVUR since 2007)
Evaluation of teaching, researching and administrative activities. Quality assurance steering

MINISTRY FOR THE ECONOMY
Economic and financial planning

MINISTRY FOR ECONOMIC DEVELOPMENT
Industrial innovation policies and technology transfer

MINISTRY FOR INNOVATION
Innovation policies in public systems

CODAU
Association of administrative directors. Promotes benchmarking of administrative activities

TRADE UNION ORGANIZATIONS
National contracts and comparisons on the development of the university system

PRESIDENT OF COUNCIL OF MINISTERS
National Research Plan

COUNCIL OF EUROPEAN HE MINISTERS
Periodic meetings for coordinating policies

INTERNATIONAL BODIES

EUA
Comparison projects for improvement

ENQA
Qualification of national teaching quality assurance agencies

ERC
Promotion funding of top research projects

REGIONAL AND LOCAL BODIES

REGIONAL COUNCILS AND GOVERNING BODIES
University policies shared with the state

REGIONAL COORDINATION COMMITTEE
Development of regional university system

LOCAL AUTHORITIES
Support teaching and research initiatives

EMPLOYERS' ASSOCIATION
Advice on new training initiatives

BANKING FOUNDATIONS
Funding for research and other activities

BODIES AND PEOPLE IN THE UNIVERSITY

ADMINISTRATIVE BOARD
Supervises administrative and financial matters

BOARD OF AUDITORS
Audits economic and administrative activities

RECTOR
Legal representative of the university. Coordinates all activities

ADMINISTRATIVE DIRECTOR
Responsible for administrative and financial matters. Carries out programs dictated by the governance bodies

UNIVERSITY SENATE
Develops and plans academic developments

EVALUATION UNIT
Internal evaluation of teaching, research and administrative activities

Ph.D. Schools
Faculties
Masters Degree Courses
Bachelor Degree Courses

Councils or committees
Planning and coordination of teaching and related resources

DEPARTMENTS
Programming and coordination of research, respecting the autonomy of academics

RESEARCH CENTERS
Carry out research for external stakeholders

ACADEMIC STAFF
Responsible for teaching and research. Members (by rights or through representatives) of faculty and degree course committees, departments, university senate and board of directors

ADMINISTRATIVE STAFF
Carry out specific administrative work. Are represented in university bodies

STUDENTS
Represented in university bodies

RSU
Local trade union representatives of administrative staff

The increase in the number of universities was due mainly to the addition of private universities and to the eleven distance learning universities created by legislation in 2003. In many cases these universities were weak and their birth sparked a great deal of discussion in the press. However, the uncontrolled growth of teaching structures was a more complex fact, as was clearly shown by the creation of new satellite universities throughout Italy by many universities that welcomed requests from local government authorities to set up courses on their premises. In all, at least 350 town councils had some kind of satellite university, with some universities having satellite activities in a number of different cities. This situation then combined with the great increase in university courses produced by the 1999 reform. There were now over five thousand different degree courses (first and second level). Measures approved during the Moratti Ministry (2001–2006) meant that agreements between universities and public bodies gave 140 out of a total of 180 credits to professionals in public bodies for their experience gained over time. The number of university staff grew equally fast, with permanent staff increasing from 50,500 to nearly 62,000. Although ways of selecting staff changed, the criteria still "seems to reproduce the old dynamics inside the disciplines" (Moscati, 2001: 124) and the application of the reform for recruiting professors meant, above all, that existing assistant professors could establish a career. State evaluation bodies became stronger and new tasks were assigned to the National Committee for the Evaluation of Universities, which took the place of the National Observatory and was responsible for the evaluation of teaching and for guiding the university evaluation units which were made compulsory even in private universities (Turri, 2007). The CIVR (Italian Committee for the Evaluation of Research) was set up for assessing the quality of research and carried out the important three-year exercise (2001–2004) for the evaluation of university research with great efficacy (Minelli, Rebora and Turri, 2008). The Bologna Process continued with the active participation of the different bodies present in the Italian system. The CUN retained and improved its advisory role for the Ministry together with its authority for checking the new academic programs. Despite its commitment, it did not manage to halt the previously mentioned phenomena of inertia and fragmentation. The CRUI made its presence more felt at national level and attempted to produce ideas and proposals for improving the system, although it was affected by strong inertia. The internal governance system of the CRUI (one vote for each university regardless of its size and history) became inadequate as the number of new universities increased and it consequently limited itself to making generic requests for more funds from government bodies.

Meanwhile, the role of the Ministry for the Economy began to grow. In the past the Ministry had had a say in matters but now its opinions became more crucial owing to the greater demand for funding. This led to conflicts with the Minister for the University, who requested more funds but with little success. The Ministry for Economic Development, dealing with technology transfer, and the Ministry for Innovation also became important interlocutors in the university system. External economic actors began to take more part in university issues and their roles became more dialectical than before. Confindustria in particular was no longer a partner in common initiatives but became a permanent, often critical interlocutor (Fortuna, 2003). During this period, and particularly in the early years of 2000, central government bodies seemed to have lost control of the situation in universities, and the various above-mentioned phenomena took the upper hand. None of the bodies in charge (the Ministry, CRUI, CUN, central evaluation bodies and local evaluation units) was able to manage the forceful processes that developed without any coordination or steering. *Steering from a distance* did not work and the market was far from able to regulate the system in the existing unchanged environment where rules were based on the legal value of degrees (access to certain professions is conditioned by obtaining a degree from a recognized university) and the university's strong economic dependence on state funding (over 60 percent of the total income in state universities compared to student enrolment fees of only 12 percent).

Universities were by now pursuing particular aims but had lost the initial shine that they had possessed during the period of the entrepreneurial rectors. University courses were unscrupulously advertised in newspapers, on the radio and on television and there was an unusual rush to give honorary degrees to well-known people in the entertainment and sports worlds. As a consequence, the university system was more affected than ever by polemics and discussions in the media. The openings offered by the reforms became the subject of (at times radical) criticism from university professors who were columnists for the most important daily newspapers. However, their opinions were often a combination of indignation about clearly contradictory choices and a less understandable regret for the bygone elitist university closed to the outside world, which, as well as no longer existing, was hard to sustain in a developed Western country. The lack of strong ideas shared by the various components of the university world and academics was obvious.

In the meantime, the universities that were more receptive to the outside world and the international environment, and also more market-oriented, gradually became more influential. Some, such as Bocconi, were private; others, like the polytechnics of Milan and Turin and the University of Bologna, were state universities (Azzone and Dente, 2004). The inheritance of the entrepreneurial rectors who had encouraged a large number of initiatives in these and other universities was not lost and seems to have generated greater internal cohesion regarding initiatives for internationalization, advanced training in Ph.D. programs and more sophisticated solutions for relationships with the economic world. In some cases foundations were set up by the universities, and in others medium- and long-term strategic planning took shape. This was an absolute novelty in Italy as far as state universities were concerned (Catalano, 2002, 2004; Bolognani and Catalano, 2007).

So the system developed in different ways and became more complex, it improved relationships with the outside world, increased in size (even if in a somewhat disorderly way), and above all left room for variety which had previously been unknown. A great assortment of different elements flew out of Pandora's box but they did not all signify decline and degeneration (unlike hers, which were all evil). The *locus of governance* in this new period was therefore characterized by a shift towards the outside that had already begun in the previous period. However, it also developed radically, taking on a plural meaning, *loci*, as a result of the widely differing drives from the local environment that were welcomed by the university, especially with regard to the development of new curricula. After the general election in 2001 the new government did not halt this tendency but accentuated it by opening up to external forces that set up new private universities (especially distance-learning ones) whose proposed curricula were generally weak. In other words, university autonomy with its great dependence on external resources opened the way for an indiscriminate search for any possible kind of support, rather than opening up only to the market. The *focus of governance*, moreover, remained incremental and negotiation-based, with an increased conflicting charge. The opening up to the outside did not improve internal cohesion as the development of initiatives highlighted internal divisions and conflicts. Some internal and external actors even made alliances and projects of various importance and significance that were difficult to accommodate in a common strategy for the individual university or the system as a whole.

This type of development clearly ended up by creating problems for the central government bodies who were caught off balance by the speed with which previously centralized administrative procedures were decentralized to the universities. In the 1980s national competitions for permanent professors were held once every four to five years and one session lasted at least two years, whereas universities now start and finish all exam procedures in a few months thanks also to the enormous use of the internet. Moreover, the excess number of suitably qualified people to be given a post put pressure on the system. The procedure for setting up new *curricula* moved just as quickly. The end of the period in which Moratti was Minister and the beginning of Mussi's ministry (2006–2008) showed the need to take measures to check the uncontrolled development of the system. Various steps were taken regarding national competitions and teaching curricula but at the end of 2006 the system virtually seized up. University governance was highlighted as a crucial issue to be addressed and was the subject of study committees at different levels, discussions in various organizations and promised plans for reform. There was thus a blockage in the national governance system. Pandora's box had been shut too late to keep the situation under control. Faced with the existing dispersion and disintegration, the necessary funds for developing new policies were lacking. It was time for a break and almost all the actors seemed to be waiting. Interpreting university governance as a "network" with strong factors of pluralism and fragmentation thus also seems an appropriate description of this period. The halt in expansion showed how unstable the situation was and how it was incompatible with the continuing great dependence on state funding, which in any case had no other means for steering or controlling the system.

Since 2007: Waiting . . .

The year 2007 was a year of waiting. The features of the university system described in the previous period were still valid but a curb was imposed on chaotic, uncontrolled development. The majority of commentators and principal actors involved, starting with the Minister himself, were convinced that university governance needed to be reformed (Potì and Reale, 2005; Cammelli and Merloni, 2006; Capano, 2008). There are high hopes for evaluation, but the new agency, ANVUR (National Agency for University Evaluation and Research), is still not operative. The Bologna and Lisbon processes continue to produce new stimuli and great attention is being paid to research, sparking off discussions, disputes and proposals. In 2005 a whole issue of the journal *Atenei* dealt with these themes. The more active centers and associations of researchers are putting pressure on the government to allocate more funds and the CIVR's evaluation exercise has roused a great deal of interest, while the idea that researchers are assessed on their results is also widely approved. At the same time the role and presence of the university in society has become more important, although this is the result of scattered aspects and initiatives on the part of individuals and groups since organized programs and policies are lacking.

In this new stage the *external locus of governance* seems already to be an established fact and almost a natural state. The university has to relate with society and be answerable to it, not only in relation to the market but by setting up a wide range of relationships paying attention to international research networks and the needs of the region where it is located. The *focus of governance* remains incremental, conflicting and negotiation-based in compliance with the cultural and social characteristics in Italy that continue to remain stable. Only a few state and private universities have managed to break away from this situation and create new strategies, but the system, with its weak governance, has not managed to do so. The advocates of new, more effective reforms where governance would become a vital force seem to be staking everything on the *steering from a distance* solution. The university system appears to have assimilated the concept of diversity particularly well, and it is difficult – and probably unproductive – to reject this concept. It is also unlikely that unified intentions, aims and viewpoints can be retrieved as this kind of unity is considered old-fashioned in the modern world.

If one accepts the idea of a network, the problem of how to overcome a fragmented locus of governance remains open. There is in fact a difference between fragmented and pluralistic networks, which are two different interpretations of external negotiated governance. In the future, the transition from conflicting interests to pluralism is crucial for overcoming the question of fragmentation. This will be possible if more concrete decision-making strategies come to the fore and if the part of the system that is able to set more ambitious objectives is strengthened.

Interpretation of Governance in Italy

Our interpretation of the development of the Italian university governance system differs from that of Gornitzka and Maassen (2000), who apply Olsen's framework (1988) to the Italian case and depict the transition of the university system from the sovereign, rationality-bounded steering model that existed before 1989 to a supermarket steering model. In their opinion the development of the system at the beginning of this century heads towards the supermarket model even if some elements are to be found in the sovereign rationality-bounded steering and the corporate-pluralist steering model quadrants:

> The dominant steering approach before 1989 in the pre-MURST period can be typified by referring to the sovereign state model: strong, top down ministerial control and regulation of the university sector . . . After 1989, the steering of higher education in Italy moved clearly in the direction of the supermarket model, with certain elements of both the sovereign state model and the corporate state model.
>
> (Gornitzka and Maassen, 2000: 278)

Our analysis claims that in Italy the foundations of the sovereign rationality-bounded steering model or a rule-governed community of scholars were incomplete even before 1989. This is due to the conflicting aims at different levels in the system and the power of chair-holders who controlled local situations depriving the national government and control bodies of formal powers. Gornitzka and Maassen's description matches Italian university governance in the period well before the one we analyzed. We feel that the period immediately before 1989 corresponds most closely to the idea of an "alliance of independent *feuds*" and prefer this definition to Olsen's, which was taken up by Gornitzka and Maassen and defined as a "corporate-pluralistic steering model" or "representative democracy." A democratic idea may have inspired the formal drafting of a series of norms and the 1980 Italian reform in particular, but it has had no real effect on outcomes. The most important decision-making processes regarding strategic decisions, allocation of funds and making a career are in the hands of centralized power and subject to the influence of negotiation between ministerial bureaucracy and the chair-holders who represent local power networks. The direct relationship between a few academic actors, ministerial bureaucracy and political power resolves issues pragmatically through negotiation. The metaphor of the feuds aptly sums up the idea of the pre-eminence of virtual powers that are predominant at various points in the system without corresponding to formal institutional and organizational structures supported by explicit rules. Those responsible for system governance come to terms with this situation, do not attempt to change it and thus adopt a model of negotiation-based governance that remains within the boundaries of the university environment.

The view of university system governance as an instrument of public policy is conceptually appropriate in the words of Olsen, who sees it as an institutional steering model and an instrument for national political agendas. This also corresponds to the political idea of the university that characterized the Italian reforms in the 1990s. However, this vision does not establish itself because the independent "feuds" use the new openings for autonomy set up by the reforms to resist attempts at steering from a distance inspired by the situation in other European countries. The ministerial techno-structures that are accustomed to managing information according to their own bargaining power are unsuitable for this task and the good intentions of some enlightened politicians are not enough. The governance structure seen in terms of an alliance of independent feuds can thus be overcome through a new opening up to the outside pushed up from the bottom, and to a much lesser degree through the adoption of a strategic rational decision-making model. This foreshadowed the further fragmentation of the system that was fully evident in the following period. Thus the 1990s and the early years of the 2000s can be seen as expressions of external negotiation-based governance, which in our opinion does not correspond to Olsen's service enterprise embedded in a competitive market vision and even less to a supermarket model. In fact the opening to the outside, which became more marked over time, only partly followed the attraction of the market and led to a great increase in relationships that were not solely economic. Within the market, individuals and groups often confront one another more than official structures and universities do. In Italy the particular features of entrepreneurial universities are weak (Clark, 1998). Olsen's scenario is therefore inadequate as it does not describe a real situation or an ideal goal. The development of the Italian case collocates itself well within the bounds of an external locus of governance (or more precisely loci – plural) with a negotiation-based conflicting focus. The analysis shows that this space can be occupied in different ways. Taking a network that is not centrally governed as a reference point, it can be divided into two different versions – fragmented and/or pluralistic. The transformation of system governance is therefore interpreted as a transition from an alliance of *independent feuds* to a fragmented and/or pluralistic network over a period of almost twenty years.

This interpretation shows an ambiguity in that the inertial shift is towards fragmentation. Looking back at the danger of fragmentation and its effects in the early years of this century, the government seems to want to re-propose public policies by attempting to govern the system in an undifferentiated way through a series of measures that the stalemate in 2007 made difficult to carry out. The overall history of the Italian situation would suggest following a different route, abandoning the ambition to develop a strategic focus of governance in the system with the necessary consequences in terms of coherence and shared aims. The alternative is to aim for pluralism which is more in line with reality and more aligned with international trends.

Conclusions

Although the initial positioning of the Italian system as an alliance of independent feuds diverges from the analysis made by Gornitzka and Maassen (2000), it does find support in the literature. According to Clark (1983: 127), Italian system governance is the result of a "combination of authority of state bureaucracy and faculty guilds in a power structure which expresses the interests of two groups: state officials and senior professors" (see also Clark, 1977). From the 1990s to the present day, system governance development is concentrated in just one of the four quadrants. The analysis shows that since the mid-1990s, if not before, the locus of governance has tended to become external and does not seem able to turn back.

The question of focus is more controversial but in our opinion the negotiation-based/incremental nature was not only acquired many years ago and engrained within the more general connotations of the national system but is unlikely to change over time.

Our analytical frameworks and Olsen's have the advantage of drawing attention to the university's opening up to the outside world and to a multiple structure of aims and objectives expressed in the "pluralistic or fragmented network." This vision includes a multitude of possible governance set-ups with extremely diverse features and differing consequences. So, if the future development of university system governance throughout the world is likely to revolve for the most part around these variables, then an even deeper analysis of the possible variants that goes far beyond such references as the "supermarket model" is necessary.

In our opinion, choosing between a fragmented or pluralistic network may provide a useful outline for future studies. A pluralistic structure of the system is a feasible alternative to the drift towards fragmentation, the development of a supermarket model or re-introduction of the "instrument of public policies" model. Truly pluralistic governance is born of the combination between the autonomous entrepreneurial drive of state and private universities supported by their own territories and the government agencies' ability to organize and stimulate the university system.

A limited number of entrepreneurial universities could become prominent, depending on their ability to appeal to local resources and attract external funding even with the support of national bodies. However, this has to exclude a return to obsolete forms of national programming and state-controlled public policies. Setting up differentiated structures and behavior in universities is deemed vital for improving the overall efficiency of the system. As far as the state is concerned, this means really "steering from a distance" and making it possible to build a platform that functions even when there are different drives and behaviors on the part of universities.

References

Agasisti, Tommaso, Michel A. Arnaboldi, and Giovanni Azzone. "Strategic Management Accounting in Universities: The Italian Experience." *Higher Education* 55 (2008): 1–16.

Azzone, Giovanni, and Bruno Dente. "Dall'Autonomia alla Governance. Il Caso del Politecnico di Milano." *Il Mulino* 54(3) (2004): 479–488.

Bevir, Mark, Rod A.W. Rhodes, and Patrick Weller. "Comparative Governance: Prospects and Lessons." *Public Administration* 81(1) (2003): 191–210.

Boffo, Stefano. "Evaluation and the Distribution of Power in Italian Universities." *European Journal of Education* 32(2) (1997): 175–184.

Boffo, Stefano, and Roberto Moscati. "Evaluation in the Italian Higher Educational System: Many Tribes, Many Territories . . . Many Godfathers." *European Journal of Education* 33(3) (1998): 349–360.

Bolognani, Mario, and Giuseppe Catalano. "Strategie Competitive e Università." *Sviluppo e Organizzazione* 222 (2007): 35–64.

Cammelli, Marco, and Francesco Merloni, eds. *Università e Sistema della Ricerca: Proposte per Cambiare.* Bologna: Il Mulino, 2006.

Capano, Gilberto. "Looking for Serendipity: The Problematical Reform of Government within Italy's Universities." *Higher Education* 55(4) (2008): 481–504.

Catalano, Giuseppe. *La Valutazione delle Attività Amministrative dell'Università: Il Progetto "Good Practices."* Bologna: Il Mulino, 2002.

Catalano, Giuseppe. *Valutare le Attività Amministrative delle Università: Aspetti Metodologici e Buone Pratiche.* Bologna: Il Mulino, 2004.

Clark, Burton R. *Academic Power in Italy: Bureaucracy and Oligarchy in a National University System.* Chicago: University of Chicago Press, 1977.

Clark, Burton R. *The Higher Education System: Academic Organization in Cross-national Perspective.* Berkeley: University of California Press, 1983.

Clark, Burton R. *Creating Entrepreneurial Universities: Organizational Pathways of Transformation.* New York: IAU Press, 1998.

Conraths, Bernadette, Kenneth Edwards, Ulrike Felt, and Gordon Shenton. *Managing University Autonomy: Collective Decision Making and Human Resources Policy.* Bologna: Bononia University Press, 2003.

Dent, Mike. "Symposium on Changing Modes of Governance in Public Sector Organizations: Action and Rhetoric." *Public Administration* 85(1) (2007): 1–8.

Egidi, Massimo. *Report of the Conference: L'Università Motore dello Sviluppo del Paese: Meritocrazia e Concorrenza.* Rome: Aspen Institute Italia, 2006.

Finocchietti, Carlo, and Silvia Capucci. "The National System of Higher Education in Italy." In *Accreditation and Evaluation in the European Higher Education Area,* edited by Don F. Westerheijden, and Stephanie Schwarz. Dordrecht: Kluwer, 2004, 251–274.

Fortuna, Silvio. "Università e Impresa: Dove c'è Integrazione c'è Sviluppo." In *Nuova Università e Mondo del Lavoro,* edited by C.R. Anfonsi, and C. Cosciotti. Roma: Fondazione Crui, 2003, 27–36.

Gornitzka, Ase, and Peter Maassen. "Hybrid Steering Approaches with Respect to European Higher Education." *Higher Education Policy* 13(3) (2000): 267–268.

Luzzatto, Giunio, and Roberto Moscati. "University Reform in Italy: Fears, Expectations and Contradictions." In *Reform and Change in Higher Education,* edited by Ase Gornitzka, Maurice Kogan, and Alberto Amaral. Dordrecht: Springer, 2005, 153–168.

Meek, Lynn. "Diversity and the Marketisation of Higher Education: Incompatible Concepts?" *Higher Education Policy* 13(4) (2000): 23–39.

Minelli, Eliana, Gianfranco Rebora, and Matteo Turri. "The Structure and Significance of the Italian Research Assessment Exercise (VTR)." In *European Universities in Transition,* edited by Carmelo Mazza, Paulo Quattrone, and Angelo Riccaboni. London: Edward Elgar, 2008, 221–236.

Moscati Roberto. "Italian University Professors in Transition." *Higher Education* 41(1) (2001): 103–129.

Olsen, Johan P. "Administrative Reform and Theories of Organization." In *Organizing Governance: Governing Organizations,* edited by Colin Campbell, and B. Guy Peters. Pittsburgh: University of Pittsburgh Press, 1988, 233–254.

Olsen, Johan P. "The Institutional Dynamics of the European University." *ARENA Working Paper Series* 15, 2005 (www.arena.uio.no).

Olsen, Johan P. "The Institutional Dynamics of the European University." In *University Dynamics and European Integration,* edited by Peter Maassen, and Johan P. Olsen. Dordrecht: Springer, 2007, 45–85.

Potì, Bianca, and Emanuela Reale. "New Tools for the Governance of the Academic Research in Italy: The Role of Research Evaluation." *Ceris-Cnr Working Paper* 13 (2005) (www.ceris.cnr.it).

Reale, Emanuela, Anna Barbara, and Antonio Costantini. "Peer Review for the Evaluation of the Academic Research. The Italian Experience." *Ceris-Cnr Working Paper* 15 (2006) (www.ceris.cnr.it).

Regonini, Gloria. "Il Principe e il Povero: Politiche Istituzionali ed Economiche Negli Anni '80." *Stato e Mercato* 3 (1993): 361–403.

Rotter, Julian R. "Generalized Expectancies for Internal versus External Control of Reinforcement." *Psychological Monographs* 80(1) (1966): 1–28.

Simon, Herbert. *Administrative Behavior.* New York: Macmillan, 1957.

Spector, Paul E. "Behavior in Organizations as a Function of Employee's Locus of Control." *Psychological Bulletin* 91 (1982): 482–497.

Stefani, Emanuela. *Qualità per l'Università.* Milano: Franco Angeli, 2006.

Steinbrunner, John D. *The Cybernetic Theory of Decision: New Dimensions of Political Analysis.* Princeton: Princeton University Press, 1974.

Streeck, Wolfgang, and Philippe C. Schmitter. "Community, Market, State and Associations? The Prospective Contribution of Interest Governance to Social Order." *European Sociological Review* 1 (1985): 119–138.

Turri, Matteo. *La Valutazione dell'Università: Un'Analisi dell'Impatto Istituzionale e Organizzativo.* Milano: Guerini editore, 2005.

Turri, Matteo. "I Fattori di Crisi dei Controlli nel Caso delle Università." In *La Crisi dei Controlli: Imprese e Istituzioni a Confronto,* edited by Gianfranco Rebora. Milano: Pearson Education Italia, 2007, 279–323.

3

Governance in German Higher Education
Competition Versus Negotiation Of Performance

DOMINIC ORR AND MICHAEL JAEGER

Introduction

In Germany and elsewhere there has been much talk about a paradigm shift within the higher education system throughout the last decade. The associated reforms have been grouped under the heading New Public Management (which also appears in German texts, otherwise: *Neues Steuerungsmodell*). This reform program was seen in Germany to encapsulate three main objectives: less state intervention, more university autonomy and, in the new space between actors (state and university) who were previously closely bound, more market and more competition. This was, to some extent, borne out of a recognition that top-down (rational) planning initiatives by the state, for instance, for study reform in the 1970s and 1980s, have not been successful (Schreiterer, 1989). In this sense, we are looking at changes in governance. "Governance" will be defined here as an umbrella term which encapsulates all collective regulations of university action within society, with a particular focus on the role of the state (see Pierre, 2000). On this very broad level, the reform program is indeed similar to the one taking place concurrently in many higher education systems of the world and in many other public services (e.g. health services).

After such a period of reform, the higher education researcher is faced with the task of finding an appropriate conceptual framework which can provide a lens through which to view and perhaps to understand better the changes and to assess the reform trajectory for the future. It is proposed that there are two main approaches to such analyses:

- *Structure model* – In this approach a basic framework for the structure of governance is proposed and changes to various aspects of this framework are analyzed. Possibly the most recent attempt to capture the multidimensionality of higher education systems through such an approach is the equalizer model developed by Schimank (Kehm and Lanzendorf, 2006: 15–16; Schimank, 2002a) with five dimensions: external regulation of universities, external guidance of universities, competition, academic self-governance and managerial self-governance. This model has already been used successfully in a number of recent comparative studies to describe change (Kehm and Lanzendorf, 2006; CHEPS et al., 2006). However, although this model describes changes in such a way that it facilitates international (and historical) comparison, the model contains no elements that *explain* change. Furthermore, its utility may be limited by the "messiness" of regulatory reform (King, 2007: 66). This is because the closer you look at all such models, the more the apparently clear "system" multiplies and diversifies: for example, we find different regulatory/governance spaces depending on the university tasks (teaching, research, administration, etc.) and the nexus (state–university, university–faculty, faculty–department, etc.) we look at (Jaeger and Leszczensky, 2008).

- *Actor-centered model* – This approach starts out from the goals and purposes of reforms as expressed explicitly by the actor or as can be deduced from actors' actions. One such approach has been developed by Guy Peters, who has applied the view that policy-makers are purposeful actors trying to solve a problem to changes in governance in public services (Peters, 2001). This understanding of policy-making echoes Pawson and Tilley's methodological arguments for a realistic form of evaluation of policies (Pawson and Tilley, 1997). According to both Peters and Pawson and Tilley, policy should be evaluated within the following chain of causes and effects. Policy-makers diagnose a problem and design policy initiatives (programs), which have the objective of affecting the target group in such a way as to solve the problems. However, since policy initiatives can best be conceived of as suggestions for action, the actual effect of policy programs is very much related to the context of the policy implementation. Naturally, the utility of this approach is also limited. Indeed, although these models set out with a problem diagnosis and look for a policy solution for implementation in the practice, Peters himself does not expect a clean top-down procedure. He emphasizes that a central characteristic of government reform has been a move away from authoritarian top-down hierarchies to cooperation and negotiation involving a variety of actors (Peters, 2002: 2). Therefore, the actor perspective also becomes reductionistic. Nevertheless – according to Peters – within this more complex structure, the state can retain a substantial amount of influence through the process of "agenda-setting" (2002: 16).

The following analysis of higher education reform in Germany will be based on Peters' actor-centered approach. In 1996 Guy Peters published an important monograph on changing states, governance and reform in the public services and distinguished four emerging models behind contemporary public reforms (Peters, 1996, 2001). Although this work was not focused on higher education reform, we know that the latter has happened in most countries within the context of general reforms of public services. For this reason, it is useful to review the utility of Peters' models for an analysis of governance changes in higher education. After a general introduction to Peters' approach and his four models of governance, the subsequent section will describe the current situation in German higher education on the basis of Peters' models, which each start from a problem diagnosis. However, it will go beyond this actor-centered perspective to describe the instruments and structures being implemented. This is because such an analysis will highlight the expected chain of reaction for policy implementation:

diagnosis of problem – plan of action – implementation of solution – assessment of effectiveness – new diagnosis of problem. This section will therefore demonstrate the governance changes which have been taking place in German higher education. Furthermore, this descriptive section will enable a full assessment of the usefulness of Peters' approach.

Much reform in German higher education has been about introducing competition and the main instrument for this has been the allocation of state funding (Orr, 2007; Orr, Jaeger and Schwarzenberger, 2007); because of this, the ensuing analysis will particularly focus on these areas of reform. The paper will show in particular that two specific issues have shaped the implementation of the above-mentioned reform triad (less state – more institutional autonomy – more market) in Germany: the insecurity regarding risks of change (e.g. the question of quality) and the issue of capabilities on the part of both universities and ministries. The prominence of these issues leads to a governance constellation, which in effect focuses more on re-organizing the existing close relationship between state and university and less on fully fledged competition. The paper will also show that Peters' actor's perspective provides useful insights into the dynamics of policy reform.

Peters' Four Models of Governance

Over ten years after Peters' publication, it is appropriate to evaluate the reality of the public reform programs which he saw as emerging; in particular the market model. A return to Peters' model goes some way to explaining the constellation to be found in German higher education, because it takes a step away from the praxis. Peters introduces his analysis of emerging models of governance with a reality check. He reminds the reader that public policy is a tricky business – if problems were easy or profitable to solve, they would be dealt with by individuals or by the private sector, respectively (Peters, 2001: 1). He notes that a major stimulus for public reform in most countries over the last twenty years is simply a drop in the stability of both the organizations, which governments mean to influence with their policies, and political groups. This instability makes an adequate definition and framing of issues and indeed policy negotiations even harder – not to mention the problems of policy implementation (2001: 16). In the second, extended, edition of his monograph, he remarks that the initial reforms of the public sector have not led to a new stability, but continue to produce further reforms. Peters differentiates in his analysis between four basic models of public service reform, which he has deduced from empirical investigations. These models provide a broad skeleton for an analysis of public reform in higher education in Germany. For each of these model approaches, Peters asks what is the diagnosis of the problem, what is the recommended structure for public services, how should they be managed, how should policy-making occur and what is seen as the focus of the public interest (see Peters (2001) pp. 21 and 178 for a summary).

For each of his models, Peters remarkably uses the term "government" rather than "governance." Although these terms can largely be seen to be used as synonyms in the following, it can only be supposed that his preference for the former when naming his models was motivated by an emphasis on the state (the government) as prime mover within the context of policy development and particularly in forging the structures for policy implementation. This leads to his approach being termed "state-centrist" within the governance literature (Pierre, 2000).

Market Government

According to Peters, the market approach is driven by the diagnosis that bureaucratic monopolies are singularly interested in self-preservation and power gain. Therefore, there is an interest in determining its own objectives (agenda-setting), but not in responding to the needs of external stakeholders. Indeed, it is not so much a question of inadequate responses to market demands, but such bureaucracies just do not want to respond to them (Peters, 2001: 33). The solution is seen in setting incentives to encourage more efficient processes in the public service that are as close to the market as possible. For institutions and agencies to become more responsive, it is seen as necessary for them to be flatter organizations and possibly more focused on specific tasks or purposes. Within this approach, it is assumed that management is management no matter where it occurs and that basic principles can be adopted anywhere in the public service sector; in particular the allocation of financial resources by performance and payment of staff by merit instead of seniority. This then goes some way to legitimizing public spending in one area of public services over another (e.g. education versus health). The public interest is seen as efficient use of taxpayers' money and there is a general focus on improvement over past performance, which drives further reform efforts (2001: 43). At the same time, Peters marks out possible difficulties in coordination of policy-making, since a pure model would leave everything up to the market and Adam Smith's invisible hand. For example, redefining citizens as consumers reduces the relationship between a service provider and a citizen to a seller and buyer. Particularly in the case of higher education, we would expect the concept of "public interest" and citizens' rights to remain important for policy-making initiatives. Furthermore, Peters highlights the weakness of the new focus on output-centered control in defining what level of performance is good enough. Additionally, it can be added that investigations into unintended effects of the market approach would be necessary (but this issue is essential for all governance constellations). However, the ability of policy-makers to react to the results of such evaluations may be more limited by the autonomy given to institutions in the market approach.

Participative Government

Participative approaches to governance take an essentially different view of the persons involved in public services, according to Peters. While the market approach sees people as driven by self-interest and especially by financial gain, the participative approach sees people's engagement with public services as interested in the collective good of the service provided. These actors are assumed to be full of talent, energy and insights into ground-level practices, but constrained by official structures. In contrast to the market model, the way to more effective work is seen in the empowerment of the lower echelons of an organization – those close to service delivery – and not the management levels. The problem is seen as hierarchy and the solution is to flatten structures in order to get more people involved through teamwork. The management task is to find ways of organizing such teamwork within a quality-focused framework. One way of achieving this is through implementing Total Quality Management programs (Peters, 2001: 54). Policy-making should therefore be a bottom-up process of negotiation and consultation involving a maximum number of stakeholders or clients. The difficulties involved in realizing this approach stem from the need to maintain coherence and coordination within such open structures. These problems lead back to a criticism of traditional bureaucracies, because participative structures may lead to policies and actions which are too slow due to extensive negotiations, too complex due to the aversion to focus and are tangled up in too much red tape as a consequence of efforts to maintain coherence and quality (2001: 59).

Flexible Government

Peters explains that this governance approach is the least clearly articulated of the four. However, it is interesting for its focus on one assumption: beyond ideological differences – for instance, between the two previous models – this approach diagnoses permanence as a central problem of the public services. This permanence manifests itself in organizational blindness and an incapacity or unwillingness to respond to environmental changes. Furthermore, it tends to lead to gradual public service expansion and incremental rises in annual public costs (budgetary incrementalism). Organizational change is indeed seen as a positive characteristic in itself (2001: 79). The implementation of this approach requires the instalment of flexible structures and, in order to avoid permanence creeping in, regulations determining the frequent termination of existing structures. One way of achieving this is to tap into inter-organizational networks (virtual organizations) for the delivery of services and policy initiatives. Another way is to change the employment conditions of workers who may then have temporary or part-time contracts. These structures will avoid organizational inertia and can then be expressed in innovative or even experimental policies (2001: 90). Regular termination of existing organizations also provides the opportunity for collective rethinking on why an organization exists and whether it should be changed or disbanded.

One weakness of the focus on permanence as a problem is that it neglects the forte of stability for organizational learning, where an existing organization may function as a repository for prior learning (2001: 80). Furthermore, the practice of employing staff on temporary contracts is likely to lead to a reduction in intrinsic commitment and the kind of self-interestedness of staff expected in the market model (2001: 95). An open question remains in how to coordinate all this flexibility. Peters would expect a superstructure beyond individual organizations in order to coordinate the field (2001: 94). However, the model makes no recommendations on accountability, presumably because it assumes that errors will be punished by organizational termination.

Deregulated Government

Public organizations often limit the actions of their members through setting rules and procedural prescriptions. Such regulations are there to improve the predictability of certain actions and as checks and balances to avoid errors. These prescriptions are based on the assumption that particular detrimental actions will happen and should be limited. Within the deregulation approach to governance, according to Peters, it is assumed that such constraining regulations prevent the effective delivery of services. The solution is to remove as many constraints as possible to give more room for organizational talent and know-how. The expertise for policy-making is seen as situated within the public services as major repositories of ideas and experience. Peters notes an acceptance of the correctness of bureaucratic hierarchies and organizational goals, which is in contrast to the participative model (2001: 117). As with the market model, the focus is on giving managers more room to be entrepreneurial. The general distrust of regulation, however, also leads to criticisms from the perspective of this model aimed at market-based models, whose instruments (information systems, budget rules) often simply introduce regulations at other levels (2001: 108).

Since regulations have often been introduced for reasons of distrust, Peters concludes that widespread deregulation would be possible only in a system with a high civil service ethos shared by managers, their employees, politicians and the public as a whole (2001: 108). In circumstances where these conditions are not found, there is likely to be a move from ex-ante regulations to ex-post controls (2001: 112). However, Peters points to the remaining problem of finding appropriate measurement and evaluation systems to cover all requirements of both politicians and heads of bureaucracies (2001: 116).

Before we turn to the praxis in German higher education in the next section, one implication within Peters' construction of his four models should be examined. The structure of Peters' analysis suggests that a policy-maker is confronted with the choice between four separate models. Peters has commented upon this assumption and suggests that it may be more appropriate to see these models as lying next to each other with reference to the garbage can model of policy development (Peters, 2002). In this way, certain choices based on one model might have implications which encourage the realization of some aspects of other models. Despite this, Peters is somewhat disinclined to expect focal points of power and authority to lessen through governance reforms, rather believing they will only be re-defined (2002: 17). Within this more complex structure, the state can retain a substantial amount of influence through the process of "agenda-setting," according to Peters (2002: 16). For this reason, we can expect that discussions on necessary reforms and paradigm shifts will be dominated by one main model according to the definition of the problem by the most powerful actor in the governance constellation, although the reality will show a rather more diverse situation.

The Practice of Higher Education Reform in Germany

This section will present the main elements of reform of German higher education with a focus on changes related to governance and particularly funding higher education. The reforms can be summarized as the following paradigm shift (Jaeger and Leszczensky, 2008; Kehm and Lanzendorf, 2005; Leszczensky, 2003).

• Until the 1990s, the regulatory and governance space was dominated by the forces of state regulation and a strong academic oligarchy. The state regulations were primarily geared to the formal level (e.g. employment of academic staff and line-item budgeting). The academic oligarchy centered on the content of teaching and research (e.g. research profiles, curricula design). This constellation signifies a governance regime in which vertical differences between universities are avoided or – under the fiction of equality of service – at least non-transparent.

• Within the context of increasingly competitive conditions, which are related to the internationalization and globalization of higher education and indeed of society in general, the governance regime has been significantly changed. The universities should now see themselves more as enterprises and take on the task of self-steering (i.e. being entrepreneurial). This is linked to a shift away from a regulatory and administrative state to a system of autonomous institutions of higher education, which are steered by the state on the basis of negotiated performance targets and results. This development is flanked by an increase in competition, in particular for financial resources.

This paradigm shift in the governance structures, therefore, consists of aspects of all of Peters' models, in particular the approaches concerning deregulated government, market government and participative government. Depending on the level on which performance occurs and the specific activity, each reform has a different focus. The changes related to governance structures for the area of funding and budgeting can be especially clearly identified, where they affect both the nexus between state–university and university–faculty (i.e. central to subordinate unit). Below, the development trends will be characterized in relation to Peters' models.

Deregulated Government: State Deregulation and New Organizational Models Within Universities

Are universities in Germany efficient? This has been and remains one of the biggest questions in German higher education. It has been argued that universities in

Germany were in fact two organizations before the reforms – the administrative arm of the university was largely controlled as if it were a part of the state apparatus and the academic arm was a "learned republic." In the name of efficiency and freeing up entrepreneurial energy this had to change – even if the universities themselves were initially reluctant (Palandt, 1993). The state administration of universities has changed substantially within the last decade and shows a rolling back of state regulations and detailed steering. This can be seen in relation to two aspects:

- *Passing on competencies to the universities* – In nearly all German *Länder* (states) there has been a shifting of tasks traditionally carried out by the state from the ministerial level to universities. For example, the responsibility for study and examination regulations (what should be learned, over how long, with what level of resources?), the recruitment of professors and the administration of the payment of staff – all tasks in which the Ministry previously had the final vote. In terms of finances and budgeting, university budgets are no longer allocated and administered as line-item budgets, but as "global" or one-line budgets. The extent of reform concerning both aspects varies from state to state. Regarding the latter reform of budget structure, almost all universities can keep residual funding for use in the next year or swap between different expense types (e.g. staff and running costs; Behrens et al., 2006). That said, significant restrictions remain in detail and have consequences for the real financial freedom which universities have.
- *Introduction of university boards of governors* (Hochschulräte) – The competencies originally held by ministries have not all been passed on exclusively to the universities, but have been partially taken up by the new boards of governors. These boards are meant to open up the universities to the wider interests of society. With the exception of Bremen, such bodies have been prescribed by law in all German *Länder*. The state's supervisory authority is passed on to this external organ, whose members are prominent representatives of university stakeholders (e.g. industry, professional bodies). However, the responsibilities of these bodies are frequently limited in practice, and they often function more like consultants to university presidential units. Two exceptions are Hamburg and Nordrhein-Westfalen, where the boards of governors authorize the universities' financial plans and the basic principles of internal finance allocations. A special case are the boards of universities that are chartered (in Niedersachsen), since here the board decides on the use of trust funds (Kehm and Lanzendorf, 2006).

The rolling back of state regulation in connection with the requirement for universities to steer themselves has led to changes in the internal organization structures of universities. This is in line with Peters' expectations for greater managerial freedom coupled with a stronger internal hierarchy.

- *Legal reforms* – The state laws for higher education in most of the *Länder* have been reformed to enable a more entrepreneurial organizational structure in universities with a strengthening of the competencies of leadership positions (Nickel and Zechlin, 2005). In some laws so-called "experiment clauses" allow institutions to adopt new forms of organization (e.g. in Berlin). The result is usually a shifting of competencies to strengthen the executive function of leadership levels (i.e. more management competencies) and the academic committees are given goal-definition and control tasks (e.g. the president or dean, rather than the senate or faculty council, respectively, decides on the allocation of funding and staff positions).

- *Organizational structures* – In conjunction with the above, many universities have reconfigured the relationship between the leadership of higher education institutions and decentral organizational units. Two trends are particularly visible (Nickel and Zechlin, 2005): either the consolidation of decentral units to larger, interdisciplinary faculties (e.g. Hamburg or Humboldt universities) or the implementation of a more detailed organizational structure with a high number of small homogeneous units. These two models vary in terms of the decentral–central distribution of competency: while the first model situates a high level of steering competency at faculty level (in particular in coordinating tasks between subject areas), the second entails a much higher degree of direct steering and coordination at central level.

Market Government: New Forms of Output-based Steering

In connection with the question of how to make universities both more efficient and more dynamic, the governments of the *Länder* have given the implementation of market-like impulses and competition a particularly high priority. Indeed, the German Monopolies Commission (2000) expressed the need for these elements and in 2004 a positional paper from the Minister of Baden-Württemberg, Peter Frankenberg, on higher education reform mentioned the word "competition" (*Wettbewerb*) in his ninety-page report thirty-nine times (Frankenberg, 2004). Two particular instruments have been introduced to enable this change from input to output or demand-led steering:

- *New report systems* – A consequence of the shift from input-led detailed steering to a steering based on targets and results is the need for more information on demand and output measures. This has led to the development and implementation of special report systems. In a number of *Länder* (e.g. Niedersachsen, Bremen) appendices to annual financial reports contain quantitative and qualitative information on the latest performance of the university (Ziegele, 2002).
- *Performance-based allocations of state grants* — Fourteen of sixteen German *Länder* utilize funding systems based at least partially on indicators. The most common indicators quantify teaching performance using student and graduate numbers and research performance by third-party funding (Leszczensky and Orr, 2004). How these procedures are embedded in the whole steering concept of a state varies:

- Some states implement a strategy of almost completely formulaic allocation of the state grant. In Rheinland-Pfalz and Brandenburg approximately 90 percent of the state grant is allocated by formula. Albeit, a large share of the respective budgets is determined by the number of staff, which is not strictly performance-led.
- Some states utilize formula-based procedures as supplementary instruments to the target agreements (contracts – see below), e.g. in Berlin and Bremen. In these cases, a part of the funding allocation contained in the respective target agreement is redistributed between universities on the basis of competitive performance as measured by formula. In Berlin this part of the grant accounts for 30 percent of the total allocation; in Bremen it is 10 percent.
- A third option is to combine formula-based allocations for one part of the budget with discretionary allocations based on the previous year's budget for the rest. In these cases the formula comprises rarely more than 20 percent of the total allocation (Mecklenburg-Vorpommern 2.5 percent; Bayern 1.5 percent).

Remarkably, the share of grant allocated by formula says little about the real redistribution effects between universities and therefore about the degree of realized competition, because of limits to university capacity to act competitively (Orr, Jaeger and Schwarzenberger, 2007) and because of the use of tolerance bands to restrict losses (Orr and Schwarzenberger, 2007). Reports from the field have shown that these redistribution effects rarely reach the plus–minus 1 percent mark of universities' state grants. A review of different allocation systems in Germany (Jaeger, Leszczensky and Handel, 2006) argues that the utilization of a combination of formula-funding and target-based steering has had the best effects in terms of the realization of competitive stimuli and transparency. Approaches based only on using formulae for the allocation of university grants have proved to be dysfunctional (e.g. in Hessen and Niedersachsen). The introduction of performance-based funding at state-university level has been accompanied by similar initiatives within universities. The motivations for using performance-based funding within universities are at least twofold:

- The strengthening of central management functions within the universities requires systems by which management can reward high performers and reduce funding in areas of low performance. Formula-based funding, in particular, provides a transparent method of achieving this. Nearly all universities have implemented such systems, but frequently for a low share of the total university budget (often under 10 percent; Jaeger et al., 2005), although current efforts to incorporate staffing costs will make these significantly higher (e.g. in Darmstadt Technical University; Schultz, 2006). However, direct competition between faculties or schools is only of limited use for university steering, which must also consider quality differences and strategic priorities (Jaeger, 2005).

- Performance-based internal allocation is also a reaction to state initiatives. The performance measure used by state funding systems can be directly linked to the performance of specific faculties or indeed of individual staff. For this reason, university management is under pressure to allocate this share of state budget to the high performers. Although many universities introduced their first procedures for formula-based funding before or at the same time as the states (*Länder*) did, most internal procedures are now closely linked to the state mechanisms (Orr, Jaeger and Schwarzenberger, 2007).

Two further changes within German higher education have increased the influence of market demand and competition on universities:

- In 2006 tuition fees were introduced and by the winter semester 2007/2008 around three-quarters of all students were paying fees of approximately €1000 per annum to their respective universities (Ebcinoglu, 2006). As in other countries, there was an interest in introducing such fees on the part of both the state and the universities. The state wanted to introduce stimuli for competition between universities and encourage students to see themselves as critical consumers and thereby strengthen the weak demand-side influence on university performance (Orr, 2007: 171). The universities saw the benefit of supplementary funding based on their relative quality.
- Third-party funding for research projects from industry, governmental bodies and research councils is, for the same reasons as for tuition fees, attractive to both sides. The importance of this funding stream has grown over the past two decades. Between 1992 and 2004 the share of income from this source has risen on average for all institutions of higher education in Germany from 14 percent to 17 percent of universities' running costs. The differentiation between universities on the basis of research profiles has also increased due to the German Excellence Initiative, which awards premium funding to top research institutes and – naturally – further increases their comparative advantage in acquiring third-party funding.

Participative Government: Contract-like Forms of Higher Education Steering

Participative structures – as seen by Peters – would seem to describe best the status quo in universities before the reforms. As Peters describes, the principle behind this model is that people (here, more specifically, academics) are driven by intrinsic motivation, which should not be constrained by official structures. Peters also points out the weaknesses of this mode of governance: it is difficult to maintain coherence and coordination within such open structures. In fact, both of these characteristics of the participative mode of governance have been seen as reasons for a necessary reform in Germany. Trust in the effectiveness of intrinsic motivation of academics was called into question and academics typified as "lazy" by media and politicians alike (see, e.g., Kamenz and Wehrle, 2007). Furthermore, there were arguments that organizational reform must lead to more cohesive management and coordination structures (Schimank, 2001, 2002a). One high-level ministerial civil servant starts out his description of organizational reform in Niedersachsen with a rhetorical question to university leaders: what are you the boss of? (Palandt, 1993).

It is clear from the sections above that the introduction of elements of deregulation and market orientation must have knock-on effects for any existing elements of participative coordination. The task for policy and practice has been to find a coordination structure which:

- is acceptable to academics used to a participatory approach and maintains the structure by which creativity can be fostered at low levels in the organization; and
- at the same time is able to reflect the newly strengthened hierarchy between university leadership and individual faculties, and between faculties and their subordinate units. This is important as the autonomy given to universities can be dealt with in this very complex organizational structure only if common goals, targets and performance measurements can be communicated effectively. This is especially important now that the organization "university" finds itself competing in a market with other universities.

The policy response has been to implement contract-like target agreements between the state and universities and between university leaderships and subordinate units:

- Target agreements between the state and universities can be found in all German *Länder* (König, 2007). In general, these agreements determine budget allocations only to a limited extent. And even then there are no agreements where an automatic link between goal delivery and budget level is clearly specified. In many cases, however, the total state grant is documented in the agreement (especially in Berlin and Bremen).
- Comparing the German *Länder*, it is interesting to note the reform trajectory regarding the two now-standard components of university funding and steering (see Figure 3.1). In the year 2000 three of the sixteen German states were using formula-based funding (Baden-Württemberg, Bayern, Rheinland-Pfalz) and four were using a target-based agreement (Bremen, Berlin, Hamburg, Schleswig-Holstein) – the latter states are typically small with high levels of institutional diversity. No state was yet using a combination of the two. By 2006 almost all states were applying combinations, with just two exceptions (Saarland, Sachsen-Anhalt). This is clear evidence of the acceptance of a complementarity between both instruments of university steering in Germany.
- The same situation can be found inside universities for the agreements between university leadership and subordinate units (Jaeger et al., 2005).

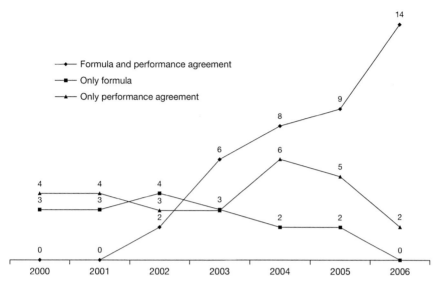

Figure 3.1 The Number of *Länder* Using Formula-funding and/or Performance Agreements, 2000–2006

Results: Tempered Autonomy and Competition

In summary, we can see how elements of each of the three models have been implemented within the context of university steering and funding in Germany. Regarding the fourth model – flexible government – elements of flexibilization have also been implemented and organizational change is certainly seen in the German debate as an expression of reform and positive progress. However, the target agreements, which structure – at least in general terms – all decisions between the state ministry and universities, are valid on average for two years. This would seem to be incompatible with the avoidance of permanence prescribed by Peters as a characteristic of the flexible government model. Indeed, in reference to funding contracts, they are often promoted for their provision of multi-year planning security. A real judgement on flexibility lies in the degree of experimentation and empowerment at the lower levels of the university facilitated by the agreements. One systematic review of the practice after ten years sees a limited implementation of agreements, which have been developed from the bottom up (König, 2007: 85), for example, in Hamburg (Nickel, 2007: 264).

In the light of the reform triad for German higher education mentioned above, we should now ask whether there is evidence of less state intervention, more university autonomy and more competition in Germany since the higher education reforms. This section has certainly shown that there is more market and that the state has devolved some of its substantial responsibilities either to universities or to other external bodies (e.g. boards of governors). The state has also certainly moved away from input-steering. However, in terms of increasing university autonomy, the current use of reporting structures and particularly of state–university bilateral target agreements suggests that the state still has an interest in institutional steering (see Lanzendorf and Orr (2006) for a comparison with other countries). This would appear to contradict the reform triad, if institutional steering means state intervention in another guise and results in less institutional autonomy and less competition between the providers of higher education. Three specific examples can be given from the process of higher education reform as initiatives which do not appear to fit the general discourse regarding a paradigm shift (see Jaeger, Leszczensky and Handel, 2006; Handel, Jaeger and Schmidlin, 2005):

- *Inconsistent handling of indicator-based procedures* – This method of funding allocation has been introduced as a way of aligning state funding to real performance. However, in Hessen, for example, the reallocations between universities according to the indicator-based procedure were not, in fact, realized consistently. Instead, they were further adjusted to take account of additional factors, which were not made transparent and had the character of discretionary – interventionist – decisions. The two main concerns on the part of the policy-maker which led to these actions were:
  - The acceptance of university and stakeholder concerns that quality of performance is at least as important as quantity of performance as a criterion for funding allocation and that indicators cannot adequately reflect the former.
  - The concern on the part of the state (the Finance Ministry) that this procedure, which allocated a set amount of funding per capita, would lead to increases in the quantity of performance across the whole sector and the state could not afford to keep pace with this quantitative growth through budget increases.
- *Continuance of discretionary funding* – Funding on the basis of particularist interests constrains the development of competition between the providers of higher education. However, in some states, for instance, Niedersachsen, the effects of an allocation model based on performance have been undermined by secondary funding decisions realized through discretionary allocations, thereby neutralizing the impact of the indicator-based funding procedure. One of the main reasons for this has been concerns regarding the consequences of formula-based allocations which do not take account of regional policy concerns, such as regional economy and town planning. The continuance of discretionary funding facilitates the "correction" of the formulaic results.
- *State initiatives to restructure university systems* – The reform program would suggest that institutional provision of higher education should be the result of a combination of market demand, comparative advantage in competition with other providers and strategic decisions on the part of individual institutions. However, in a number of *Länder*, states have initiated restructuring through policy programs. Illustrative for such actions is Niedersachsen. In September

2003 the so-called "Higher Education Optimization Concept" (HOK) was announced, which resulted in a reduction in the number of higher education institutions (from nineteen to eighteen) and the number of locations (from thirty-two to twenty-nine). Many of the changes involved moving or merging faculties from two different locations. This program is a clear example of state-led steering in a top-down manner and is evidence that performance-based funding is only one element in the steering framework.

If we take up the perspective of purposeful policy-makers who diagnose a problem and design a program to solve it as suggested by Peters (and Pawson and Tilley, 1997), we may see two main reasons behind this very tempered autonomy implemented in German higher education:

• *Insecurity regarding the effects of current reforms* – We have seen that the enacted reforms are broadly a combination of Peters' market government and deregulated government models. Regarding the issue of error detection or correction (e.g. the concerns given in the three above-mentioned examples), Peters ascribes this task either to the market, according to the first model, or prescribes "accept more errors," according to the second (2001: 178). There seems to be little willingness to do this in Germany. At the same time, other research sees this disposition in many countries, where reforms to governance have not led to decreased state intervention (Amaral and Magalhães, 2007). In many of the German states, ministries would see one of their tasks as assuring a balanced higher education system and the avoidance of risk, and their response is to remain influential even at an institutional level of steering.
• *Competencies for appropriate action* – The need for new skills and competencies emerges in connection with the new division of labor between universities and the state. Although structural reforms have occurred, the new responsibilities require the acquisition of new skills on the part of the actors at university and state levels (Nickel and Ziegele, 2006). Only then can they avoid falling back into their old roles out of lack of competency. Germany has few institutions which train new personnel for such tasks (e.g. through vocational training or Master's courses) and the situation may be further hampered at ministerial level because of the permanency of civil service staff. This also contradicts Peters' expectations for such reform programs.

Conclusion and Reflection

Much of the literature on governance continues to focus on describing structural and administrative change. This is important because it overcomes ascribing the changes to particular ideologies, for example, belief in the market, and focuses instead on the more complex results of the interaction between ideas and existing structures which result in actual policy implementation. With his four emerging models, Peters offers an approach which helps us better understand the resulting changes. This approach could be typified by Schimank (2002b), who refers to the work of Scharpf (1997) as focusing on "games real actors play."

In order to grasp reforms, Peters explicates four models and describes the basic assumptions behind each of them, for example, in reference to problem diagnosis, expected organizational structure, management approach, etc.. Naturally, this is the most useful – but possibly the most critical – part of Peters' analytic framework for governance reform. It is questionable whether the proposed models of governance would ever be found in their purest form, and as a model of governance reform "participative government" does seem a little like a straw man argument: it looks attractive but can never be achieved. Indeed, in Peters' second edition he has commented on the observable changes since reform efforts began. These second-stage reforms are characterized by at least three aspects (Peters, 2001: 21–22):

- Policy is less driven by theory ("intellectual roots") and many initiatives are based on the consequences and perceived failures of the first stage reforms.
- Following an emphasis on performance, public reform is turning back to the question of coordination, which is difficult to achieve if all actors focus on their own performance.
- Following deregulation, there is a tendency to re-regulation. However, in contrast to earlier phases, such regulation is often ex post facto, i.e. states impose controls after the assessment of actions and performance.

In order to capture these changes, it may not be enough to start out again from Peters' four models. Indeed, Peters sees these three issues as largely visible irrespective of the initial route to reform. This insight may suggest that an analytical model based on a structural framework (such as the one proposed by Schimank (2002a)) would be an important supplement to the analysis which was carried out above in order to facilitate comparative analyses over time or between countries. This chapter shows that both analytical methods are necessary to encapsulate reform and to understand better the reasons and motivations behind the resulting implementation of reform.

The second issue in reference to Peters is the implicit assumption that only one or a small number of actors influence policy and that these actors have the chance to convert their purposeful ideas into practice. Indeed, Schimank explains in a methodological note that this is a common problem for sociological theory which strives to scale-up theories to capture more of reality, but at the same time becomes a messier framework for analysis (Schimank, 2002b). Frameworks such as Peters' therefore come at a price. This assumption of one main actor has been useful for the above analysis. However, in view of the increasing number of different actors (stakeholders) influencing the university enterprise (boards of governors, third-party funders, students paying tuition fees, competitors), it is questionable whether all these "voices" can be captured in an analysis, especially a more in-depth study than the one carried out in this short chapter.

Lastly, there is the question of whether these actors are really acting purposefully, since their actions are constrained by the actions and reactions of each other. If Peters' argument that the state remains most influential through its ability to set agendas (Peters, 2002) is true, this latter point may not be so limiting for analyses. However, since many reforms are in fact based on economic arguments and the argument that universities and university systems are subjected to international competition, the influence of the state and particularly the respective ministries responsible for higher education may be decreasing. A more inclusive approach (indeed discussed by Peters (2000)) might, for instance, facilitate a better understanding of all the elements which have led to this particular flavor of governance in German higher education, especially the remaining tendency towards governmental steering at institutional level in higher education sectors.

References

Amaral, Alberto, and António Magalhães. "Market Competition, Public Good and State Interference." In *Public–Private Dynamics in Higher Education: Expectations, Developments and Outcomes*, edited by Jürgen Enders, and Ben Jongbloed. Bielefeld: Transcript Verlag, 2007, 89–110.

Behrens, Thomas, Michael Leszczensky, Christiane Mück, and Astrid Schwarzenberger. *Flexibilisierung und Globalisierung der Hochschulhaushalte der Bundesländer im Vergleich.* Hannover: HIS-Projektbericht, 2006. Available online (accessed 6.2.2008): http://www.his.de/pdf/23/Flexibilisierung_Hochschulhaushalte.pdf.

CHEPS, CHE, ESMU, and NIFU-STEP. *The Extent and Impact of Higher Education Governance Reform across Europe (part two).* 2006. Available online (accessed 6.2.2008): http://ec.europa.eu/education/doc/reports/doc/higherextent2_en.pdf.

Ebcinoglu, Fatma. *Die Einführung allgemeiner Studiengebühren in Deutschland: Entwicklungsstand, Ähnlichkeiten und Unterschiede der Gebührenmodelle der Länder.* Hannover: HIS-Kurzinformation, A4/2006.

Frankenberg, Peter. *17 Thesen zur Hochschulreform-Strategien einer ganzheitlichen Hochschulentwicklung in Deutschland.* Stuttgart: Ministerium für Wissenschaft, Forschung und Kultur, 2004.

Handel, Kai, Michael Jaeger, and Janina Schmidlin. "Evaluation der Formelgebundenen Mittelvergabe für die Niedersächsischen Fachhochschulen." *Beiträge zur Hochschulforschung* 27 (2005): 72–89.

Jaeger, Michael. *Leistungsbezogene Mittelvergabe und Qualitätssicherung als Elemente der hochschulinternen Steuerung.* Hannover: HIS-Kurzinformation, A12/2005.

Jaeger, Michael, and Michael Leszczensky. "Hochschul-Governance als Konzept sozialwissenschaftlicher Hochschulforschung-am Beispiel neuer Modelle und Verfahren der Hochschulsteuerung und Finanzierung." *Das Hochschulwesen* 56(1), 2008: 17–25.

Jaeger, Michael, Michael Leszczensky, and Kai Handel. "Staatliche Hochschulfinanzierung durch Leistungsorientierte Budgetierungsverfahren: Erste Evaluationsergebnisse und Schlussfolgerungen." *Hochschulmanagement* 1 (2006): 13–20.

Jaeger, Michael, Michael Leszczensky, Dominic Orr, and Astrid Schwarzenberger. *Formelgebundene Mittelvergabe und Zielvereinbarungen als Instrumente der Budgetierung an Deutschen Universitäten: Ergebnisse einer Bundesweiten Befragung.* Hannover: HIS Kurzinformation, A13/2005.

Kamenz, Uwe, and Martin Wehrle. *Professor Untat: Was Faul ist hinter den Hochschulkulissen?* Berlin: Econ Verlag, 2007.

Kehm, Barbara M., and Ute Lanzendorf. "Ein Neues Governance-Regime für die Hochschulen-mehr Markt und Weniger Selbststeuerung?" *Zeitschrift für Pädagogik* 50 (2005): 41–55.

Kehm, Barbara, and Ute Lanzendorf, eds. *Reforming University Governance: Changing Conditions for Research in Four European Countries.* Bonn: Lemmens, 2006.

50 • Dominic Orr and Michael Jaeger

King, Roger. "Governing Universities: Varieties of National Regulation." In *Public–Private Dynamics in Higher Education: Expectations, Developments and Outcomes*, edited by Jürgen Enders, and Ben Jongbloed. Bielefeld: Transcript Verlag, 2007, 63–87.

König, Karsten. *Kooperation Wagen: 10 Jahre Hochschulsteuerung durch Vertragsförmige Vereinbarungen.* Halle-Wittenberg: HoF Arbeitsberichte, 2007.

Lanzendorf, Ute, and Dominic Orr. "Hochschulsteuerung durch Kontrakte-Wozu und Wie? Unterschiedliche Stellenwerte von Wettbewerb, Autonomie und Indikatoren im Europäischen Vergleich." *Die Hochschule* 2 (2006): 80–97.

Leszczensky, Michael. *Paradigmenwechsel in der Hochschulfinanzierung.* Hannover: HIS Kurzinformation, A1/2003.

Leszczensky, Michael, and Dominic Orr. *Staatliche Hochschulfinanzierung durch Indikatorgestützte Mittelverteilung: Dokumentation und Analyse der Verfahren in 11 Bundesländern.* Hannover: HIS Kurzinformation, A2/2004.

Monopolkommission. *Wettbewerb als Leitbild für die Hochschulpolitik: Sondergutachten der Monopolkommission, Band 30.* Baden-Baden: Nomos Verlagsgesellschaft, 2000.

Nickel, Sigrun. *Partizipatives Management von Universitäten. Zielvereinbarungen, Leistungsstrukturen, Staatliche Steuerung.* Munich: Rainer Hampp Verlag, 2007.

Nickel, Sigrun, and Lothar Zechlin. "Die Suche nach der optimalen Organizationsstruktur." In *Management von Universitäten: Zwischen Tradition und (Post)Moderne*, edited by Heike Welte, Manfred Auer, and Claudia Meister-Scheytt. Munich: Rainer Hampp Verlag, 2005, 199–214.

Nickel, Sigrun, and Frank Ziegele. "Profis ins Hochschulmanagement." *Hochschulmanagement* 1 (2006): 2–7.

Orr, Dominic. "More Competition in German Higher Education: Expectations, Developments, Outcomes." In *Public–Private Dynamics in Higher Education: Expectations, Developments and Outcomes*, edited by Jürgen Enders, and Ben Jongbloed. Bielefeld: Transcript Verlag, 2007, 157–184.

Orr, Dominic, and Astrid Schwarzenberger. *The Position of Competition in State Models for Performance-based Funding in German Higher Education: Critical Assessment of Variations and Trends in the German Länder.* Paper presented at the annual Resup Conference, Paris, February 1–2 2007. Available online (accessed 6.2.2008): http://www.resup.ubordeaux2.fr/manifestations/conferenceinternationaleparis2007/Actes/ORR_RESUP2007.pdf.

Orr, Dominic, Michael Jaeger, and Astrid Schwarzenberger. "Performance-based Funding as an Instrument of Competition in German Higher Education." *Journal of Higher Education Policy and Management* 29(1) (2007): 3–23.

Palandt, Klaus. "'Wozu sind Sie der Boss': Probleme mit der Selbstverwaltung der Hochschulen." In *Der Ausbau der Hochschulen oder der Turmbau zu Babel*, edited by Wolfgang Körner. Wien: Passagen Verlag, 1993, 95–114.

Pawson, Ray, and Nick Tilley. *Realistic Evaluation.* London: Sage, 1997.

Peters, B. Guy. *The Future of Governing: Four Emerging Models.* Kansas: University of Kansas Press, 1996.

Peters, B. Guy. "Governance and Comparative Politics." In *Debating Governance: Authority, Steering, and Democracy*, edited by Jon Pierre. Oxford: Oxford University Press, 2000, 36–53.

Peters, B. Guy. *The Future of Governing: Four Emerging Models* (2nd edn). Kansas: University of Kansas Press, 2001.

Peters, B. Guy. *Governance: A Garbage Can Perspective.* IHS Political Science Series (No. 84), Vienna, 2002. Available online (accessed 6.2.2008): http://www.ihs.ac.at/publications/pol/wp_84.pdf.

Pierre, Jon, ed. *Debating Governance: Authority, Steering, and Democracy.* Oxford: Oxford University Press, 2000.

Scharpf, Fritz W. *Games Real Actors Play: Actor-centered Institutionalism in Policy Research.* Boulder: Westview Press, 1997.

Schimank, Uwe. "Festgefahrene Gemischtwarenläden: Die Deutschen Hochschulen als Erfolgreich Scheiternde Organizationen." In *Die Krise der Universitäten*, edited by Erhard Stölting, and Uwe Schimank. Opladen: Westdeutscher Verlag, 2001, 223–242.

Schimank, Uwe. *Governance in Hochschulen. Vortrag im Rahmen der Veranstaltung "Professionelles Wissenschaftsmanagement als Aufgabe" des Zentrums für Wissenschaftsmanagement.* Speyer:

ZWM, 2002a. Available online (accessed 6.2.2008): http://www.zwm-speyer.de/Vortrag Schimank.pdf.

Schimank, Uwe. *Von Sauberen Mechanismen zu Schmutzigen Modellen: Methodologische Perspektiven einer Höherskalierung von Akteurkonstellationen.* Hagen: Fernuniversität, 2002b. Available online (accessed 6.2.2008): http://www.fernuni-hagen.de/SOZ/weiteres/preprints/arcadeon.pdf.

Schreiterer, Ulrich. *Politische Steuerung des Hochschulsystems: Programm und Wirklichkeit der staatlichen Studienreform 1975–1986.* Frankfurt am Main: Campus Verlag, 1989.

Schultz, Volker. "Dezentralisierung durch Budgetierung: Das Darmstädter Mittelverteilungsmodell und Wege zur Personalbudgetierung." *Wissenschaftsmanagement* 4 (2006): 14–20.

Ziegele, Frank. "Reformansätze und Perspektiven der Hochschulsteuerung in Deutschland." *Beiträge zur Hochschulforschung* 24(3) (2002): 106–121.

4

Governing Disciplines

Reform and Placation in the Austrian University System

CLAUDIA MEISTER-SCHEYTT AND ALAN SCOTT

Introduction

> The principle of equality and the principle of hierarchy are facts, indeed they are among the most constraining facts, of political and social life.
>
> (Dumont, 1970: 3)

The above quotation from Louis Dumont's influential anthropology of the Indian caste system, *Homo Hierarchicus* (first published in French in 1966), provides the initial premise from which this analysis of the nature of recent reforms within a continental European higher education system commences. For Dumont, the principles of equality and hierarchy are "social facts" in Durkheim's sense; that is to say, they exist beyond the preferences and choices of individual actors, and in part form those preferences and constrain those choices. We should note straight away that for Dumont – as for Durkheim – a social fact is every bit as "real" as a physical one. Furthermore, Dumont's assertion also implies that (a) equality and hierarchy are *systems* of beliefs and practices – i.e. consistent and coherent across a wide range of actions, issues, dispositions and opinions, and (b) these two systems are *mutually exclusive* – i.e. they create different worlds of cultural practice, opinion and cognition.

Dumont analyzes a case – the caste system – in which the principle of equality is all but absent. Our case is different. We shall argue (a) in the university system both principles are present and form the poles towards which actors are drawn; (b) these two systems are in a long-term struggle with an indeterminate outcome – an ongoing war of position between the historically older principle of hierarchy and its upstart rival, the principle of equality; and (c) while, for many observers of university systems, this kind of dynamic is thought to lead to ossification – the "moving graveyards" view of university reform – we shall argue that university systems do move, though more slowly than reformers would wish, but they do so via minor, and often reversible, shifts in the relative balance between the two contrasting principles. Rather than the replacement of one principle by another, we typically observe the sedimentation of conflicting values and practices, or vacillations between them.

We take the case of current reform of Austrian higher education along the now familiar lines drawn by New Public Management (NPM). We are aware that most readers of this volume will not be seeking a detailed account of the university system of a small continental European country.[1] However, the case is interesting for a number of reasons. First, it can illustrate more general features of university reform practice. Second, it can be understood as a close to ideal type via which we can acquire analytical leverage on other cases and wider issues. We shall give the details of this particular case, but also seek to make the broader points and make clear how this case might be treated as something approximating an ideal type. Finally, the Austrian system is a variant of the German "Humboldtian" model of a university with its emphasis upon the autonomy of institutions ("institutional pillarization" in the language of modern social science) and the unity of teaching and research under the protection of a *Kulturstaat*, a state that respects these principles. This model had a profound impact upon a much larger university system operating in a very different institutional environment: that of the US.

There are specific reasons, above all in the nature of the employment contract (see Greenwood, 2007: 100), why change within a university system typically takes the form of the sedimentation of one principle upon another, or vacillation between a limited number of value options. As Max Weber recognized, the key to social change is the process of the selection (*Ausleseprozess*) of a particular type of subject (*Menschentyp*) by dominant institutions (Weber, 1988: 37). The existence of tenure, or at least of a high degree of stability of employment, within many university systems represents a limit to this process of institutional selection, which can thus operate only in slow motion via generational replacement (Kuhn cf. (1962) on the way paradigms shift). The substitution of one type of subject by another, which Weber considered both the condition for and evidence of social transformation, happens, if at all, glacially. In periods of transition – that is, almost always – the principle of hierarchy and the principle of equality are left to slog it out. The Austrian case is of interest in this context as the reforms that shifted universities from a Humboldtian model into a so-called twenty-first-century university took place over a mere thirty or so years: from the traditional autonomous university governed by professors (up to the late 1970s) via the so-called democratized university (from the 1970s to the 1990s) to the university driven by NPM principles. The last phase started slowly in the mid-1990s and was fully established – in law at least – by 2002. Hence, some of the key actors (governors, rectorial team members, deans and unit heads) have experienced all the different university governance regimes of the last two hundred years and have had to incorporate and accommodate conflicting values and principles.

The following discussion draws on Dumont's analysis in order to periodize the system's transformation and upon Mary Douglas's Cultural Theory and the use to which this has been put in the analysis of public administration by Christopher Hood in order to understand the ways in which reform aims have not been achieved or have produced "reverse effects" due to institutional path dependency and/or the necessity of placation. We focus upon the kinds of communities that are embodied in academic disciplines and on different layers of the university in terms of Douglas's criteria: solidarity (group) and the degree of ritual and rule-boundedness (grid), and on the kinds of reverse effect that Hood argues are associated with attempts to shift the management of an organization from one grid-group box to another (Hood, 1998). In the analysis that follows, we shall seek to avoid both modernizing rhetoric and backward-looking despair (see Collini (2003) for a warning).

We illustrate our argument through an empirical research project on the boards of governors, an important instrument of the new governance structure implemented by the latest reform.[2] Empirical data stem from around forty in-depth interviews with board members from a number of Austrian universities, as well as with rectors and senate chairs, covering the triad of the institutionalized governance structures. With the board of governors, a body was created that is structurally independent from the Ministry and the respective university (politicians as well as university members are not eligible) and has far-reaching competencies formerly assigned to the Ministry of Science and Research, for example, selecting and appointing the rector from shortlists drawn up by the senate, controlling the whole management staff, deciding on all strategic aspects of the university, and negotiating the performance contract between university and Ministry (see Meister-Scheytt, 2007). By creating this body, the new distance ("autonomy") between Ministry and universities should be counterbalanced, following the NPM creed that politics must not directly intervene in operational issues, but should steer and monitor the activities of (ostensibly) independent public organizations.

Tradition: *Die Ordinarienuniversität – Homo Hierarchicus*

> The whole is founded on the necessary and hierarchical coexistence of the two opposites.
>
> (Dumont, 1970: 43)

Following Dumont, hierarchy is not just a system of ranking, but a holistic system in which, as the saying goes, everything in its place and a place for everything. Such hierarchical systems are sustained via complex and interwoven discourses of purity and impurity (pollution). These are the coexisting opposites referred to in the epigraph above. In her essay on *Homo Hierarchicus*, Mary Douglas (1975: ch. 12) notes that where social differences are not established via inequality of material or power resources they will emerge via a purity discourse in which the greater the distance from mundane practices, the higher the status (1975: 186). This places the priesthood above those with political – and thus worldly – power and, in a university context, pure over applied research, disciplines above multi-disciplinary areas (for example, management studies), and creates a prestige hierarchy among disciplines.

Now, clearly we have to be very cautious in adapting terms meant to apply to a caste system elsewhere. However, as Dumont acknowledges, one can view caste in Weberian terms as a highly developed, complex and extreme form of status differentiation; as a society consisting of distinct "status groups." In the traditional Germanic university system, we are dealing with just such a system of status groups – *Stand/Stände* (estate/estates) – in a strict sense of the term. First, the professoriate, non-professorial faculty, and non-academic faculty are organized into separate *curia* with distinct rights and duties. Formally, all senior positions can be filled only by professors. This formalized status division between professorial and so-called *Mittelbau* – non-professorial faculty – is the linchpin of the hierarchical system. Second, traditionally in Austria, and in Germany still, the basic unit of university organization was the *Lehrstuhl* (chair) rather than the department. In effect, each professor is a "department" in his or her own right, claiming a monopoly of at least part of a discipline and with his/her own support staff and assistants. This organizational principle is a clear example of what Weber meant by "social closure" – i.e. monopolistic practices designed both to claim resources and fend off potential challengers. Finally, movement from a lower- to a higher-status group was tightly policed. To qualify as an independent university teacher or researcher and to undertake normal academic work (such as the supervision of doctoral or MA theses) unsupervised, university assistants have to submit a *Habilitationsschrift*: a single lengthy work or, increasingly, a collection of published papers (the so-called *kumulative Habilitation*). The process is discipline-based and the candidate has to demonstrate command of the discipline in front of all professors of the respective faculty. In this way, a simple qualification takes on other latent functions, notably a gatekeeping role and a role as ritual initiation rewarding appropriate behavior in the eyes of the community, or of powerful actors within it. It becomes a (frequently jealously guarded) gateway and pillar of hierarchy and disciplinary purity in which not only the knowledge but the personality of the candidate is key. For entry into the highest-status group (that of the professors) both the *Habilitation* and the "call" to a chair (*Ruf* or *Berufung*), normally by another university, are required.

This system reproduces the personal dependencies and associated conflicts brilliantly analyzed, from a Weberian perspective, by Fritz Ringer in his classical study of the nineteenth- and early twentieth-century German university (Ringer, 1969), possibly still the best source for anyone seeking a sense of what the system is like from within. In its pure form, such a system presupposes a high degree of institutional protection, even isolation – i.e. relatively little exposure to external influences. At its extreme, it descends into what Mary Douglas calls "backwater isolation": "insulations between individuals which prevent free transaction" (Douglas and Isherwood, 1979: 22). As one might expect from Dumont's account of caste and from Douglas's analysis of pollution (Douglas, 1966), these insulations are maintained via a discourse of purity, in this case one organized around disciplinarity and disciplinary tradition. This is a logic that is, in the first place, highly balkanizing and thus limits cooperation and "free transaction," and is, second, and relatedly, what Weber would have called *wirtschaftsfremd*: indifferent to, or even hostile towards, considerations of performance and efficiency. Within hierarchies, the maintenance and reproduction of the system and, above all, of the status hierarchy – becomes an end in itself, at least, as Weber also argued, as long as traditionally defined standards of living are maintained; that is, as often as not, until they are challenged by markets. The market, in turn, often appears in the guise of the principle of equality and of individual freedom from conditions of personalized subordination (see Simmel, 1990). The first reform wave in the

Austrian system took precisely this form: the demand for equality and freedom from the figure of the professor as chair incumbent; a position from which he – less often she – could exercise personal power over assistants based upon a monopoly claim and underpinned by the institutional arrangements of the *Ordinarienuniversität*, the university of, and for, professors.

The First Challenge: The Upstart Principle of Equality – *Homo Aequalis*

How vulnerable is the purity-scale to the blasts of the command system?
(Douglas, 1975: 192)

What distinguishes the contemporary German from the Austrian university system is that the principles of the *Ordinarienuniversität* have been only weakly challenged in the former whereas the latter underwent a period of democratizing reforms in the 1970s which aimed to improve the position of non-professorial faculty by lessening their dependence upon the patronage and largesse of the professors and giving them (and students) greater say in the running of the university. As a result, in the German system the chair system has largely persisted whereas the Austrian has gone over to something more like a departmental model, but not quite. The reforms in Austria reached their zenith in a law, the *Universitätsorganisationsgesetz* (UOG, 1975), a bold attempt by the state to work against the inherited hierarchical university system. In Douglas's terms, the law was a blast from the command system (i.e. the state) against the purity-scale.

While the reforms of the 1970s had real effects in weakening relations of dependency on the person of the professor and giving the *Mittelbau* a real say in decision-making, they left many historical structures intact. Much of the "legacy organization" (Burt, 2005) survived within the new structures for a number of reasons. First, the cohort of professors embodying traditional values did not vanish with the reforms and habitualized patterns do not necessarily or easily adapt to new rules. Nor must we forget that the cohorts of non-professorial staff empowered by democratizing reforms were themselves socialized within the legacy organization in which they had good reasons to imitate the strategies and values of the professors (see Hedström, 1998). While democracy and *Mitbestimmung* (co-determination) were the banners behind which the *Mittelbau* marched while making their claims, this does not necessarily imply a break with the professorial *habitus* once they themselves had gained access to some of these privileges. Such intermediate groups find themselves in a position typical of the middle classes for whom, as Norbert Elias noted, the characteristic motto is "The doors below must remain shut. Those above must open" (Elias, 1982: 16). Second, the resilience of the professorial status group was also maintained by the fact that the Austrian higher education system has continued to take in a relatively large number of academics who were socialized into the German chair system while there are correspondingly few academics who have been exposed to alternative (e.g. departmental) models. Third, with respect to structures, the democratizing reforms changed the relative powers of the *curia* but did not abolish them. The professorial and non-professorial *curia* continued to possess distinct powers and rights and therefore remained distinct status groups. Thus the *form* of democracy introduced by the reforms of the 1970s was highly corporatist: powers were ascribed to individuals as members of specific status groups. As Weber argued, such corporatist systems are inherently conservative (Weber, 1994). Finally, the separation of status groups was cemented by the *Habilitation* procedure which remained largely unchanged.

For these reasons, the democratizing reforms of the 1970s, and more especially their translation into practice on the ground, left the Austrian system suspended somewhere between the chair system and the departmental model. This supports our general claim that change takes place via a gradual sedimentation of one system upon another rather than via outright replacement, and illustrates path dependency in the face of reforming blasts from the command system.

However, we need to differentiate more carefully here. Thus far, we have treated the *Ordinarienuniversität* as a pure and uniform type. But the degree to which the legacy organization has been retained is uneven across universities and disciplines. Criteria of success (and failure) vary across the natural sciences, humanities, arts and social sciences (see Byrnes, 2007). This is, not least, an effect of the differential level of exposure of disciplinary areas to international standards and (scientific) competition (see Gambetta, 1998). For example, natural scientists are exposed to international rules – publish in high-ranked international journals or perish – while in areas such as the humanities and social sciences, which retain a national orientation and are less exposed to international pressures, the publication culture is different. Thus, for example, while the former have modernized the *Habilitation* in such a way as to make it compatible with international practices (for example, the *Habilitation* consisting of a collection of papers), the latter have largely adhered to the historical convention of the *Habilitation* as "the big book." These differences came even more to the fore in later reform waves.

To sum up: the answer to Mary Douglas's (1975: 192) question – "How vulnerable is the purity-scale to the blasts of the command system?" – would appear, in this case, to depend in part upon the degree of the community's contact with external systems and, correspondingly, specific scientific cultures. Blasts from the command system must necessarily make concessions to traditional practices and are weakened by the community's response and by the necessity of placation (see Hood, 1998). They are, at best, a necessary but not sufficient condition for challenging the purity-scale. Nevertheless, we can identify factors that drive on reform even in the face of placation and resistance. The reforms of the 1970s stressed democracy and equality of treatment in terms of rights. Different discipline-based cultures were thus not an issue as long as the democratic principle of equality was coupled with pluralism. However, the logic of market, or quasi-market, competition, in which the natural sciences more than the humanities and social sciences are located is antagonistic to the principles of (status) hierarchy *and* democracy. In the market, and particularly international markets, not the reproduction of existing structures but, in Douglas and Mars's vivid metaphor, grabbing the megaphone is the aim (2003: 767). These are forces that work against tradition and which can be mobilized by the command system – read "state" – in subsequent waves of the battle against tradition.

The Second Challenge: The Parvenu Principle of Performance – *Homo Meritocratus*

Dumont treats the *homo aequalis* as the opposite to *homo hierarchicus*, but equality of treatment is not the only alternative to hierarchy in its transmitted form. For our purposes, one can speak of *homo meritocratus* as a further alternative to hierarchy. Democracy and meritocracy are not necessarily incompatible, but emphasis can be placed more on the one than on the other, and, under some circumstances, they can come to be viewed as alternatives and as competitors. Where the emphasis shifts towards meritocracy, performance and the reward of demonstrable success, rather than co-determination and rights, become key aims. In the long struggle against hierarchy and tradition, the latest wave of reform shifts from a discourse of equality to one of performance and achievement; performance displaces co-determination as the key term in modernization rhetoric turning last-wave reformers into current-wave conservatives.

In our case, democracy itself (particularly in its corporatist form) has come to be viewed as an enemy of change. The inherited (democratized) structures and procedures were seen to be contributing to stasis by creating stalemate and stand-off throughout the system: any change would produce a winner and a loser, but the potential losers were in a position to stave off reform (see BM:BWK (2003) for such an analysis). The solution proposed by the latest reform, UG 2002, was the now familiar mix of autonomy (from direct state control) and strong internal leadership. The new reform sought to break from the old system in a number of key respects, for example, by weakening the powers of all *curia* and strengthening those of senior managers in order to break the deadlock; by giving each university a lump-sum budget and replacing direct state regulation with performance-related instruments: performance contracts (*Leistungvereinbarungen*) between universities and the state, and at all levels within the university; by installing a board of governors with members mostly from outside the academic world and over whose appointments the Ministry had considerable say; and by abolishing tenured and civil service employment status for all new appointments.

These changes appeared to advocates and critics alike to be revolutionary; a complete reversal of the principles of the self-governing university whether in its traditional or democratized form. It also appeared to represent a revolution in the means by which the state regulates: away from legalism (micro-management via legal rules) and towards managerialism (the setting of targets and the expression of high, but vague, expectations). But the managerialist nature of new governance and management practices introduced by the new law (*Universitätsgesetz*, UG, 2002) was in sharp contrast to the residual democratic culture of the universities. The ensuing struggle produced numerous instances of placation and reversal in the face of rejection and criticism of the reform goals at all but the highest levels of the institutions themselves.

It is, of course, too early to say what the longer-term effects of such a reform will be. The British case, for example, demonstrates that only in the course of a series of Research Assessment Exercise cycles does the behavior of actors become reoriented (see Le Galès and Scott, 2008). Nevertheless, in the remaining discussion we seek to identify a number of factors and mechanisms that may systematically undermine the reform intentions or even produce reverse effects in Hood's sense – i.e. achieving the opposite of the aim. The discussion will focus particularly on the role of the new university boards because these were intended to overcome many of the perceived shortcomings of the inherited system, but in fact end up embodying many of the key contradictions and tensions. This problem was indeed recognized by some of our interviewees. As the chairman of an academic senate and holder of a number of positions on supervisory boards in the academic as well as the corporate world noted, on the basis of his experience of board membership:

> The construction is rather analogous to the corporate world and is hierarchical. But there is a contradiction. And if this contradiction between committee-based will-formation and authoritarian-hierarchical decision-making is not well managed, then the construction will fail. Then it will go wrong and will result in continuous tensions.

But in what ways and for what reasons can the work of reform "go wrong"?

Incompatibility of Life Orders and the Conduct of Life

The first factor militating against the chances of the boards achieving the desired radical transformation of university governance practice was, to use Weberian categories, the incompatibility of life orders and life conduct between business-oriented and academic-oriented board members. For example, the new managerialist jargon, imported by the board members with a background in the corporate world, induced sharp counter-reactions among university members. One board member with a background as CEO of a company ascribed the permanent conflicts in the early stages of his board membership to the idiosyncrasies of board members from the academic world:

> There was a glaring contradiction between the academic world and the rest. The mistrust was enormous. I had no prior experience of this. I didn't know, for example, the terms that are part of academic discussions on gender issues and can make others "fume." I was familiar with gender as a general issue, but not as such a linguistically nuanced "minefield." But that was just a minor thing. The major thing was that whenever one of us used a word that implied a business term, even in the slightest way, then the hairs of my dear fellow governors nominated by the university immediately stood on end. As if it were the worst thing on earth.

Another board member from the corporate world (delegated by the Ministry) was
even more explicit:

> After I had become familiar with the law I had low expectations. Because,
> well, there are people coming from the university, from the senate. So my
> expectations were never high with respect to those persons nominated in this
> way. So, I thought this will be a board with the incompetence that usually
> characterizes boards. Actually, that's how I estimated it.

Lack of information and problems of communication across a business–academic
divide compounded these problems and tensions:

> When the board meets and the topic is resource allocation, they need to know
> how this works in universities. Or if the board talks about curricula, you
> shouldn't think of "exotic species" [laughing]. No, I am serious. We are in
> most cases confronted with a simple lack of knowledge. And I think the
> universities have the right to have informed boards.

Governors with a professional background in academia criticized those from the
corporate world who did not invest much time in their role as governors for their
dominating behavior in board meetings and general lack of engagement. Such a
lack of engagement can have serious consequences for the effectiveness of the
boards in the view of one academic governor:

> That is the typical arrogance of X [a governor with a professional background
> as CEO in a private company]. These guys never participate in meetings. Y
> therefore has to bear the whole workload, but he is a retired CEO. And the
> other members don't participate in the meetings either.

Thus, rather than smoothly introducing values and practices from the business
world into university governance – a central hope in creating the boards – the
boards have come to display the tensions between the two distinct life orders, and
thus reflect rather than resolve a conflict running through the universities
themselves. There is scope here for a gradual shift in the workings of the boards
away from their original remit – the introduction of corporate styles of governance
– towards a fire-fighting reactive role, or that of advocate. Should this become
the case, they will become part of the system rather than the intended external
control mechanism. How this pans out will in part depend on the final two
aspects of the reform implementation we wish to outline: internal developments
and the wider (national) institutional context in which higher education is
embedded.

Internal Developments: Continuity, Missing Instruments and Unintended Consequences

The seeming radicalism of the new law should not blind us to continuities, for example, local variations in international trends in university management, to the remnants and durability of the legacy organization, or to the stubborn power of hierarchy. These continuities include: (a) the retention of the *curia* (albeit with weakened powers) and of the *Habilitation* (albeit in a devalued form); (b) the persistence of small and relatively autonomous discipline-based units; (c) the fact that legalistic habits die hard and frequently the law kicks back in with respect to specific decisions and initiatives and tends (arguably, as it should) to support conservatism over radicalism; and (d) in the course of both the 1993 and the 2002 changes in the law governing universities, the *Mittelbau* had negotiated tenure for themselves in return for accepting a deterioration in the employment contracts of those generations that were to follow them, thus keeping the door to below firmly shut and slowing down the working of new selection mechanisms.

These elements of continuity between the legacy and the new organization constitute the first major obstacles to realizing the desired neo-liberalization of the university system. The second, and arguably more important, factor is that not all the instruments necessary to effect such a change – i.e. to create a quasi-market and thus internal and external competition – are in place. While much of the language of international competition between universities is empty rhetoric, there is one area in which there is real (regional, national and international) competition, namely for the most able and/or wealthiest students. One sacred cow (free tuition) was slaughtered, but another part of the social- and Christian-democratic heritage in Austria, open access (i.e. the right of any qualified person to a university place), was left intact. Whatever the social justice arguments for open access (though it has been sadly ineffective in raising the percentage of students from non-academic family backgrounds), it clearly weakens Austrian universities in the competition for high-ability and/or wealthy students and thus bars them from the reputational, and frequently material (e.g. in alumni donations), gains that a concentration of such students can bring (see Stinchcombe, 1998: 274–277). Similarly, while student fees have been introduced, these are not sufficiently high to give universities an incentive to increase their income flows via competition for, say, overseas students. Likewise, Austrian universities are barred from the kinds of estate management (not to mention property speculation) with which, for example, UK universities have sought to make good their undercapitalization. They must rent their buildings from a private company, the Bundesimmobiliengesellschaft (BIG), whose sole owner is the Republic of Austria. Autonomy without autonomous resources is empty. In a capitalist system, "self-ownership" (to adopt the Danish term – see Wright and Ørberg, 2008) must include ownership of property if it is to mean anything at all. The formal autonomy of the university scarcely disguises its real dependence on the state.

The incompleteness of the instruments for creating a quasi-market is also evident with respect to control and auditing measures. The performance contracts were meant to play this role, but it is as yet unclear what will be done with the vast quantity of data collected to measure "performance." Nor do these data establish a priority of criteria or weighting. There is, for example, no equivalent to the UK's Research Assessment Exercise (RAE); a system which has eventually changed academic practices through repetition and a clear relationship between performance measures and resources (even if the details are known only *post factum*). These preconditions, which are vital in altering behavior over time (Le Galès and Scott, 2008), are, as yet, absent in the post-reform phase in Austrian higher education.

Finally, given all this, we would expect to see the kinds of paradoxes and "reverse effects" that Christopher Hood believes normally accompany reform (Hood, 1998). In Diego Gambetta's words: "we can expect considerable resistance to change . . . Selection effects can cement bad practices and easily wreck naïve policies that focus only on agents' rationality when trying to improve the performance of institutions" (1998: 107). We can see this most clearly with respect to the old and new forms of employment contract. First, paradoxically and unintentionally, the reforms have strengthened the hand of the "old guard" of tenured civil servant academics (i.e. exactly the *Menschentyp* that the reform was targeted against) even while condemning this category to a slow death. Tenured faculty are now confronted with junior colleagues on (frequently temporary) private employment contracts over whom they are again able to exercise – or choose not to exercise – largesse. This does not merely strengthen the status quo; in some respects it reinstalls features of the status quo ante: some of the conditions prior to the democratizing reforms. Those younger faculty members on the new contracts, who should be the foot soldiers of reform on the ground, find themselves in even greater conditions of dependency. Second, ironically, the details of the career structure were left to be negotiated by an institution that is the very opposite of the NPM ideal: collective bargaining. The outcomes of this long post-reform process of collective bargaining over the details of the new career structure are unclear at the time of writing. Collective bargaining could reintroduce something approaching the level of security created by tenure through the back door. If this is the case, then many of the claims of the reformers will have turned out to be bluff.

Institutional Embeddedness

As we have already noted, in comparison to previous systems of regulation, the new law (UG, 2002) intentionally leaves more scope for actors to fill the "empty shell." As one respondent, a chairman of senate, very experienced in university governance on all levels, puts it:

> The chance [of the new law] is that we fill this "empty shell" with content – something compatible with the self-understanding of a university. However, there is the danger that this empty space is pinched by *Zeitgeist*-related, instrumental, economist approaches. And I think this is the greatest danger at the moment.

But what factors influence how the "empty shell" is to be filled? Loose regulations leave a great deal of the work to key actors within the system as university boards and rectorial teams struggle to come to terms with lower levels of state protection and increased exposure to the international business of higher education and research. Hence, it is the worldview (or the socialization) of those in senior positions which strongly influences the reform path.

However, paradoxically, this very open-endedness provided a lever for direct political intervention into the so-called autonomous universities. The higher education system is embedded in a national context, and, in the case of Austria, this is a context of neo-corporatism in which all public institutions, and particularly key appointments within them, become highly politicized, to the point where appointments are divided up between the ruling political parties; normally Christian- and social-democratic, but from 2000 until 2007 Christian democrats (ÖVP) and the right-wing Freedom Party (FPÖ). This habit of political intervention did not die out simply because of a law giving formal autonomy to one of the system's components.

Although active politicians are barred from being university governors, political allegiance has clearly been a much more important criterion for nomination than experience or competence. The parties ruling at the time of the reform implementation tried to keep ideological control by nominating people who had demonstrated their political allegiance. As some of our respondents noted, an ideological fit outweighed governance experience in the nomination process. On boards one can thus find former politicians, or relatives of active politicians, or members of the top management of state-owned companies or non-profit organizations, or known friends of government members:

> What really upsets me is the political influence. That has to be said very frankly. We [in our board] got off to a good start. But governor Z was nominated because he was at university with Minister X. I ask you! And they were best friends, therefore he got the position . . . And I know that there were lists [of possible governors], drawn up by the ruling parties. The Minister forwarded them to the government without having a look at them! She didn't give a damn about it! That means there is utmost exertion of influence by political parties, and this upsets me.

The full extent of the political influence on the boards can be imagined if we look at the proportion of governors close to political parties (see Laske et al., 2006). An analysis of publicly available information revealed that thirty-six out of fifty-nine, hence 61.5 percent, of the board members nominated by the Ministry can be clearly identified as close to the then ruling parties. Accordingly, the group of governors ideologically close to the parties that were in opposition at that time (social democratic (SPÖ) and green parties) is small: "So the government didn't nominate people like me; that is, people with my political background. Therefore, I couldn't be on the government's list of governors." As one governor observed, it was "a good political trick" by the government to enact a law that prescribes independence of governors while at the same time nominating people who are proponents of their ideologies.

But the nomination procedure was not the only means by which the work of the boards was influenced by party politics. In addition, members of both political parties as well as Ministry officials retained their influence through a number of interventions. One rector describes one method of influencing governors:

> I find it unacceptable that a government or the Ministry organizes trainings or information meetings for governors in which information stemming from specific interests is presented to participants because the Austrian Rectors' Committee could do the same saying "let's do some lobbying for our issues among the governors."

Similarly, the appointment of rectors was also subject to political intervention. The legal regulation with respect to the rector's position shows a similar pattern to that of the board of governors – once again a quite loose legal prescription. The UG law prescribes in Chapter 23 that "only persons with international experience and the necessary abilities to manage a university's organization and finances may be selected as rector." In some cases, however, there is doubt that all rectors met these criteria. For some, the "international experience" consisted of just half a year of study, or a similar stay, abroad, sometimes decades earlier. Also, the ability to manage a university's organization was questioned by some of our interviewees, for example: "I think that exactly in such a phase [of change] the rector needs to have terrific leadership qualities. And . . . well . . . that's not there to the extent I think is necessary." Accordingly, in some cases governors also questioned the abilities of "their" rectors to manage the university in the way a fundamental reform demands. Since the position of the rector is crucial for the reform path, personal qualities are identified as key to success: "I understand the law as a great chance. Naturally, it depends on the people, on the rectorate. Success always depends on people and always on the boss."

The key point about this continued politicization is that as soon as national or regional (party) political interests kick in they trump the language of internationalization, excellence and competition. It is not simply that the politicians have narrow party political interests (though, of course, they do), but that their general interest in the university is limited. Universities are interesting as potential partners in regional "growth coalitions" (Logan and Molotch, 1985), for disguising unemployment figures (Plümper and Schneider, 2007), for labor market training, for spin-off and as regional or national flagships.

In the context sketched above, the struggle between tradition and reform re-emerges as a defense of the humanities and *Bildung* (cultivation) against the onslaught of instrumentalism:

> Humanities are struggling at our university for their acceptance and legitimation. It is not the case that there are few students, but in comparison with IT, people from the humanities are disadvantaged. It cannot be doubted

that there is a bias towards engineering and sciences; of course, important fields. But I would regret it if the humanities end up as decorative disciplines,[3] because they are a significant part of what I understand as *Bildung*.

Moreover, an asymmetry in the disciplinary orientation at the highest level of university governance – that of rectors who are predominantly from the natural science, economics, etc. – is accompanied by a number of other trends via which the political goal to turn universities into instruments of economic development is pursued. For example, a change in the funding mechanisms gives applied research an advantage that can be economically exploited. As one rector complains:

> It is a fact that our universities have less money to spend. Most of the money is channeled into those areas where there is a clear research policy towards technology to the disadvantage of humanities, social sciences and the arts. And even in technology and medicine it's solely focused on very few small niches. So the responsibility to spend money reasonably is taken away from the university. They give smaller lump-sum budgets to the universities and call it an advantage. And the real steering mechanisms were externalized to other research policy institutions, like the National Science Fund. That means that universities as self-steering and regulating organizations lose influence in the higher education sector. This weakens the idea of the university.

Now, the complete picture of how universities in general, and disciplines in particular, are governed with respect to certain – politically desired, but not openly addressed – intentions becomes clearer: there is a paradigmatic shift that favors applied and technical disciplines while disadvantaging "the other," namely the humanities, social sciences, theology, etc., but also those areas of natural science that concentrate on basic research. This shift has not come about by direct intervention of the government as a direct effect of the reform. Rather, the new governance structure, loosely defined by the law, gave leeway for a majority of agents with a specific political standpoint and expertise related to the corporate world. This in turn led to an intensified focus on the economic aspects of university life and hence to the reinforcement of the reform's basic idea that universities should serve society and economy primarily as a motor of economic growth, but equally led to "blowback" from the institutions who were to be thus reshaped.

Conclusion

Rather than present the neo-liberalization of higher education as an inevitable process that will eventually roll over even ideal typical centralized state systems and universities founded upon humanistic – for example Humboldtian – principles, we have, first, tried to locate the current stage as the latest in a series of struggles between traditional and modernizing rhetoric; a struggle in which both tradition and modernization become periodically redefined. Second, we have sought to show how uneven and context-dependent the outcomes can be. Whereas the rhetoric of

NPM-based reforms sounds quite clear, the day-to-day practice looks more like a struggle between a variety of actors and life orders to determine the actual reform path. This is partially due to the particular character of universities (Meister-Scheytt and Scheytt, 2005), but equally to the fact that actors, in both politics and universities, do not always trust their own solutions. We have identified this pattern, for example, among politicians who herald a reform based on the idea of an autonomous university, while simultaneously nominating governors on the basis of their personal and/or ideological proximity to political parties, and as safeguards of the "correct" political ideology.

It is worth noting, finally, that the Austrian government is now considering a reform of the reform, and doing so in a language closer to the historical conception of the role and function of the university. According to Johannes Hahn (BM:WF, 2008: 2), the Federal Minister for Science and Research:

> No doubt the future of the universities is not a mere legal task or a mere management challenge. The future of the universities is a question of culture. It is about development, innovation and open-mindedness, being internationally comparable and globally competitive. But first of all it is about people who are extraordinary, who bring in new insights and ideas. These people must be at the center of the university. That is my central motivation for improving the international standing of our universities.

We make no predictions about the outcome beyond expressing sympathy for Nils Brunsson's wry observation that the only guaranteed outcome of any reform process is the next reform (Brunsson, 1989). But we shall finish where we started, with Louis Dumont, who elsewhere argued that the "German ideology," organized as it was around the notion of *Bildung*, was a mixed form: neither quite *homo hierarchicus* nor *homo aequalis* (Dumont, 1994). While the intentions behind the reforms we have been discussing are clearly neo-liberalizing, their outcomes may yet confirm Dumont's view.

Notes

1 We refer those interested in a more detailed account of the reforms to Burtscher, Pasqualoni and Scott (2006) from which we have drawn here.

2 We thank the Anniversary Fund of the Oesterreichische Nationalbank (OENB) for funding the research project titled "Structure and Self-perception of Austrian Universities Boards of Governors." We would also like to thank André Gingrich (Vienna) and Bruce Leslie (SUNY Brockport) for their comments on an earlier version of this chapter.

3 *Orchideenfächer*, an ironic and/or derogatory term for small subjects, or those without an immediate labor market or economic function.

References

Brunsson, Nils. "Administrative Reforms as Routines." *Scandinavian Journal of Management* 5 (1989): 219–228.

Bundesministerium für Bildung, Wissenschaft und Kultur (BM:BWK). *Aufbruch in die Autonomie: Ausbruch aus tradierten Universitätsstrukturen*. Vienna: Eigenverlag, 2003.

Bundesministerium für Wissenschaft und Forschung (BMWF). *Visionen. Perspektiven: Strategien: Zur Zukunft der Universitäten.* Vienna: Eigenverlag, 2008.

Burt, Ronald S. *Brokerage and Closure: An Introduction to Social Capital.* Oxford: Oxford University Press, 2005.

Burtscher, Christian, Pier-Paolo Pasqualoni, and Alan Scott. "Universities and the Regulatory Framework: The Austrian University System in Transition." *Social Epistemology* 20 (2006): 241–258.

Byrnes, Dolores. "Narrating the University: Values across Disciplines." In *Bright Satanic Mills: Universities, Territorial Development and the Knowledge Economy,* edited by Alan Harding, Alan Scott, Stephan Laske, and Christian Burtscher. Aldershot: Ashgate, 2007, 133–148.

Collini, Stefan. "HiEdBiz." *London Review of Books* 25 (November 6, 2003). Available online (accessed February 2008): http://www.lrb.co.uk/v25/n21/coll01_.html.

Douglas, Mary. *Purity and Danger.* London: Routledge and Kegan Paul, 1966.

Douglas, Mary. *Implicit Meanings: Essays in Anthropology.* London: Routledge and Kegan Paul, 1975.

Douglas, Mary, and Baron Isherwood. *The World of Goods.* London: Routledge and Kegan Paul, 1979.

Douglas, Mary, and Gerald Mars. "Terrorism: A Positive Feedback Game." *Human Relations* 56 (2003): 763–786.

Dumont, Louis. *Homo Hierarchicus: The Caste System and Its Implications.* Translated by Mark Sainsbury, Louis Dumont, and Basic Gulati. Chicago: University of Chicago Press, 1970.

Dumont, Louis. *German Ideology. From France to Germany and back.* Chicago: University of Chicago Press, 1994.

Elias, N. *The Civilizing Process.* Translated by Edmond Jephcott. Oxford: Blackwell, 1982 [1939].

Gambetta, Diego. "Concatenations of Mechanisms." In *Social Mechanisms: An Analytical Approach to Social Theory,* edited by P. Hedström, and R. Swedberg. Cambridge: Cambridge University Press, 1998.

Greenwood, Davydd. "Who Are the Real 'Problem Owners'? On the Social Embeddedness of Universities." In *Bright Satanic Mills: Universities, Territorial Development and the Knowledge Economy,* edited by A. Harding, A. Scott, S. Laske, and C. Burtscher. Aldershot: Ashgate, 2007, 95–118.

Hedström, Peter. "Rational Imitation." In *Social Mechanisms: An Analytical Approach to Social Theory,* edited by Peter Hedström, and Richard Swedberg. Cambridge: Cambridge University Press, 1998, 306–327.

Hood, Christopher. *The Art of the State.* Oxford: Oxford University Press, 1998.

Kuhn, Thomas S. *The Structure of Scientific Revolutions.* Chicago: University of Chicago Press, 1962.

Laske, Stephan, Claudia Meister-Scheytt, David Lederbauer, and Bernadette Loacker. *Endbericht zum ÖNB-Projekt "Struktur und Arbeitsweise österreichischer Universitätsräte."* Innsbruck: Department of Organisation and Learning, University of Innsbruck, 2006.

Le Galès, Patrick, and Alan Scott. "Une Révolution Bureaucratique Britannique? Autonomie sans Contrôle ou 'Freer Markets, More Rules.'" *Revue Française de Sociologie* 49 (2008): 317–346.

Logan, John R., and Harvey L. Molotch. *Urban Fortunes: The Political Economy of Place.* Berkeley: University of California Press, 1985.

Meister-Scheytt, Claudia. "Reinventing Governance: The Role of Boards of Governors in the New Austrian University." *Tertiary Education and Management* 13 (2007): 247–261.

Meister-Scheytt, Claudia, and Tobias Scheytt. "The Complexity of Change in Universities." *Higher Education Quarterly* 58 (2005): 76–99.

Plümper, Thomas, and Christina Schneider. "Too Much to Die, too Little to Live: Unemployment, Higher Education Policies and University Budgets in Germany, 1975–2000." *Journal of European Public Policy* 14 (2007): 631–653.

Ringer, Fritz. *The Decline of the German Mandarins.* Cambridge, MA: Harvard University Press, 1969.

Simmel, Georg. *The Philosophy of Money.* Translated by Tom B. Bottomore and David Frisby. London: Routledge, 1990 [1900].

Stinchcombe, Arthur. "Monopolistic Competition as a Mechanism: Corporations, Universities, and Nation States in Competitive Fields." In *Social Mechanisms: An Analytical Approach to Social Theory,* edited by Peter Hedström, and Richard Swedberg. Cambridge: Cambridge University Press, 1998, 265–305.

Weber, Max. "Methodologische Einleitung für die Erhebung des Vereins für Sozialpolitik über Auslese und Anpassung (Berufswahlen und Berufsschicksal) der Arbeiterschaft der geschlossenen Großindustrie." In *Gesammelte Aufsätze zur Soziologie und Sozialpolitik*, edited by Marianne Weber. Tübingen: J.C.B. Mohr, 1988 [1908], 1–60.

Weber, Max. "Parliament and Government in Germany under a New Political Order." In *Weber: Political Writings*, edited by Ronald Speirs, and Peter Lassmann. Cambridge: Cambridge University Press, 1994 [1918], 130–271.

Wright, Susan, and Jakob W. Ørberg. "Autonomy and Control: Danish University Reform in the Context of Modern Governance." *Learning and Teaching: The International Journal of Education in the Social Sciences* 1(1) (2008): 27–57.

5

Prometheus (on the) Rebound?

Freedom and the Danish Steering System

SUSAN WRIGHT AND JAKOB WILLIAMS ØRBERG

Introduction

Guy Neave and Frans van Vught, in their study of the changing relationship between government and higher education in Western Europe, liken universities to Prometheus (Neave and van Vught, 1991: ix). This was the Titan who stole fire from Zeus and gave it to humans. He also boasted that he taught humans the civilizing arts of agriculture, language, architecture, metalwork, astronomy, mathematics, divination and medicine. But it was not Prometheus as the source of knowledge that made him Neave and van Vught's symbol for the university. Nor was it Prometheus' reputation among the gods for being quick-witted, a clever talker, using guile, and having the gift of prophecy that reminded Neave and van Vught of academics. Rather, it was Prometheus' subjection to Zeus, the ruling god, and his daily torture that Neave and van Vught took as an image of the emerging position of European universities. Zeus had Prometheus chained to a rock and sent an eagle to peck out his liver each day, which restored itself during the night, ready for the next day's agony. This continued for centuries until Hercules eventually killed the eagle and broke Prometheus' chains.

Neave and van Vught provide a very strong image of the university in opposition to the state and of academic autonomy as incompatible with state control. In this image the state is holding down the ability of universities to act and fulfill their potential. They trace how this has come about historically. Their first model, the "facilitatory state" (1945–1970s) conveys an image of responsible autonomy. Even during the enormous changes associated with the massification of higher education in the 1960s, there was a stable, if implicit, agreement that government underwrote the cost of universities' work in providing higher education without much internal intervention. Their second model, the "interventionary state," was in full force by 1983–1985. It replaced negotiated coordination with central planning and rational control. Government penetrated deep into the autonomy of institutions and of higher education professionals through budget cuts, greater oversight into the efficiency and quality of outputs, and demands that universities create a strategic management capable of prioritizing the mission and resource allocation across the whole institution (Neave and van Vught, 1991: xii–xiii, 239, 243). In their third model, the current "evaluative state," governments proclaim they will dispense with detailed planning and operate instead by remote control and by "setting universities free" from the shackles of the state. That is, government focuses on the outputs – qualified students, projects completed, patents registered, articles pub-lished. Decisions about how to achieve these outputs and indeed responsibility for the whole fortune of the institution are placed in the hands of its leadership (1991: 251). Whereas such strategies depict a powerful image of increased institutional autonomy, Neave and van Vught find there is often no diminution of central planning and control (1991: xiii). This leads them to "suspect" that "behind the façade of an autonomy widely proclaimed" governments "cleave to central steering," which is as active as it ever was (1991: 250). They call this combination of "two extreme theoretical concepts" – dirigisme and autonomy – a "strange hybrid" of incompatible elements (1991: 250–251). They question if, in time, universities were to produce the kinds of products with the levels of efficiency and social relevance that meet government objectives, governments might reduce their central controls (and presumably let "real" autonomy re-emerge). But Neave and van Vught feel that, even so, self-steering on such terms may undermine the ability of universities to be "in the world but not of it" – a stance which they argue is essential to the university's role as social critic and to Prometheus' risky task of generating, organ-izing and passing on new knowledge which runs counter to Zeus' plans and rouses his wrath (1991: xiv). They conclude their book with the image of Prometheus, the Western European university, still bound to a rock, with the eagle of massive oversight and industrial relevance tearing daily at its entrails. With a note of wishful thinking, they say: "Perhaps the extension of institutional autonomy will usher in a new era for the systems of higher education in the West and that Prometheus once again will be free to apply his ingenuity and cunning without let or hindrance for the benefit of humanity" (1991: 254).

But, they ask, how might this heroic task be achieved? They do not identify any current social force that could possibly play the role of Hercules. Instead, they make a plea for governments, unlike Zeus, to have a change of heart and let Prometheus unbound (autonomous) emerge.

Their argument portrays the university as the same enduring character whether tied down or set free, and depicts autonomy and control as two stable concepts in a zero-sum relationship. While our research on Danish university reform chimes with the historical changes Neave and van Vught set out, our anthropological approach leads to a different interpretation. We focus on freedom and control as keywords. Such words are "keys" to prevailing or contested images of how society should be organized. By Gallie's (1956) and Williams' (1976) definitions, keywords are continually contested and never have a complete or final meaning. They accumulate a history of meanings, which actors select from, while also stretching or inverting existing meanings or inventing new ones. In the process of contesting the meaning of a keyword, other words with which it has been habitually associated also change their meanings. New "semantic clusters" emerge, which, as Shore and Wright (1997) argue, are the threads from which ideologies are woven. While it is a traditional feature of anthropology to focus on the complexity of meanings of keywords and how they are used in practice and with what effects, Shore and Wright argue that a focus on how keywords are contested in social arenas engaged in policy processes is a way of tracing changes in forms of governance and power.

The study of university reform, of which this research is a part, viewed students, academics, university managers, governing boards and policy-makers as all actively involved in imagining and enacting the university.[1] Although this chapter draws only on research on policy documents and interviews with policy-makers and some managers, it is clear there are multiple meanings of "freedom" and "autonomy" currently in play, just as there are different ideas of "steering" and "control." For example, how do government policy-makers genuinely think that their new steering forms are unleashing the power of universities that was held back before? What version of academic autonomy is central to their imagining of the university? Rather than labeling one state as freedom and another as control, we focus on the constant negotiation of the meanings of these terms in relation to each other. We ask, through this contested process of continually figuring out the meanings of and relationships between freedom and steering, what kind of university is emerging?

Our stance towards the object of our study can be attributed to anthropological responses to the crisis of positivism in the 1980s. Anthropologists realized that the models of society and of forms of governance that they had previously presented as true representations of how things worked among a particular people were often a ruling ideology upholding the power of particular elements in the society, most often particular categories of men (Asad, 1979). Haraway (1991) calls this the "God trick": to project a satellite image of the world as if from above or outside it. Rather than simply rejecting such models of governance or society, she questions how they are constructed and by whom, and how such partiality purports to objectivity. In what she sees as a truer kind of objectivity, she aligns herself with different actors to understand compassionately their different perspectives and their interactions. This enables her to show how a partial perspective on the world or on an object, such as the university, comes into being.

Such an approach makes models of governance appear less stable than in much of the academic literature on university reform. Danish official documents convey a model of governance, most coherently captured in the 2003 University Law, but this model is under continuous development. It is made up of a number of legal concepts and steering technologies, each of which, like keywords, has its own historical trajectory. Several of these concepts and technologies have come into conjuncture at a particular moment, informed by a particular rationality of governance, and then later reformed, with some elements downplayed and other new ones introduced, to create a new cluster or assemblage informed by a slightly different political rationale. This approach shows how each element is being reworked in relation to all the others in the present, and how they might each be continuing to move in different directions, with new meanings and associated practices, in the future. We draw here on the notion of "global assemblage" from the anthropology of globalization (Collier and Ong, 2005) to suggest a way of thinking about Prometheus' room for maneuver which is more mobile, contingent and unpredictable than a focus on the government's steering model might suggest.

The politicians and university leaders we have interviewed and studied do not see the system as complete or fixed, or as working towards a predictable end point. In interviews, policy-makers and university leaders focused on the trajectory of one

or other of the elements that make up this assemblage, to give different interpretations of the kind of university they are trying to bring about through their
particular ideas of freedom and control. Our approach is not necessarily more
optimistic than Neave and van Vught's, but it suggests a different project. Instead
of entering into a Manichean fight between essentialized concepts of freedom and
control, or scanning the horizon for a Hercules who will do so on universities'
behalf, it suggests that university freedom and autonomy have always been in
relation to government control, and that multiple actors are, as always, engaged in
identifying ways to expand the "room for maneuver" to create their visions of the
university in the present.

To explore the ways freedom and control are being negotiated in the current
process of re-forming Danish universities, this chapter will first set out the model
of university governance promoted in the 2003 University Law. There are clear
connections with neo-liberal reforms of the public sector in other OECD
countries.[2] These reforms are based on the idea that increased state steering can
be achieved through setting the framework within which institutions, their leaders
and members act with an expanded sense of autonomy and freedom. This section
explores the way the keyword "freedom" is contested in Denmark in the process
of creating new relationships between state steering and institutional autonomy.
That still does not explain how the governance model, however contested, plays
out on the ground. In the second section, we use the concept of assemblage to show
how a number of elements (ordering concepts and administrative technologies),
each with different histories and accumulated meanings, come into conjunction
in the model. We then explore how different positioned actors draw on some
elements from the steering model in the process of negotiating new relationships
between state steering and institutional autonomy. We conclude that it is through
a focus on these positioned interventions that we can understand potential
developments in the governance model and current enactments of the university.

Setting Danish Universities Free – The Model

The history of reforms that Neave and van Vught found elsewhere in Europe has
parallels in Denmark. Partly prompted by the financial crisis of the late 1970s and
early 1980s, Danish policy-makers drew on New Public Management ideas from
the PUMA section of the OECD to engage in a thorough reform of the whole of
the public sector, including universities (Wright and Ørberg, 2008). From the
1990s, Denmark also engaged actively with OECD debates about university
governance and joined the frenzy of university reforms intended to position OECD
countries strongly in the emerging global knowledge-based economy. All these
strands came together in the Danish University Law of 2003, which can be
summarized as follows:

1 The role of politicians was changed, so that they now concentrate on setting the
   policy aims for the university sector and the budget through which these aims
   are to be achieved. This "aim and frame" is then given to the relevant Ministry
   to decide how to contract out the work and achieve the required outputs and

performance. In the modernized state, politicians and ministries are no longer responsible for delivering services themselves through a bureaucracy, but for seeing that subcontracted organizations create the required policy outcomes.

2 The legal status of universities was changed. They are no longer a part of the state bureaucracy, but are "set free" by being turned into "self-owning institutions" and given the status of a legal person. A governing board with a majority of members from outside the self-owning university was made responsible for the organization's activities and finances. A self-owning university can go bankrupt, but it might not own anything – the government decided to retain state ownership of their buildings and land.

3 The Ministry enters into a development contract with the governing board of the institution, which is intended to develop the university's strategic capacity to respond to a range of government funding mechanisms and policy priorities. Although the university's fulfillment of the development contract is audited, its provisions are not directly connected to funding. Instead, funding for teaching is based on the institution's output of students, measured by the number of students who pass exams. Research funding is also increasingly being based on performance. Although the core funding for research is still a basic grant (*basisbevilling*) to support research capacity, the government is devising a method for allocating 5 percent of the basic grant competitively on the basis of an objective calculation of research performance (publications, research student completions, external research collaborations and patents). On top of this, competitive grants from the state research councils form a growing part of the universities' research budgets.

4 In New Public Management, subcontracting organizations usually have "freedom of method" to work out how to achieve their contracted outputs and performance targets. In the case of universities, the 2003 law specifies that the university is to consist of faculties and departments and the governing board is to appoint a rector, who appoints faculty deans, who appoint heads of departments. The performance targets in the university's "development contract" with the government are then subcontracted to faculties, and the targets in their contracts are further subcontracted to departments. The result is a chain of contracts running down through the organization, and the appointed leader at each level of the organization is responsible and accountable for contract compliance to the level above.

5 The Ministry audits the universities to ensure their chosen methods for meeting performance targets are within the law, and to check on the efficiency and effectiveness of their organization. Audits used to be mainly to check financial probity and to react to complaints. A draft new audit system for universities is expanding this practice in a very proactive direction, involving Ministry officials in an intensive series of meetings with universities throughout the year to check on operations and identify and spread "best practice" through the sector.

This model has many of the features identified by Neave and van Vught, and two aspects in particular are recognizable as what in political science literature is called the shift from government to governance (Clarke and Newman, 1997; Dean, 2007; Kooiman, 2003; Pierre, 2000; Rhodes, 1997): that is, a shift from government exercising state power on its own to a broader partnership between government, public, private and other civil society institutions (Harvey, 2005). The first aspect is that, in Osborne and Gaebler's terms, the state no longer "rows" the bureaucratic delivery of services (Osborne and Gaebler, 1992). Instead, it "steers" others (conceived of as free actors) to provide the desired services by granting and monitoring contracts. The aim of this contracting out, as set out in Finance Ministry documents and OECD papers, is to make those providing services at the bottom of the system much more responsive to the aims of ministers at the top. Although the previous hierarchical and bureaucratic system looked much more "joined up," various "noise factors," such as professional standards or local politicians' interests, intervened. Now these interests are much less able to interfere, as the conditions and performance indicators set out in the contract for the delivery of the service directly reflect the ministers' policy for the sector. The political science literature debates whether the model is working as intended in this respect, most notably in Britain (Wright, 2008). Some authors report that political control over the subcontracted process has increased (Saward, 1992), whereas others argue, on the contrary, that the shift from government to governance entails a hollowing out of the state (Rhodes, 1997).

A second aspect of the shift from government to governance which is evident in the Danish steering model is social regulation through contractual obligation. Within this model, universities and each of their constituent units – faculties, departments and academics – are free actors, in the sense that they are able to enter into contracts. In contracting with the Ministry, universities undertake to enact the government's policies. They then further outsource responsibility for delivering on the government's policies down the chain of contracts to the department, and sometimes through action plans to individual academics. Critics complain that autonomy is jeopardized by this intense steering that Neave and van Vught call "dirigisme."

Both of the above issues in the political science literature – whether state power is enhanced or hollowed out; and whether universities lose autonomy or are set free – echo Neave and van Vught's binary opposition between Prometheus and Zeus. Marginson (1997), analyzing the Australian university reforms which provided much "best practice" for OECD countries, argues that the state/freedom dualism is a hangover from the thinking of classical liberalism. Instead, he identified the overall rationale of the new model used to reform universities as one where state steering and autonomy emerge together. The Danish reform can be analyzed in a similar way. The state, in constituting the universities as free, both creates new kinds of free agencies at universities and new ways of controlling those agencies. Rather than, as Neave and van Vught suggest, treating this relationship as a question of the degree of the state's steering and intrusion into the autonomy of the university, Marginson shows how in the Australian reform model the two are constitutive of each other. That is, in neo-liberalism, freedom and control are interdependent. The government steers from a distance through the empowered and expanded scope of free actors. Government minimizes overt coercion and instead uses policy norms, regulations and funding mechanisms to make clear to institutions and individuals how they can optimize their performance. The work of government becomes that of enhancing the autonomy of self-managed institutions, not least through the expanded strategic role of their managers, as agents responsible for their own outcomes, while establishing the systems which frame their choices. Devolution and the power of government increase simultaneously as subjects' exercise of "regulated autonomy" facilitates the advance of central control. Indeed, this intimate relationship between control and autonomy is at the core of the steering system:

> With government and autonomy implicated in each other, it is unsurprising that state–institutional tensions are a permanent source of criticism and complaint; and that institutional autonomy and academic freedom – the shifting terrain on which these endemic tensions are played out – are never finally defined or resolved.
>
> (Marginson, 1997: 65)

If, as Marginson suggests, a focus of criticism and debate points to the core issue in the functioning of the system, then there are strong parallels between the Danish and Australian situations. A tension between government control and academic freedom has also been central to debates about university reform in Denmark. The debate has generated numerous interpretations of possible relationships between control and autonomy and of what kinds of state and university such relationships would produce.

Setting Danish Universities Free – Contested Discourses

Those who oppose the Danish university reforms appeal to an idea of institutional autonomy akin to that of Neave and van Vught as a realm free of state power and industrial influence. They see this as undermined by the influence of the state and the role and powers of the new university managers. Academic autonomy and freedom have different meanings in different countries: in the USA the focus is on freedom of speech; in the UK it includes the right to decide on staff appointments and student selection, and decisions over what to teach, as well as what to research, publish and say in public. In Denmark, the focus is on research freedom, including the choice of topic and research method. Many Danish academics, when talking about research freedom, connect it to institutional democracy. Here they are referring to a narrative about the history of Danish universities, in which the student revolt of the 1960s broke the professors' dominion (*professorvælden*) and resulted in a law in 1970 which established what is known as "university democracy." Academics, support staff and students elected the decision-making bodies and the leaders at each level, from department, to study board, to faculty, to rectorate. This academic community-cum-workplace democracy was to protect the freedom of its members, and especially the ability of academics to decide for themselves what and how to research.

As in many other university systems, university autonomy and academic freedom used to be considered interdependent, whereas the growth of strategic management in universities has meant that the interests of those who lead the institution may not be congruent with the protection of the freedom of individual academics (Shore and Wright, 2004). In Denmark, whereas universities previously came under the protection of the state, the 2003 University Law states that, as self-owning institutions, universities now have responsibility to project their own freedom and research ethics. That clause in the law does not specify how this is to be achieved, but presumably the governing board stands for "the university." The university is charged with being responsive to the needs of the surrounding society, including civil society, business and government, and presumably the governing board is to moderate somehow when the demands on the university from one of these interests become excessive. The law does not specify who is meant to protect the academic freedom of individuals, or how.

Critics focus on the legal provisions for research freedom. The research unions' magazine produced a "freedom index" which showed Denmark as having the worst institutional arrangements for protecting academic freedom in Europe. They featured Karran's comparative analysis of academic freedom in Europe, which also placed Denmark low on the list (Karran, 2007). In May 2008, the academic union, Dansk Magisterforening, sent a complaint to UNESCO that the 2003 University Law was at variance with the standards for academic freedom set out in UNESCO's (1997) *Recommendation Concerning the Status of Higher-education Teaching Personnel*. Critics focus especially on paragraph 17 of the law, which states that academics may conduct research freely in such time as they have not been allocated specific tasks by the head of department, and as long as their research comes within the strategic framework laid down by the university for its research activities (Folketinget, 2002). Members of Parliament raised the question of academic freedom during the passage of the law and were reassured by a note from the Ministry of Research, Science and Innovation, stating that the wording was virtually the same as in the previous law and did not change the legal framework for the exercise of academic freedom (Ørberg, 2006b). The Ministry guaranteed that the law would be revised if it became evident that academic freedom was threatened. Critics still doubted that freedom of research was secure when this wording came into conjunction with the new management system, which gave the head of department decision-making powers and abolished the departmental board.

The Royal Danish Academy of Sciences and Letters published a report on academic freedom and had the Minister of Research attend their annual conference in March 2007 to respond to their criticisms. This meeting vividly demonstrated the conflict. Senior Danish professors claimed that a raft of recent changes to universities reduced both institutional autonomy and individual academic freedom both formally, in the provisions of the law, and informally, in working conditions and the climate of social debate. These changes influence individual academics' freedom of action and expression, especially their ability to choose research topics and publicly discuss issues that go against academic or political orthodoxies without worrying about negative consequences for their careers (Kærgård et al.,

2007: foreword, 3, 6). The Minister rejected these arguments and maintained that the law set universities free. Neither side examined the differences between what they meant by "freedom."

When we asked in interviews what was meant by "setting universities free," a senior civil servant explained that the law was giving universities freedom from internal disputes and discussions. There had been widespread criticism, even from academics themselves, that the universities' democratic committees produced interminable arguments and few decisions, and that the elected leaders, beholden to their electorate, could not act strategically or decisively. Another interviewee, who had held a senior position in the Ministry of Education, said that external members of the new governing boards spelled an end to academic committees discussing the colour of toilet paper. A third said governing boards that had a majority of external members would end the previous jockeying between the faculties for an equal share of resources and would enable the university to prioritize emerging areas of new research. Industrial associations echoed this, arguing that the democratic system had been incapable of focusing resources on research areas of strategic importance to the country's economy, such as IT and bio-sciences, and, as they put it in one report, shortening the distance "from idea to invoice" (Government of Denmark, 2003). By introducing appointed leaders with the powers to act strategically, academics would be released from all these kinds of "fuss" and be able to concentrate their energies on more productive research.

The government's discourse in introducing the 2003 University Law also involved setting universities free from the trammels of state administration. By constituting universities as self-owning institutions, they acquired the legal status of a person, with the freedom and right to enter into contracts. As Yeatman (1997) makes clear, neo-liberal governmentality rests on a notion of individuals (whether institutions or people) as contractual persons who are able to exercise choice about who to associate with and to enter freely into agreements as legally equal parties. To Yeatman, the shift from classical liberalism to neo-liberalism involves changing the status of those who were previously dependants of patrimonial governance, whether of the family or the state. These dependants have to learn to think of themselves and manage themselves as autonomous units of social action in order to acquire the capacity to act as freely contracting beings (1997: 46). This was very much the language of the Danish government: universities were no longer to be located within the state bureaucracy. Instead they were made into "self-owning" institutions, which would manage themselves. They had to prove they could use their freedom responsibly by showing themselves capable of strategic leadership: that is, prioritizing universities' activities and resources to meet the country's current economic needs and connect universities effectively with major industrial and regional developments. In doing so, they would gain politicians' trust and might be granted further "degrees of freedom," taking over more aspects of their affairs still controlled by the state. Even some chairs of the new governing boards – directors or former directors of large companies or major Danish institutions – grew impatient with this paternalistic (even colonial) language. They complained that the Ministries of Finance and of Research continued to keep control of so many areas of decision-making and made so many detailed interventions that this seriously impeded the new governing boards in appointing the managers and setting up the new governance systems. For example, the Ministry of Finance delayed the governing boards' appointing of rectors and pro-rectors because it had to determine the salary levels. Two years later the state auditor then complained to the Ministry of Science, Technology and Innovation that the universities had set the salaries too high – as if they were abusing one of their patiently acquired "degrees of freedom" (Rigsrevisionen, 2006: 111–114).

In government discourse, freedom is linked to trust, responsibility and accountability: that is, measurable ways of demonstrating that public funding has been used efficiently and strategically for the country's economic growth. Prosperity is achieved when individuals use their freedom responsibly and strategically to exercise choice, enter into contracts and engage in markets so as to advance their own position and thence the sum of human well-being. According to Harvey, freedom in this sense seems to degenerate into free enterprise (Harvey, 2005: 37). Meanwhile, the government sees its role as steering universities to ensure they are acting responsibly, efficiently and strategically, until they are sufficiently trusted for regulation to be reduced. The current intensity of the state's intervention can be explained by the government not as a contradiction but as only a matter of degree – too much control of a newly liberated subject which is still learning how to use its freedom. Ultimately, universities will learn how to use their freedom within a framework of less visible systems of government steering and control. By this reckoning, the government is not making a categorical mistake, as Neave and van Vught suggest, or as Danish critics claim.

To academic activists, "freedom" referred to their ability to control their own work, rather than be a managed workforce, so as to secure the conditions for each academic freely to choose his or her research topic, conduct research and participate in public debate. Critics' ideas of academic freedom as linked to workplace democracy are not in the government's firmament. What we find here is a keyword, "freedom," whose meaning is being dramatically contested. Whereas academic critics associate freedom with democracy, in the government's discourse it is the keyword in a semantic cluster consisting of "freedom," "responsibility," "accountability," "enterprise," "strategy" and "trust" – whose meanings are adjusting in relation to each other. For Prometheus to find room for maneuver, it is important to distinguish between the two meanings of "freedom," each of which is a keyword for a completely different discourse with a very different political rationality. Otherwise, there is the danger of misrecognition (Wright, 2005) as when critics hear the government talking of setting universities free, and assume the word is being used with the meaning of academic freedom that they hold dear. Each idea of freedom is informed by a very different political rationality. The government's meaning has to be understood in order to be contested; otherwise critics' calls for academic freedom will continue to be answered with bland responses that the legal wording remains unchanged. That may be so, but its meaning in the context of the steering technologies in which it is located is now quite different.

Assemblage

A focus on keywords and semantic clusters makes it possible to examine the rationality underpinning the model of governance in the new law, in which freedom and control are implicated in each other. This approach, however, has two limitations. First, there is a tendency to treat the semantic cluster as stable or static, whereas the relationship between their meanings is continually negotiated. The model of governance, similarly, is made up of a range of ordering concepts and steering technologies, each of which has its own history. These elements are brought together in an assemblage,[3] which draws on an aspect of the history of some elements, while the meanings of other elements are stretched or reinvented (as seen with the shift from classical liberal to neo-liberal meanings of contractual persons above). This approach makes the conjunction of elements in the governance model seem contingent and open to negotiation and interpretation. Second, Foucault-inspired approaches, such as Marginson's analysis of Australian university reform, tend to assume that the ruling rationality constructs the subjectivity of people so powerfully that they simply act out the model "on the ground." In contrast, politicians, policy-makers, university leaders, academics, students and other people engaged in enacting the reformed university may emphasize particular elements in the model, draw on other meanings or associations for these elements, or try to introduce considerations from other aspects of their working lives and negotiate new meanings. From this perspective, the process of enactment becomes an unpredictable process out of which different interplays between freedom and control and new meanings for the university are created.

Taking this perspective, the Danish steering system can be seen as made up of a number of elements, each with its own historical trajectory.

Self-ownership

The memorandum explaining the 2003 University Law states that most of the law's provisions are effects of universities becoming "self-owning" institutions (Folketinget, 2002). The term carries very positive connotations of the peaceful land reform in the 1780s by which a debt-bonded peasantry was "set free" and became "self-owning" farmers. A grass-roots enlightenment movement inspired these farmers to establish self-owning folk high schools and to develop new methods of farming and cooperative methods for processing products and retaining their added value. The Education Ministry referred to these self-owning institutions when reviving the concept as part of the reform of technical colleges in the 1980s and the modernization of most of the rest of the education sector in the 1990s. However, when "self-ownership" was used to reform the education sector's institutions and universities, its positive images of local ingenuity and self-management were combined with the frame and aim thinking of the modernization program. Strong emphasis was placed on conditions for public funding, performance indicators and expanded auditing systems (Ørberg, 2006a). Indeed, far from its original associations with grass-roots self-organization, it was being used to conceptualize an organization with accountable and strategic management.

Development Contracts

The government first entered into voluntary development contracts with universities in 1998 as a way to encourage them to think of themselves as organizations and to develop their leadership's capacity for strategic management. The government did this as an alternative to imposing management reform (Andersen, 2006). At that time, university funding was divided between the faculties. The rectors were responsive to the senate on which faculty deans were a majority, and rectors therefore did not have much money to develop pan-university agendas. The first generation of development contracts concerned rather innocent topics, such as cross-faculty initiatives to facilitate foreign students, and commitments to evaluate different university activities (Forskningsministeriet and Undervisningsministeriet, 1999).

The creation of self-owning universities in 2003 put into legislation what the development contracts had tried to achieve as a pedagogical exercise. It became compulsory for university governing boards to enter into contracts with the Ministry of Science, Technology and Innovation, and their purpose changed: now they were to define the university's strategic aims and activities. The law states that the contracts are not legally binding agreements between the Ministry and the university, but a university's ability to deliver on the promises made in its development contract *could* be used to divide up any new money which parliament allocates to the sector (Folketinget, 2002).

After 2003, the development contract became a tool for government to hold the new top-down leadership to account for the strategic decisions, activities and spending of their institutions. The development contracts signed after the 2003 University Law also reflect much more ambition on the part of universities' central leadership to bring their strategic decisions into effect. Since 2003, the Ministry has developed the comparability of contract elements and performance indicators across the university sector to a much greater extent, and the link between government priorities and the issues included in contracts has become clearer. Far from the initial aim of getting rectors to give a few issues strategic attention, in the latest amendment to the University Law development contracts are now to encompass the whole of the university's strategy. Indeed, the government now refers to them as "performance contracts" and has started negotiations over the latest contracts by issuing a list of sixteen issues that all universities should focus on and for which they must provide numerical measures of performance. The development contracts are now also scrutinized by the state auditors, whose latest report recommended that the Ministry should make a stronger effort to ensure that the commitments universities made in the development contracts included what the auditors saw as the appropriate measures to enhance quality in education (Rigsrevisionen, 2008: 31).

These contracts have therefore transmogrified into a detailed steering technology. They are increasingly replicated at every level throughout the universities, between the rector and faculty dean, between the dean and head of department, signed personally by these leaders. Meeting the numerical performance indicators in their contract (number of international conferences held, percentage increase in Ph.D. students, number of patents, etc.) is one of the main ways that a leader is held to account. These contracts demonstrate the reversal in the line of accountability that was introduced by the 2003 law. Under the previous system, elected leaders were accountable mainly to their electorate. Now the leader at every level is accountable only to the leader at the level above, who has the power to hire and fire his or her subordinates. By continuing to use the technology of the development contract but changing its form and meaning, by 2006 it had become a tool to ensure that the new strategic leaders of self-owning universities aligned their actions with government policies, and in this way the contracts appeared somewhat to constrain the capability of self-owning institutions to act independently.

Finance and Performance

Each university used to be financed to maintain its overall capacity, and this was done by an appropriation on the national budget (that is, a right to draw from an account in the national bank). Now self-owning universities are paid as independent institutions on completion of specified activities. Although this change is very subtle, it moves responsibility for the administration of university funds and for rendering the university financially auditable away from the Ministry and towards the university leadership.

Danish universities are funded through a combination of output payments for teaching, a block grant for research based on their historical budgets, and competitive project funding from the research councils. The method for funding teaching output was introduced in 1994, when the government introduced a real-time relationship between students passing exams and universities receiving payments. This not only gave universities an objective calculation of income but power to decide over its use. It was a move to reduce government control over universities; now this same technology has been reintegrated into a renewed method of government steering.

Contrary to experience elsewhere in Europe, the new steering system for universities was not brought in to deal with a reduced budget; on the contrary, the government promised to increase funding for universities, although it is not clear when this will materialize. The government stipulates that the funding increase has to be allocated on a competitive basis. A method is under construction for allocating part of the block grant according to a system devised in Norway for awarding points for each category of research output. As universities' finances are still based to a high degree on student performance and the ability to bring in competitive funding (which, in the absence of true overhead costs, continues to bind a large part of universities' block grants) the ability of the universities' central leadership to control their budgets remains limited.

Auditing and Inspection

Because of the shift to self-owning status, the 2003 University Law set in train changes to the auditing and inspection of universities. Universities are legally required to employ a commercial company to do their own company audit and provide the information the governing board needs for strategic purposes. Accrual accounting and budgeting were introduced into universities along with the rest of the public sector after the 2003 law. A potential effect of this, which until now has been realized to only a limited degree, is that university activities can be calculated and evaluated in terms of profit. A more real consequence will probably be the abolition of activities that accrue losses. In addition, in 2007 the Ministry of Science, Technology and Innovation drafted a new system for ministerial audit and inspection of universities that included an extensive cycle of meetings with university administrators to advise them how to deliver on the university's strategy and purpose as set out in the development contracts (UBST, 2007).

This review of the elements that constitute the current model of university governance indicates that various different ideas about neo-liberal governance have been developed at different times. The output payment for teaching was initially intended to suffice as a steering mechanism on its own. It was to give the university a predictable income based on objective measures over which it had decision-making power. The development contracts were an alternative method of develop-ing management capacity, through which the Ministry could steer universities. These have both been repurposed and repackaged in a steering system which gives the Ministry directly and through the university leaders much more comprehensive oversight and control. Some of our interviewees argued that the government does not need both financial steering mechanisms and development contracts. The system is so comprehensive and interventionist that it may fail the essential art of neo-liberal government, which is not only to steer from a distance but to disguise the presence of government altogether, so that local leaders feel their capacity for action has been expanded and the political system of control just appears to participants as minimal and objective administration.

Enactment

This assemblage of steering technologies, with their different histories and current conjunctions, forms the landscape in which the university is situated. Actors, also situated in that field, each view and speak from a particular position when negotiating the relationship between state and university. Some focus their gaze on one or other of the elements in the assemblage, or combine the elements in different ways. To illustrate this, we will draw on two of our interviews with people involved in enacting the governance model, and, in the process, creating the university.

One civil servant in the section of the Ministry of Science, Technology and Innovation concerned with university finances argued that the 2003 law had not made a big difference. In his view, relations between the state and university had not changed substantially since the previous University Law of 1993. He saw a line of development over the last twenty-five years, which he described as a movement away from funding universities as a national capacity, and towards financing specific activities on delivery, almost regardless of which university produced them. In the early 1980s, the annual Finance Law included a budget line for every little item of university expenditure. Since then, there has been a shift to output payments, notably for teaching, but when the bibliometric measures are developed, research will also move more to output funding. The big change for him was the University Law of 1993 when the university itself was given the power to decide how to use these output payments. What mattered to him in asserting university freedom was not self-ownership but the amount of money the governing boards would administer and the degree of freedom they have in strategic and administrative matters. He used the research councils to exemplify how mechanisms are used to give universities more or less freedom. Initially the research councils were part of a system set up to control universities when they still had collegial governance. University freedom was constrained by claiming part of their budgets as co-funding for research projects selected by the research councils. Now that politicians have more confidence in universities, the research councils are a hindrance. They are being rolled back to give more freedom to the new management and more influence to the governing boards. So the move towards full economic costing of applications to the research councils will give university managements more resources to control and more institutional freedom. Freedom, to him, was local control over such income without direct instructions from the Ministry – this had made universities practically self-owning since the 1990s. He concluded, "politicians feel universities should have freedom, if they do what politicians think they should do . . . Otherwise, well then the whip comes out. It's the whip and carrot that's used in this system." From his position, he describes the university sector as consisting of different funding, reporting and incentive schemes, like a series of levers under continual adjustment. To him, all that happened in 2003 was the reshaping of one of the agents in this complex interplay as a more accountable subject. This sets in motion one more move in a long sequence of adjustments which are shifting budget decision-making to universities. From his position, local freedom and activity-based funding are the mechanisms through which the capacity for steering according to government priorities has been gradually developing.

In contrast, one interviewee in a top leadership position at a major university said she did not see the reforms in terms of a consistent vision but rather many partial visions to improve specific parts of the universities' performance and numerous political interventions aimed at making them happen. She was in sympathy with many of these visions, but, from her position, most government initiatives were like "medicine that kills the patient." For example, the government wanted to speed up student throughput, with which she was in agreement. But the government's mechanism for doing this, by tying the output funding for teaching to the time it took for students to complete their studies, had other, enormous repercussions. This she saw as an example of an overlap between two governance systems: while self-ownership was intended to engender active and independently acting universities, the Ministry still tried to steer universities in very direct ways. To her, the latter ran counter to the "freeing" of universities and the enactment of the new kind of leadership made possible by the 2003 law.

What had attracted her to university leadership was the growing requirement, as she saw it, that universities respond to a variety of demands from their surroundings, and to position themselves against a variety of contexts. She likened the new conception of universities to a "science wish machine" into which society was putting all its desires for the future. In order to thrive in such a situation, she thought universities needed strategic thinking and bridge-building leaders. A lot of her job, as she saw it, was about creating connections between the university and its surroundings. She was building up strong ties with the local regional government by positioning the university as important for the region's future strategy. She also lobbied private sector organizations and enterprises to take an interest in collaborating with the university; she placed a strong emphasis on creating ties with other Danish research institutions; and she entered into talks and collaborations with international organizations and developed partnerships with universities worldwide. From this point of view, the government, as the main financing partner of the university, was only one among many important stakeholders for the new free and strong university (Shore, 2007). But our interviewee thought that the government and the university did not see eye to eye on this. To her, there seemed to be an overlap of steering systems. While the university governance system was now geared to self-ownership and strategic action in relation to a variety of partners and competitors, the government still aimed to steer the universities tightly and often through very precise directives. While acknowledging that some strategic actions, like the implementation of a university-wide restructuring of buildings and facilities, had been made possible through the 2003 reform, there were also heavy government restrictions on the freedom of action of the university. This could be seen, for example, in the struggle over the right to define the university's strategy. Her university had a strategy towards all the different contexts in which it operated and a development contract concerning its relations with just one of those contexts, i.e. the government. But the University Law as amended in 2007 stated that development contracts should now include *all* of the university's activities (Ministeriet for Videnskab, 2007). To this interviewee, the government seemed to be producing even more ways to control the universities it had supposedly set free. As she put it, her university was almost like Gulliver, tied down by strings, and she did not see the strings being cut any time soon.

These two interviewees explain very different attempts to enact a relationship between freedom and control. The university leader said: "I doubt that anyone is able to go up in a helicopter and then look down and say, 'Ha! So this is what it's supposed to look like!'" Nobody had a complete view of the reform or a clear picture of where it was taking universities: there were partial visions and positioned interventions as people learned how to work the relationship between steering and autonomy. Marginson sees the discussions over control and autonomy as an outcome of a tension inherent to the governance model. We recognize that tension and the debate, but instead of seeing a model being implemented in its entirety, we see an assemblage of elements which provides a landscape in which positioned actors, with different views of freedom, continually engage in enacting the university–state relationship in different ways. In short, the relationship between the state and the university is invented through the ways differently positioned people enact it in numerous instances. Some of the actors are more powerful than others, but those in the university, just as much as those in government, are fully engaged in enacting the relationship between steering and control and inventing the university in new ways.

Conclusion

The university leader was speaking from within the government discourse about freedom. She was not appealing to an adversarial notion of academic freedom. She shared the government's vision of the university as an actor in, even a driver of, the regional and national economy. She was trying to position the university in multiple relations with the surrounding society, whereas the government seemed to be holding this back by its assumption of an over-ordinate position of control. Her image was not of Prometheus chained, waiting for unlikely salvation from Hercules. In her image, the university is still tied down, not by Zeus, but by people six inches high; and not with an iron stake and chains, but with multiple little ropes and even its own hair. This is a rich image because Gulliver found he could wriggle and loosen the ties and set himself free, but he refrained, partly because of the sting from volleys of arrows (our other interviewee's "sticks") and partly to maintain good relations with his captors. Gulliver was continually negotiating his relationship to the benefit of the emperor and himself. The university leader adopted a similar strategy of negotiation, from within the government's discourse, but with a positioned view on the limitations and constraints of the new steering system. After some time, Gulliver was granted managed freedom, where he could take specified paths, as long as he provided certain services for the emperor (carrying the mail, lifting heavy stones). Danish universities do not yet seem to have reached such a compact about how to deliver what the government wants through steered autonomy. Eventually, when an armada from the neighboring island threatened to invade Lilliput, Gulliver, who was capable of dragging the boats away, took on a new meaning for the emperor. The meaning of the university will also change as new contexts arise and positioned actors will use the elements of the governance model in conjunction with their other interests and experiences, to negotiate the relation between control and autonomy and thereby enact the university in new ways.

Our aim in this chapter has been to explore the dynamics in a model of governance. To assume that a model, albeit with inbuilt tensions, will play itself out on the ground according to its inner rationality only asks for disappointment or problems in explaining nonconformity. The reform of the university cannot be read off from the government's steering model. The approach we have developed sees clusters of keywords and assemblages of steering elements working in similar ways. Both are conjunctions of elements, each carrying a history of meanings, which are negotiated and contested by people with different partial visions and positioned stances. Through studying the ways that positioned actors in particular situations enact the relationship between control and autonomy we can understand potential developments of the model of governance and inventions of the university in multiple and changing contexts.

Notes

1   The project "New Management, New Identities? Danish University Reform in an International Perspective" is funded by the Danish Research Council. It consists of four elements: Jakob Williams Ørberg and Susan Wright are studying the debates surrounding the reforms; Stephen Carney is studying the new governing boards and strategic leadership; John Krejsler is studying academics' perspectives; and Gritt Nielsen focuses on students' participation in education and governance. This chapter is based solely on material from the first element, and does not attempt to look at the steering model from the other perspectives.
2   The Organization for Economic Cooperation and Development has a membership of the thirty wealthiest countries in the world.
3   The term "assemblage" is being used in diverse ways in contemporary academic writing. Collier's study of the neo-liberal reforms in Russia shows that in creating a new budgeting system for local government some of the elements from the constellation that made up the Soviet budgeting system were reused in conjunction with globally mobile technologies for introducing a logic of commensurate calculation (Collier, 2005). Sassen's analysis of how the mode of government and institutions of the nation-state are being transformed through a repurposing of their capabilities to function in a new "organizing logic" of globalization is even more dynamic (Sassen, 2006).

References

Andersen, Peter Brink. "An Insight into the Ideas Surrounding the 2003 University Law – Development Contracts and Management Reforms." *Working Papers on University Reform No. 4.* Copenhagen: Danish School of Education, University of Århus, 2006.
Asad, Talal. "Anthropology and the Analysis of Ideology." *Man* 14 (1979): 607–627.
Clarke, John, and Janet Newman. *The Managerial State.* London: Sage, 1997.
Collier, Stephen. "Budgets and Biopolitics." In *Global Assemblages: Technology, Politics, and Ethics as Anthropological Problems*, edited by Aihwa Ong, and Stephen Collier. Oxford: Blackwell, 2005, 373–390.
Collier, Stephen, and Aiwha Ong. "Global Assemblages, Anthropological Problems." In *Global Assemblages: Technology, Politics, and Ethics as Anthropological Problems*, edited by Aiwha Ong, and Stephen Collier. Oxford: Blackwell, 2005, 3–21.
Dean, Mitchell. *Governing Societies.* Maidenhead: Open University Press/McGraw-Hill, 2007.
Folketinget [Danish Parliament]. *Forslag til Lov om universiteter (universitetloven).* Copenhagen: Ministry of Science, Technology and Innovation, 2002.
Forskningsministeriet and Undervisningsministeriet. *Udviklingskontrakter for universiteterne – stærkere selvstyre, stærkere universiteter.* Copenhagen: Forskningsministeriet and Undervisningsministeriet, 1999.
Gallie, Walter B. "Essentially Contested Concepts." *Proceedings of the Aristotelian Society* 56 (1956): 167–198.
Government of Denmark. *Nye veje mellem forskning of erhverv-fra tanke til faktura.* Copenhagen: Government of Denmark, 2003.
Haraway, Donna. *Simians, Cyborgs and Women.* London: Free Association Books, 1991.
Harvey, David. *A Brief History of Neoliberalism.* Oxford: Oxford University Press, 2005.
Karran, Terence. "Academic Freedom in Europe: A Preliminary Comparative Analysis." *Higher Education Policy* 20 (2007): 289–313.
Kooiman, Jan. *Governing as Governance.* London: Sage, 2003.
Kærgård, Niels, Carl Bache, Mogens Flensted-Jensen, Peter Harder, Søren-Peter Olesen, and Ulla Wewer. *Forsknings- og ytringsfriheden på universiteterne.* Copenhagen: Royal Danish Academy of Science and Letters, 2007.
Marginson, Simon. "Steering from a Distance: Power Relations in Australian Higher Education." *Higher Education* 34(1) (1997): 63–80.
Ministeriet for Videnskab, Teknologi og Udvikling. *Bekendtgørelse af lov om universiteter (Universitetsloven), LBK nr 1368 af 07/12/2007.* København: Ministeriet for Videnskab, Teknologi og Udvikling, 2007.

Neave, Guy, and Frans van Vught, eds. *Prometheus Bound: The Changing Relationship between Government and Higher Education in Western Europe.* Oxford: Pergamon, 1991.

Ørberg, Jakob Williams. "Setting Universities Free? The Background to the Self-ownership of Danish Universities." *Working Papers on University Reform No. 1.* Copenhagen: Danish School of Education, University of Århus, 2006a.

Ørberg, Jakob Williams. "Trust in Universities – Parliamentary Debates on the 2003 University Law." *Working Papers on University Reform No. 2.* Copenhagen: Danish School of Education, University of Århus, 2006b.

Osborne, David, and Ted Gaebler. *Reinventing Government: How the Entrepreneurial Spirit is Transforming the Public Sector.* New York: Plume, 1992.

Pierre, Jon, ed. *Debating Governance: Authority, Steering, and Democracy.* Oxford: Oxford University Press, 2000.

Rhodes, Rod A.W. *Understanding Governance.* Buckingham: Open University Press, 1997.

Rigsrevisionen. *Beretning til Statsrevisorerne om revisionen of statsregnskabet for 2005.* Copenhagen: Danish State Auditor, 2006.

Rigsrevisionen. *Beretning til Statsrevisorerne om sikring og udvikling af kvaliteten af universitetsuddannelserne.* Copenhagen: Danish State Auditor, 2008.

Sassen, Saskia. *Territory, Authority, Rights: From Medieval to Global Assemblages.* Princeton: Princeton University Press, 2006.

Saward, Michael. "The Civil Nuclear Network in Britain." In *Policy Networks in British Government*, edited by David Marsh, and Rod A.W. Rhodes. Oxford: Clarendon, 1992, 75–99.

Shore, Cris. "After Neoliberalism? The Reform of New Zealand's University System." *Working Papers in University Reform No. 6.* Copenhagen: Danish University of Education, 2007.

Shore, Cris, and Susan Wright, eds. *Anthropology of Policy: Critical Perspectives on Governance and Power.* London: Routledge, 1997.

Shore, Cris, and Susan Wright. "Whose Accountability? Governmentality and the Auditing of Universities." *Parallax* 10(2) (2004): 100–116.

Universitets- og Byggestyrelsen (UBST). *Udvikling af universiteter – et moderne tilsyn: Udkast.* København: Universitets- og Byggestyrelsen, Ministeriet for Videnskab, Teknologi og Udvikling, 2007.

Williams, Raymond. *Keywords: A Vocabulary of Culture and Society.* London: Fontana Press, 1976.

Wright, Susan. "Processes of Social Transformation: An Anthropology of English Higher Education Policy." In *Pædagogisk Antropologi – et Fag I Tilblivelse*, edited by John Krejsler, Niels Kryger, and Jon Milner. Copenhagen: Danmarks Pædagogiske Universitets Forlag, 2005.

Wright, Susan. "Governance as a Regime of Discipline." In *Exploring Regimes of Discipline: The Dynamics of Restraint*, edited by Noel Dyck. Oxford: Berghahn, 2008.

Wright, Susan, and Jakob Williams Ørberg. "Autonomy and Control: Danish University Reform in the Context of Modern Governance." *Learning and Teaching: International Journal of Higher Education in the Social Sciences* 1(1) (2008): 27–57.

Yeatman, Anna. "Contract, Status and Personhood." In *New Contractualism?*, edited by Glyn Davis, Barbara Sullivan, and Anna Yeatman. Melbourne: Macmillan Education Australia, 1997, 39–56.

6

Reform Policies and Change Processes in Europe

CATHERINE PARADEISE, IVAR BLEIKLIE,
JÜRGEN ENDERS, GAËLE GOASTELLEC, SVEIN MICHELSEN,
EMANUELA REALE AND DON F. WESTERHEIJDEN

Introduction

Analyses of higher education reform policies and their effects on higher education systems come in different versions. In this chapter we shall explore a number of recent European reform experiences, focusing on how the reforms reflect the role of the nation-state and the relationship between states and universities. The analysis is based on data[1] from a comparative study of higher education reform in seven countries – the UK, the Netherlands, France, Italy, Germany, Switzerland and Norway – and on how steering and organization of universities have changed during the last twenty-five years (Paradeise et al., forthcoming). We start by outlining three different theoretical perspectives and their corresponding "policy narratives" to identify possible "causes" understood as sequences of events that can explain reform policies as they unfold in different national settings. Then we shall look at reform trends in the seven countries that may be regarded as common in a broad sense. We present itemized comparative reform histories since about 1980 and changes that have taken place, including central government regulation, system characteristics, organization and governance of higher education institutions (HEIs), degree structure and study programs. Then we shall focus on path dependencies and peculiarities of the national reform experiences. The analysis ends with a discussion of the implication of the reforms for three vital characteristics of political systems: multilevel governmental steering, the strength of the nation-state and the vitality of democratic institutions. Finally, we shall return to the theoretical questions raised above about how the pattern and outcome of processes of reform and change during the last twenty-five years may best be understood. In the concluding discussion we shall use these three main assumptions about the sequence of events driving the reform process as a basis for the analysis.

Perspectives and Narratives

Policy-makers and administrators responsible for evaluating pressing problems in need of solutions tend to emphasize an actor's perspective. Scholars entertaining *an actor's perspective* often claim that policies are the product of the actions of major actors, like policy-makers and affected groups, where policies are understood in terms of the preferences of the actors involved in the decision process (Ostrom, 1990; Scharpf, 1997; Tsebelis, 1999). According to these interpretations, the degree and pace of change depend on the aims of the actors and may be explained either by changing values and aims among actors or by changes in the constellation of actors involved. However, other scholars have depicted reform processes as complex, hard to delimit and difficult to interpret in terms of specific actors, choices, outcomes and consequences (Bleiklie, 2004; Bleiklie, Høstaker and Vabø, 2000; Kogan et al., 2006). Such observations have often been taken to support *an institutionalist perspective*, according to which policy change tends to be path-dependent and slow. Change becomes abrupt only if circumstances create a situation in which existing policies are considered inadequate to sustain institutionalized values, norms and practices in a given policy field (Baumgartner and Jones, 1993; March and Olsen, 1989; Maassen and Olsen, 2007). A third perspective is based on the observation that structural change tends to be based on evolving needs generated by developing pressures on social systems. According to this *functional perspective*, change depends on external pressures and how social systems respond to them in order to remain stable (Ben-David, 1971; Parsons and Platt, 1973). The specific organizational forms of concrete universities depend on how society's need for cultural functions is expressed.

These perspectives inspire some of the major policy narratives that structure current policy discourses. Narratives are "stories or description of actual or fictional events" (*American Heritage Dictionary*). Their strength is based on their internal coherence that affords cognitive frames used as policy models and theories for action (Dawkins, 1976). We shall use three different theoretical narratives in order to make explicit different ideas about change dynamics and driving forces behind current development.

The first is the New Public Management (NPM) narrative. NPM is one of the most widely used narratives in social science analyses of public sector reform in the last decades. It represents a perspective that focuses on changing beliefs, whereby public agencies are induced to change their *modus operandi* from bureaucratic to entrepreneurial and start operating as business enterprises in the market – *in casu* producers of educational and research services – rather than rule-following bureaucratic entities (Bleiklie, Høstaker and Vabø, 2000; Ferlie et al., 1996; Pollitt, 1993). The NPM perspective focuses on *changing beliefs about the instruments of governance* designed to increase the efficiency of service production. As it is applied here, the narrative assumes the following causal structure of policy-driven change processes in public higher education systems. Changing ideas about appropriateness of public steering, its purpose, its prominence and its instruments lead to redefinition of the policy problems with which governments are faced and the adoption of reforms that espouse new steering instruments reflecting the new ideas. Thus the NPM narrative bears a strong similarity to the normative or sociological institutional notion of policy change.

Second, the Network Governance (NG) narrative assumes a causal structure consistent with an actor's perspective. The NG perspective as formulated here refers to a situation where horizontally organized networks of actors rather than hierarchically organized public bureaucracies formulate, administer and implement public policies. This is assumed to have organizational implications as policies are implemented in a more non-hierarchical, discursive and open-ended fashion (Jones and Hesterly, 1997). In this case policy change is the outcome of changing actor constellations that lead to redefinition of policy problems, bring with them new ideas about the content and process of policy reform and adopt reforms intended to address these new or redefined policy problems.

Finally, the neo-Weberian narrative represents a third change model. Neo-Weberianism focuses on the *functions* of governance and reform processes whereby new aspects of public activities are formalized and made accessible to outside administrative and political control (Ferlie and Andresani, forthcoming). Whereas the two former narratives tend to assume that the changes mean that the state and public authority are weakened, the latter assumes a positive role of the state, a distinctive public service and a particular legal order. Changes, therefore, might testify to the adaptability and resilience of state structures faced with a changing environment and new challenges demanding new organizational arrangements. This line of reasoning is consistent with a functional perspective as it assumes the following causal sequence of policy-driven events. Pressures from the environment of higher education (e.g. greater demand) results in growth and differentiation that make it necessary for public authorities to implement structural change in order to stabilize the function of higher education provision by controlling costs more efficiently and strengthening the efforts to steer the increasingly diverse sector more tightly.

The two former narratives emphasize change away from traditional policy instruments and the adoption of new, more market-like instruments (NPM). This may weaken traditional state steering and represents a move towards governance by networks that include state as well as non-state actors. The latter narrative emphasizes continuity. Policy change is interpreted as an expression of the continued strength and versatility of the state. This is demonstrated by its ability to adjust to new kinds of pressure by adopting new policy instruments, yet retaining and strengthening its efforts at maintaining and extending its bureaucratic influence over an increasingly complex and costly higher education sector.

Claiming to provide a plausible account of public policies, New Public Management, Network Governance and neo-Weberian narratives "tell policy and management stories," mixing "technical, political and normative elements" (Ferlie, Musselin and Andresani, forthcoming). It is tempting to label what has occurred by the name of narratives. *Ex post*, what has occurred, may, for instance, look like the result of implementing an NPM policy, even though policy-makers made incremental changes, moving step by step without much vision on what the next moves could be, as we have seen in several countries. Only meticulous historical study can disentangle hard historical facts from *ex post* rationalization in cognitive frames built by narratives.

We shall first look at the reform histories and common trends in the organizational transformation of the steering and administration of European universities from traditional bureaucratic administration to modern management.

From Bureaucracy to Management

During the last twenty-five years national governments in Western Europe have sought to "modernize" their national system of higher education and research by introducing new regulations. From the beginning of this period policy-makers in all seven countries under study were driven by some sort of concern over resources. It became a hot issue on policy agendas with the rising burden of cost increases driven by massification processes. As a consequence, spending per student decreased, while universities were regarded as inefficient and too expensive. The efficiency issue was raised again with generally limited public budgets spurred by such phenomena as economic stagnation from the mid-1970s, followed by the development of supply-side economic policies and tax reductions during the 1980s. Finally, university missions multiplied during the 1990s when the notion of a knowledge-based economy emerged, putting higher education at the very core of economic dynamism. The problem increased as dissatisfaction with higher education rose when visions of the social and economic role of higher education in society coincided with rising unemployment. This contributed to changing perspectives on higher education and research. Where they used to be considered cultural and welfare goods, they increasingly came to be regarded as potential engines for economic growth. The central policy question moved from being one of how much we can afford to one of how we can tailor and shape higher education to serve economic needs. The idea developed that the HEIs might be used more effectively as policy instruments in this connection, and this increased the workload of public higher education and research as new missions were piled on top of existing ones.

The pace, methods and extent of reform varied across countries. Two broad groups of countries can be distinguished. The first one includes UK and the Netherlands. These countries went far, reorganizing forcefully and systematically the entire multilevel governance system of higher education and research institutions according to a general reform plan. The second group includes France, Germany, Italy, Switzerland and Norway. These countries have been late or slow movers, developing mostly incremental approaches to reform.

European universities were also affected by the idea that the proper way in which to improve productivity and quality was to transform public bureaucratic *administration* by means of public *management*. The European Union also influenced the content of reform. EU funding schemes within the Framework Programs enhanced networking of research actors with a growing involvement of academics. Furthermore, the Lisbon Strategy from 2001 onwards had a global impact on government choices. The Bologna Process, as a European intergovernmental process, also had a substantial impact on the mode in which the educational function was restructured.

The notion of a knowledge-based economy also added a fundamentally new dimension to the conception of universities, their mission in society and the nature of public spending on higher education and research. Where it previously was considered necessary in order to provide the nation with educated elites and learned professionals, and later a welfare entitlement for those who qualify for higher education and research, it is now increasingly considered an integral part of the production apparatus of the modern economy itself.

Turning Loosely Coupled Structures into Strategic Actors

In the 1980s European universities enjoyed variable degrees of formal autonomy, ranging from the high degree of autonomy enjoyed in the UK, via the autonomy and academic freedom that came with special civil service status in continental European countries like the Netherlands, Switzerland, Germany and Norway, to the Napoleonic system in France and Italy, where universities as such were locations in which overarching national disciplines ran their local teaching and research operations. University administration in all these systems was passive and reactive, and semi-dependent on professional activity. It meant partly legal control and partly administrative assistance necessary for running academic activities, but no management whatsoever. A shift from administratively supported academic communities to strategic actors first required reinforcing individual universities' internal steering capabilities. Whereas academic institutions until the 1980s had developed decision-making structures that were designed to enable institutions and their leaderships to express the collective preferences of the members of the organization within a given legal framework, the purpose of the new management structures was to enable leaders to impose their strategic goals on the organization. Thus there was a fundamental shift in the standards according to which the strengths and weaknesses of universities were evaluated, from a bottom-up to a top-down logic.

In terms of autonomy, European universities were distributed between the two extreme cases well described by the opposition between the UK and France. The UK higher education system was based on a high degree of autonomy of individual universities. They were not regulated by laws, except for common frameworks on a few matters like salaries. They were financed by a buffer funding agency, the University Grants Committee, loosely coordinated externally by an association of vice-chancellors. Until the mid-1970s, the funding agency distributed quinquennial block grants to institutions based on historic principles. Internally the distribution of power was based on professorships and collegiality. French (or Italian) universities represented the other extreme of the spectrum. They were directed by a large number of laws defining detailed substantive rules to be implemented top-down by the ministries in charge. Universities were submitted to item budgeting and *ex ante* budgetary control, implying rigid resource allocation. They were not responsible for their own human resource decisions. Academics were usually civil servants, but recruitment, although controlled by ministries, was formally or informally assisted by prominent academics representing national disciplinary communities. Definition of work contents was uniform, and degrees were nationally defined. Yet, in both extreme cases, collegiality, absence of strategic power and distributive behavior were common characteristics.

The internal structure of university governance reflected their organizational orientation. In many continental European countries a roughly common pattern of dual leadership emerged. At each organizational level (university, faculty, department) administratively appointed leaders shared the floor with elected academic leaders (France, Italy, Norway, Germany), and the jurisdictional divide between them was often unclear. In either case their authority and strategic leadership capacity were limited by the lack of tools of strategic decision-making. Consequently, presidential functions tended to turn on representation and internal consensus-building among disciplines.

Starting in the UK in the 1980s, new instruments and rules have strengthened the internal top-down managerial capacity of universities to varying extents, by developing managerial tools like strategic plans, accounting schemes, incentives, human resources managing schemes, in all the seven countries. A common feature in all seven has been the promotion of strategic planning at the level of individual universities as a basis for allocation of resources.

Towards More Tightly Coupled Organizations

Comparative results corroborate the idea that universities have changed character by becoming more clearly hierarchically integrated over the last twenty-five years. The common aim is to enhance efficiency by means of institutional autonomy and less traditional bureaucratic forms of public sector control, by substituting substantive top-down regulation by more indirect and evaluative relationships between central administrations and individual universities.

What appears at first sight as a striking convergence across European countries covers a great variety of implementation processes, in terms of rate and pace of change as well as in terms of path dependence of national patterns. The "convergence" thesis in higher education public management reform is therefore still at the very least partial and premature. At the beginning of the 1980s, communication between national university systems was quite poor and national issues were felt as very specific. Change has often been incremental rather than *ex ante* planned, as the French and Norwegian cases amply illustrate. Yet to a certain extent there was more of a creation of a "European space" later in this period. Benchmark and diffusion effects certainly increased with the role of OECD, with the development of the European dialog in associations like the European University Association (EUA) or during EU working groups – one of which achieved permanence as it grew into an organization of quality assessment agencies (ENQA) – or inter-governmental processes on higher education and research. Benchmarks are now an explicit part of the EU's Lisbon Strategy and the Open Method of Coordination. Therefore, benchmarks increased and national reforms came to use tools forged through such European processes as the Bologna Process.

The next section stresses the following point: reform efforts always somehow face forces of path dependency within local social orders (Pierson, 2000). Path dependency occurs at the macro-level of national or regional systems as well as at the meso-level of universities. Each of these levels has to be observed as political coalitions, with specific results rooted in path dependency and internal power balance (March, 1962). This section exhibits the varieties of paths to reform implementation within specific local national social orders. It will then allow us to evaluate change in relation to the narratives presented in the introduction.

National Reform Trajectories

Complaints about universities and their performance in the post-Second World War period started rising in various countries in the 1970s or even sometimes earlier. Some referred to shortages of financial resources and inflated costs in countries that experienced early massification, such as France, Italy, Germany and the Netherlands. Others blamed the supposedly decreasing quality of students, in particular in countries that did not diversify their systems of higher education, such as Italy, or where no post-high school selection occurred, such as France, Italy, Germany, Norway and the Netherlands. The third expression of discontent blamed the rising burden and inefficiency of bureaucracy. Complaints were higher where all factors cumulated, with France and Italy at the top of the scale, followed by Germany and the Netherlands. Norway, Switzerland and the UK were less affected, because they had developed some protective characteristics, such as selective admission policies, a binary higher educational system, better funding, or better administrative resources.

Repertoire

As observed above, European countries share a common repertoire of reform instruments that in principle are used to push universities towards becoming more tightly integrated and efficient organizations. Public authorities have stimulated the creation of research programs, doctoral schools and research groups as ways to promote cooperation within the academic body, contain academic freedom and create more transparency in choices. To enhance competition for excellence, they have introduced the range of tools presented above that are assumed to increase strategic action, competitiveness and efficiency of higher education and research institutions. Yet, the crucial questions of how, to what extent and with what effect these instruments have been applied remain to be answered.

Rate and Pace

With the exception of the UK, complaints did not prompt efficiency-oriented reforms until the 1990s. In spite of some diffusion of the NPM recipes and with the exception of the UK and the Netherlands, reforms that developed during the 1990s were mostly disjointed and incremental, even though some tendencies towards systematic reform have become perceptible since the turn of the century. Other countries are still trying to rebuild the new puzzle of higher education piece by piece, with policy successes and failures on the way. In many countries, such as France, Italy, Norway, Germany and Switzerland, general legislation would typically pile up without offering operational tools efficient enough to rearrange power positions. Implementation tended not to follow policy objectives. Its impact was often blunted by latent or open power struggles, and its failure discredited further reforming. Yet, deliberately or not, technical measures sometimes opened unexpected channels for change, as was the case in France.

Implementation as Performance

There are clearly major implementation differences between continental Europe and the UK, as well as between Northern and Southern Europe, building on the historical heritage of British, Humboldtian and Napoleonic higher education national systems.

However strong the display of political leadership exhibited in the UK during the Thatcher era may seem, several contextual factors also contributed to the forcefulness with which the reforms were implemented. The Benthamite British political and social philosophy helped promote reforms where quasi-markets and principal–agent relationships were accepted as substitute regulatory instruments to bureaucracy. The economic crisis at the time also bolstered the will to push through radical innovation, with consequences that broke the path dependency built into a century-long history. Continental European welfare states have been more resistant to market-oriented deregulation, fearing that competition might be more destructive than regenerative. This may explain the precautions taken in most continental countries to protect the weakest universities, for instance, by mixing input and output criteria into a single set of allocating resources, thus inviting universities to develop catch-all policies by increasing size and internal differentiation rather that specializing. It also probably explains why continental countries usually paid more attention to supporting the education of underprivileged students than the UK, where the situation only recently started to turn around with the Blair government initiative Aim Higher: Partnerships for Progress in December 2001.

Systematic reform was hard to achieve in countries characterized by institutional variation like Norway, Switzerland, the Netherlands and Germany. Frequently radical ambitions that were sought, and realized by means of new policy tools, failed because policy-makers had not considered their implications. The Norwegian Quality reform of 2002 has increasingly come to be regarded as considerably less beneficial to higher education than originally assumed. Once again Norway appears as a "reluctant reformer" where old patterns seem to reassert themselves and slow down the process of planned policy change, reproducing localism and incrementalism. Similar resistance against intended changes occurred in the Netherlands when an NPM-style policy was set up in the 1980s. By vaguely formulating research programs, Dutch academics made the prescribed idea of programming palatable as well as harmless to their disciplinary traditions. Peer review was used as a protection against outside interference threatening the established power distribution within academia. Even at present, as "NPM reforms" are strongly developed, we should not underestimate the role of old-fashioned consensus-building in Dutch decision-making at all levels (De Boer, Enders and Westerheijden, forthcoming). The same slow adaptation is apparent in Italy, where the 1989, 1996 and 1999 modernization acts created new maneuvering space for universities without achieving many of the intended effects in terms of differentiation of mission and governance. It was also the case in France during two decades starting at the end of the 1980s, where the setting of technical tools such as four-year contracts carried along incremental changes that were not fitted into a global plan and remained largely unforeseen by reformers themselves.

Yet, in all countries, managerial reforms have relaxed bureaucratic substantive rules to some extent, allowing for some strategic diversification of individual universities. Therefore, diversified adoption of reform measures within countries must be considered part of the changing landscape of universities. It may be argued that relaxation of tight substantive rules ensures diversification. However, it may also be argued that the expansion of incentives encourages institutions to imitate apparently successful arrangements introduced by pioneering institutions. Actually, both trends can be observed. Despite the common identity of basic repertoires, variations in performance – timing, rhythm, instruments selected, impact of social negotiations on implementation, unexpected effects – have all contributed to diverse, path-dependent national trajectories (Musselin, 2005).

New Steering Patterns?

Until the 1980s, the vision of university governance referred to the mix of bureaucratic steering and self-governance specifically seen in professional bureaucracies. During the 1980s, the increasing distrust in the governing capacity of the national state, widespread skepticism against the professions as well as the need to contain rising public expenditures led to reformulating the basic steering paradigm and methods of steering. The following idea became a basic premise for political action: potentially affected actors are numerous, heterogeneous and localized. Problem-solving involves emerging processes that cannot simply be steered by top-down linear processes. Therefore, decentralization by which affected actors are allowed to deal with problems in their specific contexts is required. These ideas call for a completely new design of public steering (Neave and van Vught, 1991). The commonly accepted recipe is the organizational model of the corporate enterprise, operating as an autonomous but tightly managed unit. By decentralizing micro-management to each unit, they are allowed to operate independently enough to devise their own strategies. Public steering thus becomes indirect, using *ex ante* incentives and *ex post* performance measures.

In principle the notion of a new steering system implies building coherence on its three complementary pillars. First, by pulling back the state from universities; second, by transferring micro-management to higher education "business units"; third, by basing steering on *ex ante* incentives and *ex post* performance assessment. Therefore, new models of steering cannot be assessed without considering simultaneously reorganization of universities, ministries and rules. Ferlie, Musselin and Andresani (forthcoming) have outlined three patterns of effective steering that correspond to these three complementary pillars: stronger multilevel steering, hollowing out of the state, and revitalized democracy. We examine how and to what extent they have been established below.

Stronger Multilevel Steering?

We have observed an increasing institutional autonomy, as recent and incomplete as it still may be in some countries. We have pointed out that this increased autonomy has usually been pushed by internal reorganizations such as new leadership arrangements and governing bodies, reforms of personnel structure, changes in funding models, etc. Yet, increased formal autonomy *per se* does not directly change the internal balance of power.

Turning universities into more tightly managed organizations implies turning presidents or rectors into formal gatekeepers who regulate internal and external interactions involving strategic deliberation and operational decision-making. There are definite signs that their roles did change in this direction. Nevertheless, their position often remains relatively weak in terms of leadership, especially in cases where the university leadership is unable to control agendas and reposition the internal political order. Variations in leadership are not simply a national or regional matter. They also relate to the history of each individual university (Mignot-Gérard, 2007). In a given country or region, the same set of management tools usually meets individual university path dependencies that shape their individual histories.

Enforcement of controls by assessment and accountability procedures has certainly increased the pressure on academics in Britain and the Netherlands, the only two countries where they are fully operative. But some degree of autonomy of research and influence of the academic hierarchy has remained in spite of the development of managerial programs and weakened collegiality in these two countries (Henkel, 2000). In most countries, segmentation of the academic body in terms of salaries and job content according to individual performance has not yet occurred, leaving traditional hierarchies and individual autonomy intact.

The development of the organization of the state apparatus in the sector also displays certain characteristics that support the assumption of a managerial turn in the public steering of higher education. Public authorities increasingly operate through intermediate bodies, such as the Swiss Confederation and cantons or the Network Norway council and NOKUT (the national quality assurance agency), and by developing external agencies for research funding, quality assurance, evaluation, accreditation, etc. However, their mode of operation from their inception until today has changed radically from support of individual disciplinary projects towards broader thematic pluri-disciplinary research programs aiming to produce research relevant for policy-makers, business life and the public at large. Quality assessment and accreditation agencies are more recent, but are now present in all seven countries. Although new agencies may support a new steering framework, they may nevertheless be engulfed by established patterns of practice. Thus there are clear signs that the "old administrative world" has hardly receded: new procedural rules have not eliminated old substantive ones in most countries. At the present time, each national higher education and research sector exhibits a specific mix between old and new patterns, with a variable emphasis on both sets of tools.

Each country has developed, or is in the process of developing, tools designed to enable government from a distance: performance indicators, plans, reporting, performance budgeting, etc. Altogether, the sophistication and validity of the tools vary widely across countries. Thus, new instruments do not usually provide means that are necessary and consistently used for steering from a distance. First, although the use of performance indicators and the rise of performance-based public funding can be quite impressive, it represents only a limited share of universities' total budget when both research and teaching are considered, and salaries are included. Second, steering tools may be used for different purposes. In the UK and the Netherlands, they reinforce governmental control over higher education institutions and provide support for funding allocation. In other countries, such as France, Italy and Switzerland, they are used as a source of knowledge about universities rather than as a means for funding allocation.

It would be misleading to presume that the introduction of the new steering instruments decreases state control over its activities. This has clearly not been the case in the UK, where the new policies came with less trust and a far harsher control regime than the previous "gentle attention" of government towards universities. Furthermore, the effective number of government rules and regulations remains impressive in most countries. The monitoring of targets and performance often comes in addition to traditional bureaucratic *ex ante* steering. Public authorities still keep fixing many rules of the game, such as conditions of recruitment and careers, structure and size of faculties, minimal standards for opening teaching programs. Universities remain highly dependent on the resources of public authorities. Reforms still tend to be imposed by laws and decrees. Hierarchical control is still clearly visible if not dominant, while the introduction of quasi-market rules appears to be difficult and sometimes symbolic.

These remarks show that the present-day organizational turn of universities did not usually clearly relate to an actual managerialist turn in multilevel governance. It is difficult to infer from the present mix of new and old instruments that university steering is actually moving from the old bureaucratic pattern to a managerialist one. Even where reforms have been pushed by managerialist visions, path-dependent systems reveal strong enough forces resisting implementation or transform expectations embedded into the most rational designs.

Hollowing out the Nation-state?

While principal–agent visions of multilevel steering develop, the role of the state is challenged by the emergence of new actors that are able to influence higher education system governance, the setting of new relevant levels of university governance, and the will to achieve complex objectives requiring the coordination of multiple actors. Thus public actors and especially local public authorities share the floor with private actors such as company representatives and business authorities as members of university government bodies, as in Italy, the UK, France and the Netherlands. Industrial associations advise the government on higher education policies as in Italy. Universities develop explicit attempts to strengthen ties with industry, local authorities and students in Norway, France and Switzerland. Boards of trustees and higher education institution government bodies in some cases include representatives of local authorities and private business, as in France, Italy, the Netherlands and Norway, whereas voluntary organizations, including trade unions, play a marginal role. Regional government also becomes more important in university governance. These changes often come together with a strengthening of the role of presidents, vice-chancellors or rectors, or of university associations in the Netherlands, France, Switzerland and Norway, aiming at coordinating actions and building collective agendas in order to join forces and operate more effectively politically. Students are also more directly involved in internal governance, for example, in France, Italy, Switzerland and the UK. Students' feedback impacts on both the quality assurance system and university ranking in the UK.

The relevance of multi-actor governance increased in the 2000s along with the differentiation of funding sources. The EU level is both consolidating as an important level of research funding and for professional training. Thus, competition for European funds becomes relevant for research centers and universities. Simultaneously, Europe has become a relevant level for building standards, for example, through the Bologna process with the implementation of doctoral/graduate schools that formalize the content and the structure of doctoral studies. Furthermore, within the Bologna Process, indicators are created to evaluate diplomas, with the goal of creating comparable degree structures, and periodical assessment becomes an objective for the institutions. External accreditation may impact on the national process of diploma recognition. Bibliometric assessment and peer review was developed on the UK model, in Italy, Norway and the Netherlands for some disciplines, to promote research-based university rankings.

The involvement of multiple heterogeneous actors as potential university stakeholders questions the traditional regulatory role of the state. Indeed, a new distribution of power between the various actors is observed. Vertically, stronger and more autonomous universities come together in associations to foster shared visions, share good practices and develop ways to defend their interest in relation to public authorities. So do professional managers, whose specialization, role and numbers are growing within universities. In addition the horizontal distribution of power within universities is changing as university governing bodies are opened to include new actors and stakeholders. Simultaneously these bodies often reorganize so as to clearly distinguish a board of trustees with decision-making power from a senate representing a consultative academic parliament.

The above changes invite questioning the role of the state in higher education. One possibility is that the state is becoming a stakeholder among others and will have to share its historical responsibilities for the steering of higher education systems, potentially undermining state power and authority. The alternative perspective is that these changes demonstrate the ability of the state to reposition itself in the face of new challenges represented by the new role of higher education and research in the knowledge economy. Faced with the changing role, the increased size and importance of the sector, one might assume that the state needs to mobilize the resources of actors across all sectors of society in order to meet the demands facing higher education and research today.

Observation across countries shows that state functions are repositioned rather than shrinking. The state does not lose functions, legitimacy and authority. As far as the amount of funding is concerned, the contribution of non-state actors should not be overestimated, although marginal flexible contributions may well be decisive in the shaping of specific university projects. However, public basic funding still provides, with considerable variation across individual universities, the major part of university resources in all countries, especially in continental Europe.

But financial matters are just part of the question. Other factors explain why, with a few exceptions, the new actors that have emerged have not been able to counterbalance the role of states. First, states remain central in the traditional meaning of the term. They have not yet reorganized according to a stakeholder vision of governance and still largely govern by rules. New policy instruments are added to rather than replace traditional ones. Second, states remain dominant players because they carry on setting the rules of the game. Although their way of doing it is often, progressively but slowly, shifting from a substantive to a more procedural way, using a mix of authority and negotiation with stakeholders. Inasmuch as implementation of the rules is concerned, it appears that the state in several countries is building new mechanisms for dialog and negotiation in order to ensure the legitimacy of its participation in the university system. Third, the move towards decentralization of micro-management indisputably increases the autonomy of universities. Yet, the development comes with a corresponding centralization of authority at state level by means of governance tools for steering at a distance (evaluation and accountability), even though it remains weak in most countries aside from the UK and the Netherlands. The new governing tools are often ambivalent as they are designed to serve as incentives for universities to operate as collective actors relating to multiple stakeholders, but also to provide instruments for more effective steering and control through standardization of benchmarking, evaluation and control.

Ultimately, the state does not lose authority, but shares responsibilities. The hollowing out of the nation-state certainly takes place if one considers the increasing number of actors taking part in steering higher education and research and the increasing influence of new levels of steering (European and regional) relative to the national one. Simultaneously, in most cases, this reorganization is managed by the state that "holds the ring," opens it to new players and defines the content of the relationships and responsibilities among these new players.

Democratic Revitalization?

How do new steering instruments affect the relationship between universities and civil society? Do they incite citizen participation in policy and management? Such an evolution would require pairing the traditional model of responsive public administration with collaborative public administration promoting trust in government through enhancing shared ideas, knowledge and power (DeLeon,

2005). The state would maintain its position, but experience a substantial revision of the traditional bureaucratic forms of public administration. How much is internal governance of public agencies influenced by external civil society? Such dynamics could break out of a policy in search of efficiency by participation with the idea that people or groups involved in decision-making are more likely to support the outcomes of processes they have been part of, especially in present times when citizens' level of education is much higher than previously. Such revisions can be observed as counter-effects against excessive coercive use of new instruments for vertical steering, as it has been experienced in the UK or the Netherlands. In this way, government interests can be reshaped or transformed as a result of engaging in dialog with an increasing array of actors. They can also be imposed from citizens' movements "inviting themselves," for instance, in the arena of scientific expertise and research funding and standing up for values such as equity, security, societal openness, respect of nature and mankind (Callon, Lascoumes and Barthe, 2001).

Several signs of such a process that could also be interpreted as symptoms of the hollowing out of the state may be acknowledged in higher education. Public participation and democratic renewal can also go with typical processes of managerialism, such as devolution, partnership, policy evaluation and long-term capacity-building. There are many signs that multiplying stakeholders favor a new vitality in universities. Instruments such as technology assessment arenas, consensus conferences, hybrid forums and deliberative bodies may involve stakeholders in decision-making. But, in the present period, they are not customary in the relationship between the universities as such and the state.

Higher Education Reform and Governance Narratives

In each of the countries studied, universities seem to have changed considerably, although to various degrees over the last twenty-five years. This significant shift from the expected picture of high continuity is as much due to top-down reform and shifts in steering as to bottom-up and academically driven forms of micro-institutional change. This emphasizes the need to be aware of the macro-forces shaping the higher education sector as a whole, bringing in the public management and political science literatures.

The analysis has underscored the similarities of methods used to develop management in higher education institutions, and the development of new steering tools by public authorities. It has explored the implications of what appears to be a massive trend in Europe, the position of the national (or regional) state in charge as a specific actor among several emerging stakeholders. This section goes back to the narratives at the start of the chapter, to evaluate their ability to account for local trajectories and possible convergence between countries.

Policy Narratives and Higher Education Reform Processes in Europe

Recent changes do show clear signs of universities moving from administrative institutions towards managed organizations, based on diversification of funding, development of management tools, and external steering by incentives and performance (Kogan and Hanney, 2000; Kogan et al., 2006). But change is not restricted to the rearrangement of vertical relations between central authorities and individual higher education institutions. There are also symptoms of the types of horizontal rearrangements described by the Network Governance narrative, as we observed pervasive hybrid forms across a number of the cases. Finally, the shift from *ex ante* direct regulation to indirect regulation by means of incentives, evaluation and accountability procedures in many cases demonstrates the versatility and strengths of the central government regulation capacity.

Yet, it has become all too commonplace to think of these changes in terms of the NPM narrative alone. Indeed, individual policy tools have been discussed and to a certain extent developed in all countries, which may be considered parts of the NPM narrative repertoire. The UK must be understood as an "NPM outlier," outside of which the diffusion of most radical NPM ideas proved problematic. Outside of the UK and possibly the Netherlands, policy-makers did not have the ambition of building an exhaustive system of operational instruments springing up from an elaborated *ex ante* theory of action. The interest in new policy instruments in other countries resulted mostly from the increasing cost-awareness of activities in higher education and research. This pushed governments to create or appropriate new instruments in view of reducing costs by better decentralized management, more selectivity in funding and creation of new tools of distant control by the state. Changes appeared slowly, developed step by step, and were at first largely contained in national traditions of higher education. Many supposedly new levers of action were simply digested by the environment upon which they were supposed to impact. Implementation processes tended to follow incremental rather than radical trajectories.

What public authorities actually did or did not implement over the last twenty-five years seems more consistent with processes driven by explicit or implicit pressure or resistance of actors, both from within and outside higher education institutions, than the clean design of the NPM narrative suggests. Yet, the NPM policy design contributed to the diffusion of neo-liberalism, by progressively or abruptly changing the state's agendas and the power balance among social actors. Clearly, the deployment of new instruments was a second step in that direction, taking care of the vertical relationship between central authorities and individual public institutions. They were increasingly adopted towards the end of the 1990s, and benchmarking accelerated with international circulation of public management models over the last decade. But by no means did implementation simply mean applying a systematic model of management that claimed to rebuild public service as an all-encompassing quasi-market within the NPM perspective, for at least two reasons. First, outside the UK and the Netherlands, governments did not possess the political resources required to develop such an agenda and have it effectively implemented in the very sensitive arena of higher education. Second, in some countries, like France, public decision-makers and high civil servants often could not even cognitively consider regulating the public sector through quasi-markets. It is only during the last decade that NPM as a narrative has largely invaded the reflection on change in the public sector in much of continental Europe and even here reception was locally contingent. But at the same time, competing narratives such as Network Governance (NG) have developed to make sense of the rise of horizontal rearrangements within higher education and research systems, related to the emergence of new actors in new arenas, and their impact on the regulation of higher education and research.

The comparative analysis of our seven cases suggests there is no such thing as a "natural" sequence of policy events or phases, leading from "old Weberian" bureaucracy via NPM to NG policies. The NG narrative may be evoked to counter the effect of the impact of the NPM narrative and therefore can be seen as a reaction against NPM policies, as suggested in the British national case. But NG may also directly result from shortcomings of the practice of higher education and research, while maintaining some basic axioms from the welfare state policy regime. Rather than deploying new policy instruments, the NG idea is to mobilize new actors for policy formulation and implementation. Pollitt and Bouckaert (2004) propose a similar perspective with their "neo-Weberian model" as a continental alternative to the NPM British model. The British intellectual climate, with its tradition of empiricism in philosophy and with a clear dominance of economic reasoning even when it comes to "government delivering the goods," was certainly a better breeding ground for the NPM narrative than elsewhere on the continent (Neave, 1982). In continental Europe, the overarching metaphor (and organizational culture) was not economic, but rather legalistic and procedural: as different as they were from each other, the Humboldtian and Napoleonic higher education systems shared the view of higher education and research as part of public service to its citizens. And this view has not been destroyed by the use of new management tools in higher education institutions. It should also be pointed out that many of the policy instruments that have been deployed during the last decades, such as management by objectives and results, are not necessarily market-oriented but are primarily seeking to make public bureaucracies more efficient, flexible and powerful (Christensen and Lægreid, 2007). For instance, a dominant characteristic of the new policy instruments is the attempt to formalize and measure output and input factors in higher education and research. This was a massive effort to bring the steering and management of higher education and research under a regime characterized by *formal rationality* in the Weberian sense, strengthening the control of the modern state by enhancing its ability to monitor and sanction a much wider range of activities than previously (Weber, 1978). It may be – and seems to be quite often the case in many of the countries studied – that NG developed as the result of evolutions of the classical bureaucratic state relaxing substantive constraints, for instance, in order to compensate for its loss of financial resources.

All seven countries in our study present a mix of signs and symptoms of NPM, NG and neo-Weberian characteristics. Even the index case for NPM, the UK, shows relatively strong development with regard to NG indicators. And France, which has recently become an index case for NG, equally has developed a good number of implicit NPM characteristics over the years. Altogether, extreme cases such as the UK and to a certain extent the Netherlands aside, higher education and research policy reforms are moderately strong on both the NPM and NG dimensions, and it is difficult to tell which came first. In addition, the increasingly formal rationalization of steering and management is increasingly characterized by a more pervasive formal rationality.

For many reasons, reform rationales nowadays tend to be absorbed by the NPM narrative. Yet, as we have shown, it is not a fair account of the overall historical development of new policy instruments. Indeed, our study uncovered international trends of more or less parallel movements in many countries, though two – the UK and to some extent the Netherlands – seem to be following a somewhat different trajectory. These trajectories constitute trends that may be expressed as different mixes of the two dominating narratives of this day, NPM and NG. There are also clear indications of increasingly strong formal rationalization of steering and management of the sector and a possible trend towards a stronger state in a neo-Weberian sense. The differences across countries derive mainly from path dependencies of the movements in each country. Moreover, the narratives get twisted to some extent in the different intellectual and policy debates, probably due to variation in national political and administrative traditions, to the influence of individual authors and consultants, and certainly to political coincidences, such as which political party is elected in a given country at a moment when a certain element of a certain narrative is *en vogue*.

Conclusion

The comparative analysis used in this chapter leads to some conclusions which we summarize here. First, a managerial approach to university governance has gained influence over the last two decades in all countries, with a significant acceleration towards the end of the 1990s. The repertoire of instruments appears to be shared between all governments. Yet, this does not mean that they spread by benchmarking or diffusion of good practices. This may have happened, but not always. It is only *ex post* that we can evoke a "repertoire," since it did not necessarily exist as such before.

Second, in all countries (except perhaps the UK) change does not result from linear implementation of a previous plan. There is no clear evidence indicating that national reforms will converge towards a common governance model, in spite of many similarities in discourse.

Third, the rise of management in universities is recent and far from being complete. It results from the aim of strengthening regulation of higher education by developing multilevel steering, introducing new organizations and new connections to encourage and control action within universities by the state. Yet this does not mean that organizational integration of universities necessarily leads to managerialism. Consequently, the rise of management in universities may affect a variety of links with civil and political society. Thus a variety of outcomes is possible from managerialism: stronger multilevel steering in one local context, withdrawal of the state in another, and democratic revitalization in yet another.

It is striking that the present situation displays, with varying emphasis depending upon the country and the sector, all three possible types of regulation: by substantive rules, which dominated traditional bureaucratic regulation of the "old Weberian state"; by markets or quasi-markets as described in the NPM narrative; and by institutionalization of collective action, as in the network governance model (Duran and Thoenig, 1996). As different as they may seem, these regulations coexist in the higher education sector, and all require some form of involvement by the state: to formulate the rules, to warrant markets, to offer institutional and legal devices. Thus, the weight of each mode of regulation does not *per se* automatically bring about the hollowing out or the reinforcement of the state, but different forms of expression of public authority, different ways of being a policy actor. The essential question relating to these new organizational forms is not necessarily whether they bring about more or less state bureaucracy, more or less state action or more or less civil society influence. Equally important is the extent to which they facilitate solutions to practical challenges faced by democratic societies.

Note

1   Data were collected from a variety of sources: partly documents and interviews and partly secondary analysis of previously published research.

References

Baumgartner, Frank, and Brian Jones. *Agendas and Instability in American Politics*. Chicago: University of Chicago Press, 1993.

Ben-David, Joseph. *The Scientist's Role in Society: A Comparative Study*. Englewood Cliffs: Prentice-Hall, 1971.

Bleiklie, Ivar. "Norway: Holding back Competition?" In *Controlling Modern Government*, edited by Christopher Hood, Oliver James, B. Guy Peters, and Colin Scott. London: Edward Elgar, 2004, 114–118.

Bleiklie, Ivar, Roar Høstaker, and Agnete Vabø. *Policy and Practice in Higher Education*. London: Jessica Kingsley, 2000.

Callon, Michel, Pierre Lascoumes, and Yannick Barthe. *Agir dans un Monde Incertain: Essai sur la Démocratie Technique*. Paris: Seuil, 2001.

Christensen, Tom, and Per Lægreid, eds. *Transcending New Public Management: The Transformation of Public Sector Reforms*. Aldershot: Ashgate, 2007.

Dawkins, Richard. *The Selfish Gene*. Oxford: Oxford University Press, 1976.

De Boer, Harry, Jürgen Enders, and Don F. Westerheijden. "An Echternach Procession in Different Directions: Setting Steps towards Reform in Steering of Doctoral Studies and Research Funding in the Netherlands." In *University Governance: Western Europoean Comparative Perspectives*, edited by Catherine Paradeise, Emanuele Reale, Ivar Bleiklie, and Ewan Ferlie. Dordrecht: Springer, 2008.

DeLeon, Linda. "Public Management, Democracy and Politics." In *The Oxford Handbook of Public Management*, edited by Ewan Ferlie, Lawrence E. Lynn, and Christopher Pollitt. Oxford: Oxford University Press, 2005, 103–129.

Duran, Patrice, and Jean-Claude Thoenig. "L'Etat et la Gestion Publique Territoriale." *Revue Française de Science Politique* 4 (1996): 580–623.

Ferlie, Ewan, and Gianluca Andresani. "Organisation Theory and University Governance: Towards a Neo Weberian Model." Unpublished presentation at the second PRIME Annual Conference, PRIME Scientific Days, Marne-la-Vallée, 2006.

Ferlie, Ewan, and Gianluca Andresani. "UK National Case, 1960s–2007: From Bureau Professionalism to New Public Management?" In *University Governance: Western European Comparative Perspectives*, edited by Catherine Paradeise, Emanuele Reale, Ivar Bleiklie, and Ewan Ferlie. Dordrecht: Springer, 2008.

Ferlie, Ewan, Lynn Ashburner, Louise Fitzgerald, and Andrew Pettigrew, eds. *The New Public Management in Action*. Oxford: Oxford University Press, 1996.

Ferlie, Ewan, Christine Musselin, and Gianluca Andresani. "The 'Steering' of Higher Education Systems: A Public Management Perspective." In *University Governance: Western European Comparative Perspectives*, edited by Catherine Paradeise, Emanuele Reale, Ivar Bleiklie, and Ewan Ferlie. Dordrecht: Springer, 2008.

Henkel, Mary. *Academic Identities and Policy Change in Higher Education*. London: Jessica Kingsley, 2000.

Jones, Candace, and William S. Hesterly. "A General Theory of Network Governance: Exchange Conditions and Social Mechanisms." *Academy of Management Review* 22 (1997): 911–945.

Kogan, Maurice, and Stephen Hanney. *Reforming Higher Education*. London and Philadelphia: Jessica Kingsley, 2000.

Kogan, Maurice, Marianne Bauer, Ivar Bleiklie, and Mary Henkel, eds. *Transforming Higher Education: A Comparative Study* (2nd edn). Dordrecht: Springer, 2006.

Maassen, Peter, and Johan P. Olsen, eds. *University Dynamics and European Integration*. Dordrecht: Springer, 2007.

March, James G. "The Business Firm as a Political Coalition." *Journal of Politics* 24(4) (1962): 662–678.

March, James G., and Johan P. Olsen. *Rediscovering Institutions*. New York: The Free Press, 1989.

Mignot-Gérard, Stephanie. "Gouvernance des Universités." In *Dictionnaire de l'Education*, edited by A.Van Zanten. Paris: P.U.F., 2007.

Musselin, Christine. "Change and Continuity in Higher Education Governance? Lessons Drawn from Twenty Years of National Reforms in European Countries." In *Governing Knowledge: A Study of Continuity and Change in Higher Education*, edited by Ivar Bleiklie, and Mary Henkel. Dordrecht: Springer, 2005, 65–79.

Neave, Guy. "The Changing Boundary between the State and Higher Education." *European Journal of Education* 17(3) (1982): 231–241.

Neave, Guy, and Frans van Vught, eds. *Prometheus Bound: The Changing Relationship between Government and Higher Education in Western Europe*. Oxford and New York: Pergamon Press, 1991.

Ostrom, Elinor. *Governing the Commons*. Cambridge: Cambridge University Press, 1990.

Paradeise, Catherine, Emanuele Reale, Ivar Bleiklie, and Ewan Ferlie, eds. *University Governance: Western European Comparative Perspectives*. Dordrecht: Springer, 2008.

Parsons, Talcott, and Gerald M. Platt. *The American University*. Cambridge MA: Harvard University Press, 1973.

Pierson, Paul. "Increasing Returns, Path Dependence, and the Study of Politics." *American Political Science Review* 94(2) (2000): 251–267.

Pollitt, Christopher. *Managerialism and the Public Services: The Anglo-American Experience*. Oxford: Blackwell, 1993.

Pollitt, Christopher, and Geert Bouckaert. *Public Management Reform: A Comparative Analysis*. Oxford: Oxford University Press, 2004.

Scharpf, Fritz W. *Games Real Actors Play: Actor-centered Institutionalism in Policy Research*. Boulder: Westview, 1997.

Tsebelis, George. "Veto Players and Institutional Analysis." *Governance* 13(4) (1999): 441–474.

Weber, Max. *Economy and Society*. Berkeley, Los Angeles and London: University of California Press, 1978.

7

Policy Networks and Research on Higher Education Governance and Policy

LUCIA PADURE AND GLEN A. JONES

Introduction

In his pioneering 1978 essay on policy networks, Hugh Heclo used an example from higher education to demonstrate the increasing importance of issue networks in American politics. In 1977 Harvard University employed a Washington lobbyist and joined a group called Friends of DNA in order to influence government regulation of research into the creation of new forms of life (Heclo, 1978). Over the last thirty years the concept of policy networks has been widely employed within policy analysis, political studies and comparative politics in North America and Western Europe, and while it has been less frequently used in the higher education literature, it has informed several studies on higher education policy reforms. Different interpretations and typologies of policy networks can be found in the academic literature and there is a continuing debate on whether this is a theory, an analytical tool, an explanatory device, or simply "another example of otiose social science jargon" (Rhodes, 1997: 9). Critics argue that the concept lacks forecasting power and does not explain policy outcomes. Proponents suggest that policy networks reflect the new reality of "governance without government" (Rosenau, 1992) and provide explanatory and theoretical tools for studying contemporary policy-making processes.

Our objective in this chapter is to discuss the ways in which policy networks can be used to contribute to our understanding of higher education policy and policy development. We analyze the evolution of the "policy networks" concept and review several higher education case studies in which policy networks are used to explain policy change or continuity. We argue that policy networks can and should be used as a theoretical framework in the study of higher education policy and governance in order to illuminate the nature, impact and variety of international, regional and domestic policy networks that link universities, international organizations, national governments, interest groups, epistemic communities and individuals. Policy networks can contribute to research on the effects of globalization and multi-level governance on higher education policy-making not only in industrialized nations but in developing and post-communist countries. In addition, incorporating critical and discursive policy network approaches in the study of higher education policy can increase our understanding of the politics of higher education policy development.

The Concept of Policy Networks

Defining the Concept

Four observations emerged from our detailed review of the literature on policy networks. First, there is considerable agreement among contributors to this literature on how to define policy networks and related concepts (Coleman and Skogstad, 1990b; Kenis and Schneider, 1991; Mikkelsen, 2006; Rhodes, 1997; Wilks and Wright, 1987). *Policy community* is defined as the totality of actors that have an interest in a policy area, share a common policy focus and shape policy outcomes. The term *policy network* characterizes the relationship among policy actors around a policy issue of importance to the policy community. Policy networks account for informal relations in policy-making and are created in the "gray" area between state and civil society in response to new or failed governmental policies; they may emerge as a consequence of political pressure from the civil society or as an initiative of governmental and intergovernmental organizations (Forrest, 2003; Ottewill, Riddy and Fill, 2005).

Second, scholarship in this area has tended to focus on the meso or sectoral level of the political system rather than analyzing the micro and macro levels of the system. The meso level includes "the activities of particular sectors or regions of the economy, the behavior of one part of the labor movement . . . and the decision-making of a limited set of state agencies and politicians" (Coleman and Skogstad, 1990a: viii–ix). Scholars have analyzed policy networks in various public sectors or policy areas, such as changes in water policy in Israel (Menahem, 1998) or protecting marine areas in California (Weible and Sabatier, 2005).

Third, the theoretical questions raised within the literature have evolved over time. The major theoretical debate within the literature of the 1970s and 1980s concerned differences between the policy network approach and traditional approaches to understanding the work of pressure groups associated with pluralism, corporatism and Marxism. Since the mid-1990s, research on policy networks has centered on governance, European integration, global policy networks, increasingly engaging postmodernist and critical analyses of public administration and policy networks (Grant and Edgar, 2003; Johnson, 2005; Nóvoa and Lawn, 2002; Rhodes, 1995, 1997, 2003; Sørensen and Torfing, 2003; Stone and Maxwell, 2005). In these studies, researchers examine the relationship between policy networks, policy change and policy paradigms, as well as the importance of the context in which policy networks operate.

Fourth, policy network analysis is a predominately Western discourse that emerged in the Western academic literature to explain or describe changes in policy-making in industrialized countries. Theoretical approaches to policy networks have been developed by Western European, Canadian and American scholars, and the overwhelming majority of case studies on policy networks focus on issues within Western Europe and North America. Only a few authors have recently applied the concept of policy networks to studies of democracy and international development in Eastern Europe and Africa (Anderson, 2003; Forrest, 2003).

Mapping the Discourse

The construct of policy networks grew out of theoretical debates in the 1970s and 1980s about the role of networks in modern society, and about the nature of the public policy process in the context of changing patterns of governance. Heclo, Wildavsky, Freeman and Pross were among the first to introduce the notions of policy communities and policy networks to public policy analysis in the United States, the United Kingdom and Canada. The term "network" was used to describe policy-making arrangements characterized by "a predominance of informal, decentralized and horizontal relations in the policy process" (Kenis and Schneider, 1991: 32). The *policy community* was seen as a cluster of personal relationships between major political and administrative actors in a policy area. Heclo introduced the concept of *issue policy networks* to distinguish these relations from elitist approaches in policy-making, and he suggested that policy networks should replace the "not so much wrong, as . . . disastrously incomplete" construct of "iron triangles" (focusing on congressional subcommittees, administrative agencies and lobbying groups) that was commonly used in the American political science literature (Heclo, 1978: 102). According to Heclo, *issue networks* comprised a large number of participants with variable degrees of mutual commitment or dependence on others in their environment. He believed that the increasing importance of policy networks was consistent with changes in policy-making which was "becoming an extramural activity among expert issue-watchers, their networks and network of networks" (1978: 102). Based on his analysis of Canadian political phenomena, Pross (1986: 98) argued that *policy communities* can be understood in terms of two components: the sub-government (governmental agencies, interest associations, business firms that regularly participate in policy-making) and the attentive public (media, interested individuals).

Since the 1970s the use of "networks" as a concept has spread through a wide range of disciplines, from microbiology and computer science to sociology, economics and business administration (Börzel, 1998; Castells, 2000; Kenis and Schneider, 1991). Concepts such as the network society, network systems, interorganizational networks, information networks, neutronal networks, network industries and network technologies are all attempts to describe the increasingly complex relationships associated with modern life. The network is seen as the new organizational paradigm for the "architecture of complexity," which replaces hierarchy and implies a new perception of causal relations in social processes (Simon, 1973; Kenis and Schneider, 1991). The mechanical view of the world (seventeenth century) and the bio-organic view (nineteenth century) relied on linear and functional causality, respectively, and conceived societal control as something beyond the influence of individual actors. In contrast, "the core of the network perspective is a decentralized concept of social organization and governance, in which central steering is being replaced by purposeful interaction of individual actors" (Kenis and Schneider, 1991: 26). For Castells, the new paradigm has emerged from business networks, telecommunication networking, global capital networks and nation-states, thus leading to the creation of a network society (Castells, 2000). Informational technologies and historical evolution have fundamentally changed such core processes as knowledge production, media communications, economic productivity and political and military power that are connected to global networks of wealth and power.

A number of academic fields of study that are directly related to policy analysis, such as political science, international relations and public policy, have increasingly employed concepts such as "policy networks," "policy communities," "policy universe," and "policy sub-systems" to explain changes in the public policy process. Decentralization, globalization and changing relations between the state and civil society are creating a political environment where an increasing number of actors are involved in the policy process, including new domestic actors (corporate actors, local governments and civil society) and international organizations, and horizontal governance arrangements are stressed (Coleman and Perl, 1999; Jessop, 2002; Rhodes, 1997). In the context of blurring relationships between state and civil society, the notion of policy networks is viewed as being much more flexible than general political theories, such as pluralism, corporatism and Marxism, because it accounts for variations in group/government relations that exist in many policy arenas. According to Smith (1993: 7), most theorists, including Marxists and pluralists, accept that the state is fragmented rather than unified: it is "an ensemble of many different institutions and agencies which are often in conflict. Policy networks provide a mechanism for assessing various conflicts and interests of policy actors."

Approaches and Typologies

Coleman and Skogstad (1990a) distinguished between structural, radical political economy and public choice methodological approaches to policy networks. According to the *structural approach*, the preferences and values of policy actors are shaped fundamentally by their structural position and, in contrast to the public choice approach, behavior is rule-driven rather than preference-driven (Coleman and Skogstad, 1990a). *Radical political economists* examine policy networks in the broader context of the evolution of capitalism. They study economic and political behavior and focus particular attention on macroeconomic variables (Jessop, 2002; Yates, 1990). The structural and political economy approaches share several common elements. They look at political power to evaluate policy outcomes; and, in methodological terms, both use historical analysis, elite interviewing, and the collection of qualitative data. *The public choice* or *rational choice approach* has played a major role in the American political science literature, and, as a more formal theory, links the preferences of political actors and public policy outcomes by studying the decision-making behavior of voters, politicians and government officials from the perspective of game theory and decision theory (Shaw, 2002). Institutions provide the rules of the game, but they do not determine values and preferences, which are exogenously determined by economic position, social class and/or technology. Most public choice theorists use hypothesis testing and quantitative analysis, and little attention is given to the internal workings of institutions and to differences among policy communities.

Over time, policy network research expanded significantly and became much more nuanced. Various policy network typologies have been developed by Coleman and Skogstad, Coleman and Perl, Rhodes, Wilks and Wright, Jordan and Schubert, van Waarden, and Kriesi (Börzel, 1998; Coleman and Skogstad, 1990b; Coleman and Perl, 1999; Rhodes, 1997; Wilks and Wright, 1987). The major dimensions of these typologies are types of actors (institutions and individuals), the number and cohesiveness of actors (restricted and open networks), similarity of interests and resources (homogeneous and heterogeneous), functions (producer, professional, issue and other networks), structure (more formal and less formal), and level of institutionalization (stable and unstable networks). Börzel (1998) attempted to organize the "Babylon" of different conceptions of policy networks and argued that there is an important distinction between the German conception (*governance approach*) and the Anglo-Saxon construct (*interest-intermediation approach*). She argued that German research at the Max Plank Institute (Mayntz, Schneider, Kenis) treated policy networks as an alternative form of governance to hierarchy and markets, while British and North American scholars (Rhodes, Marsh, Jordan, Coleman) used networks as a mechanism for exploring state–society relationships within a specific policy sector.

However, as Börzel acknowledges, the boundaries between the two categories are fluid, and a thorough review of the literature suggests that there is considerable diversity within each grouping. There are also differences within national schools of thought by discipline. British sociologists, for instance, have drawn on institutional methodology, but have used it to explore the power dependence between actors (Rhodes, 1997; Wilks and Wright, 1987).[1] The Canadian school on policy networks focused on the structural properties of the actors involved, but in their later work Coleman and Perl refined the distinction between public and private actors in terms of their access to power and resources (Coleman and Perl, 1999). American political economists (Benson, 1975) and structural sociologists (Galaskiewicz, 1979) examined the dominance patterns in interorganizational networks. Engaging Blau's (1964) theory on collective power as a differentiated power between dominant and subordinated actors, they studied sources of interorganizational power (such as money and authority) and the effects of dominance patterns on policy outcomes.[2]

In short, there is little agreement on how best to classify policy networks and the typologies that have emerged in the literature are frequently criticized as simplistic. Typologies of policy networks can be too general, restrictive or inconsistent; there are too many classification systems and their characteristics are difficult to apply.

At the same time, studying different types of networks contributes to our understanding of the nature of the policy process during different time periods and in different societies. Empirical research and theoretical developments in the field of critical policy analysis, which sees the policy process as complex and interactive rather than straightforward and top-down, have provided a foundation for refining typologies and focusing attention on several major characteristics of policy networks. For instance, Bleiklie, Høstaker and Vabø (2000) suggested that the idea developed by Rhodes and Marsh (1992: 122), "of policy network as a policy continuum, with 'policy communities' and 'issue networks' at two opposing ends, seems to have gained wider acceptance." Bleiklie, Høstaker and Vabø also provide the example of Marshall's analysis of Australian higher education where government–interest group interaction changed from "stable policy community" to "unstable issues networks" (Marshall, 1995). Thus, *policy communities* are characterized by limited membership, based on frequent interaction and shared values, and relatively equal power distribution, while *issue networks* are characterized by a wide range of interests, fluctuation of access and agreement, and unequal power and resource distribution.

In addition to refining typologies, policy network research evolved as scholars increasingly turned their attention to analyzing internationalized environments, the importance of state power, changes in the behavior of interest groups, the impact of new policy fashions in the context of globalization, and European integration. Recent studies focus on how different policy networks dominate various policy fields and how different types of networks can promote or obviate change. Critical accounts of policy network scholarship study power dependence and power asymmetry in networks, explore how power is exercised and who benefits from it, and examine the broader socio-economic context (Dowding, 1996; Pemberton, 2003; Rhodes, 1997). A small yet growing number of studies in policy analysis engage discursive perspectives and critique rationalist approaches to policy networks. They reject value neutrality, examine advocacy and discourse coalitions and expand qualitative research to include content and discourse analysis. According to this work, consensual knowledge, collective ideas, and specific belief systems matter in policy networks, "they are *constitutive* for the logic of interaction between the members of the networks" (Börzel, 1998: 264).

Higher Education Policy Studies: A Policy Network Approach

From State Regulation to Governance and Policy Networks

Comparative political analyses of higher education systems began to emerge in the 1970s and 1980s and these studies illuminated important differences in the relationship between the university and the state in different jurisdictions. Traditionally, continental European higher education systems were created, coordinated and almost fully financed by the state, while in the Anglo-Saxon countries universities were viewed as autonomous institutions, and governments played a smaller role in terms of regulating the sector (Amaral, Jones and Karseth, 2002). Changing economic circumstances accompanied by increased privatization, marketization and the use of business models of management in higher education brought in new conceptualizations of the relationship between universities and society. Burton Clark's (1983) "triangle of coordination" provided a framework for analyzing higher education coordination in terms of the relative influence of the academic oligarchy, the market and the state, a framework that proved useful in early comparative policy studies (Goedegebuure et al., 1994). Etzkowitz and

Leydesdorff's (1998) "triple helix" looked at the relative distribution of power within a higher education system among the university, industry and government.

The increasing use of the concept of policy networks in the higher education literature is associated with the rise of governance studies in policy analysis. Political science interprets governance in various ways: as a minimal state (diminishing public spending), as corporate governance, as the new public management, etc. Rhodes (1997: 15) argues that governance "has too many meanings to be useful," stipulating that in the case of Britain only one meaning – governance as networks – reflects changes in polity. Rosenau (1992: 4), on the other hand, clearly distinguishes between government and governance: "Government suggests government activities backed by formal authority ... whereas governance refers to activities backed by shared goals that may or may not derive from legal and formally prescribed responsibilities ..., [it] embraces governmental institutions, but it also subsumes informal, non-governmental mechanisms." Scholars in the field of higher education contributed significantly to the debate on governance. Given the special status of universities in society, characterized by institutional autonomy and academic freedom, an important body of higher education literature examined different types of institutional governance, which focuses mostly on decision-making processes within universities, as well as various modes of interaction between universities and external actors (governments, society, markets and business communities) (Baldridge et al., 1986; Jones, 2002; Meek, 2002).

In an era of commercialization and globalization, the boundaries between universities and the state have become increasingly fuzzy. The relationships between governments, society and institutions of higher education have evolved into more diverse and complex forms due to institutional differentiation, massification of higher education, and the more extensive use of research in private business and in public administration. Critical policy research by Neave (1998), Meek (2002), Huisman and Currie (2004), Gibbons et al. (1994), Bleiklie (2003), Rhoades (2001), Musselin (2005) and others has engaged such notions as the *evaluative state, steering from a distance, academic capitalism, New Public Management (NPM)*, and *mode 2 knowledge production* to analyze and describe the changing role of public authority in higher education. Rather than directly managing and funding higher education systems, governments have been steering from a distance by devolving responsibilities to the institutional level, by fixing the rules of operation in a market environment and by increasing competition within the sector.

First in selected English-speaking nations, and later in continental Western European nations, governments applied the principles of NPM to higher education; they introduced performance indicators and benchmarking, designed new budget allocation schemes influenced more by outputs rather than inputs and supported the diversification of university funding mechanisms. Governments also stimulated the creation of new actors in higher education management, such as university councils and boards, and quality control, accreditation and funding agencies. The inter-penetration of academia, local society, governments, private and public agencies, and industry created favorable grounds for the emergence of national and international policy networks. In developing the concept of *academic capitalism* in the context of US higher education, Slaughter and Rhoades described the networks of actors, "which cross boundaries among universities and colleges, business and non-profits, and the State. The boundaries became blurred among them; university is not a single entity anymore" (Slaughter and Rhoades, 2004: 4). For example, by analyzing the interconnections between the Rockefeller Foundation and the California Institute of Technology, Kay (1993) revealed how the foundation's network permeated the academic infrastructure of the leading American universities that they were funding, with many Rockefeller trustees holding senior administrative positions in universities. According to the author, by promoting various institutional mechanisms of interdisciplinary cooperation, the foundation increased its power to shape life sciences as a dominant discourse.

In Europe, the creation of national buffer bodies and regional organizations such as the European Higher Education Area (EHEA) facilitated the formation of new higher education policy networks. Critical sociology and discourse research elucidated the role of policy networks in policy production, and analyzed the asymmetrical distribution of power within networks and the formation of dominant discourses in higher education (Grant and Edgar, 2003; Lawn, 2002; Nóvoa, 2002). Grant and Edgar (2003) examined the role of hidden networks in British and Scottish research policy-making and found that powerful individuals and bureaucrats in public and private organizations "govern" the higher education policy domain and restrain the capacity of governmental institutions to steer the system. Lawn (2002) and Nóvoa (2002) utilized policy network analysis in studying higher education interrelationships with states, civil societies and international organizations from a discourse perspective in the context of European integration. Drawing on Foucault, they treated educational reforms as governing practices, while policy networks belonged to the sphere of production of policies and social relationships. According to Lawn, policy networks were "producing" the new educational space and had their own language. The discourses of globalization, knowledge society, modernization, accountability, etc., circulated on the European and national levels and legitimized certain educational policies.

Policy Networks and Higher Education Policy: Three Case Studies

The methodological contributions of policy network analysis can be demonstrated by looking at how this concept has been taken up within the existing higher education literature. In the sections below we review three case studies of higher education reforms, which engage three quite different theoretical perspectives on policy networks: the concept of policy regime which has emerged in the study of Norwegian higher education; a structural approach in the study of Canadian higher education; and a critical policy analysis approach to the study of policy reforms in Central and Eastern Europe.

Policy Regimes and Norwegian Universities

Bleiklie, Høstaker and Vabø (2000) engaged the policy network literature to develop their own theoretical approach to policy networks and to explain Norwegian higher education policy reforms. They defined *policy design* "as a set of characteristics that distinguish a given policy in one field, from policies in other fields, countries or periods" (2000: 109). They analyzed the Norwegian policy design by focusing on changes in various policy instruments, such as legislation, system organization, incentive tools and funding instruments. They argue "that a policy field like higher education is governed by *policy regimes*" which explain changes in policy (2000: 116; emphasis added). These scholars see important differences between their notion of policy regimes and how policy networks are normally understood within the literature. First, they believe that actors and their relationships change over time, so policy regimes are dynamic rather than static as interpreted by most policy network approaches. Second, policy networks are not engaged exclusively in interest politics but in all sorts of activities, which can potentially influence public policy. Finally, they believe that the policy process is driven not only by goal-oriented rational action, but by institutionalized behavior and communicative action.

In locating policy regimes vis-à-vis the pure rational and pure structural models, Bleiklie and colleagues argue that "*Actor-preference*-driven design processes and *value-structure*-driven design processes are not mutually exclusive. We expect that actual policy designs usually do not fall into one of these two categories, but are characterized by some particular mix and tensions that distinguish this process" (2000: 126). They believed that not only the constellation of actors (centralized or decentralized, pluralist or corporatist, elitist or populist, etc.) and their preferences but the dominant values shared by most actors could explain policy design. In the case of Norwegian higher education, they concluded that the growth of students, institutions and types of institutions, and increased competition among institutions from 1965 to 1995, made higher education politically more important. While the policy regime remained stable in terms of the bilateral character of coordinating forces – state versus institutions – it had changed from a cohesive, transparent network of actors to a wider, more opaque and politicized network. Parliament, students and colleges became important actors, along with universities and governments.

Given the relative cohesiveness of the Norwegian policy regime and the high level of university autonomy, the authors suggest that the higher education "reforms and policy shifts had less to do with changing constellations of actors but more with gradually changing, commonly-shared conceptions of the appropriateness of reforms that were adopted" (2000: 137). The gradual and consensual adoption of new policy instruments focusing on efficiency, quality and outcome planning was accomplished with considerable local variation in implementation. In comparing the style of higher education reforms in Norway with those in the United Kingdom and Sweden, Bleiklie and colleagues (2000: 139) described the Norwegian style as *incremental* with a gradual, consensual pattern of reform. The style of reform in the United Kingdom was *heroic* and characterized by centralized, radical, confrontational reforms in higher education, while the *adversarial style* of reforms in Sweden encountered less political stability and more confrontation between two major political blocs with different visions of higher education reform.

The Structure of Policy Networks and Canadian Universities

Several Canadian higher education scholars have analyzed the structure of policy networks in order to illuminate the complex interrelationships between universities and government and within university governance arrangements, as well as to explain policy change (or the lack of it). In a study of the interface between the University of Toronto and the provincial government of Ontario, Jones (1991) noted the university's involvement in multiple sectoral policy communities (such as healthcare policy) in addition to its involvement, both directly and through a voluntary association of universities, in the provincial higher education policy community. Individual professors participate in a range of sectoral policy networks as policy experts and advisors to governments and political pressure groups (Jones, 1994). Faculty and student organizations operating at the institutional, provincial and federal levels work to influence policy decisions by articulating member interests, though there are substantive differences in the capacity of these organizations to participate in higher education policy networks depending on their financial and human resources, and other structural characteristics (Anderson and Jones, 1998; Jones, 1995). The picture of university–government relations that emerges from this work is one of a complex web of fluid relationships, but with a relatively small number of individual and association actors with the capacity and political legitimacy necessary to influence policy decisions within the higher education policy network.

Howlett (2002) and Trick (2005) developed models to explain policy change or continuity of selected higher education policies at the federal and provincial levels, respectively. Howlett's model was grounded in network theory and evaluated network structures through an in-depth study of longitudinal policy change in four policy sectors, including federal–provincial funding of higher education. He argued that closely integrated communities and policy networks were more cohesive and better equipped to promote change than an open structure. While Trick questioned the assumptions of Howlett's model – the ability to identify and count the members of the policy network and policy outcomes at specified times – he built on Howlett's approach and used policy networks as an explanatory device. In his detailed analysis of higher education policy during the period from 1985 to 2002, Trick argued that university policy-making in Ontario had been a relatively closed policy network since its creation in the 1950s to 1960s, and had been dominated by a ministry, representatives of the university administrators, the Council of Ontario Universities and the Ontario Council on University Affairs (before its abolition in 1996). Despite political, economic and fiscal pressures in the 1980s and 1990s, the dominant policy paradigm of equality and access did not change. Due to the corporatist character of the network, the major actors were able to promote the paradigm and acted effectively to preserve accessibility to higher education in response to growing demands. However, Trick notes that the exclusion of student organizations, faculty organizations and alumni organizations from discussing many issues simplified the development of policies and excluded voices that might have helped develop alternative policies.

Instead of assuming a hierarchical relationship between governments and universities, these Canadian studies illuminate complex higher education policy environments and focus attention on structural elements of policy networks, including the relative capacity of different pressure groups to sustain involvement in networks, and network characteristics, such as the level of integration and openness.

Critical Policy Analysis and University Reforms in Central and Eastern Europe

Two important observations about the nature of policy networks in the post-communist setting of Central and Eastern Europe (CEE) in the 1990s emerge from the small number of studies that have focused on this topic. First, divided and fragmented policy networks inhibited successful reforms, and powerful international actors such as the European Union (EU) and the World Bank (WB) contributed to further fragmentation of these networks. International actors often had quite different goals than the domestic members of these policy networks, and there was little space for negotiation over the broader social implications of particular reforms.[3] Second, in these countries, dominant states and informal connections influenced network behavior. For example, Forrest argued that personal networks in Soviet Russia shaped the nature of the influence of political leaders, with negative consequences for policy implementation (Forrest, 2003).

Emerging critical policy research on higher education reforms in the region from 1990 to 2005 analyzes sources of domination, and draws attention to the sources and distribution of power in higher education (Scott, 2002; Tomusk, 2001; Brennan, 2005; Padure, 1999).[4] Educational policies in critical policy analysis are viewed as complex, multidimensional processes, but also as discourses, which represent political compromises of policy actors on the nature of educational reforms (Henry et al., 2001). In this context, the changes in university–government relations and in HE policy networks in CEE after the fall of the communist regimes are rooted in the political struggle between the dominant actors and others, and are impacted by local bureaucratic structures and international organizations. In the early 1990s, CEE governments stepped back from regulating higher education and significantly decreased funding. Various policy communities promoted important changes in higher education, such as establishing private universities, diversifying academic departments and facilitating the transition to de-ideologized curricula. Higher education policy networks, with loose memberships that were often based on personal connections, emerged from the grass roots and involved a combination of domestic actors (such as public universities, local entrepreneurs, non-governmental organizations, local governments, industrial enterprises and banks) and external actors (Western universities and foundations, such as Soros Foundation Networks).

In the mid-1990s, however, CEE governments began to reassert their role in higher education policy through the creation of accreditation bodies and by promoting the discourse of accountability and efficiency. International organizations, Western universities and experts played important roles in encouraging the neo-liberal discourse in economic and higher education reforms, and in promoting Western values and institutional solutions, such as the Dutch quality assurance model, the OECD concept of "short-cycle" or "non-university sector," and others. Local scholars and university administrators with foreign experience also became influential advocates for the adoption of NPM in higher education administration. By the early 2000s, accreditation bodies, rectors' councils, local and foreign non-governmental organizations, and international projects funded by the WB, the United Nations and the EU formed a multitude of policy networks that promoted policy issues related to quality assurance mechanisms, university internal governance and institutional autonomy. Arguably, local non-governmental organizations, universities and intermediary bodies are more vocal in the CEE nations that became EU members than in the former Soviet nations. Also, there are national variations in how higher education reforms have been formulated and implemented. However, corruption, increasing inequalities in power and wealth and weak civil institutions in these societies shaped the policy process in higher education. Policy networks seem to be more formal and centralized, while system reforms are increasingly mediated by governments and EU regional bodies rather than by local institutions.

Policy Networks and Policy Change in Norway, Canada and Central and Eastern Europe

The approaches used in examining HE reforms in Norway, Canada and CEE share several common elements, but also differ in several important ways. All of the authors engage historical and contextual analysis over long periods of time to study policy reforms. Their major theoretical assumption is that policy-making is a complex, multidimensional process rather than a hierarchical, top-down or bottom-up process. In this context, policy networks become an important element of policy-making; however, the policy outcome is influenced by characteristics of the policy network (closed or open, centralized or decentralized) and by the regional/national/local political, economic and historical contexts. There are important differences in the assumptions that the authors have used to frame their analysis of reform in these jurisdictions. Structural analyses of Canadian universities and the Ontario policy network see the policy process as mainly being shaped by the structural position of policy actors. The policy regime approach used to examine Norwegian university reforms acknowledges the importance of both institutions and individual actors in policy-making. The critical policy perspective frames the discussion on the nature of HE policies in CEE in terms of policies as processes but also as discourses. So, the three cases illustrate quite different ways of analyzing policy networks in higher education, though all three show how policy networks underscore policy change, and how the nature of this change is deeply embedded in the local, political and cultural setting.

Discussion: How Policy Network Analysis Can Contribute to the Study of Higher Education Governance

The study of higher education governance has tended to focus on the formal structures and practices that lead to the development of higher education policy at the system or institutional level. Decisions are made by government ministries, and the implementation of these decisions has an impact on the higher education system. The analysis of policy tools and instruments has become increasingly sophisticated as scholars study the impact of policies designed, for example, to stimulate the commercialization of research or create market-like competition between institutions. Based on our analysis of the literature and our previous work in this area, we believe that policy network analysis can make an enormous contribution to scholarship on higher education governance in a number of very important ways.

First, and most importantly, policy network analysis provides a conceptual foundation for exploring the questions of how policy is made and who is involved in policy decisions. These are, of course, classic questions of power and influence, but they are questions that have received surprisingly little attention within the higher education literature. Policy network analysis focuses attention on the actors and institutions which interact in the complex processes associated with policy formation, and seeks to understand who decides, and how these decisions are reached. These are not easy questions to answer, and there are complex methodological challenges associated with research in this area. For example, loose and informal arrangements and interactions may play a very important role within policy networks, but these arrangements are difficult to identify and study. On the other hand, failing to raise these questions can lead to inappropriate assumptions about the respective roles of different actors in the policy process, or lead to research that is blind to what may be dramatic debates or political conflicts underscoring policy processes. For example, the role of informal connections between major higher education actors or the impact of social discourses on reforms in higher education have been analyzed through the policy network perspective by Jones (2002), Lawn (2002), Nóvoa (2002), and Grant and Edgar (2003). Policy network analysis provides a conceptual base for looking at the roles and activities of a variety of individuals and groups that may simply be ignored within other conceptual frames, such as faculty, student and alumni associations, philanthropic foundations, unions, business organizations and private consultants.

The second reason to encourage the use of policy network analysis is that the higher education policy environment is changing and traditional assumptions about the role of the state or traditional, collegial practices within institutional governance processes are being challenged by what have been, in some jurisdictions, quite dramatic changes in authority relationships, accountability requirements and management practices. In other words, the assumptions underscoring the concept of policy networks may more accurately reflect the realities of system and institutional governance arrangements that may now provide more space for the consideration of stakeholder interests. Policy networks help illuminate certain key aspects of decision-making that are not covered by functional approaches, which focus primarily on the process of policy formulation and implementation. In the context of blurring relationships between state and civil society, policy networks provide flexibility in accounting for variations in relations between government, institutions and agencies that are often in conflict. As such, policy networks represent a mechanism for evaluating these conflicts and the various interests of policy actors.

While policy networks may more accurately reflect contemporary policy formation processes in higher education, it is important not to assume that these arrangements are increasingly open, participatory or equitable. While policy networks could enhance the principle of equity by representing and promoting the interests of disenfranchised groups of people, policy networks do not necessarily lead to improved access to the policy-making processes or more democratic practices. Actors in privileged positions may inhibit the participation of other policy actors, or even exploit the weaker network components. Rivalries between competing networks can have a significant impact on policy formation. "Openness and pluralism do not guarantee influence," as Mazey and Richardson (2003: 225) note following their analysis of European institutions. In other words, it is important not to assume that the existence of policy networks has innate advantages or disadvantages, but rather that the analysis of these networks can provide us with a clearer understanding of the voices that influence policy, and those that are ignored.

Policy network analysis can also help us understand regional/international integration within higher education. Increasingly, contributors to the policy analysis literature view the concept of policy networks as part of a theoretical portfolio (Skok, 1995; Menahem, 1998; Coleman and Perl, 1999; Peterson, 2001). In combination with other theories, such as international relations, institutionalism, policy paradigms and radical democracy, policy network analysis advances our understanding of multi-level governance and internationalized policy environments, and helps scholars escape what Caporaso refers to as the "self-constructed theoretical ghetto" (Caporaso, 1999: 161). Given the geopolitical changes in Europe, the European Union is frequently described as a special case of multi-level governance in which policy networks play an important role. While the range and diversity of international networks in higher education are vast, these networks have received surprisingly little attention, except for recent work on global knowledge networks and the influence of international organizations on policy reforms in developing countries. The emerging literature on global knowledge networks argues that they could contribute to the democratization of the international policy process; however, this literature also suggests that access can be unequal, transaction costs high, and sustainability problematic (Stone and Maxwell, 2005). There is also a growing body of literature on the role of international organizations in educational policy-making, but only a few studies have analyzed the influence that networks of international organizations have in formulating and disseminating higher education policies around the world, and the ways that these international actors participate in national policy networks

(Henry et al., 2001; Samoff and Stromquist, 2001; Torres and Schugurensky, 2002). These are important research questions that deserve further research.

Finally, policy network analysis provides the field with an opportunity to develop a more coherent theoretical base for higher education research. Higher education is a theme-focused field of study that draws on a wide range of disciplines and perspectives (Teichler and Sadlak, 2000). A great deal of higher education research is descriptive and a-theoretical, and much of the research that is theoretically grounded borrows from, without contributing to, the primary disciplines. There are those who wonder whether higher education is a "discipline, field of study, or just an opportunity for researchers in whatever discipline to earn some reputation and income" (Frackman, 1997: 18). The use of policy network analysis in the study of higher education governance and policy formation will contribute to the theoretical depth of research in this important area of scholarship and has the potential to allow higher education scholars to contribute to theoretical developments in policy analysis and political science. The repositioning of higher education as a central policy area in the context of the knowledge economy, the fact that the higher education sector has become a primary research laboratory for understanding the pressures and implications of globalization, and the dramatic changes in policy and governance arrangements in the sector over the last few decades mean that there is a broad interest in understanding how decisions in this sector (and in these institutions) are made, and there is considerable potential for the development of synergistic relationships that would further scholarship in higher education and broaden scholarship on governance and policy analysis.

Notes

1   Rhodes emphasized the structural relationship between political institutions as the crucial element in a policy network, rather than relations between individuals (Rhodes, 1997).
2   Benson (1975), for instance, distinguishes between inter-organizational networks with clear-cut dominance patterns in which one or a few organizations are powerful and exercise control, and networks with a number of minimally powerful and relatively equal parties. "Such networks are often blocked and non-cooperative because all of the agencies suffer from resource shortages and none can master power sufficient to dictate terms to others" (Benson, 1975: 235).
3   For example, the role of the EU in social assistance reforms in the Czech Republic has been analyzed by Anderson (2003), the case of the WB higher education project in Hungary has been examined by Tomusk (2004), and the role of various international agencies in pension reforms in Moldova has been studied by Padure (1999).
4   Lucia Padure's doctoral research at the University of Toronto focuses on higher education reforms in Central and Eastern Europe in the context of economic and political reforms from 1990 to 2005. She examines policy reforms in Hungary, Romania and Moldova, and analyzes the role of policy networks in promoting higher education reforms.

References

Amaral, Alberto, Glen A. Jones, and Berit Karseth. "Governing Higher Education: Comparing National Perspectives." In *Governing Higher Education: National Perspectives on Institutional Governance*, edited by Alberto Amaral, Glen A. Jones, and Berit Karseth. Dordrecht and Boston: Kluwer Academic, 2002, 279–298.

Anderson, Barbara, and Glen A. Jones. "Organizational Capacity and Political Activities of Canadian University Faculty Associations." *Interchange* 29(4) (1998): 439–461.

Anderson, Leah S. "Constructing Policy Networks: Social Assistance Reforms in the Czech Republic." *International Journal of Public Administration* 26(6) (2003): 635–663.

Baldridge, J. Victor, David V. Curtis, George Ecker, and Gary L. Riley. "Alternative Models of Governance in Higher Education." In *ASHE Reader on Organization and Governance in Higher Education*, edited by Robert Birnbaum, and Marvin W. Peterson. Lexington, MA: Ginn Press, 1986, 11–27.

Benson, Kenneth J. "The Interorganizational Networks as a Political Economy." *Administrative Science Quarterly* 20 (1975): 229–249.

Blau, Peter. *Exchange and Power in Social Life*. New York: John Wiley, 1964.

Bleiklie, Ivar. "Hierarchy and Specialization: On the Institutional Integration of Higher Education." *European Journal of Education* 38(4) (2003): 341–355.

Bleiklie, Ivar, Roar Høstaker, and Agnete Vabø. *Policy and Practice in Higher Education: Reforming Norwegian Universities*. London and Philadelphia: Jessica Kingsley, 2000.

Börzel, Tanja. "Organizing Babylon: On the Different Conceptions of Policy Networks." *Public Administration Review* 76 (1998): 253–273.

Brennan, John. "Reform and Transformation Following Regime Change." In *Governing Knowledge: A Study of Continuity and Change in Higher Education*, edited by Ivar Bleiklie, and Mary Henkel. Dordrecht: Springer, 2005, 49–64.

Caporaso, James A. "Review Section Symposium. The Choice for Europe: Social Purpose and State Power from Messina to Maastricht. Toward a Normal Science of Regional Integration." *Journal of European Public Policy* 6(1) (1999): 160–164.

Castells, Manuel. *The Rise of Network Society*. Oxford: Blackwell, 2000.

Clark, Burton R. *The Higher Education System: Academic Organization in Cross-national Perspective*. Berkeley: University of California Press, 1983.

Coleman, William D., and Anthony Perl. "Internationalized Policy Environments and Policy Network Analysis." *Political Studies* 47 (1999): 691–709.

Coleman, William D., and Grace Skogstad. "Introduction." In *Policy Communities and Public Policy in Canada: A Structural Approach*, edited by William D. Coleman, and Grace Skogstad. Mississauga: Copp Clark Pitman, 1990a, 1–13.

Coleman, William D., and Grace Skogstad. "Policy Communities and Policy Networks: A Structural Approach." In *Policy Communities and Public Policy in Canada: A Structural Approach*, edited by William D. Coleman, and Grace Skogstad. Mississauga: Copp Clark Pitman, 1990b, 14–33.

Dowding, Keith. *Power*. Buckingham: Open University Press, 1996.

Etzkowitz, Henry, and Loet Leydesdorff. "A Triple Helix of University–Industry–Government Relations: Introduction." *Industry and Higher Education* 12(4) (1998): 197–258.

Forrest, Joshua B. "Networks in the Policy Process: An International Perspective." *International Journal of Public Administration* 26(6) (2003): 591–607.

Frackman, Edgar. "Research on Higher Education in Western Europe: From Policy Advice to Self-reflection." In *Higher Education Research at the Turn of the New Century: Structures, Issues, and Trends*, edited by Jan Sadlak, and Philip G. Altbach. Paris: UNESCO; New York and London: Garland, 1997, 107–136.

Galaskiewicz, Joseph. *Exchange Networks and Community Politics*. Beverly Hills: Sage, 1979.

Gibbons, Michael, Camille Limoges, Helga Nowotny, Simon Schwartzman, Peter Scott, and Martin Trow. *The New Production of Knowledge: The Dynamics of Science and Research in Contemporary Society*. London: Sage, 1994.

Goedegebuure, Leo, Frans Kaiser, Peter Maassen, Lynn Meek, Frans van Vught, and Egbert de Weert, eds. *Higher Education Policy: An International Comparative Perspective*. Oxford: Pergamon Press, 1994.

Grant, Kevin, and David Edgar. "Using the Theory of Policy Networks and Communities to Explore who Determines the Scottish Higher Education Research Policy: Issues for Educational Managers." *International Journal of Educational Management* 17(7) (2003): 318–329.

Heclo, Hugh. "Issue Networks and the Executive Establishment." In *The New American Political System*, edited by Anthony King. Washington, DC: American Enterprise Institute for Public Policy Research, 1978, 84–127.

Henry, Miriam, Bob Lingard, Fazal Rizvi, and Sandra Taylor. *The OECD, Globalisation and Education Policy*. Amsterdam and New York: Pergamon and IAU Press, 2001.

Howlett, Michael. "Do Networks Matter? Linking Policy Network Structure to Policy Outcomes: Evidence from Four Canadian Policy Sectors 1990–2000." *Canadian Journal of Political Science* 35(2) (2002): 235–267.

Huisman, Jeroen, and Jan Currie. "Accountability in Higher Education: Bridge over Troubled Waters?" *Higher Education* 48 (2004): 529–551.

Jessop, Bob. *The Future of the Capitalist State*. Cambridge: Polity, 2002.

Johnson, Genevieve F. "Taking Stock: The Normative Foundations of Positivist and Non-positivist Policy Analysis and Ethical Implications of the Emergent Risk Society." *Journal of Comparative Policy Analysis* 7(2) (2005): 137–153.

Jones, Glen A. *Pressure Groups and Secondary Relations: A Pluralist Analysis of the Interface between the University of Toronto and the Government of Ontario*. Unpublished Ph.D. dissertation. Toronto: University of Toronto, 1991.

Jones, Glen A. "The Political Analysis of Higher Education: An Introduction to the Symposium on the University and Democracy." *Interchange* 25(1) (1994): 1–10.

Jones, Glen A. "Student Pressure: A National Survey of Canadian Student Organizations." *Ontario Journal of Higher Education* (1995): 93–106.

Jones, Glen A. "The Structure of University Governance in Canada: A Policy Network Approach." In *Governing Higher Education: National Perspectives on Institutional Governance*, edited by Alberto Amaral, Glen A. Jones, and Berit Karseth. Dordrecht and Boston: Kluwer Academic, 2002, 213–234.

Kay, Lily E. *The Molecular Vision of Life: Caltech, the Rockefeller Foundation, and the Rise of the New Biology*. New York: Oxford University Press, 1993.

Kenis, Patrick, and Volker Schneider. "Policy Networks and Policy Analysis: Scrutinizing a New Analytical Tool." In *Policy Networks: Empirical Evidence and Theoretical Considerations*, edited by Bernd Marin, and Renate Mayntz. Boulder: Westview Press, 1991, 22–62.

Lawn, Martin. "Borderless Education: Imagining a European Education Space in a Time of Brands and Networks." In *Fabricating Europe: The Formation of an Education Space*, edited by António Nóvoa, and Martin Lawn. Dordrecht: Kluwer Academic, 2002, 19–34.

Marshall, Neil. "Policy Communities, Issue Networks and the Formulation of Australian Higher Education Policy." *Higher Education* 30 (1995): 273–293.

Mazey, Sonia, and Jeremy Richardson. "Interest Groups and the Brussels Bureaucracy." In *Governing Europe*, edited by Jack Hayward, and Anand Menon. Oxford: Oxford University Press, 2003, 208–227.

Meek, Lynn. "Changing Patterns in Modes of Co-ordination of Higher Education." In *Higher Education in a Globalising World: International Trends and Mutual Observations. A Festschrift in Honour of Ulrich Teichler*, edited by Jürgen Enders, and Oliver Fulton. Dordrecht and London: Kluwer Academic, 2002, 53–71.

Menahem, Gila. "Policy Paradigms, Policy Networks and Water Policy in Israel." *International Public Policy* 18(3) (1998): 283–310.

Mikkelsen, Margaret. "Policy Network Analysis as a Strategic Tool for the Voluntary Sector." *Policy Studies* 27(1) (2006): 17–26.

Musselin, Christine. "Change or Continuity in Higher Education Governance? Lessons Drawn from Twenty Years of National Reforms in European Countries." In *Governing Knowledge: A Study of Continuity and Change in Higher Education*, edited by Ivar Bleiklie, and Mary Henkel. Dordrecht: Springer, 2005, 65–80.

Neave, Guy. "The Evaluative State Reconsidered." *European Journal of Education* 33(3) (1998): 265–285.

Nóvoa, António. "Ways of Thinking about Education in Europe." In *Fabricating Europe: The Formation of an Education Space*, edited by António Nóvoa, and Martin Lawn. Dordrecht: Kluwer Academic, 2002, 131–156.

Nóvoa, António, and Martin Lawn, eds. *Fabricating Europe: The Formation of an Education Space*. Dordrecht: Kluwer Academic, 2002.

Ottewill, Roger, Paul Riddy, and Karen Fill. "International Networks in Higher Education: Realising their Potential?" *On the Horizon* 13(3) (2005): 138–147.

Padure, Lucia. "Transitional Economies: Geopolitical Background and Patterns of Reforms." In *Economic Transition: Trends of Globalization and the Moldovan Case*. Chisinau: International Institute of Management, 1999, 18–27.

Pemberton, Hugh. "Learning, Governance and Economic Policy." *British Journal of Politics and International Relations* 5(4) (2003): 500–524.

Peterson, John. "The Choice for EU Theorists: Establishing a Common Framework for Analysis." *European Journal of Political Research* 39 (2001): 289–318.

Pross, A. Paul. *Group Politics and Public Policy*. Toronto: Oxford University Press, 1986.

Rhoades, Gary. "Introduction to Special Section: Perspectives on Comparative Higher Education." *Higher Education* 41 (2001): 345–352.

Rhodes, Rod A.W. *Towards a Postmodern Public Administration: Epoch, Epistemology or Narrative?* San Domenico: Robert Schumann Center at the European University Institute, 1995.

Rhodes, Rod A.W. *Understanding Governance: Policy Networks, Governance, Reflexivity and Accountability*. Buckingham and Philadelphia: Open University Press, 1997.

Rhodes, Rod A.W. "What's New about Governance and Why Does it Matter?" In *Governing Europe*, edited by Jack Hayward, and Anand Menon. New York: Oxford University Press, 2003, 61–73.

Rhodes, Rod A.W., and David Marsh. "New Directions in the Study of Policy Networks." *European Journal of Political Research* 21 (1992): 181–205.

Rosenau, James N. "Governance, Order, and Change in World Politics." In *Governance without Government: Order and Change in World Politics*, edited by James N. Rosenau, and Ernst-Otto Czempiel. Cambridge: Cambridge University Press, 1992, 1–29.

Samoff, Joel, and Nelly P. Stromquist. "Managing Knowledge and Strong Wisdom? New Forms of Foreign Aid?" *Development and Change* 32(4) (2001): 631–653.

Scott, Peter. "Reflections on the Reform of Higher Education in Central and Eastern Europe." *Higher Education in Europe* 27(1/2) (2002): 137–152.

Shaw, Jane S. *Public Choice Theory*. The Library of Economics and Liberty, 2002. Available online (accessed 8.31.2006): http://www.econlib.org/library/Enc/PublicChoiceTheory.html.

Simon, Herbert A. "The Organization of Complex Systems." In *Hierarchy Theory. The Challenge of Complex Systems*, edited by Howard H. Pattee. New York: George Braziller, 1973, 3–27.

Skok, James E. "Policy Issue Network and the Public Policy Cycle: A Structural–Functional Framework for Public Administration." *Public Administration Review* 55(4) (1995): 325–332.

Slaughter, Sheila, and Gary Rhoades. *Academic Capitalism and the New Economy: Markets, State, and Higher Education*. Baltimore: Johns Hopkins University Press, 2004.

Smith, Martin J. *Pressure, Power and Policy: State Autonomy and Policy Networks in Britain and the United States*. New York: Harvester Wheatsheaf, 1993.

Sørensen, Eva, and Jacob Torfing. "Network Politics, Political Capital, and Democracy." *International Journal of Public Administration* 26(6) (2003): 609–634.

Stone, Diane, and Simon Maxwell, eds. *Global Knowledge Networks and International Development*. London and New York: Routledge, 2005.

Teichler, Ulrich, and Jan Sadlak, eds. *Higher Education Research: Its Relationship to Policy and Practice*. Oxford, New York: Pergamon and IAU Press, 2000.

Tomusk, Voldemar. "Enlightenment and Minority Cultures: Central and East European Higher Education Reform Ten Years Later." *Higher Education Policy* 14 (2001): 61–73.

Tomusk, Voldemar. *The Open World and Closed Societies: Essays on Higher Education Policies "in Transition."* New York: Palgrave Macmillan, 2004.

Torres, Carlos A., and Daniel Schugurensky. "The Political Economy of Higher Education in the Era of Neoliberal Globalization: Latin America in Comparative Perspective." *Higher Education* 43(4) (2002): 429–455.

Trick, David W. *Continuity, Retrenchment and Renewal: The Politics of Government–University Relations in Ontario 1985–2002*. Unpublished Ph.D. dissertation. Toronto: University of Toronto, 2005.

Weible, Christopher M., and Paul Sabatier. "Comparing Policy Networks: Marine Protected Areas in California." *Policy Studies Journal* 33(2) (2005): 181–201.

Wilks, Stephen, and Maurice Wright. *Comparative Government–Industry Relations: Western Europe, the United States, and Japan.* Oxford: Clarendon Press, 1987.

Yates, Charlotte. "Labour and Lobbying: A Political Economy Approach." In *Policy Communities and Public Policy in Canada: A Structural Approach*, edited by William D. Coleman, and Grace Skogstad. Mississauga: Copp Clark Pitman, 1990, 266–290.

Part II
Variations on a Governance Theme

8

Effectiveness or Economy?
Policy Drivers in UK Higher Education, 1985–2005

ROGER BROWN

Introduction

There appears to be general agreement that in Britain, as in many other countries, it was in the 1980s that the national government became far more involved in determining the direction, shape and health of the higher education system than hitherto. A series of key policy pronouncements can be identified, starting with the 1985 Green Paper *The Development of Higher Education into the 1990s* (Department for Education and Science, 1985).[1] The others were:

- The White Paper *Higher Education: Meeting the Challenge* (Department for Education and Science, 1987);
- Kenneth Baker's Lancaster Speech (Department for Education and Science, 1989);
- The White Paper *Higher Education: A New Framework* (Department for Education and Science, 1991);
- The introduction of Maximum Aggregate Student Number limits, the Dearing Committee and top-up fees (1993–8); and
- The White Paper *The Future of Higher Education* (Department for Education and Skills, 2003).

It should be noted that with the exception of the last, all of these pronouncements covered the whole of the UK.

In this contribution the author proposes to ask: can an underlying pattern be discerned in these policy pronouncements? If a pattern can be seen, what is it? Do theories or models from political science, public administration or public policy help us understand what was going on? If so, what are they?

The discussion begins by looking at some previous attempts to explain government policies towards higher education since the early 1980s. It then notes a range of relevant ideas from a variety of sources. The notion of "policy drivers" is suggested as meaning continuing underlying factors shaping policy. Two such drivers – "effectiveness" and "economy" – are identified and used to account for the policies adopted. The discussion ends with the thought that the current preference for market-based approaches may dissolve the effectiveness/economy distinction by favoring policies that appear to deliver both objectives simultaneously.

Explaining Government Policies

Various attempts have been made to find a consistent rationale for government policies towards higher education since the early 1980s. Salter and Tapper, in a highly influential series of volumes, pointed to the emergence and dominance of an "economic ideology of education" so that higher education was increasingly seen in terms of its economic relevance (Salter and Tapper, 1981, 1994). In a more recent study Tapper (2007) argues that government policies for higher education reflect the crisis of the British state in the mid-1970s and the consequential move to a new model for delivering public policy. Similarly, Stevens (2005) points to the increasing role of state action and the need, in that author's view, for the universities' dependence on the state to be reduced. By contrast, Kogan and Hanney (2000: 35, 235), in what is so far the most comprehensive account of policy-making over the period – it covers the mid-1970s to the mid-1990s – professed to see no underlying thread at all:

> We therefore look for no single factor affecting change but for the interaction of actors and their historical contexts, and a constant reiteration or connection between them. Intentions were forged partly by belief systems, partly by the power of circumstances, and partly by opportunistic reactions to what might not have been planned or even rationally contemplated . . . Policy-making followed no rational model. Policies were created largely on the hoof and were, as we have said, the product of a complex interplay of context, ideologies, ministers and bureaucracies.

Similarly, Hughes noted: "Notoriously, the higher education policies of British governments have been characterised by pragmatic responses to political purposes, and not by logic, clarity and educational vision" (Hughes, 1998: 89, quoted in Archer, Hutchings and Ross, 2003: 57).

Such a conclusion would naturally be attractive to many policy-makers. For example, Richard Bird, a senior departmental civil servant concerned with higher education at the Department for Education and Science in the late 1980s and early 1990s, stated: "Most of the significant developments of the decade happened in piecemeal and pragmatic fashion. There were certainly some overall trends of policy, though these could by no means be assembled to any grand strategy" (Bird, 1994: 83). As an alternative to these somewhat skeptical perspectives, Longden (2007), drawing on macroeconomic theories of the relations between price stability, employment levels and economic growth, posits a tension, in government higher education policies, between cost consciousness, increased student numbers and quality of provision. At any one time one or two of these requirements could be satisfied but only at the expense of both or one of the others. There are two main difficulties with this. First, it is not clear that there was ever any explicit, serious or continuing concern with quality, at least at the national level (a situation that could, however, be quickly changed if we were ever to get serious price competition in the main undergraduate market – see Brown, 2006). Second, both increased student numbers and quality can easily be collapsed, without loss of explanatory power, into different forms of "effectiveness." The present author contends that, with respect to government higher education policy-making between the early 1980s and the mid-2000s, it is possible to find two underlying "policy drivers." These are called, with no great originality, "effectiveness" and "economy." Inevitably, these are often in tension, if not conflict. Before we go too much further, it may be worth offering some definitions.

Policy Drivers

The term "policy driver" is used here to note a particular kind of factor in policy-making. Such a factor is both significant and persistent. While it may not necessarily be the reason why any particular policy was adopted, it will usually be there in the background. So, to have any chance of understanding a policy properly, a policy driver is always something to be taken into account.[2] It has only been possible to find one reference to "policy drivers" in the higher education literature. This was in the recent article about post-war policy-making by Shattock (2006). But Shattock uses the term in a rather different sense, to indicate whether a particular policy was the result primarily of causes internal or external to the higher education system. When we move to the wider political science literature, however, we find some suggestive theories about how certain factors appear to persist in policy-making.

Cyclical Theories of Policy-Making

Namenwirth (1973) argues, on the basis of a study of American political party platforms between 1854 and 1964, that certain "value concerns" ("Goal states, or conceptions about the desirable level of goods"; 1973: 650) recur in both long (148-year) and short (48-year) cycles: what he calls the Wheel of Time. These value concerns include both efficiency (the use made of the means of production) and inequities in wealth distribution and access to power. Jeroen Huisman has confirmed that this theory holds true for housing planning and higher education in the Netherlands (Huisman, personal communication). De Vries (1999) sees a similar recurrent process at work in the development of post-war policies in Europe, so that "the 1980s were characterised by an emphasis on efficiency and process orientation, instead of effectiveness and goal orientation" (De Vries, 1999: 499). Linked to this is the notion that, because of the scarcity of available political resources, governments can attend to only one problem, or one aspect of a problem, at a time, what Namenwirth and Weber refer to as the "relative attention paradigm" (Namenwirth and Weber, 1987). This can be seen in the focus from the early 1990s on the issue of funding to the exclusion of wider questions, such as the overall shape and structure of the system.

There are two further ideas in the wider literature that are also relevant to British government policy-making on higher education during the period under review. These are, first, the theory of the "issue attention cycle" (Peters and Hogwood, 1985, building on Downs, 1972), based on a study of organizational change in the

American federal bureaucracy that almost all policy areas have at least one clear peak decade of organizational activity. Second, there is the notion that, very often, policy-making is a process of adjusting and borrowing "possible answers to questions which have been, seem or are expected to be, successful in other policy areas, other administrative units or even in other countries" (De Vries, 1999: 491). This can be seen in the explicit espousal of market-based policies from the late 1980s.

Effectiveness and Economy

Reviewing the different kinds of performance assessment that had by then been developed across the public sector, Pollitt (1987) drew a distinction between those that had efficiency as their main driver, and which were usually sponsored or imposed from above (what he therefore christened "efficiency from above" or "EFA" schemes), and those that were more concerned with quality and effectiveness and grew up in particular institutional settings (1987: 88–89). These two approaches were fundamentally incompatible:

> The EFA model sees individuals as needing to be formally "incentivised," and sanctioned, to ensure sufficiently rapid change. Thus it is management's task to create such a framework, and to excite otherwise subdued or dormant aspirations for improved performance. Hierarchy, competitiveness and the "right to manage" are implicit throughout this approach. The professional development model, on the other hand, is more egalitarian, less individualistic, more communitarian. Professionals co-operate to improve each other's performances, and monetary rewards (or negative sanctions for persistent under-performance) are not necessary to sustain the process.
> (Pollitt, 1987: 94; see also Elton, 1986)

The present author's use of the terms "efficiency" and "effectiveness" is somewhat different. Even though it really means the same thing – maximizing the outputs from a given level of inputs or achieving the same level of outputs with a lower level of inputs – he prefers "economy" to "efficiency" because, as will be seen, an underlying and continuing concern on the part of government has been to minimize claims on the Exchequer. "Effectiveness" in this context means the capacity of higher education – in this instance, a higher education system composed of mainly publicly funded universities and colleges – to satisfy specified needs or interests (mainly, in the period concerned, economic needs or interests). In what follows it will be found that the economy driver takes many forms, for example, rationalization of structures, the desire to limit public expenditure, or obtain as much private investment as possible for a given level of public investment. Similarly, effectiveness is sometimes seen in terms of better serving the needs of the economy, at others in terms of increasing participation generally or by certain specified groups. Unfortunately they are often to be found side by side in the same policy document, for example, in Shirley Williams' thirteen points of 1969 (see below).

The author first came across the effectiveness/economy dichotomy when he was studying the post-war planning of further and higher education in London up to the early 1970s (Howell and Brown, 1983). It was manifested in two ways. First, there was an evident tension between the lofty aspirations for post-sixteen education in the 1944 Education Act and the realities of implementation as the limitations of the post-war British economy took hold. Second, there was a contradiction, found in successive drafts of the 1965 White Paper *A Plan for Polytechnics* (Department for Education and Science, 1965), between what finally emerged as an expansionary document and the rationalizing intentions that were much more evident in the earlier drafts (Brown, 1977). The author came across the tension again in his account of the evolution of quality assurance in UK higher education after 1992, where it helped to account for the seemingly unending disputes about the national quality assurance regime up to 2001 (Brown, 2004). It is now proposed to examine the main government policies towards higher education since the early 1980s to see how far they reflect this same dichotomy.

The Origins of Effectiveness and Economy

The 1985 Green Paper on higher education *The Development of Higher Education into the 1990s* (Department for Education and Science, 1985) has been chosen as the starting point for this analysis. The author believes that it was the first government attempt to set out an agenda for higher education, to establish some criteria for determining higher education's effectiveness. We shall come to the Green Paper in a moment. The economy driver can be traced much further back. Reference has just been made to the early drafts of the 1965 White Paper *A Plan for Polytechnics.* But the author would accord a special position to Shirley Williams' thirteen points of 1969.[3] Kogan and Hanney (2000) also draw attention to the ending of the quinquennial funding system (the last was in 1972–1977), the introduction of higher fees for overseas students in 1979, and the 1981 cuts, which saw the first move towards research selectivity through the UGC allocations that year (2000: 89).[4, 5]

Kogan and Hanney argue that these various economizing policies and decisions were essentially a response to the expansion in student demand from the mid-1970s. But it seems clear that the economy driver was present much earlier. Moreover, while the expansion undoubtedly intensified concerns about the capability of the economy to sustain it, the expansion also led to questions about whether the resources allocated were being put to the best – i.e. in the government's view, the most relevant – use.

The 1985 Green Paper

Another way of putting it might be to say that, until the mid-1980s, the government's agenda for higher education – in so far as it had an agenda for higher education – was largely about "economy," namely the view that in achieving its objectives (which the government didn't question), higher education should do so as economically as possible. The Green Paper, however, attempted to suggest, for the first time, what those goals and objectives should be. The essential message was given in the first main paragraph:

> The economic performance of the United Kingdom since 1945 has been disappointing compared to the achievements of others. The Government believes that it is vital for our higher education to contribute more effectively to the improvement of the performance of the economy . . . The Government is particularly concerned by the evidence that the societies of our competitors are producing, and plan in the future to produce, more qualified scientists, engineers, technologists and technicians than the United Kingdom.
>
> (Department for Education and Science, 1985: paragraphs 1.2 to 1.3)

This shortage of appropriate manpower could be made good only if higher education was sufficiently flexible to respond quickly to new needs, which required changes in universities' management structures and practices. In addition, institutions needed to be concerned with attitudes to the world outside higher education, and in particular to industry and commerce, and to be aware of "anti-business" snobbery; to go out to develop their links with industry and commerce; and to have strong connections with their local communities. Other main themes were raising standards (by paying continuing attention to the quality of teaching), celebrating the systemic diversity offered by the polytechnics, and protecting freedom of speech within the law. But, and notwithstanding the expected decline in student numbers in the 1990s, there were also a number of economic concerns, notably that universities should reduce their reliance on public finance (by increasing their income from outside sources) and that research funding should be more efficient, which would require concentration in "strong centers." These economy themes were picked up in the final chapter. This set out what the government would take into account in determining its longer-term policy towards higher education:

(i)   the demand for initial higher education;

(ii)   the country's need for qualified manpower and the case for a continued switch of emphasis in higher education towards science and technology;

(iii) the need to stimulate in-career vocational education, professional updating and other forms of continuing education;

(iv) the need to provide adequately for fundamental and applied research and to ensure that the resources available are effectively deployed;

(v)   the scope for increased economy and efficiency in, and between, higher education institutions, including the further rationalisation of provision and the need to consider its optimum distribution between the sectors;

(vi) the outcome of the review of student support, and in particular the extent to which students, their families and other sponsors might progressively assume greater responsibility for their participation in higher education.

(Department for Education and Science, 1985: paragraph 9.11)

The 1987 White Paper and the Subsequent Legislation

This emphasis on economic relevance and links with business was continued in the 1987 White Paper *Higher Education: Meeting the Challenge* (Department for Education and Science, 1987). Indeed, "serving the economy more effectively" was stated as the first "Aim and Purpose" of higher education in the covering message from the Secretaries of State. Accordingly, the White Paper contained a number of statements such as:

> The Government and its central funding agencies will do all they can to encourage and reward approaches by higher education institutions which bring them closer to the world of business. The Government will correspondingly encourage industry and commerce to recognise the value, to themselves and more widely, of working closely with education. Significant advance on these fronts has been made in recent years – witness the doubling of universities' research income from industry since 1981 – but as yet links between higher education and industry in Britain remain less close than in many of our competitor countries.
>
> (Department for Education and Science, 1987: paragraph 1.6)

The White Paper took a more positive view of future demand than the Green Paper.[6] This could be justified by increased requirements for "highly qualified manpower" (especially scientists and engineers); by the widening of access, especially for applicants with vocational qualifications, from women and from mature entrants; and by an expansion in continuing education, especially professional updating. These effectiveness factors were balanced by economy ones. Greater attention was to be given to the quality of teaching. Research selectivity was to be taken further (the first Research Assessment Exercise was held in 1986). Tenured contracts for new appointments were to be abolished. Greater use was to be made of performance indicators and efficiency studies. There were also to be further "improvements" in institutional management.

Both effectiveness and economy were used to justify the structural changes announced in the White Paper – the incorporation of the polytechnics and large colleges and the placing of these institutions and the existing universities under two new funding councils answerable to the Secretary of State. Replacing the existing funding through grants, a new system of "contracting," would:

- encourage institutions to be enterprising in attracting contracts from other sources, particularly the private sector, and thereby to lessen their present degree of dependence on public funding;
- sharpen accountability for the use of the public funds which will continue to be required;
- strengthen the commitment of institutions to the delivery of the educational services which it is agreed with the new planning and funding body they should provide.

> (Department for Education and Science, 1987: paragraph 4.17)

Legislation to give effect to the White Paper was enacted in 1988 in the Education Reform Act.[7]

Kenneth Baker's Lancaster Speech

The overall theme of Kenneth Baker's speech at Lancaster University in January 1989 (Department for Education and Science, 1989) was the need for expansion to enable the proper development of British society and economy:

> The record of the expansion of higher education in the 1980s was a good one that stands to the credit of all who have made it possible. But there is scope over the next twenty-five years for even greater advance. Assuming an average annual economic growth rate of 2 percent, in twenty-five years' time Britain will be more than half again as rich as it is today. That is to say, our per capita income will be more or less at the same level as it is in the United States currently. This more affluent society will be built on better education and will itself be more highly educated. The foundation of London University, to which I have just referred, meant that higher education would never again be the exclusive privilege of ecclesiastics and patricians. It enabled wider aspirations to be met. So was the great expansion of the past twenty-five years. In the next twenty-five years, I have little doubt that higher education will continue to play this liberating role. We are looking to a period in which aspirations to higher education and participation in it will continue to increase.
>
> (Department for Education and Science, 1989: paragraph 7)

The government would do its part to make this possible:

> We have already indicated our intention that, notwithstanding the fall in the number of eighteen-year-olds, the numbers in higher education should be sustained in the mid-1990s. The evidence to date is that we shall succeed in this. To do so means that we will have substantially to increase the participation rate among eighteen-year-olds-from nearly 15 percent at present to something approaching 20 percent. That is [sic] a very substantial achievement.
>
> (Department for Education and Science, 1989: paragraph 10)

To sustain this demand, the government would increase the proportion of funding received for teaching by institutions coming through the tuition fee at the expense of the proportion coming through funding council grants. More importantly, the Treasury would not impose a cash limit on the funds allocated to tuition fees.

The speech was expansionary not only in terms of the government's aspirations for numbers but in terms of what was meant by higher education: "We shall have to be careful not to generalize about 'quality' on the basis of traditions of cultural exclusiveness which belongs to the world of 3 percent participation in higher education and which are neither appropriate nor sustainable in a world of 30 percent participation" (1989: paragraph 24). Again: "mass higher education will need to be more varied both in the nature of the courses it offers and in the levels at which it offers them" (1989: paragraph 25). However, this would also require a response on the part of the universities: "our higher education institutions will have to reorient themselves in new ways to recruit students not drawn from the traditional eighteen-year class, and to attract groups currently underrepresented" (1989: paragraph 10).

How would this be achieved? The Secretary of State contrasted a continental European approach with an American one. The former would involve "an increasingly state-funded and therefore state-organized 'system' of higher education". However, because public funding was limited, "the effect will be to offer a limited variety of institutional structures and missions, providing a range of broadly similar experiences to all, and producing a range of similar outcomes for all" (1989: paragraph 18). However, "if we can expand higher education on the basis of the American pattern, involving a much greater engagement of private resources, then it will be possible to secure much greater differentiation and diversity, and correspondingly greater institutional autonomy and flexibility" (1989: paragraph 32). Such "broadening [of] the financial platform for the future expansion of higher education" was also behind the government's proposal to introduce top-up loans for students (to supplement and eventually replace grants), an economy driver.

The speech also confirmed the government's selectivity policy in relation to the funding of research even if it meant questioning the assumption that all teaching in higher education should be accompanied by research and that funding for the universities should be provided on the basis that 40 percent of all academic time should be devoted to research. In a classic piece of government sophistry the Secretary of State said: "to say that the teaching and research functions may continue to be integrated is not to say that the funding of those functions must necessarily be integrated" (1989: paragraph 29).

The 1991 White Paper and the Subsequent Legislation

The 1991 White Paper *Higher Education: A New Framework* (Department for Education and Science, 1991) continued the broadly expansionary theme of the Baker speech: "More young people than ever before are staying on in full-time education after the age of 16. One in five of all 18 to 19 year olds go into higher education each year compared with one in seven at the time of the 1987 White Paper" (1991: paragraph 7). By 2000, the government expected that "approaching" one in three of all eighteen- to nineteen-year-olds would enter full-time higher education; there would also be increased demand from adults and for part-time study. Institutions had been successfully incentivized to respond to this demand by the government's decision to increase the level of publicly funded tuition fees paid as part of the student award (by reducing the level of tuition support paid through Funding Council grant). Higher education had also responded to the need to take increasing account of the country's economic requirements, though student demand for courses in science, engineering and technology had been "less buoyant than the Government would have wished" (1991: paragraph 7). Altogether, higher education was becoming more successful in responding to social and economic needs.

But the main policy announced in the White Paper, and reflected in its title – the decision to enable the polytechnics and some colleges to acquire a university title and to put these institutions and the existing universities under a single funding council – was driven by economy: "The Government believes that the real key to achieving cost effective expansion lies in greater competition for funds and students. That can best be achieved by breaking down the increasingly artificial and unhelpful barriers between the universities, and the polytechnics and colleges" (1991: paragraph 17). Paragraph 24 set out the benefits:

- all institutions will compete for funds and students on an equal basis;
- unjustified differences in funding methodologies will be eliminated. Present expenditure plans allow broadly similar levels of unit public funding for teaching costs in each sector. It should therefore be possible to eliminate differences between the sector's funding methodologies without elaborate transitional arrangements;
- for capital spending priorities and allocations will be determined across higher education;
- quality will be taken into account on a common basis in the funding of all higher education institutions;
- funds for pump-priming initiatives will be offered more readily on a comparable basis across higher education; and
- there will be increased scope for coordination and rationalisation across the whole of higher education.

Economy was also the main driver for the changes in quality assurance that accompanied the abolition of the binary line, as the present author has already shown (Brown, 2004: 39–41).[8] In one sense the abolition of the "binary line" was inevitable once the polytechnics and colleges had been incorporated. Indeed this is a classic example of what Easton (1965) once defined as a "breeder demand" whereby one policy choice leads ineluctably to another. Once the polytechnics were given essentially the same corporate status as the universities it became much harder to distinguish them. But the author also believes that the catalyst for the abolition of the binary line was the refusal of the existing universities, unlike the polytechnics, to take part in what was, in effect, an auction of funded undergraduate places by the new funding councils (Taggart, 2004). At any rate, the necessary legislation was enacted the following year.

The Introduction of Maximum Aggregate Student Numbers, Dearing and Private Funding

By 1992/3, and as a result of these policies, student numbers had rocketed. In autumn 1993 the government stated its intention to curb the expansion by introducing strict limits – Maximum Aggregate Student Numbers (or MASNs) – on the recruitment of publicly funded students. These would apply from the 1994/5 academic year. These restrictions on numbers were accompanied by restraints on expenditure more generally (the economy driver to the fore). The resultant squeeze on income led in the autumn of 1995 to a revolt by the vice-chancellors, with the Main Committee of the Committee of Vice-Chancellors and Principals (now Universities UK) agreeing that if something was not done about funding levels, individual universities should seriously consider levying (illegal) "top-up" fees. The government's response – arrived at after informal consultation with the Labour opposition – was to establish a National Committee of Inquiry under Sir Ron (now Lord) Dearing.[9] The committee's terms of reference were deliberately set very broad: it had been more than thirty years since the only previous comparable exercise, the Robbins Committee, which reported in 1965. But it was clear to everyone that the government's main purpose in establishing the committee was to find a politically acceptable means of leveraging private funding for teaching (the economy driver with a vengeance). This was reflected in the very short timescale set, not much more than a year.[10] In the circumstances the Dearing Committee report was a creditable achievement, owing much to Sir Ron's persuasive leadership and the hard work of its secretariat. Nevertheless, it is a fact that the committee's central recommendation as to how the private contribution was to be secured – by graduates in work making a flat rate contribution of around a quarter of the average cost of tuition through an income-contingent mechanism – was rejected by the government in favor of a means-tested "up-front" contribution of £1,000 in the first instance. This may have reflected the new government's decision to stay within the previous administration's spending limits. None of the committee's other recommendations represented such a significant change of policy.[11]

The 2003 White Paper and the Subsequent Legislation

The White Paper *The Future of Higher Education* (Department for Education and Skills, 2003) began with a striking critique of the policies, including particularly the funding policies, of previous governments:

- Higher education must expand to meet rising skill needs.
- The social class gap among those entering university remains too wide.
- Many of our economic competitors invest more in higher education.
- Universities are struggling to employ the best academics.
- Funding per student fell 36 per cent between 1989 and 1997.
- The investment backlog in teaching and research facilities is estimated at £8 billion.
- Universities need stronger links with business and economy [*sic*].

(Department for Education and Skills, 2003: 4)

While the economic links were by now hardy perennials (they had also featured strongly in the then Secretary of State's speech at Greenwich University in February 2000, the new government's main statement of policy in higher education prior to the White Paper), there were new or stronger messages about the need to expand the system (so that "towards" 50 percent of 18–30-year-olds were in some form of higher education at some point in their lives), widen social participation and rebuild the funding base. There was also even greater emphasis than previously on the merits of institutional diversity to permit the system as a whole to respond more effectively to the various demands made upon it.

To enable this effectiveness agenda to be implemented, the main proposal was to replace the up-front means-tested tuition contributions (by now £1,100) with fees of up to £3,000 payable after graduation on an income-contingent basis (virtually the Dearing recommendation that the previous government had rejected). There would also be a partial restoration of means-tested grants, but inflation-proof loans would continue as the main public support for students' living costs. Finally, there were to be substantial increases in funding for research and knowledge transfer. But while the effectiveness agenda may have been dominant, the economy driver was by no means absent. The planned increases in research funding would go disproportionately to a small number of institutions while the funds for knowledge transfer ("to encourage especially the non-research intensive universities") would be at a very modest level as compared with those for teaching, student support and research. There should be more research collaboration. There was to be a new Leadership Foundation to help improve institutional leadership. In spite – or perhaps because – of the failure of Teaching Quality Assessment to differentiate departments by quality of teaching, fresh attempts were to be made to link funding to teaching performance by creating new "Centers of Excellence"; there was also to be a new body, initially the Institute for Learning and Teaching, later the Higher Education Academy, to establish new national standards for higher education teachers. The rules for university title were to be changed to enable colleges without degree-awarding powers to become universities. These efforts to promote competition in teaching – alongside variability of fees – would be accompanied by "better information for students including a new annual student survey and summaries of external examiners' reports to help student choice drive up quality" (Department for Education and Skills, 2003: 7). Even the reduction in "bureaucracy and burdens," which was a major theme of the White Paper, would contribute to the better use of institutions' resources. Above all, the 50 percent participation target was to be achieved chiefly through new two-year, work-focused Foundation Degrees.[12] As the necessary legislation moved through Parliament the government agreed that there would in due course be an independent review of the £3,000 fee cap in the light in particular of the impact on widening participation. This review will take place in 2009. It remains to be seen whether effectiveness or economy will be the main driver in that process.

Conclusion

This has been a somewhat breathless excursion through successive government statements of policy on higher education over the past twenty years. The findings are summarized in Table 8.1.

TABLE 8.1 Policies and Policy Drivers, 1985–2005

Policy	Policy driver (major/minor)
Green Paper, 1985	**effectiveness**, economy
White Paper, 1987	**effectiveness**, economy
Baker speech, 1989	**effectiveness**, economy
White Paper, 1991	**economy**, effectiveness
MASNs, Dearing and private funding, 1993–1997	**economy**, effectiveness
White Paper, 2003	**effectiveness**, economy

As will be clear even from this somewhat cursory account, the main means favored by successive governments for securing economy in higher education's use of resources has been the extension of competition for students and funds. This preference for a market-based approach was first explicitly enunciated, so far as the author is aware, by Kenneth Baker: "The other route ... would see the movement towards mass higher education accompanied by greater institutional differentiation and diversification in a market-led and multi-funded setting" (Department for Education and Science, 1989: paragraph 17).

One of the major attractions of market-based policies to neo-liberal governments is the belief that, at least in principle, these will automatically resolve the conflict between effectiveness and economy. This is on the basis that the effectiveness of a good or service will be determined by the degree of market support it attracts, while economy will be secured by the need to meet that demand in as economical a fashion as possible so as to maximize revenues. The fact that even in conventional goods and services very few markets conform to this model (Kay, 2003) has not weakened its force as an idea. Nor have the warnings about the effects on higher education, such as increased stratification and reduced diversity, based principally on experiences in America and Australia (Brown, 2006), yet had any obvious impact on policy. The tension between effectiveness and economy will be with us for a while yet.

Notes

1   In the UK major statements of government policy normally take the form of White Papers. Provisional statements of policy can be found in Green Papers or sometimes in ministerial speeches.
2   Such a factor may not necessarily be explicit and therefore accessible to researchers/analysts. However, tacit assumptions can often be inferred and anyway the factors are usually made explicit at some point.
3   The points were:

   i)   a reduction or removal of student grant-aid, coupled with a system of loans;
   ii)   a similar policy at the postgraduate level only;
   iii) a more restrictive policy as regards the admission of overseas students;
   iv)   the requirement that grant-aided students should enter specified kinds of employment for a period after graduation, which might have the effect of reducing applications;
   v)   the greater use of part-time and correspondence courses as alternatives to full-time courses;
   vi)   the possibility that the most able should have the opportunity to complete a degree course in two years;

vii)   the possibility of some students not proceeding to the customary three-year course but to a different course lasting only two years and leading to a different qualification;

viii) the possible insertion of a period between school and university, which would give school-leavers a better opportunity to formulate their views as to whether or not they wished to proceed to some form of higher education;

ix)   the more intensive use of buildings and equipment, including the possibility of reorganisation of the academic year;

x)   more sharing of facilities between adjacent institutions;

xi)   more home-based students;

xii)   the development of student housing associations, and other forms of loan-financed provision for student residences;

xiii) some further increase in student/staff ratios.

(Quoted by Kogan and Hanney, 2000: 147)

The points were set out in a memorandum from the Committee of Vice-Chancellors and Principals following a meeting with Mrs Williams and the University Grants Committee in September 1969. Most of the points recurred, and some were implemented.

4   Kogan and Hanney trace the argument about research selectivity as far back as 1965, when the Department for Scientific and Industrial Research came out in favor of it. There was a similar recommendation from the Council for Scientific Policy in 1967. These concerns were echoed by the Association of British Research Councils from 1980. They were picked up by the UGC in its 1984 Strategy for Higher Education. The Research Assessment Exercise (RAE) – the classic economy measure, announced in the UGC's 1984 strategy document – was the result.

5   Michael Shattock considers (personal communication) that the origins of the RAE lie in the unforeseen costs of the subject reviews on which the UGC embarked in the early 1980s. The Oxburgh review of earth sciences had been very expensive. Chemistry, the next subject to be covered, followed by physics, promised to be even more so. The RAE would spread the adjustment costs over a longer period and put the onus on universities' budgets. The present author considers that another benefit of the RAE for the government, as compared with the subject reviews, was that it would put the responsibility for deciding which departments were to be closed or rationalized on the institutions rather than the central authorities. Remarks by the then Higher Education Minister Robert Jackson in Kogan and Hanney (2000: especially p. 100) support this interpretation.

6   The Green Paper projected falls in the numbers of students between 1989 and 1996; subsequent recovery would still mean lower numbers in 1999 than in 1989. The White Paper contained two projections for the same period. One of these showed a similar pattern while the other showed both an increase between 1989 and 1991 (in fact from 1985) and a recovery to the 1991 level by 1999. The author recalls very well the intense arguments in Whitehall about these projections. In the event, of course, student numbers rose steadily from 1985 to 1999.

7   The justification for bringing the polytechnics and colleges under the control of a new national body included the following:

•   the existing national planning arrangements are unsatisfactory. More progress needs to be made in rationalising scattered provision and concentrating effort on strong institutions and departments;

•   progress in educational planning will be even more necessary if the polytechnics and other colleges are to meet the changing needs of industry and commerce in the 1990s and provide in new ways for the wider range of students . . .;

•   this calls for a more effective lead from the centre and the reward of success and enterprise in meeting new national needs, in place of a system giving undue weight to local interests.

(Department for Education and Science, 1987: paragraph 4.6)

8   As the author has shown elsewhere, the basic aim of the new quality assurance arrangements, as with the post-binary regime generally, was to improve efficiency in resource use through greater

competition. Judgments about relative teaching quality would provide a basis for this competition for students and teaching revenues (Brown, 2004: 39–41).

9   This was the one occasion in the author's experience of higher education policy-making since the mid-1980s that the vice-chancellors really had the government, albeit temporarily, "on the run." Generally, it can be said of the vice-chancellors throughout this period that, as Byron famously said of an Irish MP, "they never miss an opportunity to miss an opportunity."

10 The committee was appointed in May 1996 and reported in July 1997.

11 As the author has argued elsewhere (Brown, 2004: 117–118), the committee's recommendations on quality and standards are a partial exception to this statement. Even though in substance they were little more than an elaboration, and in one important respect a perversion, of the Higher Education Quality Council's recommendations on graduate standards (Higher Education Quality Council, 1996), they did lead to a more comprehensive national quality assurance framework which for the first time embraced program quality, academic standards, standards of teaching, quality enhancement and, eventually, information about quality.

12 Foundation Degrees await their historian (if anyone will bother). But the present author is pretty sure that the main policy driver was the Treasury's concern at the public expenditure costs if all of the expansion to 50 percent participation, suddenly announced by the Prime Minister at the 1999 Labour Party Conference, was to be met through three-year, full-time honors degrees. Yet again, a policy driver based on economy was to be justified on the basis of effectiveness.

References

Archer, Louise, Merryn Hutchings, and Alistair Ross. *Higher Education and Social Class.* London and New York: RoutledgeFalmer, 2003.

Bird, Richard. "Reflections on the British Government and Higher Education." *Higher Education Quarterly* 48(2) (1994): 73–86.

Brown, Roger. *Policy Making in Further Education. A Critical Analysis of the Inner London Education Authority's Review of the Organization of its Vocational Further Education Service 1970–1973.* Unpublished Ph.D. thesis. London: University of London, 1977.

Brown, Roger. *Quality Assurance in Higher Education: The UK Experience since 1992.* London and New York: RoutledgeFalmer, 2004.

Brown, Roger. "Higher Education and the Market: Protecting Quality and Diversity in a Market Driven System." *Higher Education Review* 39(1) (2006): 41–54.

De Vries, Michiel. "Developments in Europe: The Idea of Policy Generation." *International Review of Administrative Sciences* 65 (1999): 491–510.

Department for Education and Science. *A Plan for Polytechnics and Other Colleges.* London: Her Majesty's Stationery Office, 1965.

Department for Education and Science. *The Development of Higher Education into the 1990s.* London: Her Majesty's Stationery Office, 1985.

Department for Education and Science. *Higher Education Meeting the Challenge.* London: Her Majesty's Stationery Office, 1987.

Department for Education and Science. *Higher Education: The Next Twenty-five Years.* Speech by the Rt. Hon. Kenneth Baker MP, Secretary of State for Education and Science, at the University of Lancaster, 5 January 1989.

Department for Education and Science. *Higher Education: A New Framework.* London: Her Majesty's Stationery Office, 1991.

Department for Education and Skills. *The Future of Higher Education.* London: The Stationery Office, 2003.

Downs, Anthony. "Up and Down with Ecology – The 'Issue–Attention Cycle.'" *The Public Interest* 28 (1972): 38–50.

Easton, David. *A Systems Analysis of Political Life.* New York and London: Wiley, 1965.

Elton, Lewis. "Quality in Higher Education: Nature and Purpose." *Studies in Higher Education* 11(1) (1986): 83–84.

Higher Education Quality Council. *Graduate Standards Program Final Report*. London: Higher Education Quality Council, 1996.

Howell, David, and Roger Brown. *Educational Policy Making: An Analysis*. London: Heinemann 1983.

Hughes, John. "Review of Pratt, John, 'The Polytechnic Experiment' (Open University Press, 1997)." *Journal of Vocational Education and Training* 50(1) (1998), n.p.

Kay, John. *The Truth about Markets*. London: Allen Lane, 2003.

Kogan, Maurice, and Stephen Hanney. *Reforming Higher Education*. London: Jessica Kingsley, 2000.

Longden, Bernard. "Affordability of English Higher Education: The Uneasy Tension between Quality and Quantity." In *Funding Higher Education: A Question of Who Pays?*, edited by Bernard Longden, and Kerri-Lee Harris. Amsterdam: European Association for Institutional Research, 2007, 79–101.

Namenwirth, J. Zvi. "Wheels of Time and the Interdependence of Value Change in America." *Journal of Interdisciplinary History* 3(4) (1973): 649–683.

Namenwirth, J. Zvi, and Robert P. Weber. *Dynamics of Culture*. Winchester: Allen and Unwin, 1987.

Peters, B. Guy, and Brian Hogwood. "In Search of the Issue–Attention Cycle." *Journal of Politics* 47 (1985): 238–253.

Pollitt, Christopher. "The Politics of Performance Assessment: Lessons for Higher Education?" *Studies in Higher Education* 12(1) (1987): 87–98.

Salter, Brian, and Ted Tapper. *Education, Politics and the State*. London: Grant McIntyre, 1981.

Salter, Brian, and Ted Tapper. *The State and Higher Education*. London: Woburn Press, 1994.

Shattock, Michael. "Policy Drivers in UK Higher Education in Historical Perspective: 'Inside out,' 'outside in' and the Contribution of Research." *Higher Education Quarterly* 60(2) (2006): 130–140.

Stevens, Robert. *From University to Uni: The Politics of Higher Education in England since 1944*. London: Politico's, 2005.

Taggart, G.J. *A Critical Review of the English Funding Body for Higher Education in the Relationship between the State and Higher Education in the Period 1945–2003*. Unpublished D.Ed. thesis. Bristol: University of Bristol, 2004.

Tapper, Ted. *The Governance of British Higher Education*. Dordrecht: Springer, 2007.

9

Good Governance and Australian Higher Education
An Analysis of a Neo-liberal Decade

LEO GOEDEGEBUURE, MARTIN HAYDEN AND V. LYNN MEEK

Introduction

The beginning of the twenty-first century saw the foundations of the corporate world shaken. Major companies such as Enron and Worldcom collapsed and reports of scandals and corporate greed made headline news for months on end. In 2008 what has become known as the sub-prime crisis not only highlights the global interconnectedness of financial markets but raises questions about oversight and control. And in many of our established democracies, governments and political parties increasingly are struggling either to keep or restore the trust of their electorates.

Taken at face value, the above description could easily be taken as a case of poor governance. And if it referred to the state of affairs in a developing nation, this most certainly would be the conclusion reached by international agencies such as the World Bank and the International Monetary Fund. But it is not a reflection on a so-called third world country but an accurate statement on the developed world. And thus it raises the question of how this has been possible, which directly links to the concept of corporate governance. It has also been the trigger for a special issue on governance in higher education, which attempted to address issues of governance, control, accountability and responsibility from a variety of perspectives in a number of countries (Goedegebuure and Hayden, 2007).

The current chapter is an attempt to take some of the insights gained in the previous exercise a step further. Rather than focusing on corporate governance *per se*, we try to explore the concept of good governance – the opposite of the poor governance identified above – and ask to what extent this can be used as an analytical, rather than a normative, instrument to address governance of a higher education system. As our empirical case we take the recently ended decade of neo-liberal governance in Australia under Prime Minister John Howard.

We start with a discussion on the concept of good governance and will propose the use of a set of principles that appears applicable to public sector governance. This is followed by a brief sketch of the policy environment and specific policy developments that have characterized the way in which the respective Howard governments over the period 1996–2007 addressed the higher education sector. In the more reflective third section of the chapter we try to put this empirical part into perspective, which will then lead us into the question of to what extent the principles of good governance can be applied and what this means for a conceptual approach to the study of higher education governance at the systems level.

Governance, Corporate Governance, Public Governance and Good Governance

Governance, though intuitively simple, is quite hard to pin down in a formal, conceptual sense. The OECD is known for its very broad and encompassing conceptualization which "comprises a complex web including the legislative framework, the characteristics of the institutions and how they relate to the whole system, how money is allocated to institutions and how they are accountable for the way it is spent, as well as less formal structures and relationships which steer and influence behaviour" (OECD, 2003: 61). Ferlie, Musselin and Andresani (2007) identify three main conceptions when it comes to higher education governance: the state's role of ensuring the autonomy of higher education; the state as a mediator of societal interests orienting the development of higher education, also known as the interventionist state; and the state as stimulator of the strength of market forces as well as the detector, preventer and repair man of market failures. This conceptualization takes us close to the familiar terrain of triangles of coordination (Clark, 1983), governmental steering (van Vught, 1989), New Public Management (Pollitt and Bouckaert, 2004; Amaral, Meek and Larsen, 2003) and markets in higher education (Dill, 1996; Goedegebuure et al., 1993). Gallagher (2001) sees governance as "the structure of relationships that brings about organizational coherence, authorized policies, plans and decisions, and accounts for their probity, responsiveness and cost-effectiveness" (quoted in Reed, Meek and Jones, 2002: xxvii). From the above it follows that governance can be seen as a relational concept that includes leadership, management and administration, and, somewhat more implicitly, a sense of purpose and direction, in our case for higher education. In other words, governance is about both structures and behavior (see Goedegebuure and Hayden (2007) for an elaboration of this point).

In the public sector, the issue of governance has been under debate for at least the last two decades. It is often tied to the debate around the introduction of New Public Management (NPM) and probably is best illustrated by the case of the United Kingdom. Here NPM featured prominently – and in its "hard" version – during the early 1980s Thatcher period. But a shift towards the more behavioral aspects of public sector governance occurred in the mid-1990s. An example of this was the establishment in 1994 by UK Prime Minister John Major of a Committee on Standards in Public Life, with a brief "[t]o examine current concerns about standards of conduct of all holders of public office, including arrangements relating to financial and commercial activities, and make recommendations as to any changes in present arrangements which may be required to ensure the highest standards of propriety in public life" (Committee on Standards in Public Life, 1994: 1). It is interesting to note that the committee, which continues to report annually, was established well before the earlier-mentioned corporate sector blow-out of the early 2000s. The need for the committee indicates that, even in the early 1990s, it was obvious that a straightforward application of NPM principles to the public sector could not stop excesses – the period prior to its establishment was one of considerable loss of public trust in the public sector in Britain because of substandard performance and the dysfunctional delivery of services. Under its first chairman, Lord Nolan, the committee developed its "Seven Principles of Public Life," to be applied to all in the public service to address the widening gap between the public and the public service. These were:

- selflessness
- integrity
- objectivity
- accountability
- openness
- honesty
- leadership.

A similar logic applied in the principles drawn up by the European Commission in its 2001 White Paper on European governance. The paper starts as follows:

> Today, political leaders throughout Europe are facing a real paradox. On the one hand, Europeans want them to find solutions to the major problems confronting our societies. On the other hand, people increasingly distrust institutions and politics or are simply not interested in them. The problem is acknowledged by national parliaments and governments alike. It is particularly acute at the level of the European Union. Many people are losing confidence in a poorly understood and complex system to deliver the policies that they want.
> (Commission of the European Communities, 2001: 3)

The Commission presented five principles of good governance, stressing that these should apply to all levels of government, underpinning democracy and the rule of law. The principles were:

- openness
- participation
- accountability
- effectiveness
- coherence.

There clearly is overlap with the UK principles of public life, though the Commission's emphasis was somewhat different in that it sought explicitly to address a need for inclusiveness in the development and execution of its policies. Importance was attached, for example, to the need to replace linear policy-making from above with "a virtuous circle, based on feedback, networks and involvement from policy creation to implementation at all levels" (2001: 11). It is in these notions of openness, inclusiveness and interaction that the main parallel with the corporate governance debate is to be found. Further work in this area also reflects this complementarity, though not all of it is equally useful for our purposes. In Australia, a joint committee (Good Governance Advisory Group, 2004) in Victoria developed guidelines for good governance by local governments. It defines good governance as participatory, consensus oriented, accountable, transparent, responsive, effective and efficient, equitable and inclusive, and law abiding. The problem with such a definition is that from an analytical perspective it is so encompassing it hardly provides guidance. More focus can be found in the six principles that form the core of the UK's Good Governance Standard for Public Services, developed in 2004 by the Langlands Committee, which further developed the Nolan principles. The six principles (OPM and CIPFA, 2004: 5) are:

1 Good governance means focusing on the organisation's purpose and on outcomes for citizens and service users.
2 Good governance means performing effectively in clearly defined functions and roles.
3 Good governance means promoting values for the whole organisation and demonstrating the values of good governance through behaviour.
4 Good governance means taking informed, transparent decisions and managing risk.
5 Good governance means developing the capacity and capability of the governing body to be effective.
6 Good governance means engaging stakeholders and making accountability real.

A recent review of the usefulness and adoption of the principles (OPM, 2007: 2) shows that "the six principles are widely accepted and that current guidance to public services is now either derived from, or is very similar to, the principles in the Standard." Though primarily intended for use in public sector organizations, the review proposes to apply good governance more widely in central government, including using the Standard as a benchmarking tool, as well as making the case for strong governance as the foundation for better public services. It continues that "This might include research into the link between good governance and good outcomes, poor governance and poor outcomes" (2007: 4). While the latter is a bridge too far for our purposes, in this chapter we intend to take up the challenge of applying these principles to analyze the way in which Australian higher education has been governed in the period 1996–2007.

A Brief Sketch of Australian Higher Education Policy, 1996–2007

In 1996, a Liberal/National conservative coalition was elected to government; it remained in power until late 2007. The Commonwealth budget statement in 1996 introduced significant new cost savings to higher education, including an increase in the Higher Education Contribution Scheme (HECS) charge (requiring a contribution from students of 20 percent of the average cost of studies), the introduction of three different HECS payment bands, the setting of a substantially lower income threshold for the repayment of HECS, the introduction of optional full fee-paying domestic student places in undergraduate courses, and the phasing out of government financial support for postgraduate courses. In addition, operating grants to universities were to be reduced by 5 percent over three years, and the government indicated that it would provide no financial supplementation for academic salary increases.

In 1998, a committee appointed by the Commonwealth to report on higher education financing and policy simply restated the policy perspectives of the government. On the matter of funding, for example, the committee argued: "The present funding framework does not assist, or provide incentives for, institutions to manage effectively. Governance structures hamper management and there are no incentives for institutions to be aware of their costs or to minimise them" (Review of Higher Education Financing and Policy, 1998: 89). Also in 1998, restrictions on the ability of universities to charge fees to domestic undergraduate students were further lifted. Universities were permitted to enroll up to 25 percent of domestic students in a course on a full fee-paying basis. In fact, less than 1 percent of domestic students ever took advantage of this option, though in some individual high-demand courses the rate of take-up was much larger than this.

In 1999, a fully performance-based funding approach was introduced for research and research training. This approach was consolidated in 2001 with the introduction of a national competitive research grants system, the establishment of the Australian Research Council as an independent statutory authority responsible for the national allocation of research funds, and the promise of the provision of a substantial boost to research spending under a policy entitled Backing Australia's Ability.

In 2000, there were further changes to the HECS. These raised the contributions students were required to make to approximately 32 percent of the average cost of studies. In 2002, the Commonwealth Minister for Education, Science and Training conducted a review of the higher education sector to determine areas in need of further change. The review involved the production of a series of discussion papers, followed by consultation with universities, student groups and other stakeholders. One conclusion reached was that "the current arrangements for funding universities were not sustainable and would, in the longer term, lead to an erosion of the excellent reputation of our universities" (Nelson, 2004: 3). However, this conclusion was not interpreted as implying that the Commonwealth should be investing more heavily in Australia's university system. Rather, it was the basis for the Commonwealth arguing that the users of the higher education system – that is, students – should be paying more, and that even more efficiencies within the system were required.

Late in 2003, the Commonwealth approved an extensive package of higher education reforms for implementation from 2005, including provisions permitting public universities to enroll up to 35 percent of domestic students in a course on a full fee-paying basis, introducing a new loans program to enable all domestic full fee-paying students to borrow funds to finance their studies, and making additional Commonwealth funding for individual universities conditional upon compliance with prescribed governance protocols and workplace reforms. It also provided for further expansion of the number of Commonwealth-funded places in higher education and for the establishment of a number of programs to allocate funds to specific areas in higher education (for example, improvements in the quality of teaching and curriculum, increased participation in higher education by indigenous peoples, and incentive schemes to encourage workplace reforms consistent with government policies on labor market deregulation).

Importantly, significant changes were made to HECS, for implementation in 2005. The three different payment bands approved in 1996 "to reflect more appropriately the balance of public and private returns to higher education, the relative costs of courses and the earning potential of graduates in particular fields" (DEST, 2002b: 7) were retained. From 2005, universities were to be permitted (except in two national priority areas: nursing and education) to add a premium of up to 25 percent to the charge imposed within these HECS bands. Approximately one-half of all universities have opted to impose the premium, which has not been popular with students. The stated intention for this initiative was that: "As student contribution levels vary between courses and higher education providers, higher education providers will become more competitive in terms of cost and quality, and will focus more on what is important to students" (Commonwealth of Australia, 2004: 6).

An undertaking given in the 2003 budget statement that the Minister would review the cost adjustment indexation mechanism for universities had not been addressed by the Commonwealth by 2007. Since 1996, the Commonwealth has not been applying a realistic cost adjustment indexation mechanism to higher education, resulting in a steady decline in real levels of public expenditure on higher education. It is estimated that in 2003, for example, the shortfall in funding for universities in terms of what they should have received from the Commonwealth had an appropriate index been applied was as much as 10 percent (AVCC, 2003: 1). As part of the 2007 election campaign, a new fund, the Higher Education Endowment Fund, was established as a permanent fund upon which individual institutions could draw for infrastructural and research investments.

Reflecting on Higher Education Governance in Australia

Having thus briefly highlighted Australian higher education policy, in our analysis we will focus on three topics that dominated the discussion during the period 1996–2007: the shift from New Public Management to neo-liberalism whereby the market "moved from means to end"; the area of institutional governance that has been very much the focus of governmental attention; and the direct control that respective Commonwealth ministers have exerted over the higher education sector.

From New Public Management to Neo-liberalism: The Increasing Importance of the Market

To be able fully to grasp what has happened over the last decade, it is necessary to trace developments back to the early 1980s. In 1983, after eight years in opposition,

Labor returned to power with a strong desire to portray itself as a sound and responsible economic manager. A particular commitment was the reform of the public service. In 1987, following its re-election, a second phase of reform was initiated. In a move clearly intended to allow direct ministerial control over the implementation of social and economic policy, the number of independent statutory authorities was slashed and many of their functions were given back to departmental heads, who reported directly to ministers. These measures were implemented in the belief that "for many purposes government departments have the decided advantage of making the relevant Minister directly responsible for the effectiveness and efficiency of administration and of saving costs through the use of long established administrative machinery" (Williams, 1988: 2).

The approach to public service management adopted by the Commonwealth at the time was by no means unique to Australia and fits the label of New Public Management. The approach entails "a preference for market mechanisms of governance, more business-like management of public agencies, the minimisation of public bureaucracy, a focus on clear responsibility and accountability for results and the empowerment of consumers of government services" (Zifcak, 1997: 107). It did not take long for this approach to impact on universities. From 1989 onwards, universities were required to negotiate directly with the Commonwealth for resources and were made more directly accountable for the expenditure of their Commonwealth grants. University managers were prevailed upon to adopt the tools of New Public Management, including mission statements, performance indicators, outcomes-based evaluation processes, systems for continuous improvement, and so on. Vice-chancellors came to be widely referred to as "chief executive officers." Academic staff willing to undertake executive and senior management functions within universities began to be offered attractive salary packages for doing so. And the rhetoric about students as consumers became widespread. The trend was fueled by the parallel development after 1989 of a market-oriented approach to the recruitment of fee-paying overseas students. Which goes to say that already, from the 1980s, the higher education sector was subject to reform and the practices of New Public Management.

In 1996, following the Liberal/National coalition's return to government, however, a new and additional dynamic became evident: the coalition's all-pervading commitment to the ideology of neo-liberalism; that is, a public policy agenda characterized by the desire to extend market relationships and private ownership to all areas of social and economic activity. Its principal manifestations in higher education from 1996 onward included a marked increase in the extent to which students were made responsible for the cost of their studies, a heightened expectation of accountability by universities to the Commonwealth for their expenditure of operating and other specific Commonwealth grants, an increased tendency for the Commonwealth to provide funds tied to specific priorities or intended to be spent in particular ways that supported the social and economic priorities of the government, and an increase in the pressure on universities to be entrepreneurial in the pursuit of resources required to remain financially viable. A further manifestation was a preoccupation in the Commonwealth with the progressive elimination of all forms of collective bargaining by the major national union representing university employees, and with workplace-based reforms to employment practices intended to result in increased efficiencies in the utilization of public funds.

It is in relation to the funding of higher education that one of the most significant manifestations of neo-liberalism is to be found. Australian higher education is predominantly "public" – there are thirty-seven public universities and only two private universities, both quite small. The system's public status derives from the fact that its assets are publicly owned and that it has always been publicly funded. Since 1988, however, but particularly since 1996, there has been a marked diversification in the funding base of the system. In 2003, for example, the system received only 41 percent of its funds in the form of Commonwealth grants (AVCC, 2004: table A21). In 1992, by comparison, 66 percent of its funds were through Commonwealth grants. Further, the absolute magnitude of the Commonwealth's total investment in higher education substantially declined over the period from 1996 to 2007.

It is evident that neo-liberalist ideology has resulted in a striking deterioration in teaching and research infrastructure over recent years, with adverse effects on the quality of academic life for staff and students (Coates et al., 2008). Staff-to-student ratios in universities have deteriorated; there is an increasing reliance upon casual academic staff appointments; academic salary levels as a proportion of average weekly earnings are in steady decline; and there is a reduced range of opportunities for academic staff to engage in research. At the same time, universities have proven to be remarkably resourceful in finding new non-government sources of funding, particularly from the sale of services overseas and from the commercialization of research. No doubt, the additional scope for them to earn more revenue from increased HECS rates and from fee-paying domestic students will confirm their resourcefulness. As the Australian Vice-Chancellors' Committee has warned, however: "the direct fee income paid by students and their families can never be a complete substitute for investment by the government in the infrastructure and resources (human and capital) that is fundamental to ensuring quality outcomes in teaching and learning" (AVCC, 2001: 2). More broadly, there is concern that the premises of neo-liberalism are incompatible with the nature and purposes of universities. A university system that is "expected to behave like ordinary profit-seeking businesses, utilising corporate management practices, serving consumers in markets, seeking measurable productivity improvements and producing services with controllable quality attributes" may not be addressing its core values and purposes (Karmel, 2002: 2).

Institutional Governance: An Area of Increasing Political and Institutional Interest

There has been a remarkable increase of interest in university councils during the past decade. There was a time when councils were largely invisible, addressing at a leisurely pace the need to provide final approval to university documentation and to address prudential considerations related to the plans brought forward by the administrative machinery of the university. This situation has dramatically changed. University councils are becoming the focus of increased interest within universities because of the importance of the decisions they are being required to make. They are also becoming of political interest, especially to the Commonwealth, because of the delegation of authority to them by the states.

Councils derive their authority from state legislation. The legislation provides them with considerable scope to affect the management, academic profile and internal quality assurance processes of a university. Of special importance is that, as trustees for the state, they can buy property, form companies, enter into partnerships, approve and grant academic awards and, most importantly, appoint the vice-chancellor. Since 1995, when the first substantial report, the Hoare Report (Hoare, 1995), was produced on university councils, various official documents have cataloged perceived weaknesses. That first report identified the need for them to have, among other things, an explicit set of responsibilities, a threshold level of professional knowledge and skills commensurate with the task of governing complex institutions, a strategic focus in their deliberations, and a more refined sense of their role in relation to asset and risk management. Also identified was the need for university councils to be smaller in size, preferably ten to fifteen members, for external members to outnumber internal members, and for potential external members to be identified through an independent professional process.

Since the Hoare Report, councils have engaged in a process of reform that has resulted in smaller memberships (of about twenty-one, on average) and increased thoroughness in the selection of external members (DEST, 2002a: 17). Examples of "best practice" are being widely produced, and annual conferences are now routinely being convened to facilitate benchmarking across universities. There are, nonetheless, perennial problems affecting councils. Within the past few years, for example, there have been well-publicized instances of factionalism within councils and of intense conflicts between councils and the senior academic management of universities. Further, there are continuing expressions of concern that councils are not well equipped to respond promptly and decisively to change, and that council members have a great deal of difficulty in being properly informed about not only the operations of a university but the activities of its controlled entities (2002a: 17–18).

Because councils appoint (and can dismiss) vice-chancellors, they have a pervasive influence on the culture of a university. This influence has for a long time gone unnoticed in most university communities. Recent celebrated cases of councils acting decisively to dismiss their vice-chancellors have provided a reminder of the strength of the latent power of a council. Most recently, councils have been in the public limelight because they have had to sign off on important decisions affecting the welfare of students and the financial health of their institution. It has been for councils to decide, for example, whether to charge the premium of an additional 25 percent on the HECS rates for students. Councils have also had to decide whether to admit fee-paying undergraduate domestic students, and, if so, in what proportions. These decisions have attracted extraordinary attention, no doubt because they have touched a raw nerve with students, who are spending longer hours in paid employment than ever before in order to meet their living expenses. A national survey reported, for example, that seven out of every ten students at university were in paid employment during university semesters – an increase by about one-half since 1984 (Long and Hayden, 2001). Among full-time students, the average number of hours worked by those in paid employment during semester was 15.5 hours per week – a threefold increase since 1984. About 20 percent of respondents in paid employment during semester reported that work adversely affected their study "a great deal," and about 10 percent reported that they "frequently" missed classes because of paid employment during semester.

In 2003, the Commonwealth introduced a statement of National Governance Protocols for Higher Education, with which universities must comply in order to secure additional Commonwealth funds. These identify generically the main responsibility of university councils and require that individual members of councils should be aware of their duties. Of note is a requirement that councils must make available a program of induction and professional development for its members, and that the size of the council must not exceed twenty-two members.

System Governance: Direct Ministerial Control

A relatively recent Commonwealth discussion paper on higher education governance states that: "Over the years Australia has experimented with 'buffer' bodies responsible for making decisions on the allocation of student places and funding, or for advising the Government on policy. Australia does not currently have such a body" (Commonwealth of Australia, 2002). What the statement is really expressing is a complete disinterest on the part of the Commonwealth in ever again having a "buffer" organization between itself and universities. The reasons for this disinterest, while they may relate to the perceived deficiencies of the Commonwealth Tertiary Education Commission during the years prior to its demise in 1987, more likely reflect a desire on the part of the Commonwealth to be able to exercise direct ministerial control over universities whenever considered appropriate. Somewhat contradictory, however, is the fact that in 2001 the Commonwealth established the Australian Research Council as an independent statutory authority to act in a "buffer" capacity in relation to research and research training. Research is not the main area of public expenditure on higher education, however, and in any case decision-making by the council must take place within a framework prescribed by Commonwealth policies, which include the creation of national research priority areas and further enhanced competition and selectivity in research funding both within and between universities. However, it should also be noted that the ARC's independent status has been seriously compromised by the direct interference of the then Minister Brendan Nelson regarding the selection and allocation of research grants, which has resulted in the current restructure of the ARC, including the establishment of an Advisory Council. In the words of the new Minister for Innovation, Industry, Science and Research: "Research is not a political plaything to be toyed with at the whim of the Government" (ARC, 2008). The Advisory Council will provide the CEO of the ARC with "non-binding strategic and policy advice" on "issues relating to the mission of the ARC; policy matters relating to innovation, research and research training; and matters relating to the evaluation of the quality and outcomes of research and research training in an international context" (ARC, 2008).

One of the major challenges of a "buffer" organization between the Commonwealth and the universities is that it must also accommodate the needs of the states. The Commonwealth Tertiary Education Commission, during its existence from 1977 to 1987, developed a complex system of "consultative arrangements" that allowed it to respond to both levels of government. Marshall (1990: 150) describes these as follows. At the beginning of each triennium state authorities and institutions prepared forward proposals which were presented to the relevant sectoral council for consideration. The reports of the three councils were then worked into a comprehensive policy statement by CTEC which was known as Volume 1. This was submitted to the Commonwealth Minister for Education who consulted with his or her state counterparts before taking a final proposal to the cabinet table. The decisions made by cabinet were termed the "guidelines" and constituted CTEC's policy directives. The guidelines became the subject of further negotiation between the commission, the advisory councils and other bodies before specific measures were finalized in Volume 2, which outlined the implementation program.

This complex process of consultation resulted in protracted negotiation and meant that decisions, when finally taken, were the product of a considerable amount of compromise. Marshall (1990: 152) reports that the process worked well for many years because it "fostered a stable and predictable policy environment" and was "internally flexible," and because for many years the commission had "a monopoly of funding, expertise and authority." During the early 1980s, this monopoly was challenged. First, the Commonwealth became convinced that the higher education system could contribute more effectively and directly to national goals than was happening under the commission's supervision. Second, other agencies, including government ministries and other statutory authorities, developed a view that the higher education system was important to the realization of their organizational goals, and so new, disparate and complex pressures from within government came to bear upon the Commonwealth's "guidelines" issued to the commission. Third, the commission itself became overloaded with intractable demands, such as having to restrain the growth of new funded places in higher education because of budgetary constraints imposed by the Commonwealth, while at the same time seeking to achieve equity goals through improvement in the participation rates of disadvantaged groups. Finally, the lengthy consultation process that was once a source of stability and strength became cumbersome against the background of a pressure for rapid political change.

Though the prospects of re-establishing a statutory authority like the commission to act in a "buffer" capacity between the Commonwealth and universities still seems remote, there are strong supporters of the return of such a body. One of these, the founding chair of the commission, has proposed establishing such a body "to promote a plurality of priorities among universities, to ensure their institutional independence, and to provide the Commonwealth Government, the universities themselves and the wider public with a source of objective expert advice on university matters" (Karmel, 2002: 18). Although the proposal was made in 2002 as a reaction to the steady increase of direct ministerial grip on the institutions, the period since then has not seen a decrease of this influence. On the contrary, and as has been highlighted in the previous subsections, in particular in the area of industrial relations the influence of the federal government on institutional affairs has been quite strong. In a cash-strapped system, providing small amounts of money with strings attached does allow the master to choreograph the institutional dancers.

The Principles of Good Governance and Australian Higher Education Governance

Having reflected in some more detail on the policy developments of the last decade and having framed these in a context that at times dates back much further (thereby highlighting the notion of path dependency in higher education), we now explore to what extent the six principles of good governance can help us in furthering our understanding of the Australian case.

Principle 1 related to focusing on the sector's purpose and on outcomes for citizens and service users. In this respect the period 1996–2007 shows a mixed picture. There is no doubt that the coalition government was clear about the purposes it saw for universities, namely as directly contributing to the realization of the government's economic and social-industrial policies. As has been argued in the previous section, the sector itself may not have liked the message, but there was no misunderstanding it in terms of intended outcomes. However, it is less clear that "users of the sector's services" – to use the Langland Committee's terminology – have received a high-quality service as ever more concerns about the impact of decreasing funding on the quality of provision have been raised. Hard data (except for proxy indicators like deteriorating staff/student ratios) do not exist to support the claim of a deterioration in quality, but there is little doubt that the system has come under severe pressure and has reached the limits of its flexibility. As to the taxpayer receiving value for money, it would appear that with the cost shifting to the "user" a sizeable proportion of the taxpayers are paying more. It is difficult to assess with any certainty whether at the system's level this has resulted in "value for money."

Principle 2 relates to clarity in roles and functions. In this respect our conclusions are also mixed. In terms of federal–institution relationships, there has been a fair amount of clarity in the sense of a hierarchical relationship with direct control exercised by the federal government over the universities. Once again, the institutions may not have been sympathetic to this approach, but from a federal perspective their role was clear and this was consistently and continually being communicated to them through ministers and ministries. Also, much of the governance within institutions has reflected that of the federal government as institutional leaders have continuously attempted to second-guess or anticipate the wishes of various ministers. As we have argued in the previous section, the relationship between the Commonwealth and the states has been less clear, which of course has resulted in mixed messages *vis-à-vis* the sector.

As to the promotion of values, putting values into practice and demonstrating values through behavior, which are some of the core elements of principle 3, there is no denying that respective ministers and their ministerial staffs have embodied the neo-liberal value system underlying the coalition's policy. We have extensively reflected on this in the previous section. To what extent this "upholds and exemplifies effective governance" is a question we find far more difficult to address. How effective has the imposition of user-pay schemes been? Effective in the sense of the students indeed paying and of institutions having diversified their income bases. But clearly questions of effectiveness have to address the long-term objectives of the sector as well. In this respect, whether the sector has been driven to the brink and is on the verge of collapse or whether it has so much resilience and has been activated to play on the international competitive stage of today's and tomorrow's knowledge markets remains to be seen. This criterion, how important it may be, is thus hard to handle. But it is safe to say that the Howard government did not well articulate an overall vision for the higher education sector beyond a simple utilitarian one. In line with its neo-liberal philosophy, government viewed higher education much more as a cost, or burden on the public weal, than as an investment in the nation's future.

Informed and transparent decision-making is a moot point. Although changes to the allocation mechanisms have certainly increased transparency, we are not too convinced through our previous analysis that this can be said to apply to the overall decision-making process. The same would be true of good-quality information, advice and support being available and used, as it is clear that a fair bit of available information has not been used and quality has to be considered in the light of ideological preferences: data contradicting or questioning policy positions systematically have been disregarded, as has been most clearly demonstrated in the denial of the underfunding of the sector in both relative and comparative terms. Whether an effective risk management system has been in operation appears an unanswerable question, given the political nature of the system. But if we examine this in relation to informed and transparent decision-making, it is worthwhile to note that government, on the one hand, removed any national authority capable of giving it independent policy advice on issues concerning higher education, and on the other put in place measures that insured that the higher education bureaucracy did nothing to challenge the political will of the minister of the day. Government, in politicizing the bureaucracy, also destroyed most of its corporate memory on issues of concern to higher education policy. This has tended to make the bureaucracy highly risk adverse, as is evidenced by the introduction of numerous compliance measures as pseudo-governance strategies.

In terms of capacity and capability-building, the stated principles appear much more geared towards an individual organization than to a sector or system as a whole. We have therefore opted to drop this principle in our approach.

Finally, engaging stakeholders and making accountability real is something that has to be seen from different perspectives. Accountability from institutions to the federal government by all accounts is something real. (If we include compliance to regulations it has become an industry in itself.) But accountability the other way around is quite absent in the Australian system in the period under study. This is very much in line with our above observation that the government viewed higher education much more as a cost that had to be managed than as a social and economic investment. The same can be said for (effective) stakeholder engagement, with consultations and notions of inclusiveness having lost much of their substance. This type of engagement rests uneasily with a command-style approach that characterized much of the federal government's approach to the sector.

A Final Assessment

Overall, we must conclude that our take on the good governance approach has resulted in mixed outcomes. We feel we have demonstrated that principles of good governance do provide (to some degree) a workable perspective on what is taking place in a particular public sector. Although not all aspects are completely applicable, and not all are easy to interpret, they offer a frame through which governance can be analyzed. Crucial in this respect is not to use the principles as a set of boxes to tick, but as a set of dimensions to apply. This is how they have been intended in their original form and how they should be used. In this sense it is not a simple scorecard, which is also why we have refrained from creating something like "an overall good governance score."

It has become clear that context matters, but that is a complete "open door" as regards policy analysis. What may have been less obvious is the difficulty of disentangling normative perspectives with observable outcomes. In the good governance literature much emphasis is placed on democratic concepts, notions of participation and inclusion, and the social institutions in which these are embedded. It is easy, especially from a normative perspective, to dismiss the Australian Commonwealth government's approach to higher education during the period 1996–2007 as harmful, counterproductive, confrontational, devastating, etc., depending on where one stands. But our analysis has also shown that it was transparent, with fairly clearly defined roles and responsibilities, and as such does portray characteristics of good governance. However, in terms of long-term outcomes, which ultimately is what higher education policy is about, it does not help us very much in our analysis. Partly this may be because of the approach adopted. Partly, we believe, it also reflects the nature of our object of study.

As a last point, we started our conceptual exploration of governance by high-lighting the complementarity of structure and behavior. Using principles of good governance clearly shifts the emphasis in the analysis to the behavioral components. Again, this has been the objective of this particular approach, as we have identified earlier in the chapter. But, of course, this should not mean a disregard for the structural aspects of governance systems. Hence, a focus on good governance can be considered an added dimension to our more traditional approaches, but cannot be considered as a stand-alone alternative.

References

Amaral, Alberto, V. Lynn Meek, and Ingvild M. Larsen, eds. *The Higher Education Managerial Revolution?* Dordrecht: Kluwer Academic, 2003.
Australian Research Council (ARC). Media release, January 7, 2008. Available online: www.arc.gov. au/media/releases/media_07Jan08.htm.
Australian Vice-Chancellors' Committee (AVCC). *Public Under-investment in Higher Education.* Canberra: Australian Vice-Chancellors' Committee, 2001.
Australian Vice-Chancellors' Committee (AVCC). "Indexation: Maintaining the Value of our Investment in Universities." In *Pursuing the Vision for 2020 – AVCC Election Issue 1.* Canberra: Australian Vice-Chancellors' Committee, 2003.
Australian Vice-Chancellors' Committee (AVCC). *Key Statistics on Higher Education.* Canberra: Australian Vice-Chancellors' Committee, 2004.
Clark, Burton R. *The Higher Education System.* Berkeley: University of California Press, 1983.
Coates, Hamish, Leo Goedegebuure, Jeannet van der Lee, and V. Lynn Meek. *The Australian Academic Profession in 2007: A First Analysis of the Survey Results.* Armidale: CHEMP, 2008.
Commission of the European Communities. *European Governance: A White Paper.* Brussels: Commission of the European Communities, 2001.
Committee on Standards in Public Life. *First Report.* London: HMSO, 1994.
Commonwealth of Australia. *Higher Education at the Crossroads: An Overview Paper.* Canberra: Commonwealth of Australia, 2002.
Commonwealth of Australia. *Information for Commonwealth Supported Students 2005.* Canberra: AusInfo, 2004.
Department of Education, Science and Training (DEST). *Meeting the Challenges: The Governance and Management of Universities.* Canberra: DEST, 2002a.
Department of Education, Science and Training (DEST). *Setting Firm Foundations.* Canberra: DEST, 2002b.
Dill, David D. "Academic Planning and Organizational Change: Lessons from Leading American Universities." *Higher Education Quarterly* 50(1) (1996): 35–53.
Ferlie, Ewan, Christine Musselin, and Gianluca Andresani. "The 'Steering' of Higher Education Systems: A Public Management Perspective." In *Higher Education Looking Forward: Relations between Higher Education and Society.* Strasbourg: European Science Foundation, 2007, 59–78.
Gallagher, Michael. *Modern University Governance – A National Perspective.* Paper presented at the Idea of a University: Enterprise or Academy? Conference. Australian National University, Canberra, July 26, 2001.
Goedegebuure, Leo, and Martin Hayden. "Overview: Governance in Higher Education – Concepts and Issues." *Higher Education Research and Development* 26(1) (2007): 1–11.
Goedegebuure, Leo, Frans Kaiser, Peter Maassen, V. Lynn Meek, Frans A. van Vught, and Egbert de Weert, eds. *Higher Education Policy: An International Comparative Perspective.* Oxford and New York: Pergamon Press, 1993.
Good Governance Advisory Group. *Good Governance Guide.* Melbourne: GGAG, 2004.
Hoare, David. *Higher Education Management Review: Report of the Committee of Inquiry.* Canberra: Australian Government Publishing Service, 1995.
Karmel, Peter. *Higher Education at the Crossroads: Response to Ministerial Discussion Paper.* Submission 14 (2002). Available online (accessed 6.17.2008): http://www.backingaustraliasfuture.gov.au/submissions/crossroads/pdf/14.pdf.
Long, Michael, and Martin Hayden. *Paying their Way: A Survey of Australian Undergraduate Student Finances, 2000.* Canberra: Australian Vice-Chancellors' Committee, 2001.
Marshall, Neil. "End of an Era: The Collapse of the 'Buffer' Approach to the Governance of Australian Tertiary Education." *Higher Education* 19(2) (1990): 147–167.
Nelson, Brendan. *Higher Education: Report for the 2004–2006 Triennium.* Canberra: Commonwealth Department of Education, Science and Training, 2004.
Office for Public Management (OPM). *Going Forward with Good Governance.* London: OPM, 2007.

Office for Public Management and Chartered Institute of Public Finance and Accountancy (OPM & CIPFA). *The Good Governance Standard for Public Services.* London: OPM & CIPFA, 2004.

Organization for Economic Cooperation and Development (OECD). *Principles of Corporate Governance.* Paris: OECD, 2003.

Pollitt, Christopher, and Geert Bouckaert. *Public Management Reform: A Comparative Analysis* (2nd edn). Oxford: Oxford University Press, 2004.

Reed, Michael, V. Lynn Meek, and Glen A. Jones. "Introduction." In *Governing Higher Education: National Perspectives on Institutional Governance,* edited by Alberto Amaral, Glen A. Jones, and Berit Karseth. Dordrecht: Kluwer, 2002, xv–xxxi.

Review of Higher Education Financing and Policy. *Learning for Life: A Policy Discussion Paper.* Report of a Committee of Review, chaired by Mr Roderick West. Canberra: Commonwealth Department of Employment, Education, Training and Youth Affairs, 1998.

Van Vught, Frans A., ed. *Governmental Strategies and Innovation in Higher Education.* London: Jessica Kingsley, 1989.

Williams, Bruce. "The 1988 Paper on Higher Education." *Australian Universities' Review* 32(2) (1988): 2–8.

Zifcak, Spencer. "Managerialism, Accountability and Democracy: A Victorian Case Study." *Australian Journal of Public Administration* 53(3) (1997): 106–119.

10
Viewing Recent US Governance Reform Whole
"Decentralization" in a Distinctive Context

MICHAEL K. MCLENDON AND JAMES C. HEARN

Introduction

By international comparison, higher education in the US appears at the lower extreme in any continuum of centralized control and coordination. Perhaps fueled historically by individualist emphases and a nationwide distrust of authority, the country has never established an empowered national education ministry. Only a few, largely military, institutions secure ongoing operating support from the federal government, and over half of all institutions are private, and thus independent of any public governance. And even in public institutions funded by the fifty individual US states, governance at many colleges and universities takes place via lay boards at some remove from full-time officials of state bureaus.

As many observers have noted, the US relies far more on marketplace forces, local authority, and professional autonomy in controlling and coordinating tertiary education. Nobel-nominated economist Kenneth Boulding (1978) even wrote "in praise of inefficiency" in US higher education, arguing that speedy, system-level steering works against effective, innovative research and successful teaching and learning. Along similar lines, numerous organizational analysts have traced, with some approval, the limitations on top-level control in a context of limited agreement regarding goals and core educational practices (Clark, 1983; Cohen and March, 1986; Weick, 1982; Meyer and Rowan, 1978).

That said, the evolution of state authority in the governance of US public higher education has been uneven. Defying stereotypes of an entirely market-driven system, many state governments throughout the twentieth century substantially deepened their oversight and regulation of public colleges and universities. Then, beginning in the early 1980s, many American states began *decentralizing* their systems of governance of public higher education; that is, moving decision-making authority from upper to lower levels of a state or a multi-institution system. These decentralizing trends continued over the next twenty-five years, manifesting in a number of ways and holding significant implications both for the management of public colleges and universities and for society at large.

Thus, decentralization in governance of higher education in the US should be viewed within the distinctive context in which it has arisen over time. Our chapter aims to qualify and, perhaps, temper perspectives on decentralization, particularly those perspectives that portray US institutions as remarkably autonomous and those perspectives that idealize US governance. We examine the evolution of different models of governance of higher education in the states, describe several major approaches to governance decentralization since the early 1980s, identify some noteworthy pressures countervailing these decentralizing efforts, and suggest some conceptual lenses for understanding these developments. Conceptually, we argue, the nation's undeniable decentralizing trends must be viewed alongside the emergence of parallel bureaucratizing pressures from governments as well as the enduring power of certain longstanding features of university organization in the states. The chapter concludes with reflections on the historical and comparative significance of the recent US trends.

A Historical Perspective on Decentralizing Trends in US Higher Education

Recent reforms in governmental oversight of higher education in the United States have occurred within a distinctive context, one whose origins date to the widespread structural changes of the 1950s. During that time, states virtually everywhere redesigned their governance systems for public higher education in an effort to address the post-war boom in college enrollments and expenditures. Prior to this period, and for much of America's history, public higher education institutions had been governed in ways largely mirroring that of private colleges (Graham, 1989; Hearn and Griswold, 1994). It is against the backdrop of these pendulum shifts that the *decentralizing* trends in US higher education over the past decade are best understood. More fully understanding the recent decentralizing developments in the US requires consideration of the distinctive nature of authority relations there.

Colleges in Britain's North American colonies emerged from shared efforts of civic, educational and church leaders. Although colonial and early state governments were active funders of these colleges, a series of legal decisions in the early 1800s declared the colleges independently controlled rather than state controlled.[1] The colleges founded in the colonial era (including Harvard, Yale, Penn, Brown, Dartmouth and Princeton) were prestigious and nationally prominent, so these private corporations came to set the institutional framework for the state colleges that were established in increasing numbers in the wake of independence, the court decisions, and the westward expansion of the nation. Most notably, governance in the new state institutions was, from the beginning, strikingly decentralized. In private institutions, boards of governors were largely composed of mercantile, religious and legal figures, and the public institutions followed suit. Direct governmental controls were minimal. Most state universities, although under law "owned" by their respective state governments, possessed great freedom. Their lay boards of trust exercised policy and fiduciary responsibility for their respective campuses, and the institutions competed with one another and with other private colleges for resources, students and political patronage in a relatively unregulated marketplace of service delivery (McLendon, Deaton and Hearn, 2007). A number of states had even written into their constitutions language which buffered public universities from governmental oversight and control.

Indeed, one of the significant developments in the surfacing struggle over autonomy and authority in American higher education was the practice, arising in the latter half of the nineteenth century, of some states granting "constitutional autonomy" to their flagship public university. This practice was pursued to remove public universities further from the reach of "meddlesome politicians" in legislatures and governors' offices. By codifying the self-governing authority of universities in the constitution, state constitutional conventions elevated the status of the flagship university to that of a "fourth branch of government" with powers, which, in theory at least, placed the university on a legal plane coordinate to that of a state legislature, judiciary and executive (Glenny and Dalglish, 1973).

Michigan, in 1850, was the first state to grant its flagship institution, the University of Michigan, constitutional standing. Over the next twenty years, California, Minnesota and a small number of other states followed Michigan's lead (Chambers, 1965; Douglass, 1992). Although, over time, constitutional autonomy in most states eroded as universities relinquished their full constitutional rights in exchange for increased state funding or as subsequent court rulings more narrowly limited the universities' authority (McLendon, 2003), the development was nonetheless an important event in the evolution of America's distinctive governance context for higher education.

By the early twentieth century, however, the governance pendulum had swung decidedly in the direction of stronger state oversight and control of public colleges and universities. Following Congress's passage of the Morrill Federal Land Grant Act of 1862, which required that federal land within each state be used to support a college providing agricultural and mechanical education, thus leading to the emergence of state "land-grant" institutions, there emerged for the first time in the nation's history a regularized pattern of state tax support for public universities. California, Illinois, Michigan, Wisconsin and a number of other wealthy states began making direct, lump-sum annual appropriations to their respective state universities. By 1908, each of these states was allocating more than one million dollars annually to public higher education (Thelin, 1982).

The accelerated growth of public universities and the increased levels of public funding they began receiving led some states to intervene more directly in the affairs of universities. One institutionalized vehicle for achieving greater central control was the creation of *statewide governing boards*. These entities were formed by consolidating the local governing boards of individual institutions into a single, state-level board responsible for all higher education, or a sector of higher education, in a given state. Under these arrangements, states granted a state board line authority over constituent campuses, empowering the board to make many day-to-day decisions for institutions within a given system, sector or state (Berdahl, 1971; McGuinness, 1997). By 1940, at least twelve states had consolidated their systems (Chambers, 1965; Berdahl, 1971).

Yet, it was during the post-Second World War era of the 1950s and 1960s when almost every state in the nation embraced reforms of governance aimed at bringing greater order, efficiency and equity to a post-secondary education system undergoing frenetic growth in both its size and scope (McLendon, Hearn and

Deaton, 2006). Some states continued the earlier consolidating trends, and thus achieved a highly centralized form of campus governance. Other states, however, pursued a distinctively new approach – that of "statewide coordination" of higher education.

Coordinating boards were designed as intermediary bodies responsible for statewide planning. Lacking direct line authority over individual institutions, these bodies instead were given responsibility for integrating planning throughout an entire state. To help state government arrive at more informed decisions about statewide needs and about the best allocation of limited financial resources, many coordinating boards (so-called "regulatory coordinating boards") were empowered to approve new academic programs (or terminate them) and to authorize institutional budgets, while other boards ("advisory coordinating boards") merely made recommendations to elected officials about programs and budget allocations. Reformers conceived of the boards, staffed by professionals possessing management expertise, as intermediary "buffering" bodies dually obligated to campus and state – a neutral third party capable of balancing campus freedoms with the public's interest in maintaining quality and access in higher education (Glenny, 1959).

Indeed, many early proponents of coordinating boards viewed these structures as rationalizing governmental involvement in higher education. Whereas in the previous era, governmental oversight often took the form of ad hoc political intrusion, the era of the coordinating board was viewed by many esteemed observers at the time as one of widespread professionalization of higher education (Glenny, 1959, 1970; Glenny and Bowen, 1977; Glenny and Dalglish, 1973). While the boards have often served as a hedge against naked political interference by legislatures or other external actors, they nonetheless represented an additional layer of external control of higher education, shifting authority and oversight of academic programs and budgets away from the local campus and nearer to state government.

The institutionalization of these new, more state-centralized models of governance was rapid. In 1950, state coordinating and governing boards existed in just seventeen of forty-eight states; by 1974, however, only three of fifty states were without them (Berdahl, 1971). The governance patterns established during this post-war era endured until the 1980s, when a new era of structural and regulatory reform emerged, one stressing more market-oriented approaches to campus and system governance (McLendon, Deaton and Hearn, 2007).

Indeed, the past quarter-century has witnessed immense change in the approaches taken by states to govern, oversee and manage public higher education in the US. McLendon (2003), for example, identified more than 100 measures by state governments to alter the governance and regulatory patterns of higher education systems between 1985 and 2002 (see also Leslie and Novak, 2003; MacTaggart, 1996, 1998; Marcus, 1997; McGuinness, 1997; McLendon, Deaton and Hearn, 2007; McLendon and Ness, 2003). By contrast with the near-universal, centralizing bent of prior decades, the past quarter-century has given rise to a mixture of reform activity, much of it focused on empowering institutions to behave more "market-like." Paralleling the rise worldwide of a public sector reform movement named the New Public Management, many American states experimented with changes to their governance systems for higher education that focused on performance rather than process, choice rather than standardization, efficiency rather than equity, and outcome rather than input measures (McLendon, Deaton and Hearn, 2007). Most notable about the period was a countervailing trend towards deregulation, decentralization and devolution of decision authority empowering local systems and campuses as against the authority of central state agencies.

Reforms in state oversight of public higher education have taken at least three principal forms, all of which may properly be viewed as falling under the "decentralization" banner because each involves transfer of decision authority closer to the campus level: the deregulation of state procedural controls; the loosening of state governance and statewide coordination; and the advent of so-called charter (or enterprise) colleges and universities.

Deregulation of State Procedural Controls

The earliest approach taken to reform occurred in the early 1980s and focused mainly on enactment of legislation promoting flexibility in *procedural* aspects of state governance and management of public campuses. Berdahl (1971, 1998) usefully distinguished between substantive and procedural controls, noting that the former involves the right and authority to decide on goals and programs (the "what" of institutional control), whereas the latter includes the procedural means (the "how") by which those goals and programs are pursued. The focus of deregulation in the 1980s involved authority over budgeting, accounting, personnel, purchasing and tuition-setting. The legislation enacted during this period typically entailed the transfer of decision authority over such areas from the state level to the system or campus level, while leaving intact much of the existing organizational apparatus supporting state coordination and governance of higher education.

The forces underlying this first wave of reform were clearly economic in nature. State fiscal stresses brought on by economic recessions in the late 1970s and the early 1980s, coupled with heightened competition from other social programs for increasingly limited public funds, necessitated major programmatic and administrative cuts in public colleges and universities, particularly in the northeast and in the Great Lakes states, whose "Rust Belt" economies were tied heavily to manufacturing and the automotive industry (McLendon, 2003). In response, campus and system officials pressed state officials for greater operating flexibility in the hope that management freedoms might enable their institutions to achieve greater operating efficiencies and to raise new, non-state revenues. For example, University of Connecticut officials advocated deregulation by arguing that, because the state was unable to provide the institution with sufficient revenue, it should at least give the university the flexibility to manage its own financial affairs and to reallocate funds internally to meet emerging challenges and needs (Hyatt and Santiago, 1984). The literature documents a sizeable number of such procedurally oriented deregulation initiatives during the 1980s, in Colorado (McCoy, 1983),

Connecticut, Massachusetts, Washington and Idaho (all Hyatt and Santiago, 1984), Kentucky (Carter and Blanton, 1983; Hyatt and Santiago, 1984), Maryland (Meisinger and Mingle, 1983), New Jersey (Marcus, Pratt and Stevens, 1997) and Wisconsin (Lorenz, 1983).

A trend of particular significance is the devolving of tuition-setting authority, a policy often pursued as a compensating strategy for declining state funding effort for higher education. In public higher education in the US, state appropriations and tuition/fees are the two primary sources of revenue for colleges and universities. Because campuses lack control over appropriations, the authority to set tuition levels provides institutions with an important policy lever for ensuring that adequate revenue is available for financing operating costs, particularly because state investment in higher education over the past twenty-five years has declined relative to changes in enrollment, state wealth, and the growth of institutional budgets. Thus, decentralization of tuition-setting authority provides public colleges and universities with greater control over their own budgets and, in many cases, greater net revenues (McLendon and Mokher, forthcoming).

The introduction of state policies to provide institutions with greater authority in the collection of revenues from student tuition and fees began in the 1980s (Deaton, 2006; Morphew, 2007). New Jersey became an early leader in the movement towards tuition decentralization by adopting a policy in 1986 which allowed all four-year colleges and universities to set their own tuition levels as long as they received approval from the state board of higher education. At least sixteen states adopted policies decentralizing tuition-setting authority between 1986 and 2003 (Deaton, 2006). There is considerable variation in the actual amount of authority granted institutions under these recent tuition initiatives. For example, while some states permit all four-year institutions to determine their own tuition levels, others have granted this authority only to research universities – and sometimes only for use in adjusting tuition for students who are not residents of the state. Despite variation in the nature and the degree of autonomy granted to colleges and universities across the states, these policies represent a notable movement away from the past practice of centralizing tuition-setting processes at the state level, and towards greater control – and responsibility – by institutions over their own financial futures.

Loosening of State Governance and Statewide Coordination

A second approach that states have taken involves the loosening, disaggregating and weakening of systems of statewide governance and coordination. By comparison with the aforementioned deregulation initiatives, these measures have involved efforts to alter the distribution of authority between state regulatory bodies and campuses in *substantive* areas such as academic programs and mission and, thus, have been more comprehensive in their scope. For example, in New Jersey's governance redesign of 1994, legislation abolished one of the nation's most powerful coordinating boards. The legislation delegated the board's authority over academic programs and budgets to the formerly regulated campuses and established a new council of state university presidents to coordinate higher education policy "voluntarily." In Arkansas, legislation passed in 1997 had a fourfold impact: replacing the State Board of Higher Education with a Higher Education Coordinating Board and reducing its staff and regulatory reach; reorganizing the board's trustee selection process to ensure greater campus influence; creating (as in the New Jersey case) an "executive council" of presidents to advise the director of the department; and empowering the executive council to hire and fire the director and to influence the board's policy agenda more easily.

The more recent case of Florida brings into sharp relief some of the complexities, ambiguities and indeed inconsistencies associated with governance "decentralization." For nearly fifty years, until 2001, public universities in Florida had been governed by a single statewide consolidated board, the Board of Regents. However, in 2000 and 2001, the Florida legislature enacted bills that dismantled the board and created local boards of trust for each of the state's eleven public universities. The legislation also established a new K-20 "superboard," the nation's first statewide structure responsible for planning, policy development and coordination across both the K-12 and higher education sectors (Trombley, 2001).

Proponents of the governance change, notably Governor "Jeb" Bush and state Republican leaders, argued that the new structure would improve campus governance by locating authority closer to the campus level and enhance accountability by lowering barriers between the K-12 and higher education sectors. Many proponents also welcomed the elimination of the Board of Regents because of its refusal to approve new programs in law, medicine and engineering for institutions located in southern sections of the state, home to growing Hispanic and African-American populations (Selingo, 2001; Schmidt, 2002; Trombley, 2001).

Prominent state Democrats claimed, however, that the board's elimination would effectively "politicize" university governance in Florida (Klein, 2001). Because the board had long served as a buffer between the legislature and local campuses, its dissolution would, these opponents asserted, lead to greater political interference in the institutions and strengthen too much the governor's role in higher education.

The governance measure was enacted in the 2000 and 2001 Florida legislative sessions (Trombley, 2001), and promptly resurfaced when opponents of the change mounted a campaign to overturn the legislation by placing the issue on the statewide ballot, permitting citizens to vote directly on the change. A prominent US Democratic senator, himself a popular former governor of Florida, led this effort. Against the backdrop of public discontent over voting irregularities in Florida during the 2000 presidential elections, Democratic Party strategists became involved in the referendum as part of a coordinated strategy to unseat Governor Bush. In November 2002, Florida voters returned Bush to office, but overturned elements of his governance initiative with more than 60 percent of voters approving an amendment to the state constitution re-establishing the Board of Regents (Hebel and Schmidt, 2002). Thus, viewed "whole," Florida may be seen as having simultaneously decentralized and re-centralized aspects of its governance regime for public higher education. Ongoing legal maneuvering over the precise authority of the reconstituted board has ensued; today much confusion surrounds the nature of governance of public higher education in Florida (Leslie and Novak, 2003; McLendon and Ness, 2003; *St Petersburg Times*, 2008).

Charter/Enterprise Colleges

The notion of the "chartered" public agency has a rich history in the theory and practice of American government. Certain political subdivisions of states, including many municipalities, have long operated under agreements with states whereby the entity created is delegated certain authorities and responsibilities to operate consistent with its state charter. These charters provide the public entity with more management discretion than that accorded traditional state agencies, often through the device of "performance contracts," which, in exchange for specified operating freedoms, obligate the administrative unit to achieve targeted goals. The application of this kind of arrangement to public colleges and universities, however, is relatively new. Indeed, while some previously enacted reforms in public governance of higher education (e.g., Hawaii and Oregon) contained elements of the emerging charter concept (McLendon, 2003), none of them focused quite as explicitly on performance contracts as a policy tool for ensuring the mutual obligations of universities and state government.

The first state to experiment with charter colleges was Maryland, which, in 1992, exempted St Mary's College, a public honors college, from the University of Maryland system following a system-wide reorganization. The action exempted St Mary's from many of the state regulatory controls that applied to other campuses within the University of Maryland system. For instance, St Mary's received a lump-sum budget and the ability to increase tuition if appropriations failed to rise at the same rate as inflation (Berdahl, 1998). Most recently, Virginia and Colorado gained national attention when they granted select public colleges and universities charter status.[2] In general, charter colleges and universities tend to have the revenue capacity, endowments and experience in local management to enable them to operate under a new partnership with the state. Notably, most of the institutions that have received these dispensations are ones already receiving low levels of state funding. For example, the Universities of Virginia and Colorado receive much less than 20 percent of their total operating revenues from state sources.

Charters essentially redefine the relationship between public colleges and universities and state government via a new operating framework. In exchange for increased management flexibility in areas such as tuition, purchasing, internal resource allocation and personnel, chartered institutions (sometimes called "enterprise universities") agree that they will receive less growth in state funding than would otherwise be expected. Institutions welcome the arrangement because they believe they will be able to compensate for waning state appropriations through increased revenues that result from the flexibility to establish market-driven tuition rates (in other words, higher tuition levels) and from the savings associated with efficiencies and reduced state reporting.

Charter colleges and universities maintain accountability to the state through performance contracts. University-specific, these contracts, also called memorandums of understanding, give concrete focus to the new operating framework by defining mutual expectations of the state and its participating campuses (AGB, 2005). In Colorado and Virginia, public colleges and universities have, as noted, entered into negotiated agreements with state government, permitting the institutions to set their own tuition and avoid much of the regulation of state agencies. In return, the institutions provide written assurances (via multi-year, renewal contracts) that they will comply with specific benchmarks for future performance. In Colorado, each public university governing board negotiates its performance contract with the Colorado Commission on Higher Education, the state's higher education coordinating agency (AGB, 2005). Each contract is signed by the campus president and chair of the board of trustees, in addition to the head of the state commission. For each institution, the contract specifies goals for student retention and graduation, enrollment of underserved students and requirements for student completion of a general education "core." The contracts also require institutions to specify whether and how financial incentives are used in the implementation of its faculty-evaluation and professional-development procedures. Lastly, the contracts stipulate institutional reporting on assessment of student learning, efficiency of campus operations, workforce development initiatives, and teacher education programs (State of Colorado, 2005).

Virginia likewise passed its Restructured Higher Education Financial and Administration Operations Act in 2005. The legislation established three levels of increased autonomy from state regulations, eligibility for which was determined by an institution's financial and management capacity (Leslie and Berdahl, 2008). The act stipulates that all Virginia public colleges and universities will develop a six-year academic, financial and enrollment plan that outlines tuition and fee estimates, enrollment projections, and detailed plans for meeting statewide objectives.[3] Each institution additionally must accept a number of accountability measures, including meeting benchmarks related to accessibility and affordability. The act provides campuses with substantial autonomy from the state in business and financial affairs, capital, procurement, personnel and information technology operations. Universities negotiate their management agreements with executive officials and submit the plans to the governor's budget for approval by the General Assembly. The initial agreements signed are for three-year terms; subsequent charters will be for five years.

In sum, the past twenty-five years have witnessed considerable change in authority relations between state governments and public higher education institutions in the US. The system, long characterized as "decentralized," particularly relative to its European peers, has found many elements of governmental oversight and regulation loosened to an even greater extent than before. At what price is decentralization achieved? Who really gains and loses in this new governance context, and how does decentralization impact on institutional decision-making? Is the move to decentralization unalloyed, or are there countervailing trends as well?

What might the changes mean for system coordination, mission differentiation, quality, affordability and access? To what extent might these changes in the locus of control influence the degree of bureaucratization at the campus level? These are empirical questions for which, unfortunately, few answers are available.

Recent Developments Viewed Whole: A Conceptualization

What conceptual or theoretical lenses might enhance understanding of recent organizational trends in US higher education, especially those arising from America's distinctive history and experience with "decentralization"? Some aspects of the trends nicely fit *structural-contingency theory*'s classic account of factors driving decision-making to lower organizational levels: growing size, increasing unpredictability, pressures for stimulating creativity and entrepreneurship, and expanding specialization in the organization (Donaldson, 1996). The global economy and technological change have brought greater unpredictability to higher education. Students are confronting a widening array of options for accessing education and, to compete creatively and aggressively in that marketplace, institutions and academic programs need to be able to make speedy, autonomous decisions. Thus, decentralization emerges as a likely response.

But can structural contingency theory also account for trends in the other direction, that is towards expanded central authority? There is little question that, even as formal regulatory structures recede somewhat in their importance, many sources of informal political control have become more assertive in recent years, threatening longstanding academic structures and processes. Indeed, one wonders whether the movement away from formal bureaucratic systems has opened the door to new forms of political intrusion.

One prominent example is the case of University of Colorado faculty member Ward Churchill, who publicly suggested that those in the Twin Towers in New York City may have deserved their fates on September 11, 2001. After Churchill's statements on this matter, Colorado legislators and governing officials began to push the institution to remove him. Rather than accede to a direct political intrusion, the university launched an investigation of possible plagiarism in some of Professor Churchill's writing. The findings led to his removal from an administrative position, and, eventually, to the termination of his employment by the institution.

Another example comes from the 2007 search for a founding dean for the new law school at the University of California, Irvine. The search seemed to have been concluded with the hiring of an accomplished scholar from Duke University, but officials of the governing board forced the university to withdraw the offer because of his putative liberal political leanings, as evidenced by an opinion piece he wrote for the *Los Angeles Times*.

These examples of threats to academic autonomy from governing boards and politicians in the US represent attempts to tighten control by groups and individuals unsympathetic to traditional levels of institutional freedom, and apparently doubtful about higher education's self-governing capacities. The efforts have not gone unnoticed. Importantly, professional associations are expressing growing concerns over the quality of governance in public sector institutions in the US, with special attention to the knowledgability and quality of trustees and concomitant concern over the "politicizing" of system governance in public higher education (AGB, 1998).

The efforts to expand top-down control in the US have also brought threats to the nation's voluntary, non-governmental approach to quality assurance via national, regional and professional accrediting associations and consortia. That approach became entrenched in the early twentieth century when the higher education community came together to resist efforts by the federal government to systematize and standardize higher education nationally. By most accounts, the voluntary approach to quality is one of the most internationally distinctive aspects of US higher education, and the most deeply institutionalized (Hawkins, 1992). Some of the first threats to it came in the 1960s, 1970s and 1980s, when the federal government began to tie its funding of research and student financial aid to certain indicators of quality, such as institutional cost controls and levels of student loan defaults. More recently, states have begun to seek expanded performance reporting from institutions, and in over half the states have tied that reporting to institutional and system funding (McLendon, Hearn and Deaton, 2006). To the extent such systems publicly raise or lower governmental support in concert with measures of effectiveness, institutions are becoming subject more directly than before to governmentally imposed quality control.

A similarly purposed effort by the federal government arose more recently. Although the Bush administration is usually considered politically conservative, and hence more resistant to expanding the federal government, its approach to higher education has been to enhance the central government's role in the interest of quality control and global competitiveness. Using language that was largely unprecedented from Washington, Secretary of Education Margaret Spellings (2006) called for a national "action plan for higher education," featuring the implementation of national information systems and tying public support to indicators of performance. Shortly afterwards came the report from her blue-ribbon Commission on the Future of Higher Education (US Department of Education, 2006), criticizing institutions for their inefficiencies and their grudging efforts at transparency. These initiatives have thus far resulted in little observable political action or institutional change, but have raised significant anxieties on campuses.[4] Some veteran observers have subsequently argued that these are *de facto* centralizing pressures and they are not going away:

> Just a few weeks ago, members of the US Senate Finance Committee sent letters to dozens of institutions with endowments of at least $500-million, demanding detailed [financial] information ... One also hears rumblings about taxing endowments or imposing price caps on tuition increases. Is it possible that such threats are linked ... to the negative and even hostile response of leading institutions to the criticisms of the Commission on the Future of Higher Education convened by Education Secretary Margaret Spellings? ... Does the Spellings report still warrant attention ...? My answer

to that question is a resounding YES. The four higher-education issues that the report emphasizes are the right ones and will continue to be with us for years: access, affordability, quality, and accountability.

(Breneman, 2008: 23)

Thus, regarding the roles of state and federal governments in the US, there are trends in opposing directions, and it is important to be precise in considering what exactly is taking place. Meyer and Scott (1983) have distinguished bureaucratization, the standardization from above of record-keeping, reporting and structuring, from centralization, moving control over actual decision-making to higher levels. Those analysts observed that decisions to bureaucratize are not the same as decisions to centralize, and indeed, moves towards bureaucratizing may be as often associated with decentralization as with centralization. Assuming this perspective, it seems fair to say that much of what states have been pursuing in recent years in performance reporting and the building of state unit-record databases may be considered more in the mode of bureaucratizing than expanding control. It is also important to bear in mind Meyer and Scott's distinction between three kinds of centralization: funding, programmatic and instrumental. While some centralizing of funding decisions may be inevitable in public higher education, it does not necessarily imply centralizing of decisions regarding specific programs and specific approaches to addressing problems.

Indeed, one can interpret the federal government's increasing attention to higher education as more of a bureaucratic reform movement (towards increased measurement and improved standardization of reporting for the public) than a movement towards dictating to institutions specific programmatic and action choices. One can interpret state governments' performance-accountability initiatives in similar ways, with the added purpose in some cases of more precisely directing funding towards quality through measurement initiatives. At the national level, for example, the Spellings Report is careful to emphasize the importance of maintaining institutional autonomy (a point perhaps pressed most energetically on the commissioners by institutional leaders), and there has been no suggestion of imposing a tightly controlling governmental hierarchy.

Thus, we can view both federal and state activism of recent years as fostering bureaucratization rather than true centralization: increasingly difficult marketplace challenges require greater autonomy at lower levels, but governmental funders and sponsors will grant that increased autonomy only in exchange for institutions and systems ensuring more comprehensive information flows and communication. In this sense, structural contingency theory can stand as a reasonably compelling account of recent trends.

Increasing board and governmental engagement in the affairs of the enterprise may be at least partially understood under the contingency theory perspective, but that perspective does not address the resistance shown by academic units and faculty both towards the widening of external controls and, at the other extreme, towards the adoption of aggressively entrepreneurial orientations that heighten internal and external competition among individuals and units. To understand those developments, it is important to review a more familiar lens for viewing authority relations in US higher education. While contingency theory suggests that organizations at various levels adapt to emerging contexts and opportunities and take action to locate decision authority rationally, *institutional theory* emphasizes the persistence of environmentally established forms and actions.

That view stresses the power of an entrenched set of norms, values and expectations among faculty and institutional leaders about what a college or university is, what faculty cherish, honor and do in their day-to-day work, and what organizational changes are legitimate and illegitimate (Meyer and Rowan, 1978). In the institutionalist view, those norms, values and expectations create counterweights against both central authority and the enduring marketization tendencies in the US. Burton Clark (1983) and others have long argued that the US system is distinctive in being coordinated more through various marketplace mechanisms (for students, faculty, government and private funding, and prestige) than through the bureaucratic, political and guild mechanisms familiar in other nations. Thus, change is often encouraged by central authorities and often compelled by the marketplace, but long-established cultural and normative views regarding the enterprise constrain both forces.

In this ongoing interaction, governments provide funding for institutions and students and strive to avoid duplication and quality deterioration, but otherwise remain largely on the sidelines. Markets, in their turn, make their own demands on the system, and produce their own effects, but there too, limits are posed by the deeply entrenched institutional culture.

Thus, from the institutionalist literature, the term "decentralized" captures only part of the reality of US higher education. Decision-making authority is indeed lower level than in most other nations, with no empowered national ministry and state-level agencies that have always been relatively weak and may be growing more so as institutions are increasingly empowered to behave competitively. But, at the same time, lower-level authority is restricted by both institutional and market mechanisms. In institutions and in their academic and administrative departments, decision-making freedom brings with it responsibility: arbitrary, unsupported and unsuccessful decisions are vulnerable to sanctions.

Those sanctions are most immediately delivered by the marketplace. Poor faculty hiring decisions lead to declining enrollments or shrinking research funding, for example. Less immediately, sanctions can be delivered institutionally, as would be the case when a structural reconfiguration (e.g., a merger of academic departments in different fields) leads to a loss of disciplinary solidarity and, over time, faculty attrition. Arguably, it is because of this dual sensitivity that the US system has historically favored the net advantages of decentralized authority over the risks entailed in hierarchical chains of command. Indeed, Karl Weick's familiar "loose coupling" notion (Weick, 1976) suggests that central authorities have deferred decisions to lower-level academic deans and faculty precisely because the latter are more attuned to both traditions and new developments in their differing knowledge arenas. In this vision of the organization, sub-units are free of cumbersome authority channels and thus able to adapt more efficiently and effectively in their own particular external environments. And the organization as a whole is served by this atomization of authority.

In what ways do the emerging organizational trends highlighted in the preceding section of this chapter refine or qualify this vision of US institutions? It would be simplistic to view the developments as indicating solely a movement towards further decentralization in the United States' already highly autonomous institutional governance systems. Instead, one can discern movement towards a new three-way equilibrium among market-driven, institutionally based and central bureaucratic forms of coordination and control. *Institutions are embracing markets in dramatic new ways, but they are also increasingly subject to public scrutiny, and attuned closely to emerging incentives posed from both directions. At the same time, institutionalized forms and processes are showing remarkable persistence. Conceptually, the recent developments chronicled in this chapter may be viewed as early elements in an engrossing three-way drama, heading towards a new but still recognizably American balance among market, institutional and bureaucratic forces.*

The most intriguing element in this drama is the pressure towards marketization. Clearly, the new marketplace demands are calling into question institutions' commitments to historically legitimated organizational forms, processes, values and cultures.[5] Undoubtedly, the marketplace for students in the US is becoming more competitive, and individual institutions are making decisions buffeted by tight budgets and growing external pressures to fill classes efficiently with a financially sound balance of full-paying and aided students. In public institutions, the push for institutional autonomy and the emergence of tuition discounting and sophisticated enrollment management systems have entailed some decline in authority for state governing boards and coordinating agencies. With that decline has come decreasing attention not only to differentiating the missions of individual institutions but to promoting equity across students and institutions. Instead, the historic US trust in marketplaces has blossomed into growing rewards for performance and merit on the part of both students and institutions.

Recent marketplace developments have brought some fault lines to historically legitimated conceptions of the enterprise. "Brand-name" institutions are renting their facilities for a variety of non-educational purposes, licensing their logos for clothing, and offering programming online and in other distance formats, not only or even primarily for degrees, but rather for certificates, credits or simply the benefits of an association and experience with the institutions. Faculty are increasingly being hired for contingent positions, either part-time or full-time non-tenure line, to the point that national associations of faculty are raising alarms (AAUP, 2003). Students are increasingly attending part-time, with some delay after high-school graduation, and with periodic starts and stops in time on campus, and increasingly attending "non-traditional" institutions (Adelman, 1999; Adelman, Daniel and Berkowitz, 2003).

In this context, the "taken for grantedness" of institutional life is shrinking. Comfortable past assumptions no longer hold quite so tightly. What is a university student? What is a credit, or a class, for that matter? How long will it take? Are certificates or even "educational passports," rather than degrees, becoming the emerging currency of record? Who is a faculty member? And what, in the end, is an institution? Each of these questions was far easier to answer in the 1950s than half a century later.

There is another sense in which institutionalized models of campus governance are being threatened. While for many years colleges have eagerly sought to adapt management approaches from other sectors, especially business,[6] the scope of the current movement to adopt not just new planning models but fundamentally new ways of organizing seems unprecedented. For example, one can interpret the surge in hiring part-time and non-tenure-line faculty as a bid for control over the historically inflexible labor-force arrangements in higher education (Rhoades, 2001). Substituting an instructor on short-term contract for a retiring tenured faculty member gives institutions the freedom to raise and lower labor-force numbers in areas of changing student demand. Any resulting loss of academic continuity and community (and some core aspects of academic norms, values and culture) can be viewed as a price to pay for increased adaptability and managerial discretion. Similarly, state officials appointing growing numbers of business leaders and political donors to governing boards can help ensure the allegiance of the institution to core values of the current state government and associated corporate and professional elites, as can the establishment of foundations affiliated to the main university but separate from its governance and legal frameworks (Roha, 2000).

Thus, institutionalized models in the US are being shaken not only from the bottom up by marketplace developments but from the top down by rising governmental attention to the enterprise. Writing three decades ago, Meyer and Rowan (1978) characterized colleges and universities as operating under a "logic of good faith" that buffered them from aggressive inspection by external authorities, the media and prospective students. Few would doubt the emergence of multiple threats to that perspective.

But it would be wrongheaded to conclude that formerly institutionalized traditions are being severely compromised. In fact, the heart of the matter is in the difficult negotiations taking place around the edges of those core traditions. While faculty in one college successfully press for removing corporate sponsorship of a course, administrators at another institution accept endowment funding for a named corporate chair, and incrementally the enterprise moves towards new configurations and postures.

Actors are important in these moves and here it is important to go beyond certain limiting views of institutional theory. That theory is often portrayed as deterministic, implying that structures are imposed by external environmental pressures and structural changes take place only gradually and largely outside of leadership control – such a view of institutionalist thinking may hinder our under-standing of recent organizational developments (Bastedo, 2007). Bureaucratization and even some forms of centralization can proceed without powerfully affecting the core values and norms of educational institutions (Meyer and Scott, 1983), and a number of new analyses have highlighted and championed the resistance on campus to market-driven pressures on institutional forms and actions (see, e.g., Levine, 2000; Stein, 2004). Universities as an organizational form have their origins in medieval times, and shades of the original form have remained relatively constant through remarkable political, social, economic, religious and cultural transitions. Clearly, such resilience has required the emergence of effective strategic leaders who can deal with new organizational realities by channeling and harnessing enduring institutional values and memories in the service of new accommodations. Will the new "market-smart" university really be so very different from its predecessors? Will the decentralizing and bureaucratizing efforts of governments fundamentally change the university? There is good reason to wonder.

Conclusion

While certain decentralizing trends in US higher education are undeniable, understanding these transitions and placing them in broader conceptual and cross-national perspective requires noting too the countervailing and qualifying trends. No simple conceptual "storyline" emerges. Marketizing is generally associated with decentralization, but governments' push towards expanded board control and increased accountability may be viewed as centralizing. And, importantly, if one wishes to portray US higher education's longstanding structures and decision approaches as buffeted by both markets and governmental intrusions, then it is important to stress at the same time the enduring institutionalization and legitimacy of those forms and processes.

It would be easy to proclaim in the US a contemporary "crisis" of either marketization or governmentalism, and no shortage of critics have arisen in both camps (see, e.g., Burke, 2002; Kirp, 2003; Washburn, 2005). Nonetheless, as organizational theorists Robert Birnbaum and Frank Shushok (2001) have persuasively argued, US higher education has *always* been characterized as being in one form of crisis or another. Some rhetorical retreat may be advisable. Without the appearance of dramatic new evidence to the contrary, history would suggest that our great-grandchildren and beyond will attend universities easily recognizable to us. In the US, decentralization may continue in concert with increasing governmental bureaucratization and efforts towards steering. But, for better or worse, these may ultimately be viewed as marginal adjustments along an established, and continuing, course.

What distinctively might the review here contribute to comparative governance analyses? Strikingly, several aspects of recent US developments resemble those in Europe and elsewhere globally. Maassen and Olsen (2007) have perceptively chronicled, conceptualized and discussed the juxtaposition of centralizing and decentralizing impulses in Europe, and there are unquestionably parallels between the nascent efforts at European integration in higher education and the efforts of the US federal government to move towards greater national presence in what historically have been affairs of the fifty states (consider, for example, the recommendations of the Spellings Commission that national action be taken regarding institutional pricing, information transparency and inter-institutional articulation in enrollments and degree programs). Academic structures and financing in the US are quite distinct from those in Europe, but many of the same organizational and political dynamics are apparently at play, and may be grounds for provocative new research and policy-maker consideration.

How, for example, do curricular articulation and degree standardization efforts in the US compare to those in Europe under the Bologna Initiative, and what might comparable experiences suggest? In what ways can US efforts towards "P-16" integration (more closely linking secondary to tertiary education, through centralized initiatives) be modeled on other nations' precedents? Most importantly, do US experiences in negotiating the boundaries of markets, institutional imperatives and governmental demands parallel those in other nations, and might frameworks be developed and refined to capture the dynamics of these ongoing adaptations?

If there is one storyline emerging from this analysis, it is the *absence* of a single, compelling storyline. US governments at state and federal levels are unquestionably pursuing ongoing bureaucratization of higher education while, just as unquestionably, committing to new experimentation in increasing institutional freedoms. When governments themselves design funding incentives and reporting systems aimed at expanding autonomy and intensifying marketization, the conceptual and practical reality is complex, and ripe for research exploration.

Notes

1   Most notable was the US Supreme Court's landmark *Dartmouth v. Woodward* decision of 1819. The *Dartmouth* dispute centered on the state of New Hampshire's effort to change the charter of Dartmouth College and, thus, to alter the college's trustee selection process. In what would become the most far-reaching ruling in the history of US higher education, the court found that the original charter granted to Dartmouth College by New Hampshire constituted a contract between the state and the college which the state could not impair (Hobbs, 1978). The *Dartmouth* decision caused widespread concern to legislatures, for, as Hobbs (1978: 34) writes, "the power of the sovereign over its corporate creation was now severely circumscribed."

2   Other less-known examples include charter initiatives in Washington, Texas, Massachusetts and Ohio (AGB, 2005).

3   See Couturier (2006) and Leslie and Berdahl (2008) for discussions of historical and political dimensions surrounding charter colleges in Virginia.

4   Interestingly, the proposed assertion of federal control has emerged in the same time period as stepped-up efforts by accrediting groups and institutional associations to demonstrate outcomes in student learning. It is interesting to speculate on the extent to which these non-governmental proposals are responding to shared interests and priorities regarding quality, as opposed to responding to unwelcome threats of federal action.

5   See, for example, Arthur Levine's essay (2000) on the threatened "soul" of higher education.

6   Often to their later chagrin (see Birnbaum, 2000).

References

Adelman, Clifford. *Answers in the Tool Box: Academic Intensity, Attendance Patterns, and Bachelor's Degree Attainment.* Washington, DC: US Department of Education, 1999.

Adelman, Clifford, Bruce Daniel, and Ilona Berkowitz. *Postsecondary Attainment, Attendance, Curriculum, and Performance: Selected Results from the NELS:88/2000 Postsecondary Education Transcript Study (PETS), 2000.* Washington, DC: National Center for Education Statistics, 2003.

American Association of University Professors (AAUP). *Contingent Appointments and the Academic Profession: Policy Statement.* Washington, DC: American Association of University Professors, 2003. Available online: http://www.aaup.org/AAUP/pubsres/policydocs/contents/conting-stmt.htm.

Association of Governing Boards of Universities and Colleges (AGB). *Bridging the Gap between State Government and Public Higher Education.* Washington, DC: AGB, 1998.

Association of Governing Boards of Universities and Colleges (AGB). *The New Interest in Charter Universities and State Performance Contracts.* Washington, DC: AGB, 2005.

Bastedo, Michael. "Sociological Frameworks for Higher Education Policy Research." In *Sociology of Higher Education: Contributions and Their Contexts*, edited by Patty Gumport. Baltimore: Johns Hopkins University Press, 2007, 295–316.

Berdahl, Robert O. *Statewide Coordination of Higher Education.* Washington, DC: ACE, 1971.

Berdahl, Robert O. "Balancing Self Interest and Accountability: St Mary's College of Maryland." In *Seeking Excellence through Independence: Liberating Colleges and Universities from Excessive Regulation*, edited by Terrence J. MacTaggart. San Francisco: Jossey-Bass, 1998, 59–83.

Birnbaum, Robert. *Management Fads in Higher Education: Where They Come From, What They Do, Why They Fail.* San Francisco: Jossey-Bass, 2000.

Birnbaum, Robert, and Frank Shushok Jr. "The 'Crisis' Crisis in American Higher Education: Is That a Wolf or a Pussycat at the Academy's Door?" In *In Defense of Higher Education*, edited by Philip G. Altbach, Patty Gumport, and D. Bruce Johnstone. Baltimore: Johns Hopkins University Press, 2001, 59–84.

Boulding, Kenneth. "In Praise of Inefficiency." *AGB Reports* January/February (1978): 44–48.

Breneman, David. "Elite Colleges Must Stop Spurning Critiques of Higher Education." *Chronicle of Higher Education*, February 15, 2008.

Brubacher, John S. "The Autonomy of the University: How Independent is the Republic of Scholars?" *Journal of Higher Education* 38(5) (1967): 237–249.

Burke, Joseph C. *Funding Public Colleges and Universities for Performance: Popularity, Problems, and Prospects.* Albany: Rockefeller Institute Press, 2002.

Carter, Edward E., and Jack C. Blanton. "Management Flexibility in Kentucky: The Passage of House Bill 622." In *Management Flexibility and State Regulation in Higher Education*, edited by James R. Mingle. Atlanta: Southern Regional Education Board, 1983.

Chambers, Marritt M. *Freedom and Repression in Higher Education.* Bloomington: Bloomcraft Press, 1965.

Christal, Melodie E. *State Tuition and Fee Policies: 1996–1997.* Denver: State Higher Education Executive Officers, 1997.

Clark, Burton R. *The Higher Education System: Academic Organization in Cross-national Perspective.* Berkeley: University of California Press, 1983.

Cohen, Michael D., and James G. March. *Leadership and Ambiguity: The American College President.* Boston: Harvard Business School Press, 1986.

Couturier, Laura. *Checks and Balances at Work: The Restructuring of Virginia's Public Higher Education System.* San José: The National Center for Public Policy and Higher Education, 2006.

Curry, Dennis J., and Norman M. Fischer. *Public Higher Education and the State: Models for Financing, Budgeting and Accountability.* Paper presented at the Annual Meeting of the Association for the Study of Higher Education, San Antonio, 1986.

Deaton, Steven B. *Policy Shifts in Tuition Setting Authority in the American States: An Events History Analysis of State Policy Adoption.* Unpublished doctoral dissertation. Nashville: Vanderbilt University, 2006.

Donaldson, Lex. "The Normal Science of Structural Contingency Theory." In *Handbook of Organizational Studies*, edited by Stewart Clegg, Cynthia Hardy, and Walter R. Nord. London: Sage, 1996, 57–76.

Douglass, John A. "Creating a Fourth Branch of State Government: The University of California and the Constitutional Convention of 1879." *History of Education Quarterly* 32(1) (1992): 31–72.

Fine, Kerry K. *A History of Minnesota Higher Education: A Policy Analysis.* St Paul: Minnesota House of Representatives, 1993.

Glenny, Lyman A. *Autonomy of Public Colleges: The Challenge of Coordination.* New York: McGraw-Hill, 1959.

Glenny, Lyman A. "Institutional Autonomy for Whom?" In *The Troubled Campus: Current Issues in Higher Education,* edited by G. Kerry Smith. Washington, DC: American Association of Higher Education; San Francisco: Jossey-Bass, 1970, 153–160.

Glenny, Lyman A., and Frank M. Bowen. *State Intervention in Higher Education.* Cambridge, MA: Sloan Commission on Government and Higher Education, 1977.

Glenny, Lyman A., and Thomas K. Dalglish. *Public Universities, State Agencies, and the Law.* Berkeley: Center for Research and Development in Higher Education, University of California, 1973.

Graham, Hugh D. "Structure and Governance in American Higher Education: Historical and Comparative Analysis in State Policy." *Journal of Policy History* 1(1) (1989): 80–107.

Hawkins, Hugh. *Banding Together: The Rise of National Associations in American Higher Education, 1887–1950.* Baltimore: Johns Hopkins University Press, 1992.

Hearn, James C., and Carolyn P. Griswold. "State-level Centralization and Policy Innovation in US Postsecondary Education." *Educational Evaluation and Policy Analysis* 16(2) (1994): 161–190.

Hebel, Sarah, and Peter Schmidt. "Voters Approve Florida Governance Shift, Major Bond Measures in California and Virginia." *Chronicle of Higher Education,* November 15, 2002.

Hobbs, Walter C. *Government Regulation of Higher Education.* Cambridge, MA: Ballinger, 1978.

Hyatt, James A., and Aurora A. Santiago. *Incentives and Disincentives for Effective Management.* Washington, DC: National Association of Colleges and University Business Officers, 1984.

Kirp, David L. *Shakespeare, Einstein, and the Bottom Line: The Marketing of Higher Education.* Cambridge, MA: Harvard University Press, 2003.

Klein, Barry. "Democrats Lead Governance Fight." *St Petersburg Times,* June 5, 2001.

Lenth, Charles S. *The Tuition Dilemma: State Policies and Practices in Pricing Public Higher Education.* Denver: State Higher Education Executive Officers, 1993.

Leslie, David W., and Robert O. Berdahl. "The Politics of Restructuring Higher Education in Virginia: A Case Study." *Review of Higher Education* 31(3) (2008): 309–328.

Leslie, David W., and Richard Novak. "Substance vs. Politics: Through the Dark Mirror of Governance Reform." *Educational Policy* 17(1) (2003): 98–120.

Levine, Arthur. "The Soul of a New University." *New York Times,* March 13, 2000.

Lorenz, Reuben H. "Improved Efficiency through Decreased Government Regulation: The Case of Wisconsin." In *Management Flexibility and State Regulation in Higher Education,* edited by James R. Mingle. Atlanta: Southern Regional Education Board, 1983, 36–44.

Maassen, Peter, and Johan P. Olsen, eds. *University Dynamics and European Integration.* Dordrecht: Springer, 2007.

MacTaggart, Terrence J., ed. *Restructuring Higher Education.* San Francisco: Jossey-Bass, 1996.

MacTaggart, Terrence J., ed. *Seeking Excellence through Independence.* San Francisco: Jossey-Bass, 1998.

Marcus, Laurence R. "Restructuring State Higher Education Governance Patterns." *Review of Higher Education* 20(4) (1997): 399–418.

Marcus, Laurence R., Barbara A. Pratt, and Jacki L. Stevens. "Deregulating Colleges: The Autonomy Experiment." *Educational Policy* 11(1) (1997): 92–110.

McCoy, Marilyn. "The Adoption of Budget Flexibility in Colorado." In *Management Flexibility and State Regulation in Higher Education,* edited by James R. Mingle. Atlanta: Southern Regional Education Board, 1983, 52–61.

McGuinness, Aims C. *State Postsecondary Education Structures Handbook.* Denver: Education Commission of the States, 1997.

McLendon, Michael K. "State Governance Reform of Higher Education: Patterns, Trends, and Theories of the Public Policy Process." In *Higher Education: Handbook of Theory and Research, Volume XVIII,* edited by John C. Smart. London: Kluwer, 2003, 57–143.

McLendon, Michael K., and Christine Mokher. "The Origins of State-policy Privatization of Public

Higher Education. Or, From whence Does Privatization Arise?" In *Privatization of the Public Research University*, edited by Christopher Morphew. Baltimore: Johns Hopkins University Press, forthcoming.

McLendon, Michael K., and Erik C. Ness. "The Politics of State Higher Education Governance Reform." *Peabody Journal of Education* 78(4) (2003): 66–88.

McLendon, Michael K., Steven R. Deaton, and James C. Hearn. "The Enactment of State-level Governance Reforms for Higher Education: A Test of the Political-instability Hypothesis." *Journal of Higher Education* 78(6) (2007): 645–675.

McLendon, Michael K., James C. Hearn, and Steven R. Deaton. "Called to Account: Analyzing the Origins and Spread of State Performance-accountability Policies for Higher Education." *Educational Evaluation and Policy Analysis* 28(1) (2006): 1–24.

McLendon, Michael K., Donald E. Heller, and Steven Young. "State Postsecondary Education Policy Innovation: Politics, Competition, and the Interstate Migration of Policy Ideas." *Journal of Higher Education* 76(4) (2005): 363–400.

Meisinger, Richard J., and James R. Mingle. "The Extent of State Controls in Maryland Public Higher Education." In *Managing Flexibility and State Regulation in Higher Education*, edited by James R. Mingle. Atlanta: Southern Regional Education Board, 1983, 17–35.

Meyer, John W., and Brian Rowan, "Institutionalized Organizations: Formal Structure as Myth and Ceremony." *American Journal of Sociology* 83 (1978): 440–463.

Meyer, John W., and W. Richard Scott, eds. *Organizational Environments: Ritual and Rationality*. Beverly Hills: Sage, 1983.

Morphew, Christopher C. "Fixed Tuition Pricing: A Solution that May be Worse than the Problem." *Change* 39(1) (2007): 34–39.

Novak, Richard J. "Methods, Objectives, and Consequences of Restructuring." In *Restructuring Higher Education*, edited by Terrence J. MacTaggart. San Francisco: Jossey-Bass, 1996, 16–50.

Rhoades, Gary. "Managing Productivity in an Academic Institution: Rethinking the Whom, Which, What, and Whose of Productivity." *Research in Higher Education* 42(5) (2001): 619–632.

Roha, Thomas Arden. *State University-related Foundations and the Issue of Independence*. AGB Occasional Paper No. 39. Washington, DC: Association of Governing Boards of Universities and Colleges, 2000.

Schmidt, Peter. "Florida's Board of Regents Wins a Reprieve (for Now) from the Legislature." *Chronicle of Higher Education*, May 19, 2000.

Schmidt, Peter. "Revamping of Education Governance in Florida Reveals a New Political Order." *Chronicle of Higher Education*, May 17, 2002.

Selingo, Jeffrey. "Florida Moves to Scrap Board of Regents in Favor of Local Control of Universities." *Chronicle of Higher Education*, May 11, 2001.

Spellings, Margaret. *An Action Plan for Higher Education: Remarks Delivered to the National Press Club*. Washington, DC, September 6, 2006. Available online (accessed 3.29.2007): http://www.ed.gov/news/speeches/2006/09/09262006.html.

State of Colorado. *State of Colorado, Department of Higher Education Performance Contract*. Denver: Department of Higher Education, 2005. Available online (accessed 3.29.2007): http://highered.colorado.gov/Academics/PerformanceContracts/final/wsc.pdf.

St Petersburg Times. "The Sad Truth on Universities." February 21, 2008. Available online (accessed 2.21.2008): http://www.sptimes.com/2008/02/21/Opinion/The_sad_truth_on_ univ.shtml.

Stein, Donald G. *Buying in or Selling out?: The Commercialization of the American Research University*. New Brunswick: Rutgers University Press, 2004.

Thelin, John R. *Higher Education and its Useful Past: Applied History in Research and Planning*. Cambridge, MA: Schenkman, 1982.

Trombley, William. "Florida's New 'K-20' Model." *CrossTalk* 9(2) (2001): 14–16.

US Department of Education. *A Test of Leadership: Charting the Future of US Higher Education*. Report of a Commission Appointed by US Secretary of Education Margaret Spellings. Washington, DC: US Department of Education, 2006.

Washburn, Jennifer. *University Inc.: The Corporate Corruption of Higher Education*. New York: Basic Books, 2005.

Weick, Karl E. "Educational Organizations as Loosely Coupled Systems." *Administrative Science Quarterly* 21 (1976): 1–19.

Weick, Karl E. "Administering Education in Loosely Coupled Systems." *Phi Delta Kappan* 63 (1982): 673–675.

Zusman, Ami. *The Legislature and the University: Conflict in Higher Education.* Paper presented at the annual meeting of the Association for the Study of Higher Education, Chicago, 1984.

11

Mapping out Discourses on Higher Education Governance

ANTÓNIO M. MAGALHÃES AND ALBERTO AMARAL

Introduction

The liberal idea of governing as the legitimate use of power to allocate resources in pursuit of political objectives has evolved with nuances throughout European nation-states' histories. Governing was conceived as emanating from the people's sovereignty, from individual freedom, from the separation of powers; in sum, from the social contract and, therefore, from rational consent – to use John Locke's expression. In parallel with the rationalization of the power of states to steer national societies politically, the concept of governance has developed in the sense of technical procedures to conduct, supervise and control the implementation of policies. The development of the separation between governing and governance had important impacts on policy-making. State officials and professional bureaucrats emerged as state apparatus managers, and the writing and development of policies became increasingly the focus and the "job" of these professionals (Peters, 2001: 10). As a result the conceptualization of policies was increasingly separated from policy implementation as a field of professional expertise under the prevalence of the former over the latter.

It was within this paradigm that both governing and governance developed as a kind of social engineering, meaning that social change was viewed as the object of a rational design and the product of its "technical" execution. This model has achieved its most developed expression in Europe within the framework of the post-1945 welfare state. It has assumed simultaneously a top-down perspective and a "moral" and "scientific" perspective with regard to the political management of social systems and institutions. A top-down perspective, since policies were designed by experts on the assumption that policies should be universal and encompassing, and the legitimacy of the processes of agenda-setting, decision-making and implementation was to be found in the interest of all citizens. Experts not only had better knowledge than individual citizens about social issues; they were also able to make more disinterested decisions. Citizens, individually and collectively, could not distance themselves from the immediacy of their interests. The ethical foundation of this governing model was based on the universal scope of social policies and also in the presence of trust in the shaping of the relationships between state/government and institutions.

During the last thirty years the main ingredients of this governing model – particularly its universality and trust – became the target for strong suspicion (Stoer and Magalhães, 2005), under the simultaneous accusation of social inefficiency and financial ineffectiveness. Alternatively, firms and corporations emerged as the "role models" for state reforms and inspiration for the reconfiguration of the governing and governance models of public institutions. When translated into governing policies, this implied more institutional autonomy, less governmental interference, a shift from public to private funding, and a move from *ex ante* control to *ex post* evaluation. Between the mid-1980s and mid-1990s, some higher education researchers argued (Neave and van Vught, 1991) that higher education played a front-runner role in the development of this governing model. In this chapter we will argue that this role is to be questioned. We will argue that the rise of higher education's "exemplary case" as a challenge to traditional state control occurred simultaneously with the configuration of the political agenda brought about by the rhetoric on the knowledge society and economy (Henkel, 2007). As knowledge management is quintessential to higher education (Clark, 1983), we will also link the changing role attributed to knowledge with the reconfiguration of "education" in "higher education." As discourses of knowledge, society and the economy put universities in a pivotal position, there are important implications not only for their autonomy but for the nature of (higher) education.

Governing and Governance

Governing as political steering acquires its legitimacy directly from democratic procedures, ultimately from the election of people's representatives. It is from the realm of "polity" that the power to allocate resources to attain certain goals derives its legitimacy. Governance, in turn, represents the management of this allocation at the various levels, its implementation and evaluation. It develops within the realm of "policies" under the aegis of government rule. Contemporary policy-making enhances the separation of governing from governance and it increasingly induces the idea that the technical approach to policy, based on the knowledge of policy instruments and their handling, features governance as the policy-making process, ranging from agenda-setting to policy evaluation. This inversion was referred to as technocracy, with an emphasis on "technical" expertise over political skills in policy formation. This is particularly visible in the area of public policies, as a research field intending to link political theory and political practices in order to understand the effective activities of governments (McCool, 1995). These activities, or public policies, are defined as governmental decisions designed to deal with social problems "where government decisions have a prospective influence on future government decisions, rather than just the immediate parties" (Nagel, 1980: 391). The dominance of expertise in the political process can be traced back to the political tendency that, at least at the discourse level, tends to subsume governing to governance.

This tendency was already identified under the designation of new managerialism (Deem, 2001; Santiago, Magalhães and Carvalho, 2004; among others), but it is not specific to higher education (Salamon, 2002: 8).[1] The political legitimacy of this process is to be found in the apparent neutrality of its technicality, based on political instruments discourse.[2] This tendency became progressively intertwined with neo-liberal perspectives and theories, such as public choice and agency theories. If we consider the redesign of the public sector that can be observed since the 1970s in OECD countries, such as the United Kingdom, Australia and the US, it is clear that there is no political neutrality in these technical approaches to policy-making. Reforms were driven by the suspicion that state bureaucracy and government officials were major obstacles to the attainment of the public interest. Public servants were represented as a group with interests of their own and committed to specific loyalties (ultimately their own interests as a professional group) other than the public interest (Ball, 1998). To deal with this source of inefficiency, public choice theory, in different strands and nuances, argued for the reconceptualization and reorganization of public institutions to make them subject to the same balance of costs and benefits that one can find in the private and corporate sectors. James Buchanan (1978), one of its main theorists, clearly defends the assertion that public finance and economics should not be independent of a theory of politics. Buchanan's analysis of public institutions constitutes an important aspect of neo-liberalism. He shares with the work of Hayek and Friedman the major conclusions of monetarism, by assuming the need to restrain the government's role, control the money supply, decrease the public sector by promoting its privatization and commercialization, and opposing full employment (Olssen, Codd and O'Neill, 2004: 154). Under this perspective, public institutions and ultimately the government cannot serve the public interest, because bureaucrats and state officials cannot act independently from their own interests as individuals and groups. On the other hand, state protection does not enact social justice with regard to the redistribution of wealth, the only way to make state action positive being to "extract . . . compliance from individuals to engineer a market order" (2004: 159).

Another perspective that endorses and enhances the divide between governing and governance and the latter's prevalence over the former is agency theory. This perspective had an extensive influence in the social and organizational reshaping that took place in the UK, Australia, New Zealand and the US (e.g., Althaus, 1997; Boston et al., 1996; Simon, 1991). This theory had its origins in the private business sector and it conceives the hierarchical distribution of authority within organizations as a set of contracts between the "principals" and the "agents" (Althaus, 1997). When translated into a management perspective it conceives organizations as a net of compliances via the control of the performance and accountability of the individual members of organizations. The chains of principals–agents can be traced in organizational contexts such as education organizations – universities included – and state agencies. Agency theory is a form of rationalizing the behaviors of individuals and organizations within a context that assumes "individual self interest maximisation, bounded rationality, risk aversion, goal conflict among members and the treatment of information as a commodity that can be purchased" (Olssen, Codd and O'Neill, 2004: 141).

For Salamon, the questioning of the cost and effectiveness of government programs and the emergence of neo-liberal theories have resulted in governments "being challenged to be reinvented, downsized, privatised, devolved, decentralised, deregulated, delayered, subject to performance tests, and contracted out" (2002: 1). The "new governance" approach is characterized by massive proliferation "in the tools of public action, in the instruments or means used to address public problems" (2002: 1–2), while attention has been shifted "from hierarchic agencies to organizational networks" (2002: 11). The state is no longer considered as having the monopoly of expertise and resources to govern (Newman, 2003). However, the increasing complexity of the multitude of tools of public action may result in "the strong possibility that the reforms they are espousing may be the source, rather than the cure, for the problems they are seeking to remedy" (Salamon, 2002: 7).

Governance theory "wrestles with the problem of how to govern complex and differentiated societies, societies in which the local and the global interact in dynamic processes of structural change" (Newman, 2003: 3). In the EU the dispersion of authority away from the central government resulting from reallocation of power upwards (to the EU), downwards (to the regions, local authorities) and sideways (to public/private networks) (Hooghe and Marks, 2001) led to the development of multi-level literature that is extensively used in the analysis of the Open Method of Coordination (OMC) (De la Porte and Pochet, 2004). Political science and public policy analysis have been dealing with the shift from the model of social engineering and state control to the new forms of governing and governance. They are trying to identify the paths and the emerging governing models both from the criticism of the bureaucratic model and, interestingly enough, from the reforms already inspired by that criticism.

Guy Peters (2001) based the rise of new forms of regulating social life in Western societies on the fact that the economies and societies that states are supposed to regulate have become less predictable and, therefore, less governable. To this he adds an increasing social and political heterogeneity among populations – and, as a consequence, the emergence of less bargainable issues – and the decline of previously stable organizations (2001: 16). He tries to clarify selected visions of possible futures for the state and its bureaucracy by proposing four models to interpret these transformations: the market model, the participatory state model, the flexible model and the deregulation model. In spite of the interpretative potential of these models, reform projects for governing the "reality" of contemporary societies are more complex than the models suggest. However, it is important to stress that each of these perspectives impinges on the way governance, in a broad sense, is to be translated into administrative regimes. The reform agendas, Peters adds, are embedded in other political and cultural movements in society, and the promotion of market models is just one tool for promoting market ideas in social institutions, including universities, while "the drive for making administration more participatory is but a part of a general ethos (largely contradictory to the market model) stressing greater opportunities for the participation in these same institutions" (2001: 17).

The changing relationship between governing and governance must also be understood in the framework of broader political and cultural movements in Western societies. In spite of Peters' theoretical and methodological cautions, the hegemony of the political proposals based on the market model is evident in the international, national and institutional panoramas. Even when we do not overestimate the ideological component of policy-making in contemporary European societies, the market model emerges as an indisputable reality. Neave (1995) stated that in Western Europe the orientation towards market (de)regulation was a pragmatic answer to the need to transfer resources to other welfare areas, such as health and social security, rather than an option determined by the inner virtues of the market acting as a regulatory mechanism. However, without denying the financial crisis of the welfare states, and their effort to "hold the line" (Scott, 1995), we should not underestimate the discourse/ideological influence brought about by the rise of neo-liberalism in Europe (and after 1989 in both Western *and* Eastern Europe) as a governing alternative.

The changing relationship between governing and governance is therefore to be understood in the framework of the reconfiguration of the state and its bureaucracy and their regulation in Western societies and of the influence of neo-liberal inspiration. Even though the advocates of a participatory model of governing put forward the general prescription to foster greater individual and collective participation by including them in the decision-making processes at various organizational levels, in a time when neo-liberalism rules over the reconfiguration of state regulation it is difficult to disentangle the claim for the "client" (individual chooser) as the center of the process and the empowerment of the "consumer" (participant citizen). This means that the political and cultural hegemony of the general approach to political steering is more important than the philosophical inspiration of a given governing model.

Changing Relationships Between State and Higher Education Systems and Institutions

In this context it is difficult to argue that higher education is playing a front-runner role. First, even if we defend higher education exceptionalism as both social and a research field, there is no evidence that the reconfiguration of governing and governance started or was inspired in higher education. Rather, the opposite is arguable. It was in the framework of the transformation of the welfare state that all social systems, education and higher education included, started to be reformed. Under the contradictory influences of increasingly strong transnational political and economic pressures (e.g. EU) and local-level claims, the European states are living simultaneously through processes of disintegration, integration and replacement (Leyton-Brown, 1996). Dale (2007) argues that this context has dictated the decline of the state as the national basis of the economy, the declining influence of borders, mainly with regard to movements of capital and to the impact of international organizations, and the recognition that state activities could/should be funded and provided by other, mainly private, institutions. The latter is particularly visible in the form of New Public Management (NPM) (Pollitt and Bouckaert, 2004) not only with regard to funding and provision but, importantly, with regard to management and administration of the activities undertaken. Since the mid-1980s the welfare state has increasingly come under political "suspicion."

In Europe, these doubts were translated into the presence and (prevalence) of neo-liberal and neo-conservative policies and discourses, though in a rather *contra natura* alliance (Giddens, 1994), in the political arenas. Peter Scott states that the "break" in welfarism should not be overemphasized, for as "this apparent backlash against the welfare state has gathered force, European higher education systems have been expanded and elaborated" (Scott, 1995: 72), and the transformation of the welfare state does not correspond to an ideological revolution but rather to the pragmatic recognition that the excessive expenditure associated with a welfare state needs to be contained. Instead of the "dismantlement" or the "rolling back of the state," Scott prefers to say that the welfare state is "holding the line" (1995: 72). He claims that there is a transition to a new form of welfare state, the "tertiary welfare state." The "primary welfare state" is described as concentrating on designing safety nets to deal with the issues of health insurance, housing, social security and unemployment benefits. The "secondary welfare state" took on a more interventionist role by combining itself with Keynesianism as the mode of economic regulation. Finally, the "tertiary welfare state," which began to emerge in the 1990s in the Western countries – in different weights and performances according to the national context – can be "described as a shift from a fiduciary state to a contractual state" (1995: 80) and as "the transition from the welfare state to a welfare society, which reflects the broader shift from the corporatist state to civil society" (1995: 81).

The changing relationship between governing and governance processes and structures in public institutions, universities included, that has occurred in the two last decades was mainly activated by the reconfiguration of the role of the state under pressures of its financial crisis and the neo-liberal rhetoric. States have started to promote an apparent deregulation – by inducing institutions to go to the market, to self-regulation and to competition between themselves – as a more effective form of regulation. This is the context within which the "evaluative state" (Neave, 1988) rose. Neave argues that while in the US the market "stands foursquare in current debate . . . over the place and responsibility of government – federal, state, and local – often expressed in terms of 'downsizing' or 'customerizing' the basic operations it has previously exercised" (1995: 59), in Western Europe it derived from pragmatic pressures for transferring resources to such welfare areas as social security and health. One way or another, the orientation towards market regulation enacted the reorganization of state sectors all over Europe.

Higher education has not been the first sector to receive the attention of NPM policies. In fact NPM, Dale (2007) argues, is equally applicable to all sectors and it is simultaneously the prescription and the diagnosis of the "problem." The health sector and the social security system were confronted with NPM at an earlier stage than the higher education system. These changes, which can be observed in various and ideologically diverse welfare states, corresponded to the emergence of the tertiary welfare state, that is "the shift from universal to selective benefits, the growing popularity of user payments, the tendency to distinguish between policy-making and service delivery (enabling the latter to be contracted out to non-state providers)" (Scott, 1995: 80). It is also true that EU policies have apparently been more effective in ensuring some degree of convergence of employment and social policy objectives across Europe while the same so far has not taken place in higher education, despite the implementation of the Bologna Process.

For Hemerijck, the rules on the limits to the public deficit have forced the reform of the welfare state "to lower the burden on the public budget and to dampen the growth of wage costs, irrespective of participation in EMU [European Monetary Union]" (Hemerijck, 2002: 22). He also argues that there are three observable trends in the EU: the liberalization of public employment service systems; the widening scope of coordination between social protection and employment provision; and emerging sub-national employment pacts in response to problems associated with regional economic conditions (2002: 27). We might say that in some European countries, higher education, to a certain extent and during a certain period, was protected from the impact of this re-composition of the state: namely, in those Southern European countries where higher education was historically "delayed" with regard to massification processes in comparison to those of Northern and Western Europe. This was the case in Portugal, which reached the stage of massification only in the mid-1990s. And at EU level, education has always been considered an "area that belongs to the core of the nation state and therefore resilient to 'Europe'" (Gornitzka, 2007: 1). This has probably delayed attempts at European convergence, although it has been unable to stop completely the creeping competence of the European Commission (Amaral and Neave, 2007). Additionally, the discursive *motto* that is pervading discourses on higher education steering and governance could also be found in general education policy proposals. Chubb and Moe (1990) pleaded for competition in education and defended the notion of choice in education to provide an equitable and effective education system.

The changes in governing and governance structures that one can identify in the field of higher education are to be understood, on the one hand, in the context of the changing nature of Western economies under the pressure of intense globalization and, on the other, in the context of the increasing complexity of societies as they evolve from the traditional concept of nation-state and become less homogeneous and predictable. The regulation in European states increasingly reflects the re-composition of national sovereignty and their position in the knowledge-based society and economy. In fact, as Carnoy argues, "knowledge production plays a definitive role (in the *network state*) . . . in managing and compensating the disequalising effects of globalisation locally" (2001: 31). Also, these are, in our view, the main "sources" (Dale, 1991) of the reconfiguration of discourses on governance in higher education.

Governing Higher Education and the Governance of HEIs

All over Europe reforms of higher education political steering and higher education governance are visible. These winds of change started in the United Kingdom under the aegis of NPM discourses and are evolving throughout Europe. For example, Austria and Portugal have recently reorganized their higher education systems, having been explicitly inspired by that perspective. For Vital Moreira, "these changes translate a change of paradigm . . . it is the so-called movement of the New Public Management . . . which simply means trying to imitate, to replicate the modes of the private sector management in the public sector" (2008: 125). And Hans Pechar states the reform has brought Austria to a leading place among the European promoters of the "managerial revolution," although there are some concerns about its consequences as "Academics, even academics in leadership positions who basically support the reform, have mixed feelings" (2005: 10).

The enhancement of institutional autonomy and the reorganization of the governance system are the cornerstones of the discourse reforms. The first dimension assumes that the more autonomous HEIs are, the more performative and the more responsive to the goals of the government and the economy they will become. The latter dimension is based on the assumption that collegial forms of governance are neither efficient nor effective. "Managerialism" is opposed to "collegiality" not only as an alternative governance structure but as a steering instrument expressing the reconfiguration of the steering role of the state (see Henkel (2007) for the UK case).

If institutional autonomy is the main driver for efficiency, social relevance and social accountability appear as the discursive ground upon which its political effectiveness is based. State retraction from institutional management does not correspond, however, to a negative perspective of the role of the state. On the contrary, the enhancement of institutional autonomy in this context, for instance, by encouraging the reconfiguration of universities from public institutions to private organizations in law, corresponds to a positive use of the state power to steer the higher education systems. As the relationship between the state and the autonomous institutions is configured as a contractual linkage ruled by the state according to governmental strategies, it appears as an enhancement rather than a retraction from system and institutions coordination. For Neave, the nation-state has compensated for its largesse in promoting institutional autonomy with "the setting up of a powerful, relatively precise and detailed instrumentality over and above that control and oversight traditionally exercised through legislative and legal procedures" (Neave, 2007: 10). Neave argues that this augmented instrumentality in higher education was the vehicle for reforms ranging from the rise of "remote steering" to the replacement of *a priori* input-based financing with *a posteriori* allocation related to institutional outputs (2007: 10). These instruments to regulate institutional autonomy, based on performance indicators, have spread all over Europe, such as incentive-led funding in Denmark, performance-driven steering in Sweden or "contracts" in France.

Interestingly enough, the diagnosis that HEIs need autonomy is a discursive strategy that has in it the remedy for such an (assumed) "handicap" that is the redefinition of universities from public institutions to self-administered bodies. This is the case of the foundational model that was proposed in some German *Länder* (e.g. Lower Saxony) and in Portugal. Under the influence of NPM, the states' strategy to reform political steering and governance transfers state supervision to the foundation, that is to its board. In the Lower Saxony case, reported by Neave (2007: 10), individual membership of the supervisory board is to be nominated by the university senate and the appointment confirmed by the Ministry. Institutional autonomy is the ultimate accomplishment of the evaluative state and the final step in its transformation from guardian to overseer (2007: 13). Apparently, Neave agrees with the interpretation that institutional autonomy advances rather than slows down the move towards a more powerful and intrusive relationship between state and HEIs in the form of a new instrumentality "more powerful, more invasive and more consequential than ever it was when the Guardian model of the relationship between government, society and the university operated through the legal construct of 'State control'" (2007: 13). In fact, as we have been arguing, these governance approaches are gradually replacing the previous state control and academic collegial governance. New governing bodies are replacing senates and other collegial bodies. New constituencies and new types of stakeholders contribute to the enactment of institutional autonomy. Discourses on the requirement that HEIs must be responsive to social and economic needs and to be socially accountable are almost universal. Mary Henkel, referring to the changing conceptions of university autonomy in Britain, finds that the "panoply of policy frameworks, institutional structures and nexuses, and policy instruments . . . substantially shape and, in some cases, restrict the choices universities make" (2007: 10).

De Boer, Huisman and Meister-Scheytt (2007) have analyzed the supervising bodies of universities resulting from the form of governance we are analyzing in three different countries, Austria, England and the Netherlands. They have focused on their roles, and particularly on how the public interest is safeguarded in this new governance structure, and conclude that it is not clear where these governance movements will lead as "we certainly lack an understanding of the 'doing' of governance" (2007: 6). This lack by the boards is exemplified in the shift in the relationship of political instruments and political goals. Boards and their governance tools are instruments whose driving logics shifted from the goals pointed out by the Ministry to their inner functioning. Probably, the reason why the boards "move in mysterious ways" (2007: 21) may not be found strictly in higher education. Without denying higher education's specificities, we can hardly sustain the argument that the paradigm of governance, and its tools that we refer to, had their origins in education, let alone in higher education. If we look at Lester Salamon's book *The Tools of Government* (2002), we easily recognize the discursive matrix of the governance model in the basic forms of government that rely on an enormous proliferation "in the *tools* of public action, in the *instruments* or means used to address public problems" (2002: 1–2) and in the replacement of the delivery of goods and services with a "dizzying array of loans, loan guarantees, grants, contracts, social regulation, economic regulation, insurance, tax expenditures, vouchers, and more" (2002: 2). Salamon stresses that the emerging approaches to public problem-solving can be characterized by two main features. The first, as we have already mentioned, involves the replacement of the concept of government by the concept of governance; the second is signified by the use of the term "new," "as a recognition that these collaborative approaches, while hardly novel, must now be approached in a new, more coherent way" (2002: 8). The "new governance" paradigm, in his words, is based upon five concepts: from agency and program to tool, focusing on governance techniques rather than on programs; from hierarchy to network, as actors play their roles in interdependent positions; from public versus private to public and private, as what is meant by "public" is currently changing; from command and control to negotiation and persuasion; from management skills to enablement skills. These narrative elements can be found in the reform of governance in the public sector throughout Western society, even though it is more visible in the NPM approaches.

Changing Governance and Changing Higher Education

According to our argument, higher education is following the same path of other social systems and subsystems. The concept of education implicit in higher education does not escape from this changing world. Peter Scott (1995) and Ronald Barnett (1994), among others, have reflected on the changing meanings of higher education and on the emerging idea of higher education. In our perspective, as the handling of knowledge is quintessential to higher education (Clark, 1983), much of this change must be found in the changing role of knowledge in the present societies and economies.

Knowledge, in the form of intense circulation of information via ICT, is pointed out as a central production factor. Some argue (e.g. Castells, 1996) that we are living through a major historical event parallel to the Industrial Revolution and an important discontinuity in the economic and cultural structure of society is being induced. "Information technology," he argues, "is to this revolution what new sources of energy were to the successive Industrial Revolutions, from steam engine to electricity, to fossil fuels, and even nuclear power" (1996: 31). But it is important to stress that in this transformation knowledge and information *per se* are not relevant, but rather "the application of such knowledge and information to knowledge generation and information processing/communication devices, in a cumulative feedback loop between innovation and the uses of innovation" (1996: 32). These assumptions about the role of knowledge gave rise to new political approaches and have repositioned higher education in the framework of political strategies, at regional,[3] national and supranational levels. They lead to changes not only in universities' strategic priorities but in governance and organization. Reichert, reporting on a research project on the role of universities in regional development, underlines that along with appeals of university members to the institutional specificities of universities, aiming at guaranteeing maximum freedom and innovating capacity for their researchers, professors and students, universities should interact with "regional agencies and knowledge based business to develop their own solutions for knowledge-friendly creative environments" (Reichert, 2006: 19).

The governance and organizational changes led by the perceived trans-formations of the role of knowledge vary according to national context. Although we do not know enough about the ultimate consequences of the governance model that we are discussing, there are some signs. Mary Henkel (2007), referring to the

UK, argues that the shift from collegial governance to management concepts, structures and methods has enabled HEIs to act more collectively and strategically, and that participation in markets can constitute an enhancement or a diminution of an institution's ability to decide about the profile of academic work they undertake. It may be that universities find more diversified sources to support their research projects and their educational programs, thus becoming less subject to state control. Or, alternatively, competing in markets means that their decision-making criteria shift "from the academic to the financial, and that their choices are voluntary but between options that distort their epistemic identities" (2007: 10–11).

The 2000 Lisbon Agenda reflects this perspective, as it assumes to transform Europe into the most competitive and socially harmonious region in the world. In fact, EU documents became populated by references to knowledge and to the advantages of competition that the handling of knowledge apparently brings to nations. A 2003 report, from the Commission of the European Communities, *The Role of the Universities in the Europe of Knowledge*, is an example of the increasing emphasis on the role of knowledge. After assuming that the EU needs increased production, transmission and dissemination of knowledge, it recognizes that this can be supported only by the excellence of its universities (CEC, 2003). Mary Henkel, elaborating on the British case, also stresses that Blair's Labour government policies have been under the influence of "theories of the knowledge society and knowledge economy," namely "in its recognition of the importance of investing in science and the scientific infrastructure in the pursuit of innovation" (2007: 7). Aiming at building a national research and innovation system, the UK government has strengthened its control and coordination of policy development and also the institutional basis in which it is funded, implemented and evaluated (2007: 7).

This enhanced mandate addressed to higher education drives, and simultaneously is driven by, the creation of the European Higher Education Area (EHEA). As the Bologna Process was appropriated by the European Commission, the EHEA has been implemented by means of "soft" law and "soft" instruments, such as National Progress Reports and National Action Plans for Recognition, Stocktaking Reports and Scorecards, and the European Qualification Framework (EQF) (Veiga and Amaral, forthcoming). These instruments are important to understand the educational change that is being induced. The EQF, for instance, is supposed to provide commonly understood reference levels on how to describe learning, from basic competences up to the Ph.D. level. The assumption is that it will not only facilitate mobility and recognition but make degrees more comprehensible to employers. A 2005 working document of the Commission of European Communities, *Towards a European Qualifications Framework for Lifelong Learning*, underlined that EQF aims at "the voluntary development of competence based solutions at the European level enabling sectors to address the new education and training challenges caused by the internationalisation of trade and technology" (CEC, 2005: 7). In this document it is expected that students will acquire a diversified set of cognitive, functional, personal and ethical competences (2005: 11).

The first evident change is the shift from knowledge as the organizer of learning to competence(s) as the capacity to mobilize knowledge to know and to act technically and socially. This focus on competences as the ability to mobilize knowledge is not new; however, its new centrality reconfigures the role of knowledge from a formative process to a teaching–learning instrument mediated by competences. The focus is now on the *mobilizing capacity* as the central educational issue. The educational process is to be realized as aiming at a product, as a "learning outcome" (Magalhães and Sousa, 2007). If educational categories (teaching, learning, students, professors, classes, etc.) were based upon the formative role attributed to knowledge, the reconfiguration of education in the framework of the creation of the EHEA is inducing an important reshaping of the educational role of knowledge, that is its formative role is being reconfigured by the potential of mobilizing it to act socially, in particular in the world of economy and labor. As HEIs are conceptualized as relevant to and accountable for economic and social changes, the need to design "learning outcomes" on the basis of internal and external stakeholders grows in proportion. "Students" are simultaneously internal stakeholders, clients of educational services, persons evolving from education to the labor market, in sum, "learners." The professor is being reinvented as an "instructional designer" (Cowen, 1996). He/she is no more the "center" of the knowledge flux and delivery, but rather the one who is responsible for creating learning opportunities for the "learners." Moreover, as an academic, he/she is giving up his/her ultimate position with regard to quality judgments on the teaching–learning processes in favor of (external) expertise on them. As "learning outcomes" are what a learner is expected to know, understand and/or be able to demonstrate after completion of learning, these outcomes are to be captured by indicators, while the assessment of the educational process moves from inside to outside HEIs and to so-called assessment experts. The rise of ICT instruments is increasingly delocalizing learning to the ether of www, with face-to-face teaching–learning being a minor proportion of the "learner's activities." E-learning is not the "death of the professor" (Nuyen, 1992) but his/her reconfiguration as a learning monitor. On the other hand, the virtual campuses are introducing new kinds of academic life whose educational impact is far from clear.

Conclusion

The role assigned to knowledge has enhanced the economic role assigned to education, particularly to higher education. The new approaches to higher education governing and governance articulate both this change in the education and economic roles and the reconfiguration of the relations between state, society and individuals in Western societies. We have argued that the rise of higher education as an "exemplary case" of the challenge to traditional state control occurs simultaneously with the reconfiguration of the political agenda brought about by the discourses on the relationship between the knowledge society and the economy. These discourses shifted the emphasis on theoretical knowledge to applied research, inducing "imperatives for government and business to involve themselves in their governance" (Henkel, 2007: 2). The fact that (applicable) knowledge became a pivotal factor in the production, distribution and consumption processes has impacted on the occupations of academics and scientists as well as the autonomy of HEIs.

The steering and governance instruments in higher education that we have analyzed reflect the new political approaches and challenge higher education to respond to such questions as "what is higher education about?" As HEIs are conceptualized as relevant to and accountable for economic and social change, and education is designed to achieve "learning outcomes" on the basis of internal and external stakeholders' expectations, demands and needs, the new forms of governance are simultaneously the explanation and what is to be explained. Thus, the changes in the governance models are a consequence of the political and social expectations put on higher education, and a driving force for their own implementation.

Traditional higher education constituencies (students, academic staff, non-academic staff, families, etc.), viewed as stakeholders, articulate the change in the educational paradigm (learners, learning monitors, competence-centered learning, etc.) and apparently this new world of higher education is to be steered and governed in a different form. We have argued throughout the chapter that in this reconfiguration of European higher education, at governance level and at educational level, there was a strong influence of the neo-liberal discourse and neo-liberal theories, even though we recognize that other discourses are also present – for instance, the participatory model narratives (Peters, 2001). In our view it is not enough merely to acknowledge that we experience a "strengthening of the management function, culture and structures" (Maassen, 2003: 33). As argued, the emphasis on governance technicality and on the expert control of its instruments does not correspond to the principle of political neutrality of traditional public administration. On the contrary, these instruments are driven by political rationales that are enacted and brought to light as they are implemented. As Salamon puts it: "what makes this development particularly significant is that each of these tools has its own procedures, skill requirements, and delivery mechanism, indeed its own 'political economy'" (2002: 2). The management of loans, grants, contracts, insurance, tax expenditure, vouchers, etc. does not work in a social and political vacuum. In fact, these changes in governing and governance are framing the shift from the higher education governance ideal of a "republic of scholars" to the ideal of a "stakeholder organization" (Bleiklie and Kogan, 2007: 477).

Notes

1 "The first of the ['new governance' defining features] signified by use of the term 'governance' instead of 'government' . . . Such an approach is necessary, we will argue, because problems have become too complex for government to handle on its own, because disagreements exist about the proper ends of public action, and because government increasingly lacks the authority to enforce its will on other crucial actors without giving them a meaningful seat at the table" (Salamon, 2002: 8).

2 This neutrality of policy-making as "technical" activity does not correspond to the principle of the "apolitical civil service" of the traditional public administration. This principle refers to the

civil servants' obligation not to have known political allegiances and to serve the government in office independently from their private political choices. The neutralism of policy-making as a "technical" activity, on the contrary, is based on its transformation into a political choice as if it could perform independently of political choices.

3   An example of the political enhancement of the role of universities at regional level is the EUA report by Sybille Reichert (2006). She argues: "Thus the university has moved centre-stage, not because the world has suddenly converted into a community of curious knowledge-thirsty citizens, but because the country or region needs the university as a source of innovation and future innovators to ensure its economic and social success" (2006: 20).

References

Althaus, Catherine. "The Application of Agency Theory to Public Sector Management." In *The New Contractualism*, edited by Glyn Davis, Barbara Sullivan, and Anna Yeatman. Melbourne: Macmillan Education, 1997, 137–153.

Amaral, Alberto, and Guy Neave. *On Bologna, Weasels and Creeping Competence.* Paper presented at the sixth Douro Seminar, The Challenges and Complexities of an Emerging Multi-level Governance System, Douro Valley, Portugal, September 30–October 4, 2007.

Ball, Stephen. "Big Policies/Small World: An Introduction to International Perspectives in Education Policy." *Comparative Education* 34(2) (1998): 119–130.

Barnett, Ronald. *The Idea of Higher Education.* Buckingham: Society for Research into Higher Education and Open University, 1994.

Bleiklie, Ivar, and Maurice Kogan. "Organization and Governance of Universities." *Higher Education Policy* 20(4) (2007): 477–494.

Boston, Jonathan, John Martin, June Pallot, and Pat Walsh. *Public Management: The New Zealand Model.* New York: Oxford University Press, 1996.

Buchanan, James. "From Private Preferences to Public Philosophy: The Development of Public Choice." In *The Economics of Politics*, edited by James Buchanan. London: Institute of Economic Affairs, 1978, 1–20.

Carnoy, Martin. "The Role of the State in the New Global Economy." In *Challenges of Globalisation: South African Debates with Manuel Castells*, edited by Johan Muller, Nico Cloete, and Shireen Badat. Cape Town: Maskew Miller Longman, 2001, 22–34.

Castells, Manuel. *The Rise of Network Society.* Oxford: Blackwell, 1996.

Chubb, John, and Terry Moe. *Politics, Markets and America's Schools.* Washington, DC: Brookings Institution, 1990.

Clark, Burton R. *The Higher Education System: Academic Organization in Cross-national Perspective.* Berkeley: University of California, 1983.

Commission of the European Communities (CEC). *The Role of the Universities in the Europe of Knowledge.* Brussels: CEC, 2003.

Commission of the European Communities (CEC). *Towards a European Qualifications Framework for Lifelong Learning.* Brussels: CEC, 2005.

Cowen, Robert. "Performativity, Post-modernity and the University." *Comparative Education* 32(2) (1996): 245–258.

Dale, Roger. "Perspectives on Policy-making." In *E333 Policy-making in Education.* Milton Keynes: Open University Press, 1991, 45–103.

Dale, Roger. "Repairing the Deficits of Modernity: The Emergence of Parallel Discourses in Higher Education in Europe." In *World Yearbook of Education 2008: Geographies of Knowledge, Geometries of Power: Framing the Future of Higher Education*, edited by Debbie Epstein, Rebecca Boden, Rosemary Deem, Fazal Rizvi, and Susan Wright. London: Routledge, 2007, 14–31.

De Boer, Harry, Jeroen Huisman, and Claudia Meister-Scheytt. *Mysterious Guardians and the Diminishing State: Supervisors in "Modern" University Governance.* Paper presented to the twenty-ninth Annual EAIR Forum, Innsbruck, Austria, August 26–29, 2007.

Deem, Rosemary. "Globalisation, New Managerialism, Academic Capitalism and Entrepreneurialism in Universities: Is the Local Dimension Important?" *Comparative Education* 37(1) (2001): 7–20.

De la Porte, Caroline, and Phillippe Pochet. "The European Employment Strategy: Existing Research and Remaining Questions." *Journal of European Social Policy* 14(1) (2004): 71–78.

Giddens, Anthony. *Beyond Left and Right: The Future of Radical Politics*. London: Blackwell, 1994.

Gornitzka, Åse. *Networking Administration in Areas of National Sensitivity: The Commission and European Higher Education*. Paper presented at the sixth Douro Seminar, European Integration and Higher Education Governance, Douro Valley, Portugal, September 30–October 4, 2007.

Hemerijck, Anton. "The Self-transformation of the European Social Model(s)." *OMC Research Forum Paper*, 2002. Available online: http://eucenter.wisc.edu/OMC/Papers/Hemerijck.pdf2002.

Henkel, Mary. *Changing Conceptions of University Autonomy in the 21st Century Knowledge Economies: The Case of Britain*. Paper presented at the University of Aveiro, Portugal, May 18, 2007.

Hooghe, Liesbet, and Gary Marks. *Multi-level Governance and European Integration*. Lanham: Rowman and Littlefield, 2001.

Leyton-Brown, David. "Political Dimensions of Regionalization in a Changing World." In *Academic Mobility in a Changing World*, edited by Peggy Blumenthal, Craufurd Goodwin, Alan Smith, and Ulrich Teichler. London: Jessica Kingsley, 1996, 7–19.

Maassen, Peter. "Shifts in Governance Arrangements: An Interpretation of the Introduction of New Management Structures in Higher Education." In *The Higher Education Managerial Revolution?*, edited by Alberto Amaral, V. Lynn Meek, and Ingvild M. Larsen. Dordrecht: Kluwer Academic, 2003, 31–54.

Magalhães, António, and Sofia Sousa. *The European Higher Education Area and the Transformation of Educational Categories in Higher Education*. Paper presented at the Annual Conference of the Society for Research into Higher Education, Brighton, December 2007.

McCool, Daniel. *Public Policy Theories, Models, and Concepts: An Anthology*. Englewood Cliffs: Prentice-Hall, 1995.

Moreira, Vital. "The Legal Status of Higher Education Institutions." In *Politicas de Ensino Superior – Quatro Temas em Debate*, edited by Alberto Amaral. Lisbon: Conselho Nacional de Educação, 2008, 123–140.

Nagel, Stuart. "The Policy Studies Perspectives." *Public Administration Review* 40(4) (1980): 391–396.

Neave, Guy. "On the Cultivation of Quality: Efficiency and Enterprise: An Overview of Recent Trends in Higher Education in Western Europe." *European Journal of Education* 23(1/2) (1988): 7–23.

Neave, Guy. "The Stirring of the Prince and the Silence of the Lambs: The Changing Assumptions beneath Higher Education Policy, Reform, and Society." In *Emerging Patterns of Social Demand and University Reform: Through a Glass Darkly*, edited by David Dill, and Barbara Sporn. Oxford: Pergamon Press, 1995, 54–71.

Neave, Guy. *From Guardian to Overseer: Trends in Institutional Autonomy, Governance and Leadership*. Paper presented at the CNE Conference on Institutional Autonomy, Governance and Leadership, Lisbon, 2007.

Neave, Guy, and Frans van Vught, eds. *Prometheus Bound: The Changing Relationship between Government and Higher Education in Western Europe*. Oxford: Pergamon Press, 1991.

Newman, Janet. *Rethinking Governance: Critical Reflections on Theory and Practice*. Paper presented at the Changing European Societies?: The Role for Social Policy Conference, Copenhagen, November 13–15, 2003.

Nuyen, Ahn Tuan. "Lyotard on the Death of the Professor." *Educational Theory* 42 (1992): 25–37.

Olssen, Mark, John Codd, and Anne-Marie O'Neill. *Education Policy: Globalization, Citizenship and Democracy*. London: Sage, 2004.

Pechar, Hans. *University Autonomy in Austria*. Klagenfurt, IFF: HOFO Working Paper Series, 2005.

Peters, B. Guy. *The Future of Governing*. Lawrence: University of Texas, 2001.

Pollitt, Christopher, and Geert Bouckaert. *Public Management Reform: A Comparative Analysis* (2nd edn). Oxford: Oxford University Press, 2004.

Reichert, Sybille. *The Rise of Knowledge Regions: Emerging Opportunities for Universities*. Brussels: EUA, 2006.

Salamon, Lester M. "The New Governance and the Tools of Public Action: An Introduction." In *The Tools of Government: A Guide to the New Governance*, edited by Lester M. Salamon. New York: Oxford University Press, 2002, 1–47.

Santiago, Rui, António Magalhães, and Teresa Carvalho. *O Surgimento do Managerialismo no Sistema de Ensino Superior Português.* Matosinhos: CIPES, 2004.

Scott, Peter. *The Meanings of Mass Higher Education.* Buckingham: Society for Research into Higher Education and Open University, 1995.

Simon, Herbert. "Organizations and Markets." *Journal of Economics Perspectives* 5(2) (1991): 25–44.

Stoer, Stephen, and António Magalhães. *A Diferença Somos Nós: A Gestão da Mudança Social e as Políticas Educativas e Sociais.* Porto: Edições Afrontamento, 2005.

Veiga, Amélia, and Alberto Amaral. "Policy Implementation Tools and European Governance." In *Bologna, Universities and Bureaucrats,* edited by Alberto Amaral, Guy Neave, Peter Maassen, and Christine Musselin. Dordrecht: Springer, forthcoming.

12

Irish Higher Education and the Knowledge Economy

KELLY COATE AND IAIN MAC LABHRAINN

The Idea

An historian of higher education in Ireland once suggested: "memories are long in Ireland and . . . the weight of history is a burden difficult to unload" (Lydon, 1991: 51). A large part of this history is the "weight" of religion and its influence on the shaping of the education system. Most memories in Ireland are imprinted with the knowledge that the largest university (University College Dublin) developed from the Catholic University of Ireland, established in 1854 with the influential John Henry Newman as its founding rector. The diversity in the system for centuries was not about academic versus vocational orientations, but rather Catholic versus Anglican (Trinity College Dublin), versus the "godless" Queen's Colleges. Indeed, it was not until the 1960s that the Catholic Church entirely lifted the ban on Catholics attending Trinity College, and the influence of religion in the education system was still being challenged by the OECD report on Irish education in 1965.

Since he wrote *The Idea of a University*, Cardinal Newman has been widely regarded as one of the strongest proponents of the ideals of a liberal education. Yet his ideas have been appropriated in ways which do not acknowledge the profound conservatism at the heart of his vision. According to Newman, the purpose of the university should be centered on teaching, rather than research (in contrast to the Humboldtian model). He felt that universities should shape the intelligence of youth, such that: "A habit of mind is formed which lasts through life, of which the attributes are, freedom, equitableness, calmness, moderation, and wisdom . . . This then I would assign as the special fruit of the education furnished at a University" (Newman, 1955: 26). In effect, his idea was that while the university would cultivate the intellect of young gentlemen through the sharing of knowledge, it would not necessarily pursue a critical paradigm or the production of new knowledge (Readings, 1997; Blackmore, 2001).

In more recent years in Ireland, any remnants of Newman's vision have been transformed by the now dominant model of economic growth driven through science, technology and innovation. The economic boom of the so-called Celtic Tiger brought rapid change. It can be hard to imagine that Ireland's recent history was one of "deep despair" with the need for a "strategy to escape from the vicious circle of stagnation, unemployment, emigration, rising taxes and debt" (O'Donnell and Thomas, 2006: 110). The economic policies of the 1980s helped fuel the socio-economic changes that included the transition from an elite to a mass system of higher education. From ideology to the knowledge economy: the changes in this small but newly affluent country have been remarkable.

While Newman was carefully shaping the minds of a few Catholic men in the mid-nineteenth century, he could scarcely have imagined the role that universities would come to play in Ireland in what has now become widely recognized as a knowledge-based society. There are nearly 180,000 students registered at about thirty-five different tertiary institutions (HEA, 2008a), with a budget of €550 million spent on research and development in higher education institutions in 2005 (Forfás, 2006). One agency alone (Science Foundation Ireland) has responsibility for the advancement of biotechnology and information and communication technologies (ICTs), and was given a budget of €1.4 billion in the National Development Plan 2007–2013. The "special fruit" that the government now wishes universities to bear is technological innovation, research and development, focusing on the skill levels necessary to create and sustain a knowledge economy.

Indeed, the rhetoric of the knowledge economy (see Bullen, Robb and Kenway, 2004; Bullen, Fahey and Kenway, 2006; Kenway, Bullen and Robb, 2004) is the key defining feature of recent change and at the core of current government policy with regards to higher education. While increased state expenditure on research and development during the 1990s was an inducement to universities to contribute to economic growth, direct state intervention in the affairs of the universities was relatively minimal throughout this time. The government has, however, been strongly criticized by some (OECD, 2006) for its lack of a unified strategy for the whole of the higher education sector. The latest Strategic Plan for the Higher Education Authority (2008–2010) does acknowledge that a national strategy for the sector is now required (HEA, 2008b), in a somewhat circular logic. This illustrates that there is a widely perceived lack of vision from government as to future directions of the system, and in such a small country the lack of coherence might be surprising to international observers.

The lack of coherence within the governance of the system is in part due to the historical growth of the sector through a patchwork of social, religious, cultural and economic interests. The concept of institutional autonomy with respect to both management and strategy is one that is deeply embedded. If institutional autonomy is seen as a means of conservative resistance to change, it is of course problematic for government and the state. However, it may also be argued that guarantees of autonomy could place the Irish universities at an advantage in comparison with other national systems, if there is appropriate reciprocity in terms of responsibility (see, e.g., Browne, 2008) and genuine efforts towards mutual collaboration when it serves the "national interest." As Gornitzka and Maassen (2000) found in their research on changing relationships between governments and higher education systems, the Irish system is in transition. This chapter will therefore suggest that the question of governance of higher education in Ireland is at a crossroads: it will either follow the path of other Western European countries in accepting a stronger evaluative role from the state, or it will pursue and defend historical traditions of self-regulation and institutional autonomy. To understand how this position has been reached, it is necessary to chart some of the recent history.

The Contemporary Landscape

The architecture of the current system was defined by the Universities Act of 1997 and consists of seven universities, thirteen Institutes of Technology (IoTs), and several specialist colleges. In an instance somewhat characteristic of the unruly nature of Irish higher education, the 1997 act designated the federal system, National University of Ireland, as consisting of four institutions in Dublin, Maynooth, Cork and Galway. Their designated, legally recognized titles are NUI Dublin, NUI Maynooth, NUI Cork and NUI Galway. Anyone familiar with universities in Ireland will know that only two of these – Maynooth and Galway – have accepted their designated titles, with the other two having retained, for operational purposes, their historical names of University College Cork and University College Dublin. Although this may be a somewhat superficial example, it seems that even a government act could not bring the universities entirely into line with their plans for a more coherent national system.

There are other historical anomalies. Trinity College Dublin (TCD) stood outside the fold for several centuries, having been founded as a charter corporation by Queen Elizabeth I in 1592. As such, it enjoyed greater autonomy than the other colleges, but was also perceived, because of its ties to the Anglican Church, as not being wholly part of Ireland (Lydon, 1991). A government decision in 1968 to merge Trinity with University College Dublin would have brought TCD into the state's legislative framework for higher education. It also would have enabled the long history of Trinity's outsider status within Ireland to be corrected. The proposal was unsuccessful, because of opposition within TCD (Clancy, 1989) and the institution continued to enjoy its special place in the higher education system until the Universities Act of 1997. This move was seen by some as a threat to the autonomy of TCD (Barrett, 2001), which until that time was governed by an academic oligarchy.

The academic opposition to the bill preceding the Universities Act of 1997 was mainly made on the grounds that it would give unprecedented power to the state to "interfere" in the running of universities. Academics from TCD were the most vocal in opposing the bill, and the Minister for Education eventually backed down on many of the powers that the act would have given to the Higher Education Authority (HEA). In particular, the proposal for an external quality assurance mechanism was dropped in favor of enabling universities to conduct their own internal quality audits. One politician at the time described the episode as "a textbook case of how not to deal with legislation" (Walshe, 1999: 152). Historically, therefore, the university sector has been very effective in standing up to increased state control. The autonomy of the individual universities is now legally safeguarded by the 1997 act.

Government plans have been more coherently and purposefully carried out in the expansion of the vocational and business-oriented arms of the sector, however. The establishment of Regional Technical Colleges (RTCs) in the 1970s, in particular, supplied distinctive vocational, technical and sub-degree provisions on a regional basis. Two institutes of higher education (the NIHEs) were also established during this phase of expansion, but were later designated as universities in 1989: the University of Limerick and Dublin City University. The RTCs were re-designated as Institutes of Technology in the late 1990s. Again, there are historical quirks in the system. The Dublin Institute of Technology is not a former RTC, it carries its own validation powers, and it awards degrees up to doctoral level. The other IoTs receive validation through the Higher Education Training and Awards Council (HETAC) and tend to focus on sub-degree provision (although there is academic drift in the sector).

The diversity within such a small system was noted by the OECD *Review of Higher Education in Ireland* which was carried out in 2003 and has been widely cited since (OECD, 2006). The report strongly recommended that some diversity is maintained through the distinctive (vocational, sub-degree) roles of the IoTs, but that the government establish a more unified steering mechanism for the whole sector. The distinctiveness of the IoTs has been a matter for recent debate: both Waterford IoT and DIT (and now, very recently, also Cork IoT) have been bidding and publicly campaigning for university status. If they are successful, the other IoTs will inevitably make a strong claim to be upgraded to university status as well, which is the pattern of events that occurred when the Waterford RTC became the first IoT. Indeed, one suggestion by the opposition political party is to unite the IoTs in a single "National University of Technology." It is interesting to note that some considerable opposition to such re-designations has come from the school teachers' unions, who fear the implications for sub-degree level vocational training and apprenticeships which historically were at the heart of the IoT sector's success and indeed their *raison d'être* (Donnelly, 2008).

In spite of the academic drift of the IoTs, the system has become larger and more diverse in recent decades. Prior to the 1970s it was dominated by the university sector, which in 1969 accounted for 78 percent of total full-time enrollments (Clancy, 1997: 87). By 1986 nearly half of all new entrants into higher education were enrolling in the non-university sector (Clancy, 1989). Today the Irish system also includes an assortment of private providers of higher education, including the Dublin Business School, which is owned by the for-profit education company Kaplan Inc. and has over 9,000 students enrolled on its courses. A fascinating example of the appearance of the private sector on the scene was the controversy generated when Hibernia College began to offer a distance learning course for schoolteacher qualifications in 2003 (Burke, 2004). The university departments of education (the traditional providers of such accredited programs) in their opposition tended to focus not only on arguments about private versus public but (and, it could be argued, somewhat counter-productively, given international experience) on the use of distance learning and online technologies, claiming that it would not be possible to provide high-quality professional programs online. Despite this, the courses were given accreditation through HETAC, and large numbers of students enrolled on the program (Walshe, 2003).

The rate of growth in the period 1970–1990 was among the fastest in Europe (Clancy, 1997). Participation rates are the envy of other nearby countries: the age participation rate is about 57 percent and completion rates are also high. Among the seven universities, historically there was limited competition for students, given that the non-Dublin universities tend to recruit largely from their regions. At University College Cork, for example, 90 percent of the full-time students are from the Cork region (HEA, 2005). However, competition for students may increase in the near future as the universities may find they no longer offer a higher education that cannot be obtained from other tertiary and private institutions. The latest strategic plan for higher education sets an ambitious participation rate target of 72 percent by 2020 (HEA, 2008b). Already, in recent years, there has been a considerable increase in advertising, branding and marketing of individual institutions, something particularly visible in the run-up to the undergraduate applications deadline (a process which is centrally administered by the Central Applications Office).

The expansion and diversification of the sector may have been recent, rapid and dramatic, but it is worth bearing in mind that the system is still relatively small. There are fewer students in the whole Irish system than there are, for example, in the Open University in the UK, or enrolled in courses through the private, US distance learning provider, the University of Phoenix. Given that the whole of the system could be managed as a single entity, it makes its quirkiness and diversity that much more remarkable and, perhaps, enviable in some senses. The role of the government in steering the state should not, in theory, be that difficult to manage. Yet institutional sensitivities around status, combined with rapid economic growth and a tradition of university autonomy (and even resistance), have resulted in a sector which the state funds relatively generously but does not control.

Who is Steering the Sector?

In principle, the HEA, which was given its statutory functions of advising and monitoring the state investment in higher education in 1972 (modeled on the British University Grants Committee, as a buffer between state and institutions), is responsible for directing the sector. The funding model in Ireland was therefore designed to enable a large degree of autonomy for the universities, which they have mostly enjoyed (Clancy, 1989), and the HEA is still evolving into a more directive, steering role.

The non-university institutions were previously funded and directly steered through the Department of Education – not the HEA – yet the HEA was given the function of advising the government on the development of the entire sector (Osborne, 1996). The historical overlapping remit of a state agency and a government department is somewhat typical of the rather *ad hoc* fashion in which the Irish system has developed. Clancy noted that "the most striking anomaly in the administrative structure of Irish higher education is that the HEA does not have any executive role with respect to a large segment of the higher education system" (Clancy, 1989: 112). This was the case even after the Commission on Higher Education's report of 1960–1967 recommended the establishment of the HEA and clearly intended that all third level colleges would be designated under the act. In the ensuing years, several reviews and reports have recommended better coordination of the sector in terms of unified strategies, most notably the influential and oft-quoted OECD review (2006) discussed above, which was finally achieved in 2006 with IoTs coming under the remit of the HEA.

Clancy (2007) has argued that such a development will add to an increasingly interventionist tendency that began in the 1990s. Ironically, it is also likely that the IoTs will now begin to enjoy greater autonomy than they had under the Department of Education, with its heavily bureaucratic structures. There will inevitably be differences of perception across the sector as to the extent to which the HEA may intervene in institutional affairs.

The overall level of institutional autonomy, however, is impressive, given that about 80 percent of the universities' income comes straight from the public purse. A further recommendation of the OECD report that has yet to be fulfilled is the diversification of funding through private income and student fees. Politically, the issue of fees is sensitive, given that they were only abolished in 1996, but the government has announced that a review will be included within the forthcoming national strategy, along with an exploration of mechanisms to encourage greater private income (Flynn, 2008a). While internationally it has been claimed that fee waivers largely benefit the middle classes, recent evidence in Ireland shows that there has been some progress in widening student diversity and participation from "non-traditional" socio-economic groups (O'Connell, 2003).

The OECD report also made it quite clear that the overall level of state support for education is too low to match Ireland's aspirations, and is poor as a proportion of GDP with comparison to other countries. The same point was raised in a recent article in the *Irish Times* co-authored by the president of UCD (the state's largest university) and the provost of TCD (the oldest university), in which they highlighted the apparent mismatch between low levels of funding and the "Government rhetoric which envisages 'world-class' institutions driving a new 'knowledge society'" (Flynn, 2008b). It is noteworthy that this criticism came from these two institutions (both of which have publicly asserted their desire to ascend the international league tables) rather than, for example, under the auspices of the sectoral umbrella organization, the Irish Universities Association.

The HEA is therefore in the driving seat for the university sector, but it has not gripped the wheel too tightly. As a buffer organization, it does not directly steer the system, but inevitably changes in its funding mechanisms and strategies do have an impact, and this will certainly be the case for the new resource allocation model which is currently being phased in. However, uncertainty in the availability of special initiative and research funds being released by the Department of Finance in previous years has also acted as a limiter on the HEA's ability to manage the sector. The additional impact of changing individual Ministers of Education and Finance Ministers can be very significant and hints at an intrinsic instability in a system that is dependent in large part on annual budgeting and planning in the absence of a longer-term strategy.

Clancy's (2007) article on the evaluative state in Irish higher education illuminates the process of a creeping state interventionism in the university sector. He points out that although the Universities Bill was substantially altered after the protest from academics, this may have been something of a Pyrrhic victory, as a managerialist ethos has still seemingly entered Irish higher education through the back door. Certainly there are voices within higher education who claim that the administrators are taking over the universities. In a collection of writings on universities in the new millennium, for example, one author states that in the 1990s, "we had a decade of unprecedented legislative, administrative and bureaucratic interference in the scholarly and collegiate functions of our universities" (Barrett, 2001: 81). Those familiar with managerialism in other systems, such as the UK's (as described in, for example, Deem, Hillyard and Reed, 2007), may find this sounds rather overblown, but within the context of rapid change in Irish higher education it probably captures how some changes have been felt by those within the system.

It is worth bearing in mind, however, that an important aspect of the contemporary Irish context is that national economic and social policy develops through the mechanism of "social partnership." Therefore, some of the evaluative and regulatory functions that the state has assumed in relation to higher education were agreed through partnerships with trade unions, employers and other participants in the process. Social partnership works through the National Economic and Social Council (NESC), which was established in 1973 with a mandate to advise government on social and economic policy, and this has become a valued aspect of Irish governmental processes. The NESC includes representatives from the employers' associations, trade unions, farmers' organizations and senior civil servants. In 1997 this was widened to include representation from community and voluntary organizations.

Issues which impinge on working practices would be part of the negotiations for social partnership, along with agreements over salary/wage increases, etc. The largest trade union in the country, SIPTU, also includes a significant number of academic staff from the higher education sector, and within individual universities it is organized into separate branches for administrative, technical and academic staff. Indeed, in at least one case the secretary of the education branch of the union ultimately became a university president, something which may well be unusual in an international context. The SIPTU education branch has been very critical of managerialism and top-down performance management systems, mainly in relation to research (SIPTU, 2007). A publication called *Universities or Knowledge Factories* is highly critical of citation indexes and the UK's former Research Assessment Exercise, even though there is little indication that Irish universities will face such a heavily bureaucratic assessment system. Yet the publication is mostly silent on the performance assessment of teaching, perhaps because in recent local partnership discussions, there has been agreement on certain measures which will encourage more transparent processes within promotion policies that include more systematic student/teaching evaluation mechanisms. Arguably, however, these initiatives are being felt on the ground to be causing greater individual anxiety about surveillance and auditing.

As with many public sector systems in Western Europe, a language of performance management has infiltrated the working practices of academic life in Irish universities. University league tables have raised awareness of how certain outputs, particularly in terms of research, can be measured. Indeed, it is the influence of global league tables with which SIPTU is most concerned, and there is a danger that some universities will start playing the game of trying to boost performance indicators for research. The system of internal quality audits that universities have established has also inevitably brought changes that are sometimes experienced (or perceived) as bureaucratic rather than academic in nature. Those who are critical of managerialism tend to perceive this shift as part-and-parcel of a neo-liberal agenda within higher education policy (see Lynch, 2006a, 2006b). This agenda brings market discourses into education and a value on the outputs and performances of institutions within a competitive environment. Others would suggest that these moves are about good management rather than managerial control. The president of DCU has recently stated that the dichotomous view of academic autonomy versus managerialism is false and that there is scope for a "pragmatic" middle ground (von Prondzynski, 2008).

The HEA's Strategic Innovation Fund, launched in 2006 (and with a total planned allocation of €510 million over seven years), provides a further example of recent trends indicative of a greater awareness of institutional management issues. The funding available is being used to facilitate (or accelerate) internal institutional restructuring and supports a large number of collaborative projects which include the development of key performance indicators, standardization of learning outcomes and program specifications in modular frameworks, and the development of structured doctoral programs with a strengthened emphasis on transferable skills and employability. Indeed, the latter of these reflects widening acceptance of the concept of "fourth level Ireland" (IUA, 2007) built on increasing uptake of Master's and doctoral programs (a target for the doubling of Ph.D. graduates is one feature of this). It is interesting to note that many such projects have come from the universities themselves (or at least senior management teams) in response to this availability of funds, and it may be that the strategy is at least to influence the shape of "the inevitable."

Certainly these are trends that are familiar in other Western countries. There have been many critical voices raised against the marketization and consumerist framework of higher education in England (e.g. Deem, 2001; Naidoo and Jamieson, 2005), and given the close ties between the UK and Ireland it is not surprising that some of the policies that now predominate in England are being discussed in Ireland. Yet governance of the Irish higher education system, in comparison with the English system, is remarkably non-evaluative and weak as an external regulator of the sector. The "creeping managerialism" is not being imposed by the state in the same way as it has been imposed in other systems. Instead, the university sector has effectively opposed managerialism in the past (through opposition to government plans for an external quality assurance system, for instance) and there is not much indication that the state has the strength to increase its control in the future. Rather than see this as a weakness in the system, as the OECD report (2006) inevitably concluded, however, it perhaps could be interpreted as a positive aspect of the Irish situation insofar as the institutions are more empowered than their equivalents in other jurisdictions to influence their future in policy terms.

What is perhaps of more concern is the rather relentless discussion of the knowledge economy and the role of higher education in fostering the knowledge-based economy. This particular emphasis within policy and strategy documents has focused on the economic contributions of higher education through research and innovation in the sciences and technologies. Yet there are problems inherent in this vision for higher education, in that the knowledge economy is more of an idea constructed through particular discourses than a coherent strategy for a higher education system. Emerging concerns highlight the emphasis on the economy at the possible expense of society; the fragmentation and lack of coordination of funding streams for research in the drive to pursue innovation; and the possible threat to the humanities and social science subject areas.

The Imperatives of the Knowledge Economy

It is difficult to find any policy or strategy documents about higher education in Ireland that do not emphasize the importance of higher education in contributing to the knowledge economy. The HEA's strategy provides a good overview of the context and the current emphasis:

> Ireland has made considerable progress economically and socially in recent years. We have done so through a mix of policies, incorporating social partnership, pro-enterprise taxation policies, the attraction of foreign direct investment and technology, and improved systems of public governance and administration . . . If Ireland as a society and an economy is to continue to develop, we must urgently adopt the strategies necessary to create a dynamic, knowledge-based, innovative and inclusive society.
>
> (HEA, 2004: 6)

This short statement captures the essence of the "received wisdom" within Ireland as to the reasons why it has undergone such an economic about-turn in the last decade or so and the individual items listed are echoed time and again in official strategy documents from various public agencies and government departments. Such language is also expected in applications for funding for research in higher education even beyond the specific subject disciplines of science, engineering and technology. It is also commonly observed that while reference is usually also made to an "inclusive society," it usually comes last in such statements.

There are many other examples of this type of rhetoric. The Science Foundation Ireland strategy, for example, acknowledges that the key challenge facing Irish higher education is the development of the knowledge economy (SFI, 2006). Similarly, the Forfás (Department of Enterprise, Trade and Employment) report on *Building Ireland's Knowledge Economy* proposed that "Ireland by 2010 will be internationally renowned for the excellence of its research and will be at the forefront in generating and using new knowledge for economic and social progress, within an innovation driven culture" (Forfás, 2004: 2). In the NESC (the social partnership agency which advises government on social policy) *Towards 2016* partnership program (Government of Ireland, 2006), the NESC's vision to develop "a vibrant, knowledge-based economy and stimulating enterprise and productivity" is set out (O'Donnell and Thomas, 2006: 129).

One of the main strategic aims of the HEA is to encourage the economic contribution that higher education makes to Irish society, describing the new role of universities as "engines of economic growth" (HEA, 2004: 20). The recent history of the Irish "economic miracle" has reinforced the perception of the important contribution that universities can make to the economy. However, the role of universities in generating the "economic miracle" can be questioned. At first glance, the increased rates of participation in higher education are hugely impressive. In the 1960s, an Irish person (twenty-five years or older) had spent on average just six and a half years in education. By 2010, it has been forecast that over 40 percent of the working population will hold a third-level qualification (Ferreira and Vanhoudt, 2004).

The incredible rate of upskilling among the young population has been attributed with fueling to a large extent the Celtic Tiger. Yet, as Ferreira and Vanhoudt (2004) also point out, increased higher education attainment levels alone do not explain the economic boom, given that Ireland's expansion is comparable to other OECD countries during this time, and is not as impressive as the growth in countries such as Norway. What was distinctive about the Irish case was the government's supply-side strategy in the technological sector and through the Regional Technical Colleges (Clancy, 1989; Ferreira and Vanhoudt, 2004). Therefore, it is perhaps not the universities which should be exhorted to fulfill the promises of a knowledge economy, but the IoTs. Yet the decisive government strategy to expand the technological sector throughout the 1970s and 1980s has not led to a firm commitment to protect that investment: instead, the IoT sector is currently somewhat in limbo until the HEA assumes full responsibility for its funding and there is greater clarity as to roles and structures within the merged system.

The link between universities, economic growth, innovation, knowledge and technological advancement seems now to be a widely held perception: "The role of the university has changed radically in the new innovation age because of the heightened strategic importance of education in a society which is now truly knowledge-driven" (Kinsella and McBrierty, 1998: 111). A key characteristic of a knowledge-driven economy is that technology is no longer just imported, but is generated. Research within the universities should support this transition in the Irish economy, according to the HEA, and a direct government role is a presumed requirement to foster higher rates of innovation.

These economic imperatives have, of course, been noted in other higher education systems. As Bullen, Fahey and Kenway (2006: 54) argue, the discourses around knowledge economies are now powerful drivers of policy in many countries: "such policies typically represent knowledge economy initiatives as the way to economic prosperity, scientific progress, social inclusion, and unprecedented global inter-connectivity." They have become especially prominent through the European Commission and the OECD, with the latter putting the term firmly on the agenda when it published its report *The Knowledge-based Economy* (OECD, 1996). Subsequently, the OECD has promoted the rhetoric of the knowledge economy in many of its publications, and certainly this is a key feature of its review of Irish higher education.

The Lisbon Strategy of the European Union has also been influential. The intention for Europe to become the "most competitive and dynamic knowledge-based economy in the world" by 2010 seems to have been embraced by the government of the day. A recent announcement of a €100 million government spend on higher education under the Strategic Innovation Fund was said to be a "key part of the Government's plan for Ireland to move towards the knowledge economy envisaged for the EU under the Lisbon Agenda" (Anderson, 2008). Knowledge-based economies depend on people with high levels of technological and scientific skills. One Irish response has been, for example, to aim to double the numbers of Ph.D. graduates by 2013 (in all disciplines, however, including arts and humanities), which is hugely ambitious given some of the infrastructural problems that are known to exist.

Worthy of note here is that probably two of the currently most influential documents in Irish higher education were produced outside of Ireland. The OECD review was conducted by international experts and the Lisbon Strategy is, of course, a development plan for the European Union. The strongest steers, perhaps, are therefore not coming from national but from supranational directives. It remains to be seen whether the proposed new national strategy for higher education may set out a vision for Irish higher education that establishes more independence and confidence within the Irish system itself.

Critical Voices

There are a few dissenting voices amid the knowledge economy rhetoric. The emphasis on the economic contribution of Irish higher education has prompted some questions about the role of higher education as a public good (see Lynch, 2006a, 2006b; Fisher, 2006). There are also some political parties outside of government who oppose the knowledge economy agenda-setting of the European Union, and the 2008 referendum on the Lisbon Treaty shows that political leaders cannot afford to be complacent. Yet Ireland generally promotes a pro-European stance: indeed, some have argued that only through membership of the then EEC did Ireland really become "independent" – its trade and financial systems being previously dominated by relations with the UK. There is more tolerance of the concept of European policy than, for example, would be the case in the UK or other larger countries. To a large extent, however, there is little academic or public debate (other than perhaps within the letters pages of the *Irish Times*) about the changing role of higher education in Ireland as envisaged through the Lisbon Agenda.

Kathleen Lynch (2006a) has raised concerns about the ways in which the social role of higher education seems to take a back seat to the economic. She argues: "Throughout the [OECD] report on Irish HE this focus is on developing a skilled workforce for the economy. There is no reference in the body of the report to the role of the universities in developing the civil, political, social or cultural institutions of society, either locally or globally" (2006a: 305). This is not necessarily a new concern, as Clancy drew attention to the lack of attention to the cultural and social roles of higher education throughout the expansion period in the 1970s (see Clancy, 1989).

Yet, a key strategic aim of the government is widening participation in higher education. Reconciling economic growth with social cohesiveness can be a tall order. Indeed, the social inclusion agenda could even be argued to be in conflict with knowledge economy policies, given that the latter tend to focus attention on technological innovation and the economic returns of education, sometimes at the expense of greater inclusivity.

As Brine's analysis (2006) of discourses around the knowledge-based economy in Europe suggests, it is the lower-skilled learners who tend to be negatively defined within knowledge economy policies. Her close analysis of European policies shows that low-skilled learners are categorized as not only "at risk" but "*the* risk" to the increased economic capacity of Europe. In other words, their very existence threatens the future of greater economic competitiveness. Furthermore, she suggests that the high-skilled learners are clearly prioritized in discourses around the knowledge *economy*, whereas the lower-skilled learners are located in the knowledge *society*. Lower-skilled members of society have little economic value, and as such are constructed through discourses of deficiency. Her clarification of these points is valuable for understanding the tensions within knowledge economy policies in relation to social inclusion.

Questions are being raised about the dual role that Irish HE might play: for some, the aim of economic advancement is not necessarily commensurate with an aim to develop social well-being (Fisher, 2006). Other social policy analysts in Ireland suggest that growth in the GDP has become an end of policy in itself, neglecting the social policies that would result in growth in people's well-being (Healy and Reynolds, 2006). Certainly there are concerns that the new-found wealth has led to new-found inequalities: Ireland scores high on inequalities of income distribution in comparison with other rich European nations (Collins and Kavanagh, 2006: 165).

One significant means through which social concerns have been partly addressed in Irish higher education is through charitable donations from private philanthropies. The largest donor has been the Atlantic Philanthropies (a charitable foundation established by the creator of the duty free system). Nearly US$7 million came into the Republic of Ireland from this charity between 1982 and 2004, and most of it went to higher education institutions for projects in non-science and technology topics (Khoo, Healy and Coate, 2007). Atlantic Philanthropies is undoubtedly promoting the role of higher education in relation to society and has funded projects on issues such as civic engagement, disadvantaged youth, and peace and reconciliation.

Important as charitable income has been, there are problems with it. To some extent, it may partly absolve the government's responsibilities in relation to the funding of those higher education projects that are oriented towards social well-being rather than economic growth (Khoo, Healy and Coate, 2007). It is also a non-strategic and non-accountable form of funding, given that donations are made largely to suit the strategies and aims of the charitable organizations rather than national priorities. Perhaps the most significant weakness is sustainability, with Atlantic Philanthropies in particular choosing to spend its entire endowment by 2020.

Another concern is the impact that market-driven strategies might have on universities themselves to pursue the production of disinterested knowledge and other forms of traditional scholarship. For example, Kenway and colleagues (2004) argue that economic imperatives for universities will damage their core, scholarly business. The academic system, they suggest, should be based on a "gift" economy rather than a knowledge economy: "Current knowledge economy policies and innovation systems tend to ignore the distinctive features of universities and scholarly communities and, in so doing, they put in peril aspects of what they seek to achieve" (2004: 331). The erosion of a "public good" ethos within higher education through the predominance of economic imperatives is arguably a hidden danger of knowledge economy discourses.

The Knowledge Economy and Research

Public investment in research in higher education institutions is still a relatively new phenomenon in Ireland. One result of the Celtic Tiger economy was a government decision to develop a research infrastructure and funding mechanism for research from the late 1990s. Within these new developments were the establishment of SFI, with its role in developing biotechnology and ICT; the creation of two research councils, one in the science and technologies and one for the humanities and social sciences; and the introduction of the Program for Research in Third Level Institutions (PRTLI) from 1998.

As with other changes in the system over recent decades, these new funding mechanisms have dramatically altered the management and development of research within the universities and the IoTs. There are several distinctive features about the ways in which these funding streams operate. First, they tend to be programmatic, cyclical, short-term and often require matched funding from the institutions. The research councils are less prone to these tendencies, given that they are more oriented towards developing general research capacity within the sector, but they operate with more modest budgets than SFI or the PRTLI. The latter two are in their second and fifth cycles of funding, respectively, and, according to some, herald an "introduction of unbridled market principles into the steering of higher education" (Clancy, 2007: 116).

SFI and the PRTLI are fairly instrumental in terms of encouraging competition between institutions for the funding of projects for which the state has given the steer. Given the small size of the higher education sector, economies of scale are deemed important and therefore institutions need to bid for these funds through collaborative partnerships. Indeed, the HEA defines one of its main roles as: "Creating a context conducive to healthy differentiation and specialisation within the sector, with competition and collaboration as appropriate among institutions in the interest of achieving efficiencies, economies of scale and critical mass across the sector" (HEA, 2004: 21). The OECD review pointed to the "dramatic way" in which the PRTLI highlighted the importance of competition and the value that "can spring from collaboration" (OECD, 2006: 64).

The resulting mix of competition and collaboration is dramatic, but perhaps not in the terms of success that the OECD and HEA would prefer to view it. The imperative to collaborate is top-down rather than bottom-up, meaning that the strategic development of funding bids has a heavily weighted steer from senior management rather than necessarily growing organically from the work of existing research teams. Collaboration is also encouraged between the universities and the IoT sector, which is laudable in theory but in practice raises a host of sensitivities. Although the funds are for collaborative efforts, only one institution can be the lead partner, thereby increasing the competitive aspect of bidding between institutions who desire to come out of the funding cycle with the most monies in their coffers.

The sustainability of funded initiatives and ongoing evaluations of how the funds are spent are also large concerns that have yet to be truly tackled. Especially in comparison to the monitoring that takes place elsewhere (such as through EU funding), there is a very low level of evaluation or assessment of how public funds are spent through these programs. In addition, the various funding mechanisms for research and development are fragmented rather than coordinated. The recent strategic plan for the HEA (2008) certainly makes it clear that the HEA has a key role to play in terms of ensuring accountability for the efficient expenditure of public funds. These statements may precipitate a greater evaluative role of the state in future; the resistance in the past to these types of move may again create challenges for the state.

Conclusion: A System at the Crossroads?

Ireland is a small, monolithic and centralized state (no regional devolution or strong local government, for example) with a successful economy and a small number of geographically distributed universities, and a larger number of other higher education providers whose offerings are strongly linked with industrial and commercial needs. On paper, then, government steering and management of the sector and its embedding within, for example, the National Development Plan should be straightforward and provide the country with the basis of a nimble and agile approach to policy and practice that many larger states cannot achieve because of their size, complexity, historical tradition, and cultural and economic inertia.

In practice, however, few will recognize this as a realistic picture of the Irish situation, and perhaps cultural factors play more strongly than is sometimes appreciated by external observers such as the OECD review team. Irish civil society is partially fragmented along geographical/regional lines and there is a strong tradition of (non-party political) associations, organizations and other groupings (including the Catholic Church) having a voice in the public sphere, even when in the current situation it would seem that the language of the so-called neo-liberal agenda seems at face value to have gained hegemonic acceptance. Any understanding of the Irish situation requires consideration of its "non-ideological" politics and the widespread acceptance of populism and economic opportunism as major factors in decision-making and strategy formulation as well as the historical particularities of the development of Irish identity and the relations of citizens to the state (e.g., Tovey and Share, 2003; Inglis, 2000; Keohane and Kuhling, 2004).

The higher education system is substantially funded by the public purse and provides a service for the state in educating largely an Irish population of students, and yet politically the state espouses much of the rhetoric, at least, of a market economy. However, the associated evaluative function of the state is minimal in comparison with, for example, its closest neighbors in the UK (who have set the global standard for managerialism in higher education). An associated irony is that the most decisive government strategy of recent decades, the supply-led expansion of the technological sector, has not fully resulted in a commitment to protect the distinct role that the IoTs have contributed to the economy.

One interpretation of the situation could be that academics in Irish universities, thus far, have appropriately managed to resist an erosion of their core scholarly business and more centralized state control. The imposition of an external quality assurance mechanism, for instance, was not deemed necessary and the resulting internal quality assurance procedures have maintained a degree of professional autonomy within the sector that would probably be welcomed elsewhere, given the choice. The enshrining of academic freedom in the Universities Act of 1997 was also an important gain. What is perhaps most interesting about the Irish context is the mixture of a government that is populist in its orientation with a fairly weak state control over universities, and a relatively strong voice in favor of university autonomy. Indeed, the Minister of Education who came under fire for the proposal of the Universities Bill, which provoked such a strong protest from TCD, acknowledges that this bungled maneuver may have been the reason for her downfall. When she unsuccessfully campaigned for re-election in 1997, she recalls that: "It came up on the doorstep in a number of cases – little old dears asking me what I was trying to do to Trinity" (Walshe, 1999: 140).

As regards governance, then, Kearns (2002) suggests that the relationship between the Irish state and universities is "loosely coupled," allowing latitude and scope for maneuver by either party. Historically, however, we have noted how the state has pushed one way on the universities and the universities have pushed back, reacting to perceived threats from proposed new laws, for example. State steering on a more routine basis has come through the agency of the HEA in the form of funding incentives and special initiatives rather than direct policy implementation. In addition, the governance of higher education in Ireland seems to have been strongly shaped by external influences, such as the OECD review and the aims of the Lisbon Agenda, rather than through the development of an indigenous, Irish vision for the system, despite the fact that there is space within the system for such a unique and self-conceived vision to take shape.

However, the economy, globalization and other international contextual factors have moved on considerably since 1997 and the key issue is which direction is

Ireland set to follow in shaping the future of its education systems. With government's enthusiastic adoption of the Lisbon Agenda, the embedding of the Bologna Process and a renewed focus on performance indicators and outcomes measures it might be presumed that it will follow the dominant pattern in much of the developed world of asserting the primacy of the knowledge economy, league tables and the commodification of education. The proposed new national strategy will be eagerly awaited, but whether there is sufficient proactive leadership and enough self-confidence within the sector to shape a strategy that is significantly different to the pattern in other developed nations is a very pertinent question. In addition, the particular roles of the arts, humanities and social sciences and their contribution to society need to be continuously reinforced and reflected in a higher education that values the transformative potential of the learning experience in terms other than the purely economic.

If it is to be more than a restatement of the prevalent economic values, the new strategy consultation process must facilitate a broader debate which seeks clarification of some of the tensions institutions face in terms, for example, of their regional versus international orientations; their contributions to the well-being of society versus their contributions to economic growth; their focus on academic development versus collaboration with industry; and maintaining academic freedom in the face of increased demands for accountability. If the strategy concentrates instead only on technical aspects of funding mechanisms (with fees likely to be mooted as one possible solution to financial constraints), implementing new performance measurements and statistical analysis, then it will be a missed opportunity for Ireland to strike out on a different and highly distinctive path; an opportunity which, unlike other countries, is still available to the sector should it choose to seize it.

References

Anderson, Paul. "€100m Higher Education Funding Unveiled." *Irish Times*, February 19, 2008.

Barrett, Seán D. "The End of University Autonomy in Ireland." In *Beyond the Ivory Tower: The University in the New Millennium*, edited by Angela Hoey-Heffron, and James Heffron. Cork: Mercier Press, 2001.

Blackmore, Jill. "Universities in crisis? Knowledge Economics, Emancipatory Pedagogies, and the Critical Intellectual." *Educational Theory* 51(3) (2001): 353–370.

Brine, Jacky. "Lifelong Learning and the Knowledge Economy: Those That Know and Those That Do Not – The Discourse of the European Union." *British Educational Research Journal* 32(5) (2006): 649–665.

Browne, James. "University Autonomy – Safeguarded by Appropriate Accountability." Keynote presentation at the Galway Symposium on the future of universities, Galway, June 5–6, 2008. Available online: http://www.nuigalway.ie/celt/webcasts/JimBrowne/Jim%20Browne.html.

Bullen, Elizabeth, Joanna Fahey, and Jane Kenway. "The Knowledge Economy and Innovation: Certain Uncertainty and the Risk Economy." *Discourse: Studies in the Cultural Politics of Education* 27(1) (2006): 53–68.

Bullen, Elizabeth, Simon Robb, and Jane Kenway. "'Creative Destruction': Knowledge Economy Policy and the Future of the Arts and Humanities in the Academy." *Journal of Education Policy* 19(1) (2004): 3–22.

Burke, Andy, ed. "Teacher Education in the Republic of Ireland: Retrospect and Prospect." *Standing Conference on Teacher Education North and South (ScoTENS)*, Center for Cross Border Studies, Armagh, 2004.

Clancy, Patrick. "The Evolution of Policy in Third-level Education." In *Irish Educational Policy: Process and Substance*, edited by D.G. Mulcahy, and D. O'Sullivan. Dublin: Institute of Public Administration, 1989, 99–132.

Clancy, Patrick. "Higher Education in the Republic of Ireland: Participation and Performance." *Higher Education Quarterly* 51(1) (1997): 86–106.

Clancy, Patrick. "Resisting the Evaluative State: Irish Academics Win the Battle but Lose the War." In *A Cartography of Higher Education Policy Change: A Festschrift in Honour of Guy Neave*, edited by Jürgen Enders, and Frans van Vught. Twente: University of Twente, CHEPS, 2007, 111–118.

Collins, Micheál L., and Catherine Kavanagh. "The Changing Patterns of Income Distribution and Inequality in Ireland, 1973–2004." In *Social Policy in Ireland: Principles, Practice and Problems*, edited by Seán Healy, Brigid Reynolds, and Micheál Collins. Dublin: The Liffey Press, 2006: 149–170.

Deem, Rosemary. "Globalisation, New Managerialism, Academic Capitalism and Entrepreneurialism in Universities: Is the Local Dimension Still Important?" *Comparative Education* 37(1) (2001): 7–20.

Deem, Rosemary, Sam Hillyard, and Mike Reed. *Knowledge, Higher Education, and the New Managerialism: The Changing Management of UK Universities*. Oxford: Oxford University Press, 2007.

Donnelly, Katherine. "Union Concern at Rush to Achieve University Status." *Irish Independent*, March 28, 2008.

Ferreira, M. Luisa, and Patrick Vanhoudt. "Catching the Celtic Tiger by its Tail." *European Journal of Education* 39(2) (2004): 209–235.

Fisher, Sandra. "Does the 'Celtic Tiger' Society Need to Debate the Role of Higher Education and the Public Good?" *International Journal of Lifelong Education* 25(2) (2006): 157–172.

Flynn, Seán. "New Strategy for Third-level Sector Under Way." *Irish Times*, February 5, 2008a.

Flynn, Seán. "University Heads Warn of Crisis through Lack of Funding." *Irish Times*, March 18, 2008b.

Forfás. *Building Ireland's Knowledge Economy*. Dublin: Forfás, 2004.

Forfás. *Forfás Annual Report 2005*. Dublin: Forfás, 2006.

Gornitzka, Åse, and Peter Maassen. "Hybrid Steering Approaches with Respect to European Higher Education." *Higher Education Policy* 13(3) (2000): 267–285.

Government of Ireland. *Towards 2016*. Dublin: Stationery Office, 2006.

Healy, Seán, and Brigid Reynolds. "Progress and Public Policy: The Need for a New Paradigm." In *Social Policy in Ireland: Principles, Practice and Problems*, edited by Seán Healy, Brigid Reynolds, and Micheál Collins. Dublin: The Liffey Press, 2006: 1–24.

Higher Education Authority. *Strategy Statement 2004–2007*. Dublin: Higher Education Authority, 2004.

Higher Education Authority. *Higher Education: Key Facts and Figures 2004–05*. Dublin: Higher Education Authority, 2005.

Higher Education Authority. *Higher Education: Key Facts and Figures 2006–07*. Dublin: Higher Education Authority, 2008a.

Higher Education Authority. *Strategic Plan 2008–2010*. Dublin: Higher Education Authority, 2008b.

Inglis, Tom. "Irish Civil Society: From Church to Media Domination." In *Religion and Politics: East–West Contrasts from Contemporary Europe*, edited by Tom Inglis, Zdzislaw Mach, and Rafa Mazanek. Dublin: UCD Press, 2000, 49–67.

Irish Universities Association (IUA). *Fourth Level Ireland – Your Future Graduate and Postdoctoral Experience in Irish Universities*, 2007. Available online: http://www.iua.ie/publications/documents/publications/2007/4thLevelIreland.pdf.

Kearns, Noreen. *Governance Reform and Value Change in the University Sector – An Institutional Analysis*. Unpublished Ph.D. thesis. Cork: National University of Ireland, 2002.

Kenway, Jane, Elizabeth Bullen, and Simon Robb. "The Knowledge Economy, the Techno-preneur and the Problematic Future of the University." *Policy Futures in Education* 2(2) (2004): 330–349.

Keohane, Kieran, and Carmen Kuhling. *Collision Culture: Transformations in Everyday Life in Ireland*. Dublin: The Liffey Press, 2004.

Khoo, Su-Ming, Carol Healy, and Kelly Coate. "Development Education and the Development of Research at Third Level in Ireland." *Policy and Practice* 5 (2007): 5–19.

Kinsella, Raymond P., and Vincent McBrierty. *Ireland and the Knowledge Economy*. Dublin: Oak Tree Press, 1998.

Lydon, James. "The Silent Sister: Trinity College and Catholic Ireland." In *Trinity College Dublin and the Idea of a University*, edited by C.H. Holland. Dublin: Trinity College Dublin Press, 1991, 29–53.

Lynch, Kathleen. "Neo-liberalism and Education." In *Social Policy in Ireland: Principles, Practice and Problems*, edited by Seán Healy, Brigid Reynolds, and Micheál Collins. Dublin: The Liffey Press, 2006a, 297–328.

Lynch, Kathleen. "Neo-liberalism and Marketisation: The Implications for Higher Education." *European Educational Research Journal* 5(1) (2006b): 2–17.

Naidoo, Rajani, and Ian Jamieson. "Empowering Participants or Corroding Learning? Towards a Research Agenda on the Impact of Student Consumerism in Higher Education." *Journal of Education Policy* 20(3) (2005): 267–281.

Newman, John Henry. *The Idea of a University*. London: Cambridge University Press, 1955.

O'Connell, Philip J. *A Review of Higher Education Participation in 2003*. Dublin: Economic and Social Research Institute, Fitzpatrick Associates & the Higher Education Authority, 2003.

O'Donnell, Rory, and Damian Thomas. "Social Partnership and the Policy Process." In *Social Policy in Ireland: Principles, Practice and Problems*, edited by Seán Healy, Brigid Reynolds, and Micheál Collins. Dublin: The Liffey Press, 2006, 109–132.

OECD. *The Knowledge-based Economy*. Paris: OECD, 1996.

OECD. *Review of Higher Education in Ireland*. Paris: OECD, 2006.

Osborne, Robert D. *Higher Education in Ireland: North and South*. London: Jessica Kingsley, 1996.

Readings, Bill. *The University in Ruins*. Cambridge, MA: Harvard University Press, 1997.

Science Foundation Ireland (SFI). *Strategy for Science, Innovation and Technology 2006–2013*. Dublin: Science Foundation Ireland, 2006.

SIPTU Education Branch. *Universities or Knowledge Factories?* Dublin: SIPTU, 2007. Available online (accessed 2.28.2008): http://www.siptu.ie/education/output/.

Tovey, Hilary, and Perry Share. *A Sociology of Ireland*. Dublin: Gill and Macmillan, 2003.

von Prondzynski, Ferdinand. "The Modern University – Corporate or Academic." In *The Diary of a University President*, 2008. Available online: http://universitydiary.wordpress.com/2008/06/11/the-modern-university-corporate-or-academic/.

Walshe, John. *A New Partnership in Education: From Consultation to Legislation in the Nineties*. Dublin: Institute of Public Administration, 1999.

Walshe, John. "Teacher Colleges Urged to Compete On-line." *Irish Independent*, November 15, 2003.

Part III
The Invisible Hand of Governance

13

The Effectiveness of a Dutch Policy Reform

Academic Responses to Imposed Changes

HARRY F. DE BOER

Researching the Effectiveness of University Reform

In 1997, the Dutch legislature passed a new Act on University Governance. The basic principles of universities' internal authority structure were substantially changed with the objective to increase the quality of teaching and research, the decisiveness of university management and institutional autonomy. This 1997 act is usually referred to as the "MUB" (*Modernisering Universitaire Bestuursorganisatie*). Designing and successfully implementing policy reforms is a most difficult assignment, with no guarantee of success (e.g. Cerych and Sabatier, 1986; Pressman and Wildavsky, 1974). It is a difficult and emotive business and often the stakes are high, with clear winners and losers resulting from the reform. Institutions themselves are not value-free and actors intend to protect their vested interests (see, e.g., Scharpf, 1986). By the same token, institutions are durable and resist constant, day-to-day transformations. Bringing reforms into force often involves considerable conflict and energy. In other words, the achievement of the goals of legislative reforms such as the MUB cannot be taken for granted.

The difficulty of institutional reform can manifest itself in several ways. Bardach (1977: 3), for example, points to several difficulties of reform policies:

> It is hard enough to design public policies and programs that look good on paper. It is harder still to formulate them in words and slogans that resonate pleasingly in the ears of political leaders and the constituencies to which they are responsive. And it is excruciatingly hard to implement them in a way that pleases anyone at all, including the supposed beneficiaries or clients.

So, first, it is far from easy to design a reform successfully and to get it accepted. Others have to be convinced of the benefits of change. Second, the implementation of the reform is no simple task. For reasons of aversion to risks and uncertainty, actors usually do not welcome substantial change. Most of the time they will act to protect their own interests. Reformers have to rely on people who are used to and have knowledge of the old structure. These people are not always willing to relinquish the old rules. Third, even after clearing the other two hurdles, the outcomes of the policy reform can be disappointing. Often, the intended benefits do not occur and perverse effects appear more often than not. If this is the case, the "theory" of the reformers appears to be incomplete or proven wrong. The focus of this chapter is on this third phase. It is interesting to inquire whether the reformers' goals of the MUB Act have actually sunk into university practices.

If the interest is in the assessment of the effectiveness of a (policy) reform, at least three questions should be asked (see Kiser and Ostrom, 1982; Scharpf, 1986). First, it is necessary to ascertain whether the proposed changes have actually been implemented. Have the universities met the requirements of the government's policy reform? This question is not as odd as it seems. For example, more than five years after the 1970 Act on University Governance came into force, many governing bodies had not yet been installed. This is not the case with respect to the 1997 MUB Act, however; here the "objective" requirements appear to be met. The universities have indeed formally changed their authority structure (e.g. Committee Datema, 1998). The second question in an analysis of a reform is whether in practice the imposed new rules of the game have an impact on actors' behavior. The MUB reform can be considered effective if, and only if, the university actors have changed their behavior in accordance with the intentions and expectations of the legislation. Behavioral modification is a prerequisite for a successful reform. When it can be observed that behavior has changed, the third question is to what extent the altered behavior contributes to the realization of the goals of the reform. Is goal achievement realized through the changes in behavior intended by the legislation? If all three questions are answered in the affirmative, the MUB reform can be regarded as effective. However, if the answers to one or more of the questions are negative, then the effectiveness of the MUB Act must be questioned.

In this chapter, the focus is on the second question and therefore seeks to determine the effects of the MUB Act on the behavior of individual actors. The focus is on one of the main formal goals of the MUB Act: the enhancement of the quality of research. The analysis concentrates on the consequences of the reform for the actual behavior of professors with respect to faculty-level research policy. Responses to the faculty-level research policy reforms of the MUB Act are selected for two reasons. First, the MUB Act clearly specifies significant changes in this area (see the next section). Second, it is argued that research is an area where professors have strong interests, and, hence, an analysis of their behavior with respect to the changed research policy framework will constitute a powerful indicator of the effectiveness of the MUB Act.

The assumption in our approach is that an actor's assessment of the effects of the reform will affect his or her actual behavior. This implies that the views of professors must be identified with respect to the *formal* rules on governance and management of research policy at the faculty level. Also the professors' perception of the *informal* rules associated with research policy at the faculty level must be examined. As argued by Ostrom (1990 and 2005), the rules that people use are not solely made up of formal rules. Informal rules may guide action too. While the formal rules are articulated by the act, the informal rules are more nebulous. The informal rules examined here relate to the preservation of the professional autonomy of the professoriate. In analyzing the consequences for the institutional reform of the professoriate's attitudes and perceptions of the formal and informal rules pertaining to faculty research policy, a theoretical framework will be employed that is derived from social psychology: *the theory of reasoned action* developed by Fishbein and Ajzen (1975). The use of this theory emphasizes the individual discretion to explain the effectiveness of macro (policy) reforms. It explicitly acknowledges the relevance of the linkages between the macro and micro levels in explaining social phenomena. In fact, if follows the path of methodological individualism in which macro phenomena are broken down into their smallest parts (e.g. Boudon, 1981; Coleman, 1990). However, before turning to a more detailed discussion of the theory, the MUB Act is set in the historical context of Dutch higher education governance policy reforms.

Background to University Governance in the Netherlands

Prior to the 1970s, Dutch university governance was, on the one hand, dominated by state bureaucrats and, on the other, by the professoriate. It constitutes a clear example of Clark's (1983) description of the continental higher education model (for a description of change and continuity in Dutch internal governance, see also de Boer, 2007). Authority for academic and non-academic affairs was clearly separated into different bodies. At the universities, government was represented by a board of curators, responsible for upholding laws and regulations, personnel policies and the administration of the university finances. The other pillar in this pre-1970 structure was the senate, consisting of all full professors. This senate epitomized academic self-governance (Arriëns, 1970).

The 1960s saw a growing concern in the Netherlands, as elsewhere, about the effectiveness and efficiency of traditional forms of university governance in an era of unprecedented growth of participation in higher education. The academic senates, for instance, were subject to severe criticism. Worries about the effectiveness and efficiency of universities, however, were overshadowed by demands for democratic participation in university decision-making by junior academics, non-academic staff and students. The spirit of this democratic movement left a deep imprint on the new Act of University Governance, passed by the Dutch Parliament in 1970: the *Wet op de Universitaire Bestuurshervorming* (WUB). Though the WUB Act attracted criticism from the beginning, it generally constituted the formal governance framework of universities until 1997.

In the WUB Act, the emphasis was upon external and internal democratization, though there were other, mostly forgotten, objectives, including effectiveness and efficiency. The WUB Act introduced a system of functional representation through university and faculty councils. Academics (professors and other academic staff), non-academics and students were given the right to elect representatives to these legislative bodies. In addition, a limited number of lay members representing the general public were appointed to the councils. A five- (later three-) member Executive Board (*College van Bestuur*, CvB), including the *Rector Magnificus*, was responsible for the executive functions.

The relationship between the University Council (UC) and the CvB created under the WuB Act was complicated, and there were many disputes because of a lack of clarity about the authority of these two decision-making bodies and power struggles between them. Basically, the structure in the early 1970s could be typified as a system of representative leadership within which the UC held most of the decision-making power. The UC had the authority to regulate and administer all matters of the university as a whole, insofar as these were not entrusted by the act to the CvB. The CvB was in charge of daily management and non-academic matters (buildings, finance, personnel matters, etc.) and had to prepare, publish and execute the decisions taken by the UC.

The WUB Act was evaluated in the late 1970s (Committee Polak, 1979). One of the main concerns was the relationship between the UC and the CvB. For reasons of effectiveness, efficiency and decisiveness, it was recommended that the powers of the CvB should be increased at the expense of those of the UC. This advice was followed in the 1980s when the laws concerning the Dutch universities were changed. A new act – *Wet op het Wetenschappelijk Onderwijs* – in 1986 did not question the *raison d'être* of the participatory mode of governance as such, but the balance of power between the UC and the CvB was shifted to the CvB. Compared with the structure in the 1970s, the formal powers of the representative councils were reduced. From 1986 onwards, all powers were assigned to the CvB, with the exception of those assigned to the UC that were exhaustively detailed in the act. The governance structure of Dutch universities in the 1980s and early 1990s can be described as a system of "mixed leadership"; decision-making was supposed to be based on "co-determination."

In the mid-1990s, interrelated problems regarding the prevailing governance system were identified by an *ad hoc* committee chaired by the Minister of Education, Culture and Science. These problems were: (1) the inadequacy of the governance structure pertaining to the organization of teaching; (2) the lack of transparency regarding responsibilities (in collective decision-making, individuals did not seem to accept personal responsibility); (3) the dispersal of authority; (4) the structure of co-determination, particularly at the faculty level, created confusion in decision-making; (5) the strong orientation towards research at the expense of teaching; and (6) the inadequacy and incoherence of communication between the various organizational levels. These issues at the time were of concern to a wide audience. They contributed to a new act in 1997 – the MUB Act.

The MUB Act promoted efficiency and effectiveness in university decision-making, and was in line with the overall governmental steering strategy that aimed to enhance institutional autonomy. In general, it embraced several notions of new public management (de Boer and Huisman, 1999). It abolished the system of co-determination by board and council. Most powers regarding academic and non-academic affairs were now allocated to executive positions at central and faculty levels. In addition, the structure became less decentralized in several ways, such as through the abolition of the organizational third layer – the previously powerful *vakgroepen* (discipline-based teaching and research groups). From 1997 on, the dean was given the authority to arrange the faculty's organization.

The MUB Act provided for a form of executive leadership of universities. At the institutional level, nearly all powers regarding both academic and non-academic affairs were assigned to the CvB, which continued to consist of three appointed members (including the *Rector Magnificus*). The CvB members are now appointed by and accountable to a new supervisory body, the *Raad van Toezicht* (RvT, a lay body of five people appointed by and accountable to the Minister). The representative councils were retained but lost most of their former power and became mainly advisory bodies. To summarize, the main changes in the management structures of Dutch universities due to the launching of the MUB Act are:

- the strengthening of executive positions *vis-à-vis* the position of representative councils at both the central and faculty levels;
- the university and faculty councils becoming representative advisory bodies for students and employees instead of "heavily equipped governing bodies";
- the integration of governance and management/administration (the new structure combines governance and management functions into one body);
- the abolition (at least formally) of the disciplinary research groups (*vakgroepen*), which until 1997 had been quite powerful;
- the increase in the power of the deans at the faculty level; and
- the introduction of a new governing body, the supervisory board (*Raad van Toezicht*).

The legislation explicitly gives the universities the option to create internal institutional arrangements to meet their specific circumstances within the confines of the MUB framework. With the introduction of the MUB Act, for the first time in their history, Dutch universities had a monocephalic structure. The new governing bodies comprise a system where executive and legislative powers are concentrated. Compared to the past, the academic community has little formal say in final decisions. All members of the crucial governing bodies, *Raad van Toezicht* (Supervisory Board), *College van Bestuur* (Central Executive Board) and *decaan* (dean), are appointed by the body above it. Thus a new hierarchical management system based on appointments replaced the old, democratic arrangements. The MUB reforms initiated a shift in the control over research from the prerogatives of individual professors to the collective setting of research agendas in line with faculty priorities and strategic plans, under the direct stewardship of the dean. However, the professoriate, individually and collectively, traditionally has been reluctant to relinquish its direct control over the content of research, how it is to be pursued, and by whom. Since at least the early 1980s, research programs and their funding have increasingly become conditional on national priorities, with the intention that research contributes more directly to solving national economic and social problems. Research has become more applied and problem-oriented, with the expectation that within the universities it proceeds in a more coordinated and managed fashion in line with national needs and priorities.

Professors, however, have not been docile followers of these changes. They have reacted to such pressures in at least three general ways (de Boer, 2003). First, they questioned the efforts to set research priorities externally, because, as they argued, academic work requires freedom. It is not possible to steer and program creativity

and serendipity. Second, they have already been able to ignore externally determined research priorities and programs for they were mostly very broad in nature,
giving professors ample room to make their own decisions. Third, professors have
countered threats to their autonomy through the very mechanism used by
government to steer the research agenda. Peer review has remained the basic
instrument for evaluating and funding research, with the professoriate still mainly
in control of the peer review process. By the 1990s, Dutch professors no longer had
complete control over the research agenda, but they nonetheless maintained a
powerful voice.

The 1997 MUB Act can be interpreted as another attack on the professors'
position regarding control of the research agenda. Compared to its predecessors,
it can be typified in terms of (vertical) integration, coherence, hierarchy, centralization and concentration of powers. According to the MUB Act, as previously
stated, the *vakgroep* – frequently dominated by professors – lost its legal basis (i.e.
it is no longer an entity that can take binding decisions). The dean becomes
responsible for the teaching and research programs, sets the general guidelines for
the practice of science, (ultimately) settles the yearly research program, and
supervises the implementation of that program. However, the degree to which
professors have actually relinquished, willingly or otherwise, control of the research
program is the subject of this chapter.

Theory of Reasoned Action

The theoretical model used to explain the behavior of professors in this study is
the *theory of reasoned action*, developed by Martin Fishbein and Icek Ajzen. The
theory assumes that actors are in principle rational and systematically use available
information in making decisions. According to this model, the best way to explain
behavior is to discover an actor's intentions to perform (or not to perform) an act.
Although there will not always be perfect correspondence between behavior and
intention, an actor will usually act in accordance with his or her intention.
Subsequently, the theory of reasoned action distinguishes two factors explaining
intentions: an actor's attitude towards a behavior and the subjective norm that s/he
perceives with respect to that behavior. An attitude is described as a person's "total"
evaluation of a behavior; it is a person's judgment that performing the behavior is
good or bad (Ajzen and Fishbein, 1980: 56). An attitude is measured by ascertaining
a person's salient beliefs that performing the behavior will lead to certain outcomes
(B), and an evaluation of the outcomes (E) (for more details see Fishbein and Ajzen,
1975). Thus, attitude A is defined as $A = \Sigma B_i E_i$. The perceived subjective norm (SN)
is also a function of beliefs, but of normative ones (Ajzen and Fishbein, 1980: 73).
An actor takes into account the normative expectations of others in his or her
environment (NE). What are, according to the actor, the beliefs of relevant
referents? The perceived evaluations of others are weighted by the motivation to
comply with each of the others' normative position (MC). Thus, the subjective
norm SN is defined as $SN = \Sigma NE_i MC_i$. Contextual variables are assumed to
influence behavior only indirectly: that is, they may have an impact on beliefs and

norms of the actors and their referents. The basic elements of the theory of reasoned action are depicted in Figure 13.1.

The theory of reasoned action assumes that behavior is under volitional control. However, a number of factors can limit an individual in realizing an intended action – for example, a lack of resources (time, money or information) may block behavior or intentions. For this reason, the model should take into account possible barriers or obstacles to willful behavior. This is in fact Ajzen's *theory of planned behavior*: the original model is extended with the factor "perceived behavioral control" (Ajzen, 1985). The perceived behavioral control can have an impact on the relationships between the three independent factors (attitude, social norm and informal rules) and the dependent variable (intention). Thus, perceived behavioral control might be included as an interaction variable. For this study issues such as time pressures, lack of administrative and managerial skills and supposed complexity of research policies could be seen as barriers for professors to act according to their attitude or subjective norm. However, the outcomes of the analyses of this research (which will be presented later) show that most of the professors say that they do not experience these kinds of barrier. This is not surprising since professors are generally self-confident. I conclude that their behavior is mostly under volitional control. Therefore, perceived behavioral control will not be taken into account for further analysis. In other words, I will use the theory of reasoned action instead of the theory of planned behavior.

However, another explanatory variable should be taken into account, given the purposes of my analysis. Apart from the formal rules that stem from the 1997 MUB Act, informal rules constrain or enable behavior as well. Therefore, the basic model of reasoned action is extended with a third factor to explain the actor's intention,

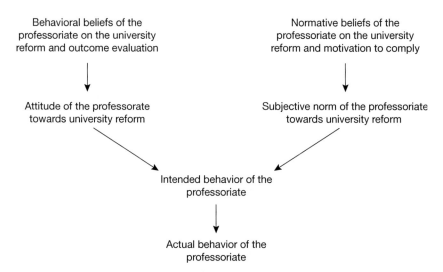

Figure 13.1 The Basic Elements of the Theory of Reasoned Action

which are the informal rules that hold safeguards to maintain professional autonomy. These informal rules are important if, and only if, they are at odds with the formal ones. If the informal and formal rules are largely identical, then an analysis based on the formal rules will be sufficient. If they differ, and the informal rules appear to have an impact on the behavior of professors, then the formal rules (in this case of the MUB Act) cannot be considered as being effective. This means that the theoretical model to explain the behaviors of Dutch professors in order to assess the effectiveness of the institutional reform looks as it is depicted in Figure 13.2.

This theoretical model assumes that there are three explanatory variables, which are supposed to have a positive impact on professors' intention to act in accordance with faculty research policy. In other words, it can be expected that the extent to which professors are intending to act in keeping with the faculty research policy increases when:

- they have a more positive attitude towards the formal rules of the MUB Act (hypothesis 1);
- they perceive a more positive subjective norm about the formal rules of the MUB Act (hypothesis 2);
- they encounter informal rules safeguarding their professional autonomy (hypothesis 3).

Methodology and Research Design

Operationalization

The theoretical model contains five variables that need to be operationalized: the behavior of professors, the intended behavior of professors, the attitude of professors towards formal rules, their perceived subjective norm towards formal rules and the experienced informal rules within the faculty (see Figure 13.2). One

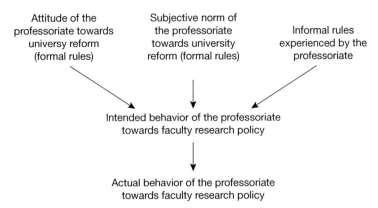

Figure 13.2 The Theoretical Model Based on the Theory of Reasoned Action Explaining the Behavior of the Dutch Professoriate

of the consequences of the MUB Act is that the dean is responsible for setting the general guidelines for faculty research and for the faculty's annual research program. Compliance with these formal rules implies that professors take these guidelines and research programs into account in their research practices. Intentional and actual behaviors of the professors are made operational by asking them a limited number of questions to find out their readiness to act in keeping with the research policy of their faculty. Do they (intend to) confine their research to topics set within the faculty program? Do they (intend to) pursue their research in accordance with the basic principles of the research policy of their faculty? By asking the professors these questions, I used the method of self-reporting. Bias may be one of the consequences, but under the assumption that the behavior under investigation here is not very sensitive I follow Ajzen (1988: 103), who indicated that "when the behavior of interest is not particularly sensitive, self-reports tend to be quite accurate." For both intentional and actual behavior of professors as regards faculty research policies a scale is used that ranges from 1 ("absolutely not") to 5 ("absolutely").

The attitude of professors regarding the formal rules of the MUB Act has been measured as follows. First, twenty-three potential effects have been selected based on a literature search. Having used a factor analysis, these twenty-three items have been reduced to six factors; they represent a set of potential behavioral beliefs of professors with respect to the MUB Act. The six distinguished factors are: academic freedom, diffusion of authorities, democratic content, decisiveness, scientific relevance of research, and social relevance of research. For each factor a scale is used ranging from −2 ("strong decrease") to 2 ("strong increase").

Second, the professors have been asked to evaluate the effects of the formal rules. How important, for instance, is academic freedom to them? To what extent do they value decisiveness or democratic content of decision-making? To measure the attitudes, the expected effects of the formal rules (step 1) and the assessment of these effects (step 2) are multiplied. Thus, the six factors weighted for their favorableness form together the overall attitude of the professoriate towards the formal rules of the MUB Act. In Table 13.1 one can find an example of this procedure for a single professor (who in this example has a positive attitude towards the formal rules).

Subjective norms reflect the extent to which professors value the positive or negative views of relevant others. What views, according to professors, do others hold about the consequences of the MUB rules? Are professors willing to comply with these views and opinions? If they are, the perceived social norms may have an impact on the intentions of professors to act in accordance with faculty research policy. I have selected seven potential referents for professors: professors from their own faculty, other academics from their own faculty, professors in the same field outside the faculty, faculty management, central management, scientific directors (if appropriate), and members of faculty representative councils. What, according to professors, is their overall judgment of the MUB Act, ranging from very negative (−2) to very positive (2). Next, I have asked them to what extent they are motivated to comply with the beliefs of these referents, ranging from not at all

TABLE 13.1 Example of a Positive Attitude of a Single Professor

Factor	Effect		Weight		Attitude
Decisiveness in decision-making	1.33	×	2	=	2.66
Democratic content of decision-making	−1.50	×	0	=	0
Scientific relevance of research	1.00	×	3	=	3.00
Separation of powers	0.25	×	2	=	0.50
Societal relevance of research	1.33	×	1	=	1.33
Academic freedom	−1.50	×	4	=	−6.00
				Σ	1.5
Total attitude				Σ/6	0.25

Note: Effects range from −2 to 2; weights range from 0 to 4. This professor believes that because of the rules of the MUB Act academic freedom will decrease. Since he values academic freedom highly, this has a serious negative impact on his attitude. Because the other factors are positive, his overall attitude towards the formal rules is positive.

(0) to very much (4). Then a similar procedure as applied to measure and calculate the attitude, was applied to calculate the subjective norm (see also the example provided in Table 13.2).

The third factor that might explain the behavioral intentions of the professors towards faculty research policies is the informal rules in the faculty. As argued above, informal rules, like formal ones, influence the readiness of professors to act in accordance with the faculty research policy and they can be important if they are at odds with the formal rules (otherwise, there is no need to take them on separately). Taking this into account, three items relating to professional autonomy have been used to construct the composite variable "informal rules with respect to faculty research policies." The three items are: keeping research policy intentionally vague and abstract in day-to-day practice; pursuing research that in

TABLE 13.2 Example of a Negative Subjective Norm of a Single Professor

Referent	Assessment of formal rules		Motivation to comply		Subjective norm
Professors from their own faculty	−1	×	2	=	−2
Other academics from their own faculty	−2	×	3	=	−6
Professors outside their own faculty	0	×	0	=	0
Faculty management	2	×	1	=	2
Central management	2	×	0	=	0
Representative councils in the faculty	−2	×	1	=	−2
				Σ	−8
Total subjective norm				Σ/6	−1.33

Note: Assessments range from −2 (very negative) to 2 (very positive); motivation to comply range from none (0) to very much (4). This professor thinks that the other academics of his faculty have a very negative view of the formal rules and since he is motivated to comply with their opinions, it has a negative impact on his subjective norm that in turn may affect his intentional behavior. Opinions about the formal rules from actors outside the faculty are not taken into account.

practice is merely the summation of individual professors' interests; and conducting research in such a way that it interferes with the research domains of faculty colleagues as little as possible. When such informal rules are daily practice in a faculty, the formal rules are not threatening and, more importantly, they cannot be seen as effective. The MUB Act intends to call for coherence, integration and strategic programming, which stands in sharp contrast with vagueness and maintaining individual research preferences. The composite variable "informal rules" has proven to be reliable (using Cronbach's Alpha; $\alpha = .58$). The scale of this variable ranges from "no informal rules experienced" (1) to "informal rules experienced" (4).

Research Design

Two sources of data have been used. First, several secondary sources, such as the relevant texts of law, institutional and faculty by-laws, explanatory memoranda and, of course, previous research on the subject, have been examined. Second, data have been collected by means of a written survey, sent to a proportion of the Dutch professoriate in April 2001. Reliable, up-to-date statistics on numbers of professors (rather than full-time equivalents) from one single source were not available. Moreover, there are several kinds of professor at Dutch universities. This study is only interested in professors of whom it may be expected that they are actively involved in the faculty's business, especially in the research of the faculty. Professors of the medical faculties and of the agricultural university of Wageningen are excluded because they are partly covered by other legislation. Additionally, deans are excluded because they are considered to be managers rather than academics. Given these restrictions to determining the exact size of the population, the Dutch almanac *Universities and Research Institutes in the Netherlands 2001* was used to select the sample. According to this source, there were at the time approximately 3,200 professors in the Netherlands (excluding those identified above).

The written questionnaire was sent to all professors in half of the Dutch faculties (forty-seven in total). In the end, the nominal sample of this study contained 1,352 professors (42 percent of the population). The questionnaire was completed by 475 professors (a response of 35 percent), indicating that roughly one out of six professors of the total population completed the questionnaire. Based on the analysis of the response and the non-response, it is concluded that bias was limited. Therefore, findings are generalized without the assignment of weights to the results. To test the hypothesis, the multi-linear regression method has been used.

The Outcomes of the Study: The Dutch Professoriate and the Changed Rules of the Game

To assess the effectiveness of the institutional reform concerning a new governing regime of Dutch universities, the intentional and actual behaviors of the Dutch professoriate have been determined. Do they comply with the new regime that intends, among other things, to strengthen the position of faculty management? As mentioned earlier, the dean is supposed to set the guidelines for faculty research

TABLE 13.3 Extent to Which, According to Dutch Professors, their Research Practice Conforms to the Faculty's Research Program and Policy (%)

Not at all	To some degree	Completely
30	41	30

Note: N = 460

and to program it. Professors are supposed to show conformity in doing their research. Table 13.3 gives a rather fragmented picture. It shows that about 70 percent of the Dutch professors do not use or only use to some degree the new rules on the organization of research at the faculty level. Thus, over two-thirds do not act as intended by the MUB Act. Faculty practice and legislative intentions differ. This is a first indication that the institutional reform is not fully effective, as it did not modify the behavior of a substantial number of professors.

This scattered picture is not surprising. In the past, when changes in the organizational structures of universities were discussed, the opinions of professors on the desirability of such changes greatly differed. For instance, when the Minister presented his initial ideas that eventually led to the institutional reform in 1997, professors expressed various views, although most of them remained silent. First, there was a group that would embrace the institutional reform because it would free the university from its "democratic" and politicized structure, in which decisiveness, in their eyes, was lacking most of the time. Second, some professors pointed to the high implementation costs (given similar experiences from the past), the uncertain outcomes of the reform and the fact that the prevailing system was not too bad after all. Third, some professors were (completely) ambivalent, since they argued that they had weathered many storms in the past and that this governance reform would be just another, so why worry about it? The outcomes presented in Table 13.3 support this heterogeneity of views among the Dutch professoriate.

According to the theoretical model, three factors could explain the behavior of the professoriate: their attitude towards the formal rules; the subjective norm towards the formal rules that they perceive in their direct environment; and the existence of informal rules. All three factors have explanatory power with respect to the intentional behavior of professors[1] (Table 13.4). As expected (hypotheses 1 and 2), attitudes and subjective norms have a positive effect on intentional

TABLE 13.4 Multiple Linear Regression Analysis to Explain the Intentional Behavior of Professors

Independent variable	Hypothesis	Effect (β)	Significance	t-value
Attitude	+	+ .21	*	+ 3.96
Subjective norm	+	+ .08	**	+ 1.56
Informal rules	+	− .30	*	− 6.49

Notes: N = 392; R^2 = .17; F statistic = 26.05*; * < .01; ** < .05

behavior: that is, those professors who positively assess the consequences of the MUB Act and/or feeling "social pressures" in favor of the MUB rules are more willing to comply with faculty research policies, while negative attitudes and negative subjective norms lead to less cooperative behavior. Particular attitudes explain compliance with the formal rules. The attitudes of professors and their subjective norms are related (r = .49), which means that the impact of attitude and subjective norms on behavior is even greater than the outcomes in Table 13.4 suggest. It is also clear that the attitude towards the formal rules is much more important than the subjective norm: that professors are not too receptive to the views of others in determining their actions. It confirms the general image that professors are well able to arrange their own affairs.

The most important factor explaining whether professors intend to conform to faculty research policies consists of the informal rules experienced within the faculty. However, the expectation that the existence of informal rules would have a positive effect on behavior is falsified. Those professors who experience informal rules that protect their professional autonomy are less willing to comply with the faculty research policies. The expectation was that if informal rules exist, professors would have substantial leeway in conducting their research; there would be no need to disregard the formal ones. It seems likely, however, that the existence of informal rules to safeguard professional autonomy legitimizes that they do not take notice of formal research guidelines set by faculty management. In this respect faculty research policies can be seen as a means to seal off professional activities from external interference.

About two-thirds of the professors have a negative attitude towards the formal rules and one-third hold a positive attitude. On average, the attitude of the Dutch professoriate is negative. Table 13.5 shows the weighted effects Dutch professors experience with respect to the institutional reform ($A = \Sigma B_i E_i$). The most important effect (highest absolute value in Table 13.5) of the MUB Act they see concerns academic freedom. On average, professors hold the view that academic freedom has diminished because of the MUB Act. Furthermore, five out of six effects have been assessed negatively. Besides the perceived decline in academic freedom, particularly the increase of power concentration and the decrease of democratic content indicate that the Dutch professoriate, on average, negatively judges the MUB Act with respect to research matters at the faculty level. The only positive effect identified by the professorial body concerns an increase in the decisiveness in decision-making at the faculty level. It is clear, however, that most

TABLE 13.5 Average Scores on Six Factors Regarding the Effects of the MUB Act, Including Overall Attitude

Aspect of faculty research policy	Average*	Sd	N
Academic freedom	−1.51	2.55	454
Fusion of powers/responsibilities	−1.45	2.92	451

Note: * < .01

professors have a negative attitude towards the formal rules. Also noticeable is the fact that, according to the professoriate, the MUB Act has had little effect on the kind of research conducted. It seems to have limited consequences for the extent to which faculty research contributes to disciplinary knowledge growth or solving social problems. Does this indicate a lack of relationship between the internal governance structure and the research processes? If so, the goals of the MUB Act with respect to changing the research process are unlikely to be achieved.

More than a quarter of the Dutch professoriate does not perceive social norms with respect to the MUB Act. They either do not care or not know what their referents think. In other words, the "direct environment" does not influence their (intentional) behavior. Of those remaining, half of the professors perceive that they are influenced by positive subjective norms, whereas the other half are influenced by the negative opinions of relevant others towards the MUB Act. Thus, some professors perceive a social norm that should stimulate them to act in conformity with faculty research policy; others feel a kind of external "pressure" to act otherwise. But, as reported earlier, the effect of the subjective norm on intended behavior is small.

Table 13.6 gives an overview on the subjective norms of the Dutch professoriate ($SN = \Sigma NE_i MC_i$). In the eyes of the "average professor," academics have a negative opinion of the effects of the MUB, whereas s/he believes that "leaders and managers" hold opposite views. The views of council members are not considered as very important. This outcome is not surprising as the general opinion with respect to the institutional changes is that the position of management was meant to be strengthened vis-à-vis representative and professional committees (see above). Managers gained where others lost powers, and this is reflected in the professors' subjective norm.

Our third independent variable concerns the informal rules that, in the way they have been operationalized, can be seen as safeguards to maintain professional autonomy. Two-thirds of the Dutch professoriate perceive the presence of such informal rules within their faculty (see Table 13.7). The results indicate that research policies of faculties are intentionally kept vague and broad and that they are actually a sum of individual preferences of faculty professors, who wish not to be engaged in the research of their colleagues. It is clear that such informal rules

TABLE 13.6 Average Scores of Weighted Views of Relevant Others

The perceived, weighted views of:	Average*	SD	N
Academic staff	−1.19	2.22	461
Dean	1.13	1.63	459
Scientific director	.97	2.16	456
Executive Board of the university	.88	1.39	463
Professors of their own faculty	−.72	2.12	461
Professors from outside their own university	−.69	2.13	457
Council members	−.34	.97	465

Note: * Average score on a scale from −8 to 8; N = 467

TABLE 13.7 Extent to Which, According to Dutch Professors, the
Research Policy of Their Faculty is Characterized by Informal
Rules that Create Safeguards for Professional Autonomy (%)

Absolutely not			Absolutely
12	23	25	41

Notes: N = 442; X = 2.95 (1.05); scale from 1 to 4

enable professors to utilize their professional autonomy and to sideline strict formal
rules that intend to program their research. Arguably, as far as it concerns faculty
research policy, the MUB Act has far from extinguished the importance of
professional autonomy. Where professional autonomy is maintained, no behavioral
modification as intended by the MUB Act has taken place.

Thus, a significant number of Dutch professors do not conform or only conform to a limited degree their research practices to the formal rules concerning
faculty research policies. This indicates that the institutional reform is not fully
effective. This result – limited effectiveness of the formal rules – is supported
by the fact that about two-thirds of the professoriate say they encounter informal
rules that enable them to maintain their professional autonomy. In further support
of this conclusion, it should be noted that a majority of the professoriate has
a negative attitude towards the MUB. Many hold the view that because of the
MUB Act, academic freedom, fusion of powers and democratic representation
in decision-making have declined. These negative assessments explain why they do
not comply with faculty research policies. Given the crucial role of professors
in universities, their willingness to implement a new set of rules at the shop-floor
level is vitally important for the reform's success; such willingness is, however,
limited.

Discussion

In the analyses of institutional effects, this study employed a theoretical model that
originates from the field of social psychology. This is a specific and relatively
original application of such a model. The results obtained through the application
of the theory of reasoned action appear promising, and the approach deserves more
attention in the area of institutional analysis. It provides a useful handle to
increase our understanding of the effectiveness of national reform policies and may
contribute to the renewed interest in implementation studies in higher education
(Gornitzka, Kogan and Amaral, 2005). By using this theoretical approach, the
importance of the perception and interpretation of the subjects of change at the
shop-floor level to make policy reforms a success is demonstrated once more.

Therefore, it seems worthwhile to test further the usefulness and applicability
of the theory with respect to governmental reform policies. There are several
opportunities for this. An attempt could be made to falsify the assumption in the
theory of reasoned action that context variables have no direct impact on behavior.

It might be useful to extend the theory through the incorporation of additional variables, such as faculty type, faculty size, disciplinary background, administrative experience, amount of time spent on research, level of trust in managers, reputation of the department and so forth. It is important to see if the theory also provides useful insights when the focus is on teaching instead of research. And, of course, it would be interesting to see the results if the theory were applied to investigate reforms outside the field of higher education. These kinds of research will without doubt increase our understanding of the applicability of the model used in this study.

One of the government goals of the university reform, in which executive leadership is formally strengthened, is an increase in the quality of the primary processes of research. It is argued that this can be achieved only if the main actors inside universities are willing to play the game by the new rules. With respect to the MUB Act, the study highlighted in this chapter indicates that this happens not to be the case, at least not entirely. A substantial proportion of Dutch professors do not act in accordance with the faculty research policy that is established on the basis of the formal rules. Moreover, a majority of the Dutch professoriate remains guided by informal rules that enable them to exploit their professional autonomy. The use of these informal rules that contrast with the formal ones implies the ineffectiveness of the government reform.

In light of all the problems that reformers face, one might ask "Why reform at all?" It seems only too obvious that there is a price to be paid when a university is seriously reorganized. Policy reformers should think twice before acting, especially because policy reform is "difficult to achieve, its outcomes are hard to predict and its benefits are likely to be realised only in the longer term while the short-term costs are not negligible" (Scharpf, 1986: 187).

This study underlines the problematic nature of policy reform if we look at the impact at the shop-floor level. The study seems to support professors' excellent record in resisting imposed changes. However, at least two caveats to this pessimistic conclusion are necessary. First, the study stresses just one aspect of the reform: that is, the effects of the MUB Act on the research policy of faculties. The practice of science is, however, probably the most impregnable fortress of higher education. The professorial body holds "absolute" sway when it comes to the practice of science. The conclusion may have been more positive had the study focused on other aspects of the reform, such as teaching. A more positive picture emerged from a comprehensive national evaluation study conducted in 2005 (de Boer, Goedegebuure and Huisman, 2005). In this national evaluation it was concluded that on average governors, decision-makers, staff and students were, with some reservations, satisfied with the MUB-based governing structure of their universities.

Second, the study presented in this chapter on the effects of institutional change is a snapshot of a reform taken at a given moment in time. The empirical data were collected three years after the introduction of the MUB Act in the universities. With the passage of time, the rules imbedded in the act may have become more accepted and institutionalized. The impacts of reforms often manifest themselves only in the longer term. Actors need time to learn new rules and to understand new relations and balances of power. Consequently, the conclusion that the MUB Act has failed to achieve (one of) its goals may need adjustment as time goes by.

Note

1   There is a strong correspondence of intentional and actual behaviors (confirmed by a linear regression that supports a strong relationship between the two). Therefore, for the further analysis we will use the variable "intentional behavior."

References

Ajzen, Icek. "From Intentions to Actions." In *Action-control: From Cognition to Behavior*, edited by J. Kuhl, and J. Beckman. Heidelberg: Springer, 1985, 11–39.

Ajzen, Icek. *Attitudes, Personality, and Behavior*. Chicago: The Dorsey Press, 1988.

Ajzen, Icek, and Martin Fishbein. *Understanding Attitudes and Predicting Social Behavior*. Englewood Cliffs: Prentice-Hall, 1980.

Arriëns, Th.E.H. *Universitaire Bestuursorganizatie*. Alphen aan den Rijn: Samsom, 1970.

Bardach, Eugene. *The Implementation Game: What Happens after a Bill Becomes a Law*. Cambridge, MA: MIT Press, 1977.

Boudon, Raymond. *De Logica van het Sociale: Een Inleiding tot het Sociologisch Denken*. Alphen aan den Rijn and Brussels: Samsom Uitgeverij, 1981.

Cerych, Ladislav, and Paul A. Sabatier. *Great Expectations and Mixed Performance: The Implementation of Higher Education Reforms in Europe*. Stoke-on-Trent: Trentham Books, 1986.

Clark, Burton R. *The Higher Education System: Academic Organization in Cross-national Perspective*. Berkeley: University of California Press, 1983.

Coleman, James Samuel. *Foundations of Social Theory*. Cambridge, MA: Harvard University Press, 1990.

Committee Datema. *De Kanteling van het Universitaire Bestuur (Rapport van de Commissie Klankbordgroep Invoering Mub)*. Zoetermeer: Ministerie van Onderwijs, Cultuur en Wetenschappen, 1998.

Committee Polak. *Gewubd en Gewogen: Tweede Kamer der Staten-Generaal, Zitting 1978–1979, 15 515*. 's-Gravenhage: SDU Uitgeverij, 1979.

de Boer, Harry F. *Institutionele Verandering en Professionele Autonomie: Een Empirisch-Verklarende Studie naar de Doorwerking van de Wet "Modernisering Universitaire Bestuursorganizatie" (Mub)*. Enschede: CHEPS, 2003.

de Boer, H.F. "Change and Continuity in Dutch Internal University Governance and Management." In *Towards a Cartography of Higher Education Policy Change: A Festschrift in Honour of Guy Neave*, edited by Jürgen Enders, and Frans van Vught. Enschede: CHEPS, 2007, 31–37.

de Boer, Harry, and Jeroen Huisman. "The New Public Management in Dutch Universities." In *Towards a New Model of Governance for Universities? A Comparative View*, edited by Dietmar Braun, and Francois-Xavier Merrien. London: Jessica Kingsley, 1999, 100–118.

de Boer, Harry, Leo Goedegebuure, and Jeroen Huisman. *Gezonde Spanning: Beleidsevaluatie van de Mub. Beleidsgerichte Studies Hoger Onderwijs en Wetenschappelijk Onderzoek 114*. Den Haag: Ministerie van OCW, 2005.

Fishbein, Martin, and Icek Ajzen. *Belief, Attitude, Intention, and Behavior: An Introduction to Theory and Research*. Reading: Addison-Wesley, 1975.

Gornitzka, Åse, Maurice Kogan, and Alberto Amaral, eds. *Reform and Change in Higher Education: Analysing Policy Implementation*. Dordrecht: Springer, 2005.

Kiser, Larry L., and Elinor Ostrom. "The Three Worlds of Action." In *Strategies of Political Inquiry*, edited by Elinor Ostrom. Beverly Hills: Sage, 1982, 179–222.

Ostrom, Elinor. *Governing the Commons: The Evolution of Institutions for Collective Action: The Political Economy of Institutions and Decisions*. Cambridge and New York: Cambridge University Press, 1990.

Ostrom, Elinor. *Understanding Institutional Diversity*. Princeton and Oxford: Princeton University Press, 2005.

Pressman, Jeffrey L., and Aaron Wildavsky. *Implementation: How Great Expectations in Washington Are Dashed in Oakland; Or, Why It's Amazing That Federal Programs Work at All*. Berkeley: University of California Press, 1974.

Scharpf, Fritz W. "Policy Failure and Institutional Reform: Why Should Form Follow Function?" *International Social Science Journal* 108 (1986): 179–190.

14

The Graduate System in Transition
External Ph.D. Researchers in a Managerial Context?

CHRISTINE TEELKEN, KEES BOERSMA AND PETER GROENEWEGEN

Introduction

The Ph.D. is the last step in the academic training of researchers, future lecturers, entrepreneurs and the intellectual elite. In an era in which knowledge and knowledge workers are increasingly important, the effectiveness and quality of this type of education is crucial (Pearson, Evans and Macauley, 2004; Barnacle, 2004). Understanding of the current functioning and future operation of this system and how it is interrelated with societal developments can guide government policy and university strategy. This is of particular urgency because in the near future the Ph.D. system will be redesigned as a last step of university reform laid down in the Bologna Declaration.

In the Bologna Declaration the (European) aim is stated that an increase in the number of higher educated citizens is necessary to be competitive. A compatible system (on the level of Bachelor's, Master's and Ph.D. degrees, also called the first, second and third tier) has been adopted in order to improve the quality of national and European-wide study programs (Kettunen and Kantola, 2006; Kehm and Teichler, 2006; Keeling, 2006). This means that the current restructuring of the Ph.D. system is part of the Europe-wide policy for educational innovation. Since September 2003 (ministerial conference in Berlin), the third tier has been brought on to the agenda. Two years later the Bergen communiqué put the need for a structured doctorate program on the policy agenda. A common European framework, clearly defined in guidelines, codes and regulations at the highest institutional level, which provides detailed rules on recruitment, supervision, exams, evaluation and defense of the thesis, is considered highly beneficial and innovative by the European University Association (EUA, 2005), as it frames further national and institutional restructuring of the doctorate system.

Theoretically speaking, these trends will likely lead to an integration and unification of Ph.D. systems in Europe. However, it has been argued that this system still has many faces due to internal diversity of higher education institutes and external variety with regard to national economies and higher education systems (Enders, 2004; see also EUA, 2007). In addition: "an agenda is not yet a concrete policy, let alone real change" (Bartelse and Huisman, 2008: 103). The actual impact of the Bologna Process on doctoral education (e.g. on the relation between education and research) and the rapidity of change are still limited (Bartelse and Huisman, 2005). This contrasts with the rather swift pace of the implementation of the Bachelor's/Master's structure in the Netherlands (Dittrich, Frederiks and Luwel, 2004).

Until now, not much is known about the "best way" to train Ph.D. students. In part, this is a consequence of the specific European situation where attention in higher education has been directed more extensively to the lower levels of university education. In the US, at the research-intensive universities, the Ph.D.s and their training schemes are the core of universities (Clark, 1995). A significant larger population of Ph.D. graduates is forced to seek non-academic employment. Continued academic careers are highly uncertain and therefore other occupations are frequently a further career step (Stephan and Levin, 1992). In contrast, a first analysis seems to suggest that the European Ph.D. trajectories are aimed primarily at the continuation of work within the academic arena. For access to industry it has been noted that the career paths of Ph.D. students depend highly on whether they collaborated with industry or any other private sector during their Ph.D. (Mangematin, 2000; see also Slaughter et al., 2002).

Recently, there has been a growing plea for making the Ph.D. trajectory more flexible and heterogeneous. One possibility could be that a full and purely "academic" dissertation becomes less relevant for future Ph.D. graduates. Instead, a portfolio of research courses, publications and relevant work experience (also) outside the academic, approved by an authority, could be enough to gain a Ph.D. (Rip, 2004). It was first and foremost in the Anglo-Saxon world that the traditional doctorate was criticized; the knowledge and skills of Ph.D. holders have not always matched the needs of the labor market. Since the Bologna Declaration, which emphasized the importance of the third tier, the European-based universities have been forced to look beyond traditional Ph.D. systems. To change the Ph.D. tradition will not be easy, since, although the environment of higher education institutions (HEIs) has been subject to change (as will be clear in this chapter), "seemingly the doctorate has been most resistant to change" (Huisman and Naidoo, 2006: 4).

In this chapter, we are especially interested in policies concerning external researchers pursuing a Ph.D., a special and underresearched group within the Ph.D. system. We focus our empirical research on the external Ph.D. in the Netherlands. These graduates work outside the university, for example, in the public or private sector as a manager in (the financial) industry or as an instructor at a professional higher education institution, and pursue their Ph.D.s mostly part-time. Barnacle (2004) carried out one of the few studies in this area. As she has shown, for the external Ph.D.s (or the "practice-based" and "professional" doctorates, as they have been called; see Huisman and Naidoo, 2006: 6), pursuing a Ph.D. means an opportunity to gain and develop knowledge that is valued both for its relevance to their work and to academia. Sometimes, it is presented as a program to become a reflexive practitioner (Schön, 1983; Cunliffe, 2004). For the candidates, it is an opportunity to develop skills and to gain knowledge with which they can critically reflect upon their professional lives.

Before dealing with the Dutch graduate system we will elaborate on the general changes in university organization, in order to explain the political and organizational contexts. Subsequently, we will give details of our empirical findings. We will end the chapter with conclusions and a discussion.

Changes in the University Organization

It is generally recognized that universities are among the most stable and change-resistant social institutions in Western society, with their roots going back to medieval times. Among leaders in higher education consensus exists that the core functions of higher education – to educate (knowledge transfer), to do research (knowledge production) and to provide community service (outreach, emanating from the knowledge base) – must be preserved, reinforced and expanded. However, although universities are longstanding institutions with a respected reputation, they are nevertheless in a process of transforming both in identity and structure.

An important element of that transformation lies in the sphere of governance. A common view on governance is an increased focus on alternative forms of control (Hood and Peters, 2004), not through direct involvement, but in an indirect manner, replacing input and output control by performance-driven steering. Management based on rules and procedures is gradually being replaced by a system based on performance measurement and decentralized decision-making. While some national governments aspire to become more accountable to their citizens, public and semi-public organizations are being required to demonstrate the results of their activities to their customers (Pollitt and Bouckaert, 2000). Higher education is one of the public sectors where such shifts in governance have been witnessed (de Boer, Enders and Leišytė, 2007).

Through the stronger but more indirect role of government, universities feel forced to adapt their organizational strategies, structures and values to such managerial characteristics as budget transparency, output measurement, increased competition, and use of private sector management influences (see Aucoin, 1990; Hood, 1991, 1995; Pollitt and Bouckaert, 2000, 2004) in order to meet the societal requirements for accountability of quality. The shifts in governance manifest themselves in, for example, management of performances and accountability, such as the Research Assessment Exercise (UK) and quality assurance through accreditation schemes (the Netherlands). Discussions about educational quality emphasize the diagnosis and assessment of quality, leading to more intensive, extensive and elaborate quality assessment (Pollitt and Bouckaert, 2004). We distinguish two important policy developments, which should be seen in the light of these shifts of governance.

First, performance measurement is increasingly present in higher education (Teelken and Braam, 2002). The organization of quality care and assessment has been a topic of discussion for many years, in the Netherlands especially since the *Higher Education: Autonomy and Quality* White Paper (1985). Since the signing of the Bologna Declaration in 1999, European universities have committed themselves to achieve comparability in systems of quality care. The quality care in education roughly has three different functions: monitoring and improvement; accountability; and provision of information. The performance element is also visible in league tables. In the Netherlands, these are published every year on the basis of questionnaires completed by students and professors in various areas of higher education (e.g. the yearly Elsevier-magazine website for the Ministry of Education, Culture and Science: www.minocw.nl). The 1985 White Paper laid the foundation for a system of external quality care, and a number of important elements of that White Paper were introduced in the 1992 Higher Education and Research Act (*Wet Hoger Onderwijs en Wetenschappelijk Onderzoek*, WHW). To fulfill the external quality demands, institutions had to improve their internal quality care as well. Attempts to form national graduate schools were stimulated, in order to improve the quality of Ph.D. teaching. This encouragement occurred usually at the level of the discipline. These national research schools still exist in areas such as the environmental sciences and are accredited by a committee of the Royal Academy of Sciences, but they have disappeared in other disciplines. The increased competition between universities and reorganizations of their faculties into larger units have directed more attention to local graduate schools. Yet, to date, there is no binding qualification system at this level in the Netherlands. The decision is very much left to the *ad hoc* committees that evaluate the Ph.D. manuscript.

The second important development is that the former system of "visitations" (evaluations including analysis and recommendations based on peer visits at the program level) have been replaced by a more rigid system of accreditation (with an emphasis on meeting accreditation criteria). Accreditation of programs (Bachelor's and Master's degrees) will be a condition for obtaining financial means, the right to award Bachelor's and Master's degrees and the accessibility to financial assistance for participating students. Programs should obtain accreditation by producing a self-evaluation report and through a visitation of an inspection committee. There are also various international accreditation schemes, which may be increasingly attractive for universities to obtain. We agree with Bartelse and Huisman (2008) that we do not expect the Ph.D. system to go through similar changes as have occurred in the first and second tier, but it is likely that Ph.D. courses will also be subject to accreditation (EUA, 2007).

In the above, we have alluded to the general policy changes. However, the interpretation of the effects of such changes has to be based on the manner in which they work out for academics. For the Ph.D. system, this includes the direct effects on supervisors and working environment. Their situation can be characterized by the fact that faculties experience, on the one hand, more autonomy; on the other hand, they are increasingly funded on the basis of their output, in terms of research as well as education. This changes the conditions under which they operate; while the national government remains an important anchoring device, there is a greater need to shift attention to other stakeholders (Neave, 2003). As has been argued by Bleiklie and Kogan (2007), the main principles in steering universities have shifted from collegial control to a significant influence of various stakeholders. Current changes in the system of higher education involve various organizing principles that are sometimes tangential to each other. With still large sums of money being distributed by national governments directly to universities, output measurement has increased and remuneration based on output performance has become more important. Moreover, in Europe, elaborate assessment and accreditation systems are being developed and directly used to replace central control in many countries. This system change is suggested to increase the freedom of manoeuver for institutions. Accompanying internal changes relegated collegial control and invested in managerial steering, creating an almost corporate image for some universities and faculties. This last managerial reform appears as a dominant theme in much of the recent literature. However, the effects still show significant differences between countries (Bleiklie and Kogan, 2007).

Measuring output may include numbers of graduates, numbers and impact of publications and *ex post* evaluations. The number of annual Ph.D. graduates forms an important part of the faculty output. If the group of external researchers aiming for a Ph.D. is of growing size and relevance, they may therefore soon be within the reach of the policy-makers and management of faculties and research groups. Alternatively, their needs may lead to a consolidation of attempts to invest in the content of graduate schools. Besides, for many (research) universities it is another way to generate additional income – a reason to see the development of external Ph.D. students in connection with income generation policies (Huisman and Naidoo, 2006).

Particularly interesting is the explicit attention given to the managerial side of the doctorate system, such as quality care, transparency and equal possibilities for development of the participants. This may be a consequence of growing attention given to the educational quality of Ph.D. training in general, stimulating it more in the direction of an actual third tier of the student programs (EUA, 2007), which has been absent in many European universities outside medical and natural sciences. Moreover, it fits well with the general pattern of "managerial" steering of higher education systems, and within that the Ph.D. system. We agree with Leišytė (2007) that new managerialism is visible in stronger, hierarchical leadership, a more top-down structure at the cost of the professional role in decision-making, which coincides with a more tightly coupled university organization (de Boer, Enders and Leišytė, 2007).

The evolving university system encompasses the Ph.D. system. This system appears to develop in policy terms towards conforming more to the general pattern of increased transparency and quality control and increased managerial control. However, attention to such changes assumes that they are pervasive and have an effect that is uniform across groups and institutes. So far, the managerial influences of HEIs seem not to have had much impact on the functioning of external researchers pursuing a Ph.D. We will provide more insight into the managerial influences on this specific group of external Ph.D. students. Our working hypothesis is that new institutional rules concerning this group of Ph.D. students are merely emerging from the day-to-day practices at a local level (Mintzberg, Quinn and Ghoshal, 1998). We suppose that the national governments and local university policy-makers are rather ambiguous with regard to modes of control (Gornitzka and Maassen, 2000); actors at the local level are provided with ample room to set their own rules and standards, especially concerning groups of Ph.D. students, that are not (yet) part of the formal graduation system. This means that in this chapter we will present the paradoxical situation of *ad hoc* managerial rules and styles surrounding this group within the broader context of an increasing managerial rhetoric in the environment of the Dutch universities.

The Dutch Graduate System

After a brief general description of the Dutch graduate system and its requirements, we will focus on the most relevant changes. The thirteen universities in the Netherlands provide teaching and research in a wide variety of disciplines. Some universities specialize in technical, economic or agricultural studies, but most cover a wide range of subjects. The university system is based on a three-cycle degree system: Bachelor (180 ECTS), Master (60, 90 or 120 ECTS) and Ph.D. The most recent strategic agenda for higher education, research and science policy (Ministerie van Onderwijs, Cultuur en Wetenschap, 2007) emphasizes the importance of a good-quality higher education system, with a relevant contribution to the knowledge society and a clear connection with the current labor market. The intention is to transform the training of researchers into an American model, with a clear starting point and orientation within research schools. HEIs should function as suppliers of highly educated professionals, as well as of knowledge in a closely knit network of teaching, research, innovation and public services. This view of HEIs is part of strategic thinking that in general terms is directed at understanding and steering the processes of knowledge creation (see, e.g., Etzkowitz and Leydesdorff, 2000) and reflects a strategic reorientation of knowledge creation and diffusion in the economy and society.

Within the higher education system, Ph.D. students form a very important, hybrid group. While doctoral programs are considered the third cycle of the Bologna Process, they form at the same time the first phase of young researchers' careers, constituting the main link between higher education and research areas (EUA, 2007). To acquire a doctorate is a testimony of scientific competence, based on an original contribution to scholarship, resulting in the publication of a thesis or dissertation, which should be publicly defended. Generic final achievement standards for a doctorate involve (VSNU, 2004: 25):

- the successful candidate has made an original contribution to academic research of a quality which stands up to peer review at the level usual in the Netherlands;
- the successful candidate has demonstrated the ability to apply the academic methods used in the discipline concerned for developing, interpreting and putting into practice new knowledge;
- the successful candidate has acquired and worked with a substantial body of knowledge which, at the very least, embraces the principles and methods of international academic practice and of theorization, methodology and study in the discipline concerned;
- the successful candidate possesses the ability to design and implement a substantial project for the purpose of developing new knowledge.

The Dutch Ph.D. system was implemented in 1985 with Ph.D. students being temporary employees. They are supervised by a professor (the *promotor* and often one or more *co-promotors*) and are often supposed to attend various courses. They may also be required to teach undergraduate students. Until the establishment of this system, the doctorate system appeared "a black box" and the exclusive domain of the individual supervisor (Bartelse and Huisman, 2005: 24). Obtaining a Ph.D. used to be an informal arrangement between the professor and the Ph.D. student. This apprenticeship model was gradually replaced by the appearance of more structured forms of postgraduate education (Enders, 2004), such as research or graduate schools (VSNU, 2004). A relatively large percentage of Ph.D. students are now trained in research schools, which are defined as centers of high-quality research offering young researchers a structured education. Some research schools managed to obtain accreditation from the KNAW (Royal Netherlands Academy of Arts and Sciences). These research schools achieve high graduation rates (Sonneveld and Oost, 2005), while there is great heterogeneity between and also within these schools (Sonneveld and Oost, 2006). Also, because of increased managerial pressures, the Ph.D. trajectory has generally become more closely supervised and controlled (e.g. selection after the first year of the Ph.D., publication pressure, etc.).

As an alternative to regular Ph.D. programs there is an international trend towards producing "industry-ready" graduates with links to the needs of non-academic environments, that is industry (Harman, 2004). Although this is not new – there have been many Ph.D. programs embedded in or funded by industry – its massification occurred only recently. Universities, facing the pressure to increase the number of Ph.D.s awarded, are looking for new ways to attract graduate students. The current managerial developments necessitate a radical rethinking of the doctorate experience and consequently a reconceptualization of doctorate candidature as a "form of knowledge-producing work contributing a complex mix of personal, social and economic benefits" (Pearson, Evans and Macauley, 2004: 352).

External Ph.D. Students in the Netherlands

In order to obtain an impression of the current situation of Dutch external Ph.D. students, we carried out interviews and document analysis at two faculties in two different Dutch universities: the Faculty of Management Sciences of the Radboud University Nijmegen and the Faculty of Social Sciences of the *Vrije Universiteit* (VU University Amsterdam). We held interviews with the vice-dean responsible for research, with the coordinator of the Ph.D. training center and with several professors who supervised many external Ph.D. students. In addition to this in-depth study, we performed an internet review through scanning the websites of all Dutch universities. We used Google to find information on the institutionalization of external Ph.D. students for which we used the search terms *buitenpromovendus* and *buitenpromovendi* (the Dutch terms for external Ph.D. students). After going briefly into the general characteristics of these external Ph.D. students, we will present our findings with the help of three dimensions that emerged from our empirical data gathering. The first dimension concerns the financial aspects and discusses whether external Ph.D. students should be considered a welcome addition to the faculty's increasingly tight financial situation or a risky factor in the extracurricular activities of individual professors. Second, we will explore the tension between control versus autonomy at the individual level. Our third dimension concerns (a lack of) faculty strategies and policies.

External Ph.D. students are defined here as researchers working on a Ph.D. thesis under the supervision of a professor from the Radboud University Nijmegen or VU Amsterdam but without an employee contract with the university. Candidates should have at least a Master's degree. The website of the Radboud University mentions a contact-person who can assist in finding a promotor (provided that the candidates develop a research proposal), but it appeared during the interviews that she is contacted only a few times a year. External Ph.D. students are entitled to follow a number of courses, for example, in the field of academic writing, presenting research and didactics. They may apply for membership of the university library and get some funding for the printing of their thesis (to a maximum of €2,200). At the VU Amsterdam there are no formal arrangements – the supervision is left to an individual arrangement between *promotor* and the Ph.D. student. Some professors draw up an agreement including a fee for supervision on an annual basis. Usually arrangements are less formal and more open.

Unfortunately, national statistics concerning the number of external Ph.D. students or graduates do not exist, but it is clear that their numbers are extensive. In some subjects external Ph.D. graduations can add up to one-third or even half the total number of graduates (e.g. at the Radboud University Nijmegen, management studies; at the Tilburg University, law studies).

The backgrounds of external Ph.D. students are very diverse: some candidates are already retired and see the achievement of a Ph.D. as a conclusion of their career by composing their *magnum opus*. However, most external Ph.D. students are employed elsewhere, for example, in policy research, which means that they can use their various findings of research reports to compose a Ph.D. thesis as proof of their ability to conduct academic research. Others may be employed in professional higher education, a category that receives special support in order to increase the number of qualified scientists in this higher education sector.

On the basis of our internet scan we can conclude that the universities and faculties deal in three different ways with external Ph.D. students. Some universities (e.g. the University of Amsterdam, the University of Groningen and the Radboud University Nijmegen) facilitate external Ph.D. students actively; they recruit them (among others) through advertisements and provide various facilities. For example, at the Radboud University Nijmegen, the "Center for Doctoral Research" gives unemployed researchers the opportunity to complete their Ph.D. studies. The center is particularly assisting the integration of women and ethnic minorities into paid employment. Potential researchers can apply to the center on the basis of a research proposal (approximately eight pages), which should be supported by a *promotor* from the Radboud University Nijmegen. The researchers are not employed by the university, nor do they receive a salary, but they are entitled to various facilities, such as the library, work space, personal computer and a range of courses. They should devote at least twenty-four hours a week to their Ph.D. research. There are also funds for traveling, visiting conferences and seminars.

There are about ten places available, and there is also a waiting list of about ten to fifteen potential researchers. The area of research concerns the arts and philosophy (40 percent) and social sciences (60 percent). Other universities express the intention to recruit more external Ph.D. students (e.g. Maastricht University) but provide no institutional support as yet. A third group only mentions the possibility of supervision by a full professor and that potential external Ph.D. students should contact a suitable professor directly (e.g. Leiden University).

Financial Assets Versus Risks

From our interviews in both faculties, it becomes very clear that external Ph.D. students are currently a relevant source of additional funding, at the faculty level but also for the individual supervisors. Research at universities is financed progressively in a more restricted manner. The former annual rounds, when six to eight new Ph.D. students could be appointed at the Faculty of Management Sciences, were abolished in 2003. At the VU University Amsterdam, formal attachments of positions to departments were abolished around the same time. Currently the only direct support is in the form of Ph.D. posts attached to newly appointed professors or as a conditional funding for proposals to be submitted to the Dutch research council. Most of the financial means for internal Ph.D. students should be obtained through external funding (national or European research councils). Other examples of financial restrictions are that staff are encouraged (or even forced) to earn part of their own wages externally; at the Radboud University Nijmegen future targets are set for approximately 30 percent of the annual salary.

The national funding allocation mechanisms put a premium on completed Ph.D. theses. Universities have translated these mechanisms locally. Faculties receive approximately €35,000 (Radboud University Nijmegen) and €25,000 (VU Amsterdam) for every completed Ph.D. thesis. This is the common fee for Ph.D. graduations in the arts and social sciences. In the natural sciences and medical sector, the fees are usually much higher, about €70,000-100,000 for the natural scientists and engineers and sometimes as much as €135,000 for dissertations in the field of medicine. The salary costs of an internal Ph.D. student add up to about €240,000, but for external Ph.D. students the fees received will always exceed the costs.

Currently, this financial system at the VU Amsterdam is under revision, with the intention to abolish the difference between the various faculties (arts, sciences, social sciences, medicine) and introduce one uniform financial reward for all graduations of €50,000. It will be paid sooner after graduation, making the relationship between performance and reward clearer and more direct. At the Faculty of Management Sciences at the Radboud University Nijmegen, the number of external Ph.D. students is relatively large: of the 109 graduations which took place between 1995 and 2007, thirty-five (32 percent) were external Ph.D.s. There is no clear increasing tendency over time. The financial rewards are transferred to the faculty in two to four portions, with the first portion usually rewarded two years after graduation, and the other portions following in subsequent years. Figures from the VU Amsterdam are not known, according to the respondent at faculty level. Only if an external Ph.D. student makes use of the educational system of the VU University Amsterdam, for example, if he or she follows additional methodology courses, do they become visible to the administration and faculty management. However, the *promotor* is able (and by law authorized) to offer a candidate professional training. There are no records at the VU Amsterdam about the actual number of external Ph.D. students at faculty level. Although we asked several people in key positions about the financial arrangements concerning external Ph.D. students, we had to rely on oral information because no formal documents could be retrieved.

An important difference between the two faculties is that at the Faculty of Social Sciences at the VU Amsterdam, half of the funding is retained at faculty level, while only €12,000 is transferred to the research group. At the Faculty of Management Sciences at Radboud University Nijmegen, it is explicit policy that graduation premiums are transferred to individual professors. As the vice-dean at the Radboud University Nijmegen explained: "Imagine that you are very good at supervising Ph.D. students, and good at organizing, and then the funding is not returned for your efforts. That can be very frustrating."

Control Versus Autonomy at Individual Level

In contradiction to the external Ph.D. students, internal Ph.D. students have to function increasingly in a more controlled and embedded system. We found various forms of control and support in the different stages of the Ph.D. process. At the Faculty of Social Sciences at the VU Amsterdam, which comprises seven different disciplines, graduation projects are now centrally administered. More emphasis is being laid on the recruitment and selection of Ph.D. students. Consequently, upon employment, Ph.D. students have to compose a training and supervision plan, there are courses at faculty (the Radboud University Nijmegen, VU Amsterdam) or even university (VU Amsterdam) level that they can follow in order to prepare themselves thoroughly for their work.

Courses may involve generic skills, methodology, particular theories or thematic training. Ph.D. students are entitled to yearly performance interviews with their supervisor. But most importantly at both universities, internal Ph.D. students have to submit a research proposal (theoretical and methodological framework) after nine or ten months. This then has to be approved by a faculty committee in order for the student to continue their Ph.D. For research projects which are in a preliminary phase and not developed in detail by the supervisors (e.g. when they have to go to the Dutch research council for assessment), this can be a stressful and demanding pursuit. However, some consider this a form of academic freedom – allowing time and scope for Ph.D. students to create and thoroughly think through their research proposals is considered the ultimate example of the academic profession. Unfortunately, the nine or ten months they are allowed can be considered insufficient (interview with the vice-dean at Radboud University Nijmegen).

All these more strictly enforced regulations do not apply to external Ph.D. students. The only control (in terms of content, quality, etc.) they experience is through the supervision of their *promotor* and eventually the thesis committee. According to the doctorate regulations (VU Amsterdam, article 21) the thesis shall be subject to the appraisal of the supervisor, who can take into account the assessment of a co-supervisor, if applicable. After the thesis has been approved by the supervisors, it will be submitted to a relevant thesis committee. This committee will be appointed by the doctoral examination committee (appointed by the professor of the faculty), and consists of a minimum of four (VU Amsterdam) or three (the Radboud University Nijmegen) members, at least one of them being a member of the faculty in question. Committee members should hold a doctorate or preferably have the *ius promovendi* (meaning they are eligible to act as supervisors). The thesis committee shall consequently assess the quality of the doctoral research as a whole, particularly the research questions, the treatment of the subject, the command of the literature and the systematic presentation of the research (article 12.5). Decisions shall be taken on the basis of a majority vote. The committee should not attach conditions to its decisions, although individual members are free to add suggestions and/or recommendations to their assessment.

The success rates of the internal Ph.D. students have been quite low, with both faculties showing high drop-out rates and on average long periods before graduation, which are supposedly typical of the social sciences (interview, VU Amsterdam). There is evidence, though, that success rates have increased due to the more managerial approach towards internal Ph.D. students. As far as external Ph.D. students are concerned, they are seemingly (and surprisingly) more successful than internal students and make it to graduation in a shorter period of time.

Faculty Policies Versus Local Initiatives

Looking closely at the managerial side of the doctorate system, we found that despite the increasing importance of external Ph.D. students, there was hardly evidence of formal policies concerning this group: "There are actually no policies in the supervision of external Ph.D. students, nor are there any systematic arrangements on how to deal with partners, with organizations whose employees may be interested in obtaining a Ph.D." (interview with the vice-dean at the Radboud University Nijmegen). (There are, however, contacts between individual supervisors and organizations.) Even the financial arrangements concerning external Ph.D. students seem vague, to say the least.

This lack of any formal policy and absence of stimulation and encouragement at the faculty level were recognized by Ph.D. supervisors:

> It is not stimulated, it is an individual activity. You are allowed to do it, but not compensated in time. All you get is the graduation premium, but that is after the graduation. It is considered a completely individual activity, which I carry out in my spare time.
>
> (Interview, Radboud University Nijmegen)

With respect to external Ph.D. students, the individual professors are still completely autonomous in the supervision process, despite the possible increased importance of external Ph.D. students.

However, while no formal policies at faculty level could be found, we did come across several initiatives at departmental or research group level which involved the provision of a framework for supervision and courses for (external) Ph.D. students. Remarkably, though, interviewees at faculty level were unaware of these local initiatives. Initiatives at the VU Amsterdam involved the annual €3,000 fee, requested by several department heads to be paid by the external Ph.D. student. Another initiative suggests setting up an academy, which would offer executive courses in cooperation with large organizations that have their headquarters close to the VU Amsterdam campus. At the Radboud University Nijmegen an initiative for a Ph.D. training center was turned down by the university's executive board despite receiving consent from the faculty dean. It was supposedly too commercial and insufficiently embedded in academic research. The initiators intend to resubmit their proposal. Three employees (two full professors, one associate professor) from the Faculty of Management Sciences at the Radboud University Nijmegen initiated a post-academic course titled "The Responsible Organization." The intention is to support potential external Ph.D. students by offering them courses in methodology and research capacities, which should result in a research proposal. The course consists of six modules and lasts one year (fee of €10,000). The idea is that after the course, participants carry on with their research individually, under supervision of a *promotor*.

All in all, it seems that the local initiatives are more directly influenced by international developments, such as the Bologna Process, the three-tier system and the creation of a structured doctoral system, while there is a lack of policy initiatives at the faculty and university levels.

Conclusions and Discussion

External Ph.D. students, compared to internal Ph.D. students, are not (yet) part of increasingly pervasive managerial control systems. Attracting external Ph.D. students can be seen as a financially lucrative activity (see Harman (2004) on similar developments in Australia). However, despite the increasingly tighter finance and the financial rewards for external Ph.D.s, few faculty or university policies concerning external Ph.D. students have been developed so far. Inviting potential external Ph.D. students is still left to the individual supervisors (*promotors*) or occurs as a result of the initiative of the potential students themselves. Various local initiatives have been developed, with the intention to explore and to benefit from this attractive market, but with mixed success and limited awareness. In contradiction to the tendency of increased steering through managerial and quality control, external Ph.D. students are still subject to the autonomous supervision carried out by their *promotor* and are not under the influence of the increasingly pervasive market- or businesslike activities of the current higher education system. While the general suggestion of New Public Management is that control and assessment efforts are comprehensive, our study shows a more variegated landscape. The logics of collegiate control still dominate this area, and the fact that external Ph.D.s are both outside and inside the system may contribute to a lack of attention from New Public Management.

Another explanation may be that with the evolving set of instruments connected to the Europeanization of higher education policy, education and regulation practices are not yet fully implemented for the third tier. In our case the changing logic of national financing of the Ph.D. system seems to stimulate the attraction of Ph.D.s. It suggests moreover that for new control and managerial mechanisms to be effective, some degree of control over academic loyalty is necessary. This is more easily achieved with respect to the employee status of internal Ph.D.s.

A final explanation might be that the current university system in transition is exhibiting a variety of conflicting dynamics. External Ph.D.s in this light represent a clear external link to stakeholders in practical, professional or corporate areas that are therefore in essence a different breed than internal Ph.D.s precisely because of the increased paradoxical demands from two different logics that are part of New Public Management (Hood and Peters, 2004). It shows a tinge of the old-fashioned call for academic freedom, which coincides with an operational connection to stakeholder importance. Therefore, the external Ph.D. is in itself a contradictory category, and forcing academic quality control would not only diminish income but damage a valuable, legitimate group. This situation, combined with the non-employee character of the external Ph.D., might be temporary, and will decline when a third-tier transformation leads to strengthening graduate education. However, the actual practice of Ph.D. training might be very different from the policy ideals of Bologna (see, e.g., Neave, 2002).

References

Aucoin, Peter. "Administrative Reform in Public Management: Paradigms, Principles, Paradoxes and Pendulums." *Governance: An International Journal of Policy and Administration* 3(2) (1990): 115–137.

Barnacle, Robyn. "A Critical Ethic in a Knowledge Economy: Research Degree Candidates in the Workplace." *Studies in Continuing Education* 26(3) (2004): 355–367.

Bartelse, Jeroen, and Jeroen Huisman. "Over de Kracht van Nietszeggende Communiqués: De Promotieopleiding in Europees Perspectief." *Thema* 12(5) (2005): 23–26.

Bartelse, Jeroen, and Jeroen Huisman. "The Bologna Process." In *Toward a Global Ph.D.: Forces and Forms in Doctoral Education Worldwide*, edited by Maresi Nerad, and Mimi Heggelund. Washington, DC: UW Press, 2008, 101–113.

Bleiklie, Ivar, and Maurice Kogan. "Organization and Governance of Universities." *Higher Education Policy* 20(4) (2007): 477–493.

Clark, Burton R. *Places of Inquiry: Research and Advanced Education in Modern Universities.* Berkeley: University of California Press, 1995.

Cunliffe, Ann L. "On Becoming a Critically Reflexive Practitioner." *Journal of Management Education* 28 (2004): 407–426.

De Boer, Harry F., Jürgen Enders, and Liudvika Leišytė. "Public Sector Reform in Dutch Higher Education: The Organizational Transformation of the University." *Public Administration* 85(1) (2007): 27–46.

Dittrich, Karl, Mark Frederiks, and Marc Luwel. "The Implementation of 'Bologna' in Flanders and the Netherlands." *European Journal of Education* 39(3) (2004): 299–316.

Enders, Jürgen. "Research Training and Careers in Transition: A European Perspective on the Many Faces of the Ph.D." *Studies in Continuing Education* 26(3) (2004): 419–429.

Etzkowitz, Henry, and Loet Leydesdorff. "The Dynamics of Innovation: From National Systems and 'Mode 2' to a Triple Helix of University–Industry–Government Relations." [Introduction to the special Triple Helix issue.] *Research Policy* 29(2) (2000): 109–123.

European University Association (EUA). *Doctoral Programmes for the European Knowledge Society, Final Report.* Brussels: EUA, 2005. Available online (accessed 1.3.2008) http://www.eua.be/fileadmin/user_upload/files/EUA1_documents/Doctoral_Programs_Project_Report.1129278878120.pdf.

European University Association (EUA). *Doctoral Programmes in Europe's Universities: Achievements and Challenges.* Brussels: EUA, 2007. Available online (accessed 1.3.2008) http://www.eua.be/file admin/user_upload/files/Publications/Doctoral_Programs_in_Europe_s_Universities.pdf.

Gornitzka, Åse, and Peter Maassen. "Hybrid Steering Approaches with Respect to European Higher Education." *Higher Education Policy* 13(3) (2000): 267–285.

Harman, Kay M. "Producing 'Industry-ready' Doctorates: Australian Cooperative Research Centre Approaches to Doctoral Education." *Studies in Continuing Education* 26(3) (2004): 387–404.

Hood, Christopher. "A Public Management for All Seasons?" *Public Administration* 69 (1991): 3–19.

Hood, Christopher. "The 'New Public Management' in the 1980s: Variations on a Theme." *Accounting, Organizations and Society* 20(2/3) (1995): 93–109.

Hood, Christopher, and B. Guy Peters. "The Middle Aging of New Public Management: Into the Age of Paradox?" *Journal of Public Administration Research and Theory* 14(3) (2004): 267–282.

Huisman, Jeroen, and Rajani Naidoo. "The Professional Doctorate: From Anglo-Saxon to European Challenges." *Higher Education Management and Policy* 18(2) (2006):1–13.

Keeling, Ruth. "The Bologna Process and the Lisbon Research Agenda: The European Commission's Expanding Role in Higher Education Discourse." *European Journal of Education* 41(2) (2006): 203–224.

Kehm, Barbara M., and Ulrich Teichler. "Which Direction for Bachelor and Master Programs? A Stocktaking of the Bologna Process." *Tertiary Education and Management* 12(3) (2006): 257–267.

Kettunen, Juha, and Mauri Kantola. "The Implementation of the Bologna Process." *Tertiary Education and Management* 12(3) (2006): 257–267.

Leišytė, Liudvika. *University Governance and Academic Research: Case Studies of Research Units in Dutch and English Universities.* Enschede: University of Twente, 2007.

Mangematin, Vincent. "Ph.D. Job Market: Professional Trajectories and Incentives during the PhD." *Research Policy* 29(6) (2000): 741–756.

Ministerie van Onderwijs, Cultuur en Wetenschap. *Het Hoogste Goed: Strategische Agenda voor het Hoger Onderwijs-, Onderzoek- en Wetenschapsbeleid.* Den Haag: Ministerie van OCW, 2007.

Mintzberg, Henry, James B. Quinn, and Sumantra Ghoshal. *The Strategy Process* (revised European edn). London: Prentice Hall, 1998.

Neave, Guy. "Anything Goes: Or, How the Accommodation of Europe's Universities to European Integration Integrates an Inspiring Number of Contradictions." *Tertiary Education and Management* 8(3) (2002): 181–197.

Neave, Guy. "The Bologna Declaration: Some of the Historic Dilemmas Posed by the Reconstruction of the Community in Europe's Systems of Higher Education." *Educational Policy* 17(1) (2003): 141–164.

Pearson, Margot, Terry Evans, and Peter Macauley. "Editorial. The Working Life of Doctoral Students: Challenges for Research Education and Training." *Studies in Continuing Education* 26(3) (2004): 347–353.

Pollitt, Christopher, and Geert Bouckaert. *Public Management Reform: A Comparative Analysis.* Oxford: Oxford University Press, 2000.

Pollitt, Christopher, and Geert Bouckaert. *Public Management Reform. A Comparative Analysis* (2nd edn). Oxford: Oxford University Press, 2004.

Rip, Arie. "Strategic Research, Post-modern Universities and Research Training." *Higher Education Policy* 17(2) (2004): 153–166.

Schön, Donald A. *The Reflective Practitioner: How Professionals Think in Action.* New York: Basic Books, 1983.

Slaughter, Sheila, Teresa Campbell, Margaret Holleman, and Edward Morgan. "The 'Traffic' in Graduate Students: Graduate Students as Tokens of Exchange between Academe and Industry." *Science, Technology and Human Values* 27(1) (2002): 282–312.

Sonneveld, Hans, and Heinze Oost. "Het is Tijd, Maar Waarvoor? Promotiesucces en Kwaliteit van Onderzoekscholen in Nederland." *Thema* 12(5) (2005): 32–38.

Sonneveld, Hans, and Heinze Oost. *Het Promotiesucces van de Nederlandse Onderzoeksscholen: Afsluiting van een Drieluik.* Utrecht/Amsterdam: IVLOS/ASSR, 2006.

Stephan, Paula E., and Sharon G. Levin. *Striking the Mother Lode in Science: The Importance of Age, Place, and Time.* New York: Oxford University Press, 1992.

Teelken, Christine, and Geert Braam. "From Myopia towards a New Strategic Performance Management System: Controlling for Potentially Dysfunctional Consequences of Performance Measurement in Organisations in Higher Education." *East London Business School Working Papers* 2002: 1–27.

Vereniging van Nederlandse Universiteiten (VSNU). *Reforming the Research Training System, Position Paper.* Den Haag: VSNU, 2004.

15

Governance and the Autonomous University
Changing Institutional Leadership in UK and Australian Higher Education[1]

DAVID N. SMITH AND JONATHAN ADAMS

Introduction

This chapter is about university leadership and its complex relationship with organizational development and state steering approaches. Its primary focus is the changing role of second-tier institutional leaders in a selection of universities in the UK and Australia. Those in the second tier, typically designated pro-vice-chancellors (PVCs) or vice-presidents (VPs), comprise a key layer of executive and academic leadership with cross-institutional responsibility for how the university interprets its core functions and makes its way in response to the policies of national and state legislatures. Drawing on recently completed research (Smith, Adams and Mount, 2007) into those occupying such posts in the UK, the chapter extends the empirical analysis to provide some comparative Anglo-Australian perspectives on the structures and strategies of institutional leadership.

We argue that the structures and practices of this leadership tier are diffused through universities in ways not easily predicted by the particular features of state steering systems. It strikes us that there is a significant isomorphism (similarity): a reflexive interplay between state, university and academics that leads to similar organizational outcomes in different locations. The balance of action and objective between the players is evolving as institutional environments change, shaped (among other influences) by different variants of state steering. Yet we see evidence of universities adopting similar organizational responses. In different theaters we see the appearance of a model of supposed strengthening of "academic management" at faculty level through, for example, "super deans." Yet, despite this assertion of the benefits of overt management, we also detect an emerging recognition that this is the age of the "brand" and the reification of value in organizational goals. Our research suggests that in the autonomous university PVCs remain culturally embedded within their organizational communities, their contribution to leadership anchored in dual roles: responsibility for driving institutional change and for maintaining continuity of academic vision or "brand." The delivery of "brand" value, we suggest, lies not simply with enhanced top-down executive "direction" but with agile and responsive "influence" mediated through far-from-redundant cross-institutional academic leadership.

Our argument draws on an institutionalist approach to organization theory, connecting this to an evidence base combining documentary and other secondary literature, statistical data on PVCs since the 1960s, and in-depth semi-structured interviews with seventy-three PVCs and their senior colleagues. The majority were based in thirteen UK universities, while the remainder included fourteen vice-presidents and senior colleagues in six Australian universities, a smaller sample of six interviews with pro-rectors in continental European universities (two Danish, two Swedish, one French and one Swiss) and informal meetings with PVCs in New Zealand. A further six key-informant interviews were held with EU-based respondents with system-wide perspectives from significant senior leadership experience. The interviews were conducted during 2006–2007 and focused on how PVCs arrived at their posts, their learning experiences en route and how they perceive and interpret their roles.

State Steering Traditions and Governance Approaches

In all Western countries, governments have been developing new, or recalibrated, steering mechanisms for public policy. A primary goal of state steering in higher education is to "stretch" institutional missions beyond traditional teaching and research into a wider embrace with the economy and society, through enterprise, interactions with business and industry, community reach-out, regional skills development and widening participation. Local inflections of this global meta-narrative on knowledge and innovation illustrate the importance attached to governance arrangements as national and regional states seek to condition and canalize what goes on. In models of state steering the basic dichotomy is between state "control" and state "supervision" (van Vught, 1989; Neave and van Vught, 1991; Goedegebuure et al., 1994; Olsen, 1988). Although these models vary in their complexity and subtlety, they tend to focus on "how tight or loose the links between central political authorities and organizations of higher education are (or are supposed to be)" (Gornitzka and Maassen, 2000: 269). However, as HE systems across the globe have faced the twin challenges of mission stretch and funding crises, this basic dichotomy in state steering approaches has begun to break down. More subtle blends of approaches – "supermarket steering" – have emerged in its place, combining "different steering instruments, institutional structures, and steering relationships" (2000: 283). In some neo-liberal systems – Australia, New Zealand and the USA are examples – state support for access, including a system of grants and loans, plus public funding to secure wider economically oriented goals, is combined with growing reliance on private sources of funding. Other systems, mostly in continental Europe, persist with the principle of public investment in free HE access, in some cases with continuing grants to students. In its purest form – typically but not exclusively in some Scandinavian countries – justification for continued investment rests on HE's contribution to the production of high-skill labor supply. It is a major challenge, however, to match the costs of public access with the needs of increasing enrollments, as well as simultaneously stimulating international excellence in research. In some systems – Germany, for instance – the national state and several of the *Länder* have started processes to encourage greater institutional differentiation, in part to create a hierarchy of internationally excellent research universities. The New Zealand government has similar objectives. In the UK the steering system appears more transitional and seeks a line between overtly liberal and public service orientations. In this mixed model, public funding is primarily formulaic and target-driven. It is placed alongside private contributions from students, though the balance between public and private sources is expected to shift over time.

One of the problems associated with such meta-level accounts of state–society–system relationships is that they rarely capture local and meso-level inflections of policy, particularly at the level of the institution. Instead, the emphasis tends to be on the general directions of change as many states, particularly in continental Europe, begin to move away from direct interference in higher education affairs towards more "evaluative" approaches, "steering from a distance." We suggest that there is a missing analytical link in the relative neglect of the organization within the literature of higher education. Clark (2000) argued that there is a need for a better understanding of how institutions make their way amid growing complexity. In his own work, Clark had already picked up this gauntlet, pointing to various institutions that have restructured themselves to adapt to turbulent environments (Clark, 1998). Other important questions emerge. How is restructuring being approached? What changes occur in the formal organizational structures of universities? Who are the key leadership actors and how are their roles reconfigured within institutional structures and strategies? To what extent do contemporary universities, in their organizational dimensions, achieve diversity or, conversely, to what extent do they display the momentum of institutional isomorphism (DiMaggio and Powell, 1983) that makes universities in different national HE systems so closely resemble one another?

Our aim, in addressing these questions, is to explore the way that meta-level relationships between state authorities and the HE system are played out in the empirical setting of the institutions. We are interested specifically in process and change at the deepening levels of steering approaches, institutional missions and leadership cultures. Despite a growing interest in the transformation, and transforming potential, of HE leadership, studies of ideological and policy influences on the intellectual identities, purposes, structures and values of universities are comparatively rare (Smith, 2008). We therefore seek to give some attention to how the "room to manoeuvre" (Gornitzka and Maassen, 2000: 268) is maintained by actors within higher education organizations.

Institutional Isomorphism and the Problem of Leadership

The application of concepts derived from institutional theories to the study of organizational structures and behaviors has diverse disciplinary roots. The evolution of such theories across the social sciences is complex, with numerous twists and turns, and has been told in detail elsewhere (Scott, 2001). This section delves selectively into this diverse literature to highlight some theoretical ideas that we consider helpful in delineating the organizational dispositions of universities and the nature of the leadership problem in such settings. Although the role of agency is ambiguous within some formulations of institutional theory, it is generally acknowledged that institutional actors have scope to "take action to create, maintain, and transform institutions" (2001: 75). Bureaucratic hierarchies, of course, are not immune to the "invisible" hand of the market. But in setting strategies to build business empires and in creating internal hierarchical structures to maximize efficiency, institutional leaders provide an alternative "visible hand" to guide organizational development (Chandler, 1977). From a structural-functionalist perspective, the leaders' role is to steer the organization through internal constraints and to restrain the impact of the external environment. However, leaders also become involved in defining and defending values, because over time the organizations they represent acquire distinct identities and characters (Selznick, 1957). Hence leaders must contend not just with technical aspects of production or efficiency but with cultural-cognitive elements of institutional arrangements. Meaning systems, cultural rules and beliefs are important social resources (and constraints) for institutional leaders and can be influential in the design and operation of organizational procedures (Meyer and Rowan, 1977).

From a macro-level view, neo-institutional theory has also been used to explain how organizations evolve and become more similar in adapting to their environments. Influential in this genre is the theory of "institutional isomorphism." Developing the earlier observations of Hawley (1968), who noted how units interacting in similar environmental conditions evolved similar organizational forms, DiMaggio and Powell (1983: 148) contend that: "Once disparate organizations in the same line of business are structured into an actual field (. . . by competition, the state, or the professions), powerful forces emerge that lead them to become more similar to one another."

Three mechanisms are identified that propel institutional effects through organizational fields. The first – *coercive* isomorphism – stems from political influence. The state's steering powers may be seen as a source of coercive isomorphic tendencies. Decisions about generic technical, legal, performance and other requirements restrict, to varying degrees, the room for maneuver of entire groups of institutions. The second mechanism – *mimetic* isomorphism – is propelled by uncertainty. It refers to the processes that lead an organization to seek to adopt the form of another similar, but perhaps more successful, organization in its field. The final mechanism – *normative* isomorphism – relates to professionalization and the shared backgrounds of those who reach the top posts of influence and control within organizational life (1983: 150).

The resonance of institutional isomorphism with concepts of evolution in natural environments will be obvious. What may be less familiar are the parallels that might also be drawn between ecological and educational organizations in the value and challenge of diversity (Stirling, 2007). Indeed, the paradox of institutional isomorphism, as DiMaggio and Powell (1983: 147) explain, is that rational actors seek to make their organizations similar to others in the field while at the same time trying to change them. The notion of organizational isomorphism has considerable, though not necessarily simple, purchase as an explanation of how competitive and institutional pressures shape organizations in the context of higher education. As Scott observes: "one university tends to resemble closely another university" (Scott, 2001: 153). Certainly there is some evidence to suggest that, irrespective of state steering systems or compliance frameworks, HEIs as organizations have core similarities in structures, cultures and processes. From a macro or environmental perspective, the state–institution relationship is a primary axis with coercive potential. HEIs are located within politically constructed, though increasingly marketized, arenas amenable to formal and informal state pressures. As an organizational "field" there are claims to HEIs being a special case by virtue of the separation of, on the one hand, the academic or professional life of the disciplines from, on the other, the corporate or institutional needs of the brand. We discuss this separation further below. Despite their core organizational similarities universities are also highly differentiated partly because they are loosely coupled, a requirement driven by the need to respond to diverse demands expressed by different agencies and stakeholders (Scott, 2001: 157). However, government seems frustrated that universities do not operate consistently or sufficiently in business-oriented ways, with executive structures and styles of decision-making. Leadership, in this discourse, is construed as a problem: universities and their academics need better motivation, clearer direction and continuous reassurance. Change management and new managerialism, once seen as suitable responses, are no longer deemed sufficient. What is required, according to the UK version of the thesis, is better organizational "leadership" (Cabinet Office, 1999, 2000; Storey, 2004).

System governance and organizational leadership, it seems to us, are connected themes, although the complex relational patterns between the two are difficult to distill from the respective disciplinary literatures. Organizations may have lives of their own, but it is the function of executives to "coordinate, appraise and plan" (Chandler, 1962: 8). It is legitimate, therefore, to probe for a better understanding of the balance between state and institutional leadership in guiding and controlling the destiny of the organization. However, the special nature of the HE system also needs to be acknowledged. For example, there seem to be few substantial differences between the job description for a lecturer in solid state materials in a school of chemistry and that for a medievalist in a school of history. Both will be responsible for researching, teaching, some administration and, perhaps, knowledge transfer in their respective fields. In this milieu, the critical difference is the field, the discipline in which each academic is an expert. Steeped in the discipline, its cultures and training (Mintzberg, 1979), they seek through self-motivation to perform within the expectations of the community or "tribe" (Becher, 1989; Becher and Trowler, 2001). The tribe extends its influence and identity beyond the university and beyond the nation, and thus the discipline remains recognizable between systems and states. In this inner, private world of the disciplines, the head of department may be reasonably close to the academic expert. The dean is a more distant colleague. The university, the institutional entity, is more distant still. A locus for the state can only be dimly conceived. Neither institution nor state has anything meaningful to say about the inner world of the discipline or even how the job must be done. Removed from any simple notion of command and control, the key issue within the academic's professional practice is self-motivation. The primary task of institutional leaders and managers should therefore, arguably, be to select people with the highest motivation and provide the context within which they will work to best effect. The consensus and cultural rules of the academic community provide the primary steers for the academic worker in this world of self-motivation and professional autonomy. This consensus is derived from a complex cocktail with two principal ingredients. The first is "tribal" – the disciplinary canon identifies the cutting-edge at which to work and demands the ability to problematize and to advance knowledge, understanding and inter-pretation. The second ingredient is institutional, the broader community that holds the cultural rules or norms that set the parameters of how people work. Status, or esteem, comes from signing up to these: disciplinary norms for professional advancement; institutional norms for career advancement.

Although this description is heavily influenced by the UK model, it is broadly recognizable in broader European, Australasian and American HE. However, while the tribal or disciplinary influences are similar across many HE systems, we contend that institutional or community influences are more variable. This is the arena within which academic leaders attempt to intervene or exert influence, to ensure that academic outcomes are aligned with the goals of the department, the faculty and the institution more broadly. This second arena (the "community" or "institutional") is also the space where the system of governance or steering has most potential for impact. If the state intervenes to guide the institution in particular directions, it sets a framework that is passed down through the institu-tion to the department or academic front line. In this genre of steering the opportunity for individual action is constrained. It is not something that is open to debate or non-compliance. Freedom to maneuver is minimized. The outcome, if state and academic objectives are misaligned, is low discretion and low motivation. Although the system appears to assert the highest common standards, in effect it operates at the level of the lowest common denominator because the standard is set at the level at which the majority of staff can normally operate. Conversely, if the state withdraws, then the institution has to think for itself. Senior leadership, the executive team and the system of independent institutional governance are placed in sharper relief. The balance of power and responsibility shifts from the system to the institution. Key decisions about curriculum and staffing, for example, reside within the institution rather than beyond it.

The boundaries between institutional autonomy and accountability are shifting, some suggest at the expense of the former (Moses, 2007). Salmi (2007: 223) notes that "many governments have granted increased institutional autonomy to public universities, often combined with increased accountability toward the state." In both the UK and Australia, it is this rebalancing which is associated with government signals of a preference for business-derived management models to increase leadership effectiveness. In other states, notably across continental Europe, there is a perception that the missing element is institutional autonomy. The European Commission suggests that effective universities require independent leaders to exert influence within institutional governance and management (Commission of the European Communities, 2006). States should, in its view, progressively pull back from the institutional arena to allow an enhancement of consensus processes.

As corporate governance and leadership are strengthened, is the influence of academics – notably the deans but also the professors – diminished? Although the disciplinary or "tribal" steer remains, in terms of the community that drives learning, teaching and research, the responsibility for goal-setting and internal coherence within the academic community is progressively relocated to the corporate center (Salmi, 2007: 239). A principal rationale for this shift in the location of institutional power is the spreading notion of an international market in HE and global positioning within it. It is reflected in the transitional state of many "research" universities as they compete to acquire the characteristics of a so-called emerging global model (Mohrman, Ma and Baker, 2008). In this model, paradoxically, dependence on governments tends to be reduced as the proportion of funding derived from public sources declines. Yet, despite the declining direct influence of nation-states and despite the fact that the top research universities constitute only a small number of institutional entities, globally they exercise a great influence on other institutions as new models of knowledge conglomerate (Mohrman, Ma and Bakar, 2008: 5). The appeal of such models is based on the "brand" of the institution itself. It is based on the coherence of organizational goals and values and no longer purely on the discipline(s). Students and other clients are drawn by the ability of the institution to "sell" the value and the values it associates with its brand. Promoting the brand is an activity reflected in a crude but potent form, in the jostling for position within the league tables of top universities (HEFCE, 2008). It is also increasingly captured in university advertising, sports sponsorship and other media more normally associated with soap powder and baked beans. It is furthermore also about the ability of institutional leaders to reorganize for increasing complexity and global reach (Mohrman, Ma and Baker, 2008), yet at the same time still being able to understand and protect traditional academic values and activities from poor decision-making, unethical activities, or indeed anything else that might undermine their institutional vision and strategic direction (Salmi, 2007: 234–237).

So, the key question around system steering and institutional leadership is: how best to achieve some convergence around the primary change areas? What does the state seek to govern? What are its cultural attributes? The argument is that academics are talented, highly motivated people. Therefore, management and governance of the system must be of a particular kind, relying more on the building of a consensus rather than a command model.

Enter the Pro-vice-chancellor

We have argued that, irrespective of state steering systems, universities as organizations have certain core similarities in terms of their structures and processes. We might claim that HE makes a special case, among organizational fields, by virtue of the duality of academic or professional life in the disciplines and the corporate or institutional needs of the brand. HEIs are located within politically constructed arenas amenable to the formal and informal pressures of the state. The steering powers of the state are a source of isomorphic tendencies via systemically applied decisions about technical, legal, performance and other requirements. The "coercive" influences of the state may exert only weak effects, however, with change occurring less by coercion than by "stimulating other institutional mechanisms such as normative and identity processes" (Scott, 2001: 208–209). We suggest that "normative" and "mimetic" sources of isomorphism drive HEIs to model themselves on similar organizations that are perceived to be successful (DiMaggio and Powell, 1983: 152). These conditions transfer across boundaries and reinforce tendencies towards organizational homogeneity regardless of different state-imposed models of steering. The configuration of PVC roles, as key actors who embody conflicting dynamics and interests in organizational change, reflects both the internal (normative and mimetic) academic continuities that preserve prevailing structures and processes and the countervailing external (coercive) pressures for change that challenge them. We suggest that these forces are played out at institutional level: state steering systems are not in themselves obviously causal factors.

Normative Sources of Iomorphism: Pathways to the Post of PVC

The academic domains of senior university leaders exhibit some of the principal forms of filtering that encourage normative isomorphism. DiMaggio and Powell (1983: 152) identify two important sources of normative isomorphism: formal education and legitimation derived from university-recognized cognitive bases; and professional networks that span and diffuse rapidly across organizations. Longer-term trends in PVC posts in the UK and Australian systems[2] illustrate these tendencies, despite a proliferation of the numbers in this leadership "class." Table 15.1 presents a simple profile over a fifty-year period using data for sample years derived from the Association of Commonwealth (ACU) yearbooks.

The secular trend shows a steady increase in the overall count of academic posts represented in the senior management team (SMT). The size of SMTs gradually increased over the decades with a progressive expansion of the numbers of PVC posts. PVCs (and their equivalent titles) rose in the UK from just eighteen posts across all eligible institutions at the start of the period to 284 by the end. When the number of PVC posts is scaled against institutions for each of our sample years, the rising trend is still quite evident.

The pattern has a remarkably similar profile in the UK and Australia. Taking all institutions into account, in the UK at the start of the period there were just 0.39 PVC posts per HEI but by 2005 the corresponding figure was 2.41 per institution. In Australia the growth was slower at the outset but the final ratio, of 2.25, is similar to that of the UK. However, the abundance of Deputy VCs in the Australian system suggests some different concepts about management and the labeling of roles.

The growth of PVC roles is of an order of magnitude, certainly, but it takes place over five decades and it is steady and progressive. This is not a sudden and sharp

TABLE 15.1 Membership of Senior Management Teams (SMTs) in Australian and UK Universities

	HEIs	Senior management team posts				Posts per HEI	
	ACU count	Total posts	PVCs	DVCs	Deans	PVCs	DVCs
Australia[3]:							
1960	11	17	3	3	0	0.27	0.27
1970	15	35	8	12	0	0.53	0.80
1980	19	56	8	22	6	0.42	1.16
1990	25	95	27	38	0	1.08	1.52
2000	43	181	68	70	0	1.58	1.63
2005	40	208	90	75	0	2.25	1.88
UK:							
1960	46	65	18	3	2	0.39	0.07
1970	57	143	59	7	17	1.04	0.12
1980	69	175	96	9	5	1.39	0.13
1990	71	218	120	18	4	1.69	0.25
2000	117	420	248	44	12	2.12	0.38
2005	118	468	284	64	6	2.41	0.54

Source: ACU Yearbooks[4]

reaction but an evolutionary, adaptive and broadly simultaneous change in both jurisdictions. Apart from comparative continuities in the statistical profiles of second-tier roles, the data provide evidence of other similarities. The biggest factor in PVC backgrounds would appear to be academic prestige. PVCs, in both Australia and the UK, are drawn almost exclusively from the ranks of established academics. As with vice-chancellors (VCs), whose characteristics and pathways into the top leadership post are similar (Bargh et al., 2000), most PVCs are professors. In the UK, the largest proportion typically have an Oxbridge, London or big civic pedigree. Slightly under half (381 out of 781) of Australian PVCs had an overseas qualification, mostly from the UK or the USA, Canada, New Zealand and South Africa, plus a few Europeans. For the UK data, fewer than 10 percent (just 141 out of 1882) had overseas qualifications (though many records have no indication of awarding institution). Pervasively, across the HE systems we sampled, we encountered strong assertions from experienced staff that senior leadership could be effective only if it was practiced by those with significant track records as academics – a track usually, though not exclusively, conceived as research. The background qualifications are not happenstance but selected characteristics.

Other continuities transcend national boundaries. The majority of PVCs in our research had not undertaken any formal leadership skills or preparatory program prior to taking up their posts. "Extractive training" involving courses, manuals or procedures was rare. Our UK research aligns with Australian findings (Anderson and Johnson, 2006). What explains this? The answer in part is connected to how

TABLE 15.2 Appointment Characteristics of PVCs

Part-time (in theory)	*Full-time*
Fixed-term secondment	Permanent post
Internal appointment	External appointment
Appointed by VC and/or academic community	Appointed by VC and/or council

universities identify and select their PVCs. Appointment systems are important. These are portrayed in Table 15.2.

In general the left-hand column represents practice in UK research-intensive (i.e. pre-1992) institutions, in other European systems and in some (mainly research-intensive) Australian universities. The features in the right-hand column reflect the pattern in the former UK polytechnics (post-1992 institutions) and also practice in many Australian universities. A somewhat opaque variable is the notion that the job might be considered part-time where practice made this frequently not the case. It is a key signifier: that the post-holder is a continuing academic as researcher and/or teacher. The division in the table is blurring. We found evidence that characteristics in both columns can be found across all types of institution. Some universities with previous commitment to part-time appointments by secondment are shifting to full-time, permanent and, sometimes, external appointments. System changes do not appear to be a significant predictor of the timing of shifts in organizational practices. However, if we turn to practices of identifying and selecting suitable candidates, the picture suggests some divergent practices. In essence there are three approaches:

- *By invitation.* The VC/president in effect is patron of the PVC. Names "emerge"; there is a tap on the shoulder. This system was defended on the grounds not only that it brings a wider pool of suitably experienced candidates into the field of vision, but that it subsequently engenders loyalty. Several critics claimed it increased loyalty to the VC but at the expense of the institution. Such "invitation" approaches are still the norm in the pre-1992 UK institutions.
- *Competitive recruitment – either internal or external.* The VC/president will usually be chairing or at least advising the appointment committee. The trawl for talent is theoretically opened to a wider pool. This is the dominant approach in both Australian universities and the UK. It is also found in some European institutions, though usually recruitment is internal.
- *Election.* Still found in many European institutions, but a much less common model in the UK and Australia (but still at present used for some institutional positions). Election systems nominally at least remain in place to reflect the interests of academic self-government and collegiality in the appointment of executive leaders. In several European systems (as practiced still in some Swedish and Swiss institutions) they may also be designed to allow input from government (both political and civil servant/local, regional and national) and other stakeholders. But election processes appear also to depend on nominations

procedures, some more arcane than others, which may retain an ultimate right of veto in the hands of the rector.

There is some evidence to indicate trends towards convergence among these divergent practices. In the UK, the opaque, informal approach is under pressure from a more widespread shift in academic recruitment and promotions criteria towards formalized and transparent processes. In several European systems, reform to governance arrangements appears to be stimulating a shift towards granting to rectors the right not just to nominate but to select their senior executive colleagues, including the pro-rectors. In the Danish system, for example, the 2003 higher education reform has ushered in independent governing bodies with responsibility for appointment of the rector passing from the state to boards.

Mimetic Sources of Isomorphism: PVC Roles

We suggest that the congruence of organizational norms around the professional development experiences deemed important in making PVC appointments tends to create a pool of potential candidates of similar orientation and disposition. In our interviews in both UK and Australian contexts it emerged that job horizons straddled higher education systems. Several interviewees in Australia recounted experiences of competing for jobs in the UK and North America, and the increasingly global orientation of the professional head-hunting firms appears to be reinforcing this process. However, although normative pressures are evident, a recognized limitation of the typology of isomorphism as advanced by DiMaggio and Powell (1983: 150) is that the types are not necessarily empirically distinct. The typology is primarily analytic. Hence in our empirical setting, although normative pressures appear to induce universities to conform to their peers through the specification of attributes and skills required of those deemed responsible for institutional performance, it would seem perfectly feasible to suggest that mimetic pressures are also influencing preferences for how leadership talent is identified and appointed. The sense that isomorphic mechanisms intermingle is reinforced if we consider the homogenization of a basic organizational model across systems. Arguably the top research-intensive institutions exert a predominant mimetic influence, with other (invariably) less research-intensive institutions looking to them as models. It is not an "iron cage," in the Weberian sense of a rationalist organizational momentum (Weber, 1952), but it propels homogeneity through mimetic processes, especially in environments that are increasingly uncertain and when goals are ambiguous or poorly understood (DiMaggio and Powell, 1983: 151). In such conditions of uncertainty, as DiMaggio and Powell explain, organizations resort to modeling:

> The modeled organization may be unaware of the modeling or may have no desire to be copied; it merely serves as a convenient source of practices that the borrowing organization may use. Models may be diffused unintentionally, indirectly through employee transfer or turnover, or explicitly by

organizations such as consulting firms or industry trade associations. Even innovation can be accounted for by organizational modeling.

(DiMaggio and Powell, 1983: 151)

Within each of the university's domains, especially teaching and research, there are enduring and often highly distinct professional practices, procedures and cultures that define the organization (Smith, Adams and Mount, 2007: 5, 33–34). Such continuities in the ways members of academic communities define their organization holistically, the coherence with which they make sense of "who we are" (Santos and Eisenhardt, 2005: 500), reinforce not just the external boundaries of the university but the nature of academic identity and the importance of tradition and cultures (Silver, 2003, 2007). Arguably the salience of this model, essentially medieval in origin (Rashdall, 1936), may limit possibilities for organizational innovation. To be sure, challenges to the classic disciplinary arrangement are not unknown, especially in the context of new foundations – classically, the period of the English new universities of the 1960s. But maintaining a commitment to innovation is comparatively rare, with radical early goals gradually subsumed into more conventional dispositions (Bastedo, 2007). While universities have undoubtedly gained corporate capacities to innovate, traditional governing patterns may remain substantially intact (de Boer, Enders and Leišytė, 2007) with academics retaining a role in strategic decision-making (Huisman, de Boer and Goedegebuure, 2006). In each of the systems we investigated we found that the post of PVC both reflects and reinforces the resilience of the university's basic organizational arrangements and its social structures. While the university vice-chancellor or president acts in the role of chief executive responsible for the broader vision, it is the PVCs who must build and facilitate the academic consensus necessary to ensure stability and give meaning to organizational behavior. They must maintain value and values: the efficiency of the operation and the standards applied to the academic enterprise. They are in essence the arbiters of the external brand and the values inside the institution as a whole.

The traditional role of the PVC is facilitating and cross-institutional. One of influence, not command. The traditional role lacks direct management levers. Many PVCs and their equivalents, regardless of HE system, do not hold budgets or line-manage staff. Their authority does not emanate from a source of control. Their roles, and (often onerous) responsibilities conventionally at least, are not exercised in simple, directive ways. However, the conceptualization of the traditional PVC role is under pressure. We found that in some Australian and UK institutions the vice-chancellor/president had reconfigured the academic structure, sweeping many small departmental units into fewer colleges or faculties (usually between five and seven). This is a trend that has been present since the early 1990s. Now, the new role emerging to lead these new entities is an executive or "super dean," freshly appointed to meld the new structure together and drive it in particular directions, their terms of reference granting them strong directive and managerial influence, often accompanied by clear financial control. This is a reification of red-in-tooth-and-claw management that challenges what we have described thus far. The apparent strengthening of faculty deans contrasts with the theme in all our site visit institutions of a need for a senior role that can take a cross-institutional view, to balance the desires of different operating units, to push through changes through facilitation and persuasion (consensus-building) while maintaining the commonality of value.

So now there is a tension, possibly even a conflict, between the executive authority of a budget-wielding "super dean" and the "authority of influence" of the traditional academic PVC. If the latter role is to be effective, then it is essential for senior management to recognize and moderate the inherent tensions in the system to achieve both the financial goals that enable the disciplinary structure and the wider goals that enable overall strategy. The emergence of the faculty "super deans" might be a threat to the traditional role, even to the existence, of the PVC because a more "executive" alternative superficially offers the delivery of short-term objectives. This should not be overstated, nor does the variability in organizational structures necessarily undermine the thesis of isomorphism, but it is a change to be monitored. The effect of these shifts is to stretch the second leadership tier as several variants of the PVC role have emerged. The principal models are presented in Table 15.3.

In Australia we found evidence of the appointment of DVCs to take on distinctive executive roles. These are "provost"-type roles, some with title attached, with responsibility for the academic direction of the institution. Some variability is to be expected in a decentralized system of autonomous institutions. In one institution the PVCs continued to take on broad policy portfolios but reported to the DVC. In another, the DVC would lead the "super deans." The shifts in the Australian system led some key informants to talk in terms of a split second tier, with the emergence of a hierarchy of DVC and policy PVCs, the latter forming a "mezzanine" layer below the executive DVC/PVCs, but located uncertainly with respect to "super deans." Similar tendencies are evident in the UK. However, in our sample of other European institutions the move towards the strengthened faculty with a "super dean" was not directly replicated. Historically, in these systems, deans

TABLE 15.3 Models of Second-tier Leadership Roles

Type	Designation	Responsibilities
DVC	Academic or non-academic	Budget and line management responsibilities; policy steer
PVC Executive	Academic	Budget and line management responsibilities
PVC Policy	Academic	No budget or line management responsibilities
PVC Dean	Academic	Faculty or other unit line management combined with cross-institutional role
PVC Service	Academic or non-academic	Primarily but not exclusively to lead administrative or professional services with line management responsibilities

of faculty have held significant academic management posts for rather longer than is typical in Australia or the UK. Although the "new deanship" can be portrayed as a reflection of a wider "manager–academic" phenomenon across HE systems (de Boer, 2008; Deem, 2004), the "super dean" model developing in several UK and Australian universities appears more exaggerated in conception. Certainly the pattern of relationships between deans of faculty and the rectorate in continental Europe and between "super deans" and the vice-chancellorship in Anglo-Australian systems appears rather complex.

Despite state-led reform processes, several of our respondents at rectorate level in Danish, French, Swedish and Swiss universities presented a picture of systems that are still struggling with the continuities of previous systems of academic self-governance. Symbolized in the post of elected dean, there is more entrenched resistance to executive attempts to lever-in corporate change. Deans are often appointed through elaborate processes of nomination and "democratic" election, as representatives of the academic caucus (usually the senior professors) rather than the corporate institution. Though these processes are sometimes proclaimed for their place in the preservation of academic self-governance, pro-rectors were critical of the constraining effects on corporate ability to drive change. Protracted appointment processes to professorships, continued provision of courses in areas considered non-viable and the refusals of some deans to implement change were three examples of frustrations cited.

Conclusions

We have suggested that there is a reflexive interplay between state, university and academics that is leading to similar outcomes in terms of leadership structures and practices across institutional types and jurisdictions. We found evidence to indicate a convergence or isomorphism in Anglo-Australian systems around the problem of aligning the leadership of academic structures, exemplified in the faculties, with the leadership of the wider corporate institution. What we found empirically fitted not just with our sense of how universities as professional organizations tend to operate, particularly the intervention of the academic in the definition of work, but in the competition between dual controlling structures derived from academic and corporate sources of power and legitimization.

The salience of isomorphism needs to be carefully delineated. We do not imply a simplification of the university as a complex social system, reduced merely to the existence of structural isomorphism. We are attempting, instead, to advance a more comprehensive understanding of why models of second-tier leadership structures and practices exhibit similar tendencies almost irrespective of detailed differences in state steering systems. In Anglo-Australian systems this group of senior leaders are under pressure and the sources of pressure are diverse: their relationship with the broader institutional structure, the problems of coping with mission stretch and complexity, the reconfiguration of academic roles, the demands of accountability, and so on. Yet diversity does not disrupt fundamental continuities and similarities: where the PVCs originate, how they get into the post, their learning experiences, and how they approach the practice of senior institutional leadership. Nor, we contend, are the similarities (or pressures) confined to Anglo-Australian systems, though the persistence of national idiosyncrasies can easily overshadow them. It is also clear that universities speak to multiple communities and it is to be expected that there will be specific elements of differentiation, according to the precise balance of which stakeholders hold the highest cards in conferring legitimacy or demanding accountability.

There is mounting evidence from other sources that institutions are jostling to adopt the features of a so-called "emerging global model" – that top stratum of research universities worldwide (Mohrman, Ma and Baker, 2008). In the competitive struggle to implement the changes necessary to give their institutions either the reality or the rhetoric of global reach we found evidence of VCs and presidents increasingly frustrated by the perceived shortcomings of traditional models of academic leadership. In many institutions there is a palpable challenge being mounted to the continuance of the disciplinary model as the appropriate reference point for change. This traditional model accords precedence to the academics carrying out research, learning and teaching. Scholars organize themselves inside disciplinary boundaries largely for reasons of intellectual convenience. More recently, this model is challenged by a reconceptualization of how and where disciplines might be organized and located. The driver of change in this respect is not managerial convenience but the emergence of an undefined notion of the value of interdisciplinarity in the quest for new knowledge. Expectations of future advance now hover at the edge of disciplines and at the interface between novel combinations of knowledge bases. It is therefore the adherence to a (pejoratively) senescent disciplinary core that, for some critics of European systems in particular, is allegedly dragging down the intellectual status of the old Europe.

Recent governments have sought to build on the tradition of institutional autonomy to bring about more innovative HE systems in the UK and Australia. They have set out a preference for stronger institutional leadership and management. They have signaled the need for, and actively promoted, models derived from business that they believe will increase leadership effectiveness. Internally as well, institutional leaders have become restless with the apparent ineffectiveness of the second leadership tier to drive changes in the increasingly complicated internal architecture of the university, particularly in relation to integrating the diverse elements of interdisciplinary research, the student experience and organizational infrastructures. In different HE systems we found evidence too of an emerging model of strengthened "academic management" at faculty level ("super deans"). At one level this appears a fairly blunt assertion of the benefits of more executive styles of management over academic or collegial models. Yet, despite the appeal of more overt managerialism embodied in the "super dean," we also detect an emerging recognition – a convergence – around the notion that in a world where university missions transcend the boundaries of the nation-state, this is the age of the "brand." The paradox of the emergence of the brand as a dominant institutional concern, almost irrespective of state steering systems, is that it reinforces isomorphic tendencies in terms of organizational configurations. This in turn places a premium on some of the traditional virtues of the pro-vice-chancellorship as an academic leadership post.

The assertion of brand values and the delivery of brand value lies not with direction but with responsive influence mediated through the far-from-redundant cross-institutional leadership of the pro-vice chancellors. Indeed, a major criticism of the reconfiguration of structures and roles where they lead to the creation of powerful executive deans is that it undermines institutional cohesiveness. Deans inevitably compete with one another and – at the extreme – disrupt institutional outcomes. We observed, of course, that the PVC role is preserved – no institution in our study had taken the formal decision to abolish the role of PVC/pro-rector/vice-president. Among the rationales for persevering with the PVC role is that it retains the essential institutional perspective and academic credibility deemed crucial to delivering the non-financial bottom line that characterizes the higher education (and generic third-sector) mission. That the PVC should continue to be such a pervasive figure in higher education leadership reflects the realization that, for a university to be successful, there are in practice few alternative models of influencing a collegial organization from which to choose.

Notes

1   This chapter draws on the findings of research reported in Smith, Adams and Mount (2007). The authors acknowledge the UK Leadership Foundation for Higher Education (www.lfhe.ac.uk), which funded the research and granted permission to quote from the final report.
2   We were unable to examine comparable data for the European systems represented in our sample universities.
3   In 1988, the Labor Minister John Dawkins announced a restructuring of the Australian HE system. This replaced a cooperative system of two vertically segmented sectors into a unitary system of universities in which all institutions competed for teaching and research resources. Only comprehensive universities with over 8,000 students would be fully funded, a decision that led to a series of mergers and restructurings. This created a unified national system but one based on mixed public–private funding (see Marginson, 2007).
4   The number of UK HEIs with data recorded in the ACU yearbook has increased over the period, with a marked growth in both countries after the abolition of the binary divide. For the UK there is a maximum of 135 institutions, and for Australia a maximum of forty-four for which data might have been available by the end of the period. The number for which data were in fact available for each sample year is shown in Table 15.1.

References

Anderson, Don, and Richard Johnson. *A Review of Proposals from the "Leadership for Excellence in Teaching and Learning Programme."* Chippendale: Carrick Institute for Learning and Teaching in Higher Education, 2006.

Bargh, Catherine, Jean Bocock, Peter Scott, and David Smith. *University Leadership: The Role of the Chief Executive.* Buckingham: SRHE and Open University Press, 2000.

Bastedo, Michael N. "Bringing the State Back in: Promoting and Sustaining Innovation in Public Higher Education." *Higher Education Quarterly* 61(2) (2007): 155–170.

Becher, Tony. *Academic Tribes and Territories: Intellectual Enquiry and the Cultures of Disciplines.* Buckingham: SRHE and Open University Press, 1989.

Becher, Tony, and Paul R. Trowler. *Academic Tribes and Territories.* Buckingham: SRHE and Open University Press, 2001.

Cabinet Office. *Modernising Government.* Cm 4310. London: HMSO, 1999.

Cabinet Office. *Strengthening Leadership in the Public Sector: A Research Study by the PIU.* London: Cabinet Office, Performance and Innovation Unit, 2000.

Chandler, Alfred D. *Strategy and Structure: Chapters in the History of the Industrial Enterprise.* Cambridge, MA: MIT Press, 1962.

Chandler, Alfred D. *The Visible Hand: The Managerial Revolution in American Business.* Cambridge, MA: Harvard University Press, 1977.

Clark, Burton R. *Creating Entrepreneurial Universities: Organizational Pathways of Transformation.* Oxford: IAU and Elsevier Science, 1998.

Clark, Burton R. "Developing a Career in the Study of Higher Education." In *Higher Education: Handbook of Theory and Research,* Vol. XV, edited by John C. Smart. New York: Agathon Press, 2000, 1–38.

Commission of the European Communities. *Delivering on the Modernisation Agenda for Universities: Education, Research and Innovation.* Com (2006) 208final. Brussels: CEC, 2006.

de Boer, Harry F. *On Increasing Our Understandings of the Deanship in Modern Times.* Paper presented at the Leadership in Higher Education: Facts, Fictions and Futures seminar, St George's House, Windsor Castle, March 31–April 1, 2008.

de Boer, Harry F., Jürgen Enders, and Liudvika Leišytė. "Public Sector Reform in Dutch Higher Education: The Organizational Transformation of the University." *Public Administration* 85(1) (2007): 27–46.

Deem, Rosemary. "The Knowledge Worker, the Manager-academic and the Contemporary UK University: New and Old Forms of Public Management?" *Financial Accountability and Management* 20(2) (2004): 107–128.

DiMaggio, Paul J., and Walter W. Powell. "The Iron Cage Revisited: Institutional Isomorphism and Collective Rationality in Organizational Fields." *American Sociological Review* 48 (1983): 147–160.

Goedegebuure, Leo, Frans Kaiser, Peter Maassen, Lynn Meek, Frans van Vught, and Egbert de Weert, eds. *Higher Education Policy: An International Comparative Perspective.* Oxford: Pergamon Press, 1994.

Gornitzka, Åse, and Peter Maassen. "Hybrid Steering Approaches with Respect to European Higher Education." *Higher Education Policy* 13(3) (2000): 267–285.

Hawley, Amos. "Human Ecology." In *International Encyclopedia of the Social Sciences,* edited by David L. Sills. New York: Macmillan, 1968, 328–337.

HEFCE. *Counting What is Measured or Measuring What Counts? League Tables and Their Impact on Higher Education Institutions in England.* Issues paper No. 14. Bristol: HEFCE, 2008.

Huisman, J., Harry F. de Boer, and Leo Goedegebuure. "The Perception of Participation in Executive Governance Structures in Dutch Universities." *Tertiary Education and Management* 12(3) (2006): 227–239.

Marginson, S. "Australia." In *International Handbook of Higher Education. Part Two: Regions and Countries,* edited by James J.F. Forest, and Philip G. Altbach. Dordrecht: Springer, 2007, 587–611.

Meyer, John W., and Brian Rowan. "Institutionalized Organizations: Formal Structures as Myth and Ceremony." *American Journal of Sociology* 83 (1977): 340–363.

Mintzberg, Henry. *The Structuring of Organizations.* Englewood Cliffs: Prentice-Hall, 1979.

Mohrman, Kathryn, Wanhua Ma, and David Baker. "The Research University in Transition: The Emerging Global Model." *Higher Education Policy* 21(1) (2008): 5–27.

Moses, Ingrid. "Institutional Autonomy Revisited: Autonomy Justified and Accounted." *Higher Education Policy* 20(3) (2007): 261–274.

Neave, Guy, and Frans A. van Vught, eds. *Prometheus Bound: The Changing Relationship between Government and Higher Education in Western Europe.* Oxford: Pergamon Press, 1991.

Olsen, Johan. "Administrative Reform and Theories of Organization." In *Organizing Governance: Governing Organizations,* edited by Colin Campbell, and B. Guy Peters. Pittsburgh: University of Pittsburgh Press, 1988, 233–245.

Rashdall, Hastings. *The Universities of Europe in the Middle Ages: A New Edition in Three Volumes,* reissued by F.M. Powicke, and A.B. Emden, Vol. III: *English Universities – Student Life.* Oxford: Oxford University Press, 1936.

Salmi, Jamil. "Autonomy from the State vs Responsiveness to Markets." *Higher Education Policy* 20(3) (2007): 223–242.

Santos, Filipe M., and Kathleen M. Eisenhardt. "Organizational Boundaries and Theories of Organization." *Organizational Science* 16(5) (2005): 491–508.

Scott, W. Richard. *Institutions and Organizations.* Thousand Oaks: Sage, 2001.

Selznick, P. *Leadership in Administration.* New York: Harper and Row, 1957.

Silver, Harold. *Higher Education and Opinion Making in Twentieth-century England.* London: Woburn Press, 2003.

Silver, Harold. *Tradition and Higher Education.* Winchester: Winchester University Press, 2007.

Smith, David N. "Eric James and the 'Utopianist' Campus: Biography, Policy and the Building of a New University during the 1960s." *History of Education* 37(1) (2008): 23–42.

Smith, David, Jonathan Adams, and David Mount. *UK Universities and Executive Officers: The Changing Roles of Pro-vice-chancellors.* London: LFHE, 2007.

Stirling, Andrew. "A General Framework for Analysing Diversity in Science, Technology and Society." *Interface Journal of the Royal Society* 4(15) (2007): 1–13.

Storey, John, ed. *Leadership in Organizations: Current Issues and Key Trends.* London: Routledge, 2004.

van Vught, Frans A., ed. *Government Strategies and Innovation in Higher Education.* London: Jessica Kingsley, 1989.

Weber, Max. *The Protestant Ethic and the Spirit of Capitalism.* New York: Scribner, 1952.

Index

academic: capitalism 113; drift, 201; freedom 75–6, 78, 85, 92, 94, 113, 212–13, 227–8, 231, 233, 246, 249; oligarchy 39, 112, 200; profession 22, 246; staff 39, 152, 194, 204. 221

accountability 5, 38, 78, 81, 97, 100, 102, 114, 117, 119, 135, 145, 147–8, 151, 157–8, 167, 169, 172, 176, 184, 189, 211, 213, 239, 257, 265–6

accreditation 97, 99, 113, 117–18, 201, 239–40, 243

Adams, J. 252, 263, 267n1

Adelman, C. 174

Agasisti, T. 22

agenda-setting 34, 36, 38, 182–3, 208

Ajzen, I. 7, 221, 224–5, 227

allocation: funding 42, 46, 98, 245; model 46, 203; resource 60, 69, 92, 168, 203

Althaus, C. 184

Amaral, A. 47, 112, 146, 188, 192, 233

Andersen, P.B. 80

Anderson, B. 116

Anderson, D. 260

Anderson, L.S. 108, 121n3

Anderson, P. 208

Andresani, G. 90, 96, 146

anthropology 52, 70–1

Archer, L. 130

Arnaboldi, M.A. 22

Arriëns, T.E.H. 221

Asad, T. 71

assemblage 5, 71–2, 79, 82, 84–5, 86n3

Aucoin, P. 239

audit 73, 81–2, 200, 205

Australia, higher education: Australian Research Council (ARC) 149, 154–5; Australian Vice-Chancellors' Committee (AVCC) 150, 152; Commonwealth Tertiary Education Commission (CTEC) 154–5; Higher Education Contribution Scheme (HECS) 148–50, 152–3; Hoare report 153; Howard 145, 157; Nelson 154

Austria, higher education: Austrian Rectors' Committee 64; Board of Governors 54, 58, 64; Habilitation 55, 57, 61; Hahn 66; Ministry 54, 58, 60, 63–4; *Mittelbau* 55–6, 61; *Ordinarienuniversität* 54, 56–7; rector 54, 64–5; senate 54, 59–60, 62

autonomy: academic 69, 71, 75, 170, 205; institutional 35, 46, 70, 72, 75–6, 93, 97, 113, 118, 137, 172, 174, 183, 189–90, 199, 203, 219, 222, 257, 266; professional 7, 161, 212, 220, 226, 228, 230–4, 257; university 19, 22, 26, 33, 45–6, 76, 115, 190, 202, 212

Azzone, G. 22, 25

Baker, D. 258, 266

Baker, Kenneth 129, 136–7, 141

Ball, S. 184

Bardach, E. 219

Bargh, C. 260

Barnacle, R. 237–8

Barnett, R. 191

Barrett, S.D. 200, 204

Bartelse, J. 237, 240, 243

Barthe, Y. 101

Bartlett, W. 2

Bastedo, M. 175, 263

Baumgartner, F. 89

Optimization Concept (HOK) 47;
Mecklenburg-Vorpommern 42;
Ministry 40, 45–6; *Neues
Steuerungsmodell* 33; Niedersachsen
40–2, 44, 46; Rheinland-Pfalz 42, 44;
Saarland 44; Sachsen-Anhalt 44;
Schleswig-Holstein 44
Ghoshal, S. 241
Giddens, A. 187
Glenny, L.A. 163–4
globalization 6, 39, 71, 86n3, 107, 110,
112–14, 121, 188, 212
Goedegebuure, L. 112, 145–6, 234, 253, 263
Gornitzka, Å. 3, 13, 27–9, 188, 199, 233,
241, 253–4
governance: corporate xxv, 60, 113, 145–6,
148, 258; good 6, 145–8, 156, 158;
horizontal 110; interactive 2; internal
25, 99, 101, 118, 221, 232; multi-actor
2–3, 99; multi-level 2–3, 6, 107, 120,
185; negotiation-based 15–16, 26–9;
network (NG) 5, 89, 102–4, 105; state
6, 165–6; strategic 15–16; system 5,
14–17, 28–30, 98, 154, 164, 171, 256;
without government 107
government: central 25–6, 88, 102, 148,
185; federal 156, 158, 161, 171, 176;
market 36, 39, 41, 47; national 28, 29,
240; participative 36–9, 43–4, 48
governmentality 77
governors 40, 45, 48, 53–4, 58, 60, 63–4,
66, 162–3, 234
Graham, H.D. 162
Greenwood, D. 53
Griswold, C.P. 162

Handel, K. 42, 46
Hanney, S. 102, 130, 133, 142n3, 143n4
Haraway, D. 71
Harman, K.M. 243, 248
Harvey, D. 74, 78
Hawkins, H. 171
Hawley, A. 255
Hayden, M. 145–6, 154
Healy, S. 209–10
Hearn, J.C. 162–5, 171
Hebel, S. 167

Hedström, P. 56
Heffen, O. van 2
Hemerijck, A. 188
Henkel, M. 97, 183, 189–92, 194
Henry, M. 117, 121
Hesterly, W.S. 90
Hillyard, S. 204
Hoare, D. 153
Hobbs, W.C. 177n1
Hogwood, B. 6, 131
Hood, C. 2, 4–5, 54, 57, 62, 239, 249
Hooghe, L. 185
Høstaker, R. 89, 111–12, 114
Howell, D. 133
Howlett, M. 2, 116
Hughes, J. 130
Huisman, J. 113, 131, 190, 222, 234, 237–8,
240–1, 243, 263
Humboldt 5, 41, 53, 65, 95, 103, 198
Hutchings, M. 130
Hyatt, J.A. 165–6

Inglis, T. 212
International Monetary Fund 145
invisible hand 4, 7, 36, 255
Ireland, higher education: Celtic Tiger 198,
206, 210; Department 202–3, 206;
Forfás 199, 206; Higher Education
Authority (HEA) 199–200, 202–3,
205–7, 210–12; Higher Education
Training and Awards Council
(HETAC) 201; Institutes of Technology
200–1; Irish University Association
203; National Economic and Social
Council (NESC) 204; Regional
Technical Colleges (RTC) 200–1, 207;
Science Foundation Ireland 199, 206,
210; SIPTU 204–5
Isherwood, B. 55
isomorphism 253–5, 259, 262, 264–5
Italy, higher education; Administrative
Board 17–18, 20, 23; Berlinguer 21–2;
Campus Project 21; CODAU 20–1, 23;
Confindustria 21–24; Italian
Committee for the Evaluation of
Research 24; Ministry 17–20, 24–6;
Moratti 24, 26; Mussi 26;National